COLLABORATION IN AUTHORITARIAN AND ARMED CONFLICT SETTINGS

For over 100 years the *Proceedings of the British Academy* series has provided a unique record of British scholarship in the humanities and social sciences. These themed volumes drive scholarship forward and are landmarks in their field. For more information about the series and guidance on submitting a proposal for publication, please visit www.thebritishacademy.ac.uk/proceedings.

PROCEEDINGS OF THE BRITISH ACADEMY • 248

COLLABORATION IN AUTHORITARIAN AND ARMED CONFLICT SETTINGS

Edited by
JUAN ESPINDOLA AND LEIGH A. PAYNE

Published for THE BRITISH ACADEMY
by OXFORD UNIVERSITY PRESS

Oxford University Press, Great Clarendon Street, Oxford OX2 6DP

First edition published in 2022

British Library Cataloguing in Publication Data
Data available

Library of Congress Cataloging in Publication Data
Data available

Typeset by Newgen Publishing UK
Printed in Great Britain by TJ Books Ltd, Padstow, Cornwall

ISBN 978-0-19-726705-9
ISSN 0068-1202

Contents

List of Figures and Tables

Figures

Tables

Notes on Contributors

Gerson Iván Arias is the Director for Social Dialogue of the Commission for the Clarification of Truth, Coexistence and Non-Repetition of Colombia. Before assuming this post, he was Thematic Director of the Office of the High Commissioner for Peace of the Presidency of the Republic of Colombia and Adviser to the Office of the High Adviser for National Security. In these positions he participated on behalf of the national government in the exploratory stage and in the public phase of the negotiations between the government and the Revolutionary Armed Forces of Columbia – People's Army (FARC-EP) in Havana, Cuba. He also participated on behalf of the government in the exploratory stage and in the public phase of the process between the government and the National Liberation Army (ELN). In 2009, together with the journalist María Teresa Ronderos, he founded the investigation portal www.verdadabierta.com, which reconstructed the truths of the paramilitary groups in Colombia within the framework of the transitional justice process known as Justice and Peace.

Ksenija Bilbija is Professor of Spanish American Literatures at the University of Wisconsin-Madison specialising in cultural studies, gender criticism, post-traumatic memory, and *cartonera* publishing. Her publications include *Cuerpos textuales: Metáforas de la génesis narrativa en la literatura latinoamericana del siglo XX*, and *Yo soy trampa: Ensayos sobre la obra de Luisa Valenzuela*. She co-edited *The Art of Truth-Telling about Authoritarian Rule*, *Accounting for Violence: Marketing Memory in Latin America*, *Academia cartonera: A Primer of Latin American Cartonera Publishers*, and most recently *Poner el cuerpo: Rescatar y visibilizar las macros sexuales y de género de los archivos dictatoriales del Cono Sur*. From 2001 to 2006 she was the editor of *Letras femeninas: Revista de literatura femenina hispánica*, and from 2007 to 2012 she directed the Latin American, Caribbean and Iberian Studies Programme at the University of Wisconsin-Madison.

Shane Darcy is a professor and Deputy Director at the Irish Centre for Human Rights in the School of Law at the National University of Ireland Galway. He is the author of *To Serve the Enemy: Informers, Collaborators and the Laws of Armed Conflict* (2019) and *Judges, Law and War: The Judicial Development of International Humanitarian Law* (2014). He is on the editorial boards of the *Business and Human Rights Journal*, the *Irish Yearbook of International Law*, and *Criminal Law Forum*. From 2019 to 2020 he was a Japan Society for the Promotion of Sciences Visiting Professor at Doshisha University, Kyoto.

Luis De la Calle is an associate professor of political science at Centro de Investigación y Docencia Económicas (CIDE), Mexico City. His broader research interests include terrorism, conflict dynamics, legacies of violence, and warfare and state capacity. His book *Nationalist Violence in Postwar Europe* (2015) examined why some sub-state nationalist movements turned to terrorism during the second half of the 20th century whereas others remained peaceful. Together with Ignacio Sánchez-Cuenca, he is working on a book-length project that lays out an original theory of terrorism. His previous work has been published in journals such as the *Annual Review of Political Science*, the *Journal of Politics*, the *Journal of Conflict Resolution*, and the *Journal of Peace Research*.

Andrea L. Dennis is Associate Dean for Faculty Development and holder of the John Byrd Martin Chair of Law at the University of Georgia School of Law, where she teaches criminal law, evidence, family law, and juvenile law. Her scholarship explores criminal and juvenile defence lawyering; race and criminal justice; and the impact of criminal justice on the lives of families, children, and youth. She is co-author of *Rap on Trial: Race, Lyrics, and Guilt in America* (2019), and author of numerous articles and shorter works. She is a graduate of the University of Maryland at College Park and of New York University School of Law.

Jacob Dlamini teaches African history at Princeton University. He is the author of *The Terrorist Album: Apartheid's Insurgents, Collaborators, and the Security Police* (2020), *Safari Nation: A Social History of the Kruger National Park* (2020), *Askari: A Story of Collaboration and Betrayal in the Anti-Apartheid Struggle* (2014), and the memoir *Native Nostalgia* (2009). He obtained his Ph.D. in history from Yale University in 2012.

Mark Drumbl is the Director of the Transnational Law Institute of Washington and Lee University, USA. He has held visiting appointments and has taught at Queen's University Belfast; University College, Oxford; Université de Paris (Panthéon-Assas); VU Amsterdam; and various other universities. His research and teaching interests include public international law, global environmental governance, international criminal law, post-conflict justice, and transnational legal process. His articles have appeared in the *NYU, Michigan, Northwestern, George Washington, Tulane*, and *North Carolina* law reviews, and many peer-reviewed journals, including *Human Rights Quarterly*, with shorter pieces in the *American Journal of International Law* and numerous other periodicals. He is the author of *Atrocity, Punishment, and International Law* (2007) and *Reimagining Child Soldiers in International Law and Policy* (2012).

Ron Dudai is Senior Lecturer in the Department of Sociology and Anthropology at the Ben-Gurion University of the Negev. He received his Ph.D. from the Institute of Criminology and Criminal Justice, Queen's University Belfast. His research interests include human rights, transitional justice, political violence, and the sociology of punishment. His work has been published in journals such as the *British Journal of Sociology*, *Law & Social Inquiry*, and *Punishment & Society*. He was co-editor of the *Journal of Human Rights Practice*.

Juan Espindola is a Research Fellow at the Institute for Philosophical Research at the National Autonomous University of Mexico. He was trained as a political theorist at the University of Michigan. His research focuses on complicity, violence, and transitional justice. He is the author of *Transitional Justice after German Reunification: Exposing Unofficial Collaborators* (2015). His work has appeared in journals such as *Studies in Philosophy and Education*, *Theory and Research in Education*, *Education Policy Analysis Archive*, *German Studies Review*, *Res publica*, *Ethical Theory and Moral Practice*, the *Journal of Social Philosophy*, and others.

Oren Gross is the Irving Younger Professor of Law at the University of Minnesota Law School. He is an internationally recognised expert in the areas of international law and national security law. He is also an expert on the Middle East and the Arab–Israeli conflict. Professor Gross holds an LL.B. degree *magna cum laude* from Tel Aviv University, where he served on the editorial board of the *Tel Aviv University Law Review*. He obtained LL.M. and S.J.D. degrees from Harvard Law School while a Fulbright Scholar.

Kevin Hearty is a Lecturer in Criminology at the School of Social Sciences, Education and Social Work at Queen's University Belfast. His research interests include criminal justice, policing, and transitional justice. He has published widely on political violence, state violence, and police reform in the north of Ireland. His monograph *Critical Engagement: Irish Republicanism, Memory Politics and Policing* (2017) critically examines police reform in the north of Ireland through an interdisciplinary lens of critical criminology, memory studies, and transitional justice. More recently, he has published in the *British Journal of Criminology* on debate around innocence and victimhood in Northern Ireland, and in *Social & Legal Studies* on the right to remember in transitional justice contexts.

Barbora Holá works as Senior Researcher at the Netherlands Institute for the Study of Crime and Law Enforcement (NSCR), and as Associate Professor at the Department of Criminal Law and Criminology at Vrije Universiteit Amsterdam. She has an interdisciplinary focus and studies transitional justice after atrocities, in particular (international) criminal trials, sentencing for international crimes, rehabilitation of war criminals, and life after trial at international criminal tribunals. Besides her research and teaching in the master's programme International Crimes and Criminology at VU Amsterdam, Barbora is a co-director of the Center for International Criminal

Justice, a knowledge centre dedicated to interdisciplinary studies of mass atrocity crimes and international criminal justice, and a co-chair of the European Society of Criminology Group on Atrocity Crimes and Transitional Justice.

Colleen Murphy is the Roger and Stephany Joslin Professor of Law and Professor of Philosophy and Political Science at the University of Illinois at Urbana-Champaign, where she also serves as Director of the Women and Gender in Global Perspectives Programme in the Illinois Global Institute. She is the author of *The Conceptual Foundations of Transitional Justice* (2017), which received the North American Society for Social Philosophy Book Award, and *A Moral Theory of Political Reconciliation* (2010), as well as more than 50 articles and book chapters. She has also co-edited three volumes. Dr Murphy is an Associate Editor of the *Journal of Ethics and Social Philosophy*, the *Journal of Human Development and Capabilities*, the *Journal of Moral Philosophy*, and *Science and Engineering Ethics*.

Leigh A. Payne is Professor of Sociology and Latin America at St Antony's College, Oxford. She has written extensively on right-wing movements, transitional justice, and human rights. Her work on collaborators emerges from two projects. Her book *Unsettling Accounts: Neither Truth nor Reconciliation in Confessions of State Violence* (2008) explores when civil society collaborators confess to past violence. Her recent co-authored book, *Transitional Justice and Corporate Accountability from Below: Deploying Archimedes' Lever* (2020), with Gabriel Pereira and Laura Bernal-Bermúdez, examines economic actors who collaborated in past state and armed conflict violence. She holds a Ph.D. from Yale University.

Gabriel Pereira is a researcher at the Consejo Nacional de Investigaciones Científicas y Técnicas of Argentina (CONICET) and an affiliated researcher to the Latin American Centre of the University of Oxford. He is also a Professor in Human Rights at the School of Law at the National University of Tucumán. He has written in journals and books on fields including transitional justice, business and human rights, human rights, and judicial politics. He is a co-founder and member of the human rights organisation Andhes.

Carlos Andrés Prieto is a former adviser to the Office of the High Commissioner for La Paz and part of the government delegation in the negotiation talks with FARC and ELN. He was also the former coordinator of the area of conflict dynamics and peace negotiations of the Ideas for Peace Foundation (FIP) and the Open Truth portal between 2011 and 2014.

Acknowledgements

This volume would not have been possible without the generous support of multiple institutions and persons. First of all, it benefitted from a generous grant from the Newton Advanced Fellowship of the British Academy (NAFR2180049). This grant allowed us to hold a workshop in Mexico City in 2019 (just a couple of months before the world went into lockdown) where the first drafts of the chapters were presented and discussed. A second iteration of the workshop was supposed to take place at the University of Oxford a few months later. Owing to the pandemic, the opportunity never came. Instead, the final versions of the chapters came to full fruition in virtual workshops held several months later.

We express our gratitude to the reviewers of the Proceedings of the British Academy. We would also like to thank Helen Flitton, Portia Taylor, Dorian Singh, and Robert Whitelock for their wonderful editorial support. We also thank Kiran Stallone for her brilliant translation of Chapter 7, originally written in Spanish.

We are grateful to our home institutions – the National Autonomous University of Mexico and the University of Oxford – for their support.

Most important of all, we thank the contributors to the volume – our collaborators – for the work they put into their texts.

1

Coming to Terms with Collaboration: An Introduction

JUAN ESPINDOLA AND LEIGH A. PAYNE

A Story of Betrayal and 30 Coins?

JUDAS ISCARIOT IS the iconic collaborator. The Gospels tell a simple story about his motivations for betraying Jesus. In the Gospel of Matthew, the assumption is that he did so for 30 pieces of silver, while the Gospel of Luke and the Gospel of John refer to Satan's possession over him. Judas is recorded as taking his own life out of remorse for his actions, which ended in Jesus's crucifixion. In this version, Judas himself recognised the wrong he had committed. For Dante Alighieri (1935 [1320]), that wrongdoing renders Judas famously frozen in Cocytus, the ninth and lowest circle of hell, along with others who betrayed relatives, country, rules of hospitality, and lords and benefactors. The location in the lowest of circles is of course significant, given that the structure of hell in *Inferno* embodies a moral hierarchy of possible wrongs. If that were not enough, Judas is perpetually chewed by Lucifer in the pit of hell – the most severe punishment of all. This Judas story is thus a warning about the evils of collaboration.

Yet not all versions of Judas portray him as supremely evil, immoral, or deserving of harsh punishment. An alternative perspective casts him as a man who loved his country, a patriot, who believed Jesus had provoked conflict and discord that would undermine and threaten it. Jesus had to be stopped. Judas's seeming betrayal of Jesus was, thus, motivated by virtue and loyalty to his land and people. Others contend that Judas, as part of his connection to the priestly class, originally aimed to spy on Jesus with the aim of protecting his class from harm, but unexpectedly became Jesus's most devout disciple. In this version, the 30 coins were a paltry sum, a symbolic reward for a rich man. He did not betray Jesus for money; he did so out of commitment to his community. In this interpretation, Judas took his own life when he came to terms with the results of his actions; his misguided

Proceedings of the British Academy, **248**, 1–26, © The British Academy 2022.

beliefs, which led him to commit an atrocity; and his subsequent love for Jesus. He could not live with himself and his acts (Borges 1944). Or perhaps, as in yet another version, it was Judas, 'the most loyal of all Apostles', who persuaded Jesus to travel to Jerusalem, where he would perform the miracle of descending from the cross. Judas' treason, if this is to be considered treason, happened at the moment when Jesus died and Judas lost faith in him (Oz 2014).

These versions of Judas's acts leave doubt and ambiguity over what has tended to be interpreted as a clear story of treachery and material self-interest. They show the complexity of the deceptively simple subject of collaboration. Who is the collaborator, or in whose eyes? What is the motivation to collaborate: for material gain, for ideology, for duty? When is collaboration betraying a hated enemy, and when is it something else: personal revenge or an instrumental, rational, or even coerced response to a situation, for example? Why do collaborators meet such harsh punishment and stigma when they are revealed as such? Can they ever atone or find redemption? Beyond the perception of the stakeholders involved, how harmful is collaboration? Does it exacerbate or abate violence? Is it always evil or can it sometimes be seen as mitigating wrongs?

The chapters in this book explore these thorny questions through a set of case studies, disciplinary approaches, and temporal and regional contexts. They show the range of the types of collaboration; the ubiquity of collaboration across time, countries, political systems, and political and cultural conflicts. Underlying each of the chapters is the foundational question, what is collaboration?

The Problem of Collaboration

Grappling with the concept of collaboration, as the example of Judas shows, is not a simple task. Two simple understandings stand in opposition. To collaborate, in one meaning, involves the action of working with someone to produce or create something. This connotes a positive relationship, of working toward a productive end. The synonyms are alliance and partnership. We, the authors in this volume, collaborated to produce it. The other meaning, the cooperation with an enemy, traitorous or not, assumes a negative and destructive relationship synonymous to collusion, consorting, conspiring, and betraying. That this one word has such contradictory understandings exposes part of the 'problem of collaboration' examined in this book. We attempt to unpack the concept in its positive and negative light, identify its complexity, and bring greater depth and clarity to its comprehension.

This is not the first study of collaboration. On the contrary, previous studies have illuminated the importance of collaborators in perpetuating extremist violence in historically poignant examples. The previous scholarship has thus defined collaboration as time- and context-dependent.

An important literature on Holocaust collaborators has made key contributions to understanding the term. And, yet, each contribution is distinct without building a generalisable concept around the phenomenon as a whole. Jewish collaborators in Nazi concentration camps, for example, contribute to an understanding of collaborators as victim-perpetrators in a 'grey zone' (Levi 1996, 2017; Card 2002). Studies of non-Jewish citizens who collaborated with the Nazi system are perceived not as operating in a grey zone, but rather as 'willing executioners' (Goldhagen 1996) and 'ordinary men' who commit atrocity (Browning 1992). Hannah Arendt's (1994) concept of 'the banality of evil' has also been used to understand motivations behind Nazi collaborators. These types of collaboration do not all fit a narrow notion of 'traitorous cooperation with an enemy', but neither do they necessarily conform to the connotation of collaboration as working together to create or produce something. They suggest a degree of coercion emerging from a complex set of social codes; upbringing (Adorno *et al.* 1950); or an innate tendency toward self-protection, protection of others, and a sense of duty and obedience to authority (Milgram 1974). Applying existing definitions thus reveal more complexity in the term. What does 'traitorous' mean? Who is the enemy? According to whom?

Vichy France is another key historical reference that has defined collaboration. Indeed, one study of the etymology of the word 'collaboration' locates its negative usage only in 1940 to mean 'traitorous cooperation with an occupying enemy', referring first to the Vichy Government of France (Webster 1999). Prior to the Vichy era and the Holocaust, and beginning in the 1860s, collaboration had a positive connotation. It 'acquired a pejorative and/or polemical connotation signifying primarily the collaboration of native political forces with the Axis occupiers during the Second World War. In its most polemical dimension, the term has become synonymous with treason and the adoption of a Fascist or Nazi ideological position' (Kalyvas 2008: 109). Indeed, the only philosophical writing we have found specifically focused on collaboration is by Jean-Paul Sartre (2017 [1976]), referring to the Vichy period.

Defining collaboration in a way that emphasises wrongdoing is time- and context-specific, especially in the Europe of the 1940s, the period of Nazi Germany and Vichy France.[1] But it also took on a similar hue during the period of Communism in eastern Europe.[2] There are films, memoirs, novels, and academic studies examining the extensive network of elite and everyday informers and spies who collaborated with Czech, East German, Hungarian, Latvian, Polish, Romanian, Yugoslav, and other Communist authorities wilfully, instrumentally, or under duress (Apor *et al.* 2017). Outing those individuals in the post-Communist era through lustration efforts have revealed a painful part of the past still denied, condemned, and debated (Connelly 2005; Nalepa 2010; Espindola 2015; David 2018).

---

[1] A notable exception is Thiranagama and Kelly's *Traitors* (2010). The book is rooted in anthropology and cultural sociology. It presents a very broad array of historical cases, and ties collaboration to questions of state-building (whether collaborators are identified and punished is a function of the anxieties of new nations) and intimacy (betrayal is ubiquitous in social life, but is turned into treason and confronted violently in specific regimes and periods).
[2] Narvselius and Grinchenko's book (2018) is narrow in its territorial scope, focusing only on eastern Europe.

To capture the variation in types of collaboration requires greater comparative and analytical precision to develop a concept that applies to a range of contexts. This book attempts to do so; it marks a shift in collaboration studies. It recognises that the time has come to broaden the framework to examine collaboration across territory and time, to acknowledge its geographical and historical ubiquity, and to contribute to building a stronger theoretical foundation. The contributions to the volume include historical references to the Holocaust (Gross) and Communism (Drumbl and Holá), but it looks at similarities and differences with other times and places of collaboration: Argentina's period of state terror (Bilbija; Pereira); Chile under the Pinochet dictatorship (Murphy); Spain and the struggle in the Basque Country (De la Calle); Northern Ireland's Troubles and the aftermath (Dudai and Hearty); South Africa's apartheid era (Dlamini); Colombia's armed conflict (Arias and Prieto); slavery in the United States (Dennis); and even the international community's articulation of humanitarian and human rights law (Darcy).

The volume not only offers an array of examples to demonstrate the ubiquity of collaboration and its extension over territory and time; it also teases out a framework for examining collaboration. This framework emerges from the multidisciplinary approach taken in the book, merging the social sciences and the humanities: specifically history, philosophy, political science, sociology, law, and literary studies. This framing chapter, and the empirical case studies that follow, probe novel questions that have not been fully explored in previous work.

This set of case studies and approaches additionally connects the project to the multidisciplinary field of transitional justice, where collaboration remains a neglected subject of enquiry compared to other subjects. As 'the full range of processes and mechanisms associated with a society's attempt to come to terms with a legacy of large-scale past abuses, in order to ensure accountability, serve justice and achieve reconciliation' (United Nations 2010), transitional justice offers a lens for how collaboration fits, or not, into responses to atrocity. These chapters grapple with those questions.

The book questions how collaboration is defined and how the concept changes across time, events, and borders. It further asks who counts as a collaborator, according to whom, and for what reasons. The volume probes causal processes, or how ordinary people become entangled in a web of collaboration; the steps that lead to active participation; and the discursive explanations made for the involvement that rarely admit to treachery and, instead, emphasise survival or reward motives, altruism (protection of others), and heroism. The volume takes a dynamic approach, recognising that views of collaboration and its moral valence can change over-time. These changes may be internal, personal, and individual to the collaborators themselves. They may also involve dramatic social and political shifts. The book also questions assumptions that collaborators actively engage in social or political processes that contribute to conflict. While this is true in some cases, this volume illuminates cases where collaborators – even when traitorous – mitigate conflict, attempt to rebuild social and political order, and contribute to the public good, rather than undermining it. It thus explores the long-term consequences of collaboration. It considers the ways in which retributive and restorative justice systems might address collaboration's harm but also the possibilities of redemption for the collaborator. In sum, the book thus examines, across a range of contexts, *who* are the collaborators, *what* makes a collaborator, *where* have they emerged, *why* do they collaborate, *how* have they been appraised and dealt with by states and societies, and *when* a response to collaboration is necessary or desirable.

In this conceptual chapter we set out some of the broad contours of the notion of collaboration that the chapters address: the who, what, where, why, how, and when of collaboration. We then provide brief descriptions of the chapters. In the conclusion to the volume, we return to these themes, bringing the contributions within it into a comparative framework for understanding collaboration.

The Making of a Collaborator

Collaboration in its negative sense is typically understood as the act of supporting an enemy in betrayal of one's community, with detrimental consequences for that community. This definition goes some way into defining collaboration, but it can also be profoundly misleading. Like kin and sometimes overlapping terms such as treason (Fabre 2020; Dudai 2021), betrayal (Margalit 2017) and complicity (Kutz 2000; Lepora and Goodin 2013), collaboration is a contestable notion. By this we mean that the act of branding individuals or groups as collaborators is always mediated by irresolvable disputes: ideological, political, and of other kinds. These are the disputes that we seek to shed light on in this introduction, and that the authors address throughout the book.

Despite ambiguity in the definition of the term, despite alternative versions of their acts – such as the Judas story – collaborators, just like informers (Natapoff 2009) tend to be despised figures stigmatised as evil doers. They are a kind of 'folkdevil' (Dudai 2012). The labels ascribed to them speak for themselves: snitch, turncoat, tout, *cipayo*, *impipi*, *chivato*, quisling, *Spitzel*, Benedict Arnold, *botifler*, frog. Black collaboration in the United States has produced a lexicon of its own: house slave, Uncle Tom, sell-out, Oreo (Dennis, Chapter 6). Yet one of the insights that this volume unveils is that collaboration is poorly understood within narrow parameters of treason or betrayal.

Avishai Margalit (2017) is one to propose viewing collaboration through the lens of betrayal. Margalit argues that collaboration is an act of betrayal when it weakens or destroys 'thick relations', that is, those basic social relationships modelled after the family (the clan, the ethnic community, nation) that rest on a sense of shared belonging and on shared memory. This is just what, in Margalit's eyes, Pétain, the paradigmatic collaborator, did. Margalit writes: 'Pétain betrayed ... the people with whom he felt he shared strong thick relations by debasing the values of their shared past' (2017: 216).

While defining collaboration in this way, Margalit identifies what may be one of the central and most controversial questions about collaboration – who has the authority to judge who is a collaborator and, most importantly, does collaboration always mean betrayal? If, Margalit asks, Pétain enjoyed the support of many of his fellow countrymen, which he did, in what sense did he betray them? And who is entitled to call him a collaborator? Margalit invokes the figure of what he calls the *gestor*, an 'agent of necessity', who is in the best position to interpret the common good in a given historical juncture. In his example, Charles de Gaulle occupies that role. His leadership determined the coordinates of resistance and collaboration.

Views such as Margalit's are quite extensive in the scholarship on collaboration. Yet their orientation ignores a central concern that the authors in this volume consider to be critical to the analysis of collaboration. The point of departure of conventional studies is that collaborators ought to have shown allegiance to a community and to an identity of shared belonging and memory, readily recognisable and acceptable to every stakeholder. When collaborators fail to maintain such an allegiance they become the subject of examination and condemnation. According to this view, any group that assists our enemy is a collaborator, while those assisting groups that we value will not. Those who 'collaborate' with the groups we support are seen as brave and defiant, as standing up for principles: the resistance, the righteous among nations, rescuers, whistle-blowers. These notions presume that a collaborator should have been on one side, but for some set of reasons (usually reflecting poorly on the character of the collaborator) changed loyalties.

While these views of collaboration as 'betrayals of trust and loyalty' (Ben-Yehuda 2001) reflect part of the phenomenon, they fail to do justice to its complexity. The problem is that in many contexts where collaborators are at work, crystallised communities and identities are not always present. And the use of the label of 'collaborator' may be precisely a way in which political actors try to crystallise them, or to challenge them if they do exist. This is not to say that disputes around the notion of collaboration cannot thrive where political identities have cemented over decades or centuries. In the archetypical, extreme case, such as the Occupation under the Axis powers and, more generally, the foreign occupation by a patently unjust regime, the demarcations between the the community and the outgroup (us and them) may be clearer. But even then, in times of political upheaval, boundaries are in perpetual influx (for an example of this, focusing on the case of China and Taiwan, see Strauss (2010)). Identities are also multiple and overlapping. Put succinctly, the collaborator label is not ascribed above the fray of politics. The attribution of the label can be part of a power struggle and, more specifically, a tool of (de)legitimation. Political actors (ETA, the IRA, Black activists in South Africa, to name a few of those that appear in this volume) may try to weaponise the label and identify other political actors as collaborators in a battle of public narratives.

Along similar lines, calling someone a collaborator can be a way to isolate or eliminate them. When something goes wrong, it is useful to blame collaborators, rather than to self-blame. Damage to the group itself, moreover, can be attributed to informants, double-agents, or collaborators rather than to the internal erosion of support. Establishing consequences for those identified as 'informants' is also a way to silence internal opposition.

Notions of the 'exceptional' collaborator as traitorous evildoer ignore how ubiquitous collaboration is. It is unlikely that any armed group – within or outside the state – can survive without informers. The intelligence they provide can undermine operations on one side and help the other. They have the information that can lead to an ambush that can advance one side over another. The same is true beyond armed conflict. If such collaboration helps our side, those involved are our heroes. If they betray our side, they are collaborators. It is not the act of collaboration, but rather whom it helps and whom it harms that matters in determining who is the collaborator.

Another reason why the notion of collaboration is not productively examined through the lens of betrayal is that collaborators may not *intend* to betray their community, and may not hurt their community, or hurt them as badly as alternative actions might. Beyond the motives of the collaborators, which we discuss below, the collaborator may be circumstantially placed in the position to collaborate by factors outside her control. The case of Jewish leaders in the *Judenräte* (an archetypical site of collaboration) or the Jewish police is a good example of this. In his study on the behaviour of Jews in the ghettos of Minsk, Krakow, and Białystok, Evgeny Finkel (2017: 69–97) brings attention to the prewar political regimes under which the Jews lived, and particularly to whether collaborators did or did not have prior political experience. According to Finkel, those who engaged in prewar political activism were more likely to engage in cooperation and public collaboration.[3] Not only did political activism reflect their prior commitment to protecting their communities, it gave them skills and experience for organisation and mobilisation. It made them visible members of the community and therefore inclined them to assume or be assigned leadership roles, especially when it came to cooperation and public collaboration. Conversely, people who engaged in private and clandestine (and sometimes public) collaboration were lacking in previous political experience and rather were consciously willing to increase their chances of survival by harming the community, and therefore reducing those of other Jews. Corrupt *Judenrat* chairs, paid informers for the Nazi security services, and Jewish policemen who helped the Germans round up Jews for deportation to death camps in exchange for a promise of personal safety fall within this category.[4] The point is that narrowing collaboration merely to those acts that harmed the collaborator's

---

[3] Finkel (2017) distinguishes between cooperation and collaboration. Cooperation – which he defines as being open and visible – was geared toward preserving the community and its members. Collaboration – which could be public or private – knowingly worked to the detriment of the community's or individual Jews' survival.

[4] The vast majority of Jews within ghettos fell between the two ends of this spectrum, choosing compliance, coping, and evasion.

community improperly reduces the phenomenon, distorting its historical significance. Some collaborators were not treacherous in the sense of intending to harm their communities (if they in fact identified with one): quite the opposite.

What this discussion shows is the layered nature of allegiances to nation, ethnicity, family, ideology, class. When these allegiances come into conflict, notions of loyalty and betrayal are not always clear. People may feel the 'pull' of one allegiance over another (Shklar 1984; Lifton 1993). Priorities can shift over time, as a result of internal or external dynamics. More radically, it is sometimes the case that a collaborator becomes one not because he or she violated a group's trust, with deleterious consequences for that group. Rather, the group construes the collaborator's acts as treacherous so that it can benefit from the attribution of that role to others, with positive consequences for the group. Collaboration – or the accusation thereof – is not a burden, but an asset to extract political benefit. The collaborator is not, then, a fixed type. Indeed, the collaborator can be made, is brought into being: crafted as it were from the materials of the society in question.

This volume avoids facile assumptions about who is a collaborator. It adds complexity and nuance. It considers these and other ambiguities. The definition we adopt captures the range of people, situations, and dynamics over time embodied in this single term. We refer to collaboration simply and broadly as *the set attitudes, actions, or omissions that converge to assist a group undertaking or seeking to undertake actions that appear contrary to the community's interest.* The type of assistance and its motivation vary. Collaborators in this sense may be members of the threatened community. When they are, they usually earn the narrower label of 'collaborationist' (although the terms collaborator and collaborationist are commonly used indistinctly). The bonds of loyalty that demarcate the contours of the collaborationist group or individual, and therefore the outside group, are open to controversy – in the present and in retrospect.

We consider our definition to broaden existing definitions to apply to a range of contexts, overcoming previous geographically and temporally fixed, and normatively rigid conceptualisations. It may be argued that broadening the notion in the way we propose simply means supporting institutional wrongdoing, rendering any perpetrator a collaborator. By emphasising the 'appearance' of betrayal, the definition suggests that motivation for collaboration is often constructed by others, rather than by the collaborators themselves. The point of the definition and of this volume is to call attention to the fact that judgements invoking betrayal rest on certain assumptions about what it means to belong to a community and which kinds of actions harm it. These assumptions shape the way in which we identify collaborators, the motivations we attribute to them, and the accountability measures we think best suit their deeds. We think it is worth exploring these assumptions in a diverse array of contexts.

Similarly, it may be argued that under this definition the acts of, say, a German law professor 'collaborating' with the regime in Nazi Germany in the 1930s, and a French law professor 'collaborating' with German authorities during the Occupation in 1942 would fall under the same types of acts and would be given the same moral valence. Our definition does not intend to convey this idea. In the examples just mentioned, it is clear to us that occupied people, who tend to be under duress, are less blameworthy for their acts (see Lepora and Goodin (2013: 128)) than people who face no such constraints – presumably the case of the German law professor. What the two cases have in common, however, is the impulse on the part of political actors and observers to identify some persons or groups as collaborators, an impulse that arises from a legitimation strategy or unexamined beliefs. It is worth examining these sources, because they have political implications with respect to how 'collaborators' are reckoned with, historically and politically.

A final critical point about collaboration, albeit one that is orthogonal to the challenges of application discussed before, is the gendered nature of the attribution of the label of collaborator. Collaborators tend to be characterised as male figures who seemingly take advantage of a difficult situation to save themselves by exerting power over others. Because collaborators tend to be seen as marginal figures who join forces with powerful groups over weaker enemies, their masculinity is often questioned. Sartre made the controversial statement that collaborators, content with their subordinate role and recognising their 'weakness', had recourse to 'cunning', which in Sartre's view is one of 'the weapons of the weak – women's weapons' (2017 [1976]: 61). Feminising collaborators, however, fails to recognise the female collaborator. When she does emerge, she is often villainised for using her sexual prowess – her cunning – as a weapon to protect herself while selling her people short, literally 'screwing' them. An emblematic, if mythical, instance of this is the Malinche, a native of pre-Conquest Mexico who served as a translator and adviser to the Spanish conquistadors; she 'was considered a hero' in the aftermath of the Conquest but over time was 'increasingly regarded as a traitor, a whore, a racial turncoat who collaborated with the Spanish invaders' (Ben-Yehuda 2001: 271). The chapters in this volume present the gendered notions of collaborators in a much more complex manner than previously examined, particularly in the case of female victim-collaborators (Bilbija; Murphy; Dennis) but also with regard to the economic or structural conditions in which females may be induced to collaborate (Dudai and Hearty; Drumbl and Holá; Dennis).

Collaboration Motives, Collaboration Moments

Some classic scholarship has illuminated relevant distinctions among collaborators. In his work on the Nazi Occupation of France, Stanley Hoffman distinguished between collaboration 'for reasons of state' (*collaboration d'état*), meant to safeguard French interests in interstate relations between vanquished and victorious power, and collaboration with the Nazis, which Hoffman referred to as 'openly desired co-operation with and imitation of the German regime' (Hoffman 1968: 376). Within *collaboration d'état*, he further distinguished between voluntary and involuntary collaboration – roughly: uncoerced and coerced, respectively. Along similar lines, Sartre argued that there were 'disinterested collaborators' who preferred German victory without seeking to derive any advantage. Sartre (2017 [1976]: 56) criticises these collaborators for what he calls their ill-conceived realism, that is, for endorsing a debased pragmatism and for judging historical events, such as Nazi victory, as unavoidable and therefore acceptable. He also recognises the disillusioned idealists: for example, pacifists who believed *pax germanica* would be the only road toward peace.

As this taxonomy suggests, collaboration takes many forms. It may be spontaneous and not presuppose any formal tie between the collaborator and the group she or he assists. Alternatively, it may stem from a premeditated plan whereby the collaborator has a clear institutional role within this group. The collaborator may receive a material reward of some kind: a salary or single payment (in a pay-per-give model); a work permit; a lenient sentence or legal exculpation for a defendant; residence benefits where migratory status is irregular; a favourable environment to conduct business transactions, in the case of corporate complicity; or something else. Non-material rewards also exist, such as postponing imminent death, as in the case of Jewish informers in Italy who helped Nazis track fellow Jews for deportation and certain annihilation, only to be annihilated themselves once they had outlived their usefulness (on this last point see Sullam 2020). Collaboration can be carried out in secret or openly, as when the sheer co-participation in economic or other kinds of activities with a rival group is grounds for the accusation of collaboration.

Interestingly, collaborators may offer intangible but critical assistance in the form of ideological support. Sometimes a collaborator will not merely provide auxiliary and secondary assistance – however crucial – by lending legitimacy to decisions that a strongly institutionalised regime or group has already taken. Instead, the collaboration may occur in the context of weak institutions, and the collaborator may be a close adviser or provider of critical information, steering the course of the conflict or inflicting great damage.

Individuals may become collaborators for many reasons. Collaborative acts are usually regarded as being motivated by ideological affinity to the outside group, by pure self-interest, by the perception on the part of the collaborator that collaboration might mitigate harm (to oneself or one's community), by the perception that collaboration makes no difference, that no one will be harmed, or by resentment or fear.

Self-interested reasons for collaboration are salient in contexts of asymmetrical relationships between rival political or ethnic groups, and where members of the weaker group stand to gain from collaboration as a valued resource. Hillel Cohen offers an example of this in discussing the collaboration of Israeli Arabs with Israel. Cohen argues that this group faced a cruel dilemma: 'They could help their own people, acquaintances, and sometimes even members of their families, in violation of Israeli law and at personal danger to themselves, or they could collaborate with those who pursued the infiltrators, in violation of their fidelity to their people and families' (Cohen 2010: 68).[5] Those who collaborated with the Israeli regime did so for a variety of reasons, such as receiving compensation in the form of a residence permit for a relative, financial rewards, a bargain to avoid criminal charges, and so on. But Cohen also notes that not all of those who *resisted* collaboration, assisting infiltrators by providing them with a place to hide or refusing to alert authorities, did so for principled reasons (e.g. nationalism). Some aided infiltrators for self-interested reasons as well (2010: 69ff.). This example illustrates some of the predicaments collaborators face, as well as challenging the false dichotomy between self-interested collaborators and selfless members of the resistance.

As Stathis Kalyvas's (2012: 330–63) work shows, malice is a pervasive driver of some collaborative acts, especially denunciations. In his view, it is a mistake to presuppose that malicious denunciations are atypical or a deviation from the purportedly more common ideological ones. He provides ample evidence suggesting that malice is in fact a main motivating force of denunciations. The desire of political actors for information (combatants in a civil war, repressive forces in authoritarian regimes, even security agencies in democracies) presents individuals with an opportunity to castigate intimate others (neighbours, co-workers, 'friends', even relatives and spouses). In return for protection and the mediation from the political actor (who metes out 'punishment' for the act that is denounced, thus allowing the denunciator to keep his or her hands clean), denunciation gives men and women the opportunity to exact vengeance on others whom they would not otherwise have treated in this way. Intimacy, then, while seemingly an inauspicious ground for denunciation, is in fact very hospitable to it. Intimacy breeds envy and resentment just as much as it breeds more noble passions, and such negative emotions often lie at the core of denunciations.[6]

Other motivations seem to be salient in cases of collaboration. Sartre notes that describing collaborators as purely self-interested and ambitious persons crudely

---

[5] Cohen charts the attitudes of Israeli Arabs in the face of this predicament along a spectrum that resonates with other cases of collaboration: 'At one end was the classic nationalist position that the refugees had the right to enter the country and that the Arab citizens of Israel were morally bound to assist them. At the other extreme was the collaborationist approach, which advocated unconditional assistance (in operations, intelligence, and propaganda) to the state and its institutions. Most of the country's Arabs found themselves at various points along this spectrum, influenced by personal and family loyalties, by utilitarian considerations growing out of the authorities' policies of reward and punishment, and by ideological and economic factors. Some helped the infiltrators, some ignored them, and some took advantage of their vulnerability to defraud them' (Cohen 2010: 69).

[6] Vandana Joshi (2002) explores the active denunciation of wives during the Third Reich: wives in abusive marriages, divorced wives, and even women with extramarital affairs who wished to get rid of their husbands denounced their partners, telling the Gestapo that they listened to foreign radio or that they cursed against authority at home, less out of ideological conviction than as a way of pushing back against violent husbands, taking revenge on former husbands to whom they might still be connected (for example, through alimony), or simply to rid themselves of them. For these women, the Gestapo was a 'conflict resolution agency', and denunciation was an extra-legal, extra-judicial stick with which to discipline current or previous spouses (2002: 435).

simplifies the problem. He puts forth sociological and psychological explanations for collaboration during Vichy's France. He argues that collaborators are usually 'social outcasts' who were marginal in their societies in times of peace, but who regarded occupation as an opportunity to become somehow relevant. Similar motivations may explain entirely different cases of collaboration (Van Onselen 2007).

While the motivations for collaboration discussed before illuminate part of the phenomenon, there is much that escapes categories such as ideology, self-interest, class resentment, duress, and so on as the incentives for collaboration. Some may sit somewhere between political good and private personal gain. There is a tendency to put large-scale or significant forms of collaboration on a par with small acts. Indeed, the place for opportunistic social navigation has escaped attention within transitional justice processes, as will be argued extensively in some of the chapters of the book.

Some feel that the organisation that they once supported has betrayed its origins. They become disillusioned and more susceptible to collaboration. Or some argue that they remain loyal to their nation or organisation, but betray specific policies, leaders, or organisations (Ben-Yehuda 2001: 15). Pure opportunism is also evident in some forms of collaboration. An example is Joe Mamasela in apartheid South Africa, who may have been a member of the liberation army in exile that he later betrayed. His handlers claimed he extracted a handsome price for that betrayal from his new employers in the apartheid police, but then he offered to sell the truth about the police to the highest bidder at the end of apartheid. His funds were cut off and his testimony deemed worthless when it became apparent that Mamasela 'could not separate fact from fiction' (Payne 2008: 218; see also Pauw 1997).

In other words, the idea of 'born collaborators' – those with particular personalities, social deviance, or avarice – is less convincing than understanding the situations that may lead individuals to collaborate. The context in which one begins to collaborate is thus critical to understanding the act. A broader conceptualisation of collaboration that is not relegated to a specific time and place, but exposes the pathways taken in a variety of country and historic contexts, reveals a more compelling set of patterns of understanding.

Supposed collaborators are often mistakenly branded as such, even under a simple understanding of the term. This was the case of Jean McConville, who was kidnapped, murdered, and disappeared by the Provisional Irish Republican Army in 1972 after being accused of passing information to the British authorities. It is disputed whether she was, in fact, an informer; if she ever gave any information to the British authorities; if she was even capable of doing so, given that she was a widow, poor, and mother of 10 children; if she even had any information to give; and, if she did indeed give up information, whether it could have any way harmed the Republican cause (Keefe 2018).

Perceptions about who is a collaborator may not only be factually false; they may shift over time. The (in)famous phrase 'treason is a matter of dates' is commonly attributed to Charles Maurice de Talleyrand. Indeed, the passage of time, and the change in circumstances that accompanies it, may render some acts permissible or impermissible to the stakeholders. What constitutes an act of collaboration might vary as socio-economic conditions worsen or improve. The case of Palestinian collaborators, as discussed by Tobias Kelly (2010), is a case in point. When Palestinians were undergoing economic hardship, Kelly argues, cooperation with Israel was tolerated; by contrast, in times of prosperity, such cooperation was deemed inadmissible collaboration. Similarly, after transitions from autocracy or civil war, society might move away from old, negative connotations around citizen denunciation and come to praise them. An act that was regarded as objectionable in the past (particularly because it was regarded as supporting an oppressive regime, as in Communist countries, or perpetuating violence) comes to be seen as a civic act.

In keeping with the question of what constitutes collaboration and the dynamic aspect of the question, frequently there is a *post facto* redrawing of the category tied to memory politics. Narvselius and Grinchenko (2018) bring together in their book several instances of *post hoc* efforts to revise and reinterpret cases of past betrayal. For instance, it can be argued that what seemed like changing sides really is not, as when Nazi collaborators in occupied France came to be regarded as protectors of the nation trying to avert the worst. The valuation of the deeds of collaborators may be inverted, as when, in cases of 'horizontal collaboration', Soviet women involved with Germans come to be admired rather than despised for running enormous risks. The boundary between betrayal and non-betrayal may be presented as thin, situational, or blurred. Additionally, there may be attempts to suspend denunciations by arguing that the betrayed state was morally corrupt or that disloyalty toward it was superseded by higher moral reasons (e.g. democratic values or religious principles).

Timing is also relevant in coming to terms with collaborators. Informers may, for instance, be first seen as an occupational hazard during civil strife, but as traitors in the aftermath of conflict, once-suppressed hatred against them emerges. In Northern Ireland, Martin McGuinness, who had once called for 'death to the informer', appealed to his community to pass on information to the police about a violent splinter group that threatened the peace accord. 'Informing' thus became an act of good citizenship (See also Keefe 2019).

Collaboration on Trial?

Communities reckon with collaborators in different ways, both during and after the conflict in which the collaboration is embedded. Those who are identified as collaborators – and those who are not identified as such, but acted in similar or even more damning ways (as we reference towards the end of this section) – are usually judged and treated harshly, sometimes more harshly than the 'principals' of wrongdoing, e.g. leaders, police-officers, military personnel, or even torturers. Whether in the form of legal or informal punishment (e.g. public shaming or lustration), or in the form of a-posteriori reprobation or stigmatisation, collaborators join the annals of infamy more frequently than other political actors. What accounts for the severity of the treatment? Is it justified? And how do collaborators respond? Is punishment morally appropriate?

Beginning with the question of harshness: at one level, as other studies have shown, part of the reason explaining the level of condemnation of collaborators may be that they are perceived as traitors who violated their fellow citizens' trust. As Kelly and Thiranagama (2010: 2) argue, 'the acts of treason seem to threaten and destabilise the fragile moral and social relationships that hold us together and bind us to the perhaps otherwise abstract notions of nation, people, or community'. The implied treason in collaborative acts is felt by members of the community as touching them too closely, as it were (Dudai 2021).

Severe punishment of collaborators may also be a disciplinary measure on the part of a group (an armed non-state actor, a regime, an oppressed minority) to control its ranks, maintain and accrue legitimacy, or resist oppressive policies, particularly in cases where collaboration is understood to pose an existential threat. The greater the threat, the harsher the punishment. Assaf (2002) describes a pattern of assassinations of Jewish informers by their own communities in the Russian Pale of Settlement in the 1830s, illustrating how the severity of the treatment of collaborators may reflect the community's perception of the menace their collaboration poses to it. Similarly, the desperate members of the resistance in the Warsaw Ghetto executed everyone whom they regarded as collaborationist (Arens 2011).

In the case of armed political groups, harsh punishment has additional functions. Severely punishing collaborators may simply be a part of a communicative strategy – sending a message of 'zero tolerance' for collaboration attempts to gain territorial control. Along these lines, Ron Dudai (2018) argues that informal punishment of informers by the Irish Republican Army (IRA) during the Northern Ireland conflict can be understood as an effort to convey a state-like image, to exert social control over its members, and to legitimate its actions. In the McConville case mentioned previously, it is hard to imagine that the victim/possible collaborator was much of a threat to the IRA. Her punishment, however, was significant in thwarting any would-be collaborator.[7]

In the aftermath of the conflict, the severity of the condemnation may reflect the attempt by some political actors to scapegoat collaborators for their complicity in wrongdoing, for which those same actors share an equal or perhaps even greater part of the responsibility. This was the case of many collaborators in post-Communist regimes. In the German Democratic Republic (GDR), for instance, *inoffizielle Mitarbeiter* (unofficial collaborators, or IM) were singled out and publicly shamed

[7] Keefe's (2019) study of the IRA emphasises the tensions felt by those who had to carry out the execution and disappearance of collaborators, particularly those who became double collaborators (working for the British as spies on the IRA and working for the IRA as spies on the British) and even advanced the Republican cause. There was simply no room for any kind of collaboration with the British, meaning that even low levels of collaboration, false collaboration, useful collaboration, or meaningless collaboration faced severe punishment.

for their complicity with the Stasi (Espindola 2015: 140–83). Exposing them, or rather *only* them, oversimplified the repertoire of responsibilities for political action and attitudes that made the activities of IM possible in the first place. Other types of contributions to, and other varieties of complicity with, the Stasi, were left outside the scope of moral scrutiny in German public discourse as a consequence of the narrow focus on the public shaming of IM.[8]

Finally, severe treatment of collaborators may be owed to gender considerations. Women may receive a punishment that is disproportionately harsh compared with that received by men who collaborated in comparable ways – perhaps even in more compromising ways. In the infamous case of the *femmes tondues*, after the Liberation in France in the aftermath of the Second World War, female collaborators were publicly humiliated by having their heads shaved, even when in many instances they did nothing but maintain intimate relationships with German soldiers. These punishments took place across France. They were not sporadic and spontaneous events, but rather premeditated and organised, however minimally, which speaks more loudly of their gendered motivation (Rouquet and Virgili 2018). French society 'sexualised' the 'épuration' in this manner to re-establish their lost virility and to exonerate themselves for having failed to prevent French women from being with German men. Voisin (2018) discusses the 'collaboration' of Soviet women with German combatants, and how they were treated after the Red Army liberated Soviet territories.

Collaborators often seek to atone for their actions. What exactly do they apologise for? Who is their audience and what is the uptake for their apologies? Collaborators are rarely forgiven. Even when they participate in truth and justice processes, providing information that only they are able and willing to reveal, they continue to face the stigma of traitorous betrayal. In the case of Jean McConville, those who opposed her disappearance as particularly cruel for the 10 surviving children nonetheless remained silent until her body was eventually found. They then risked prosecution by revealing their role in her disappearance. Even in the case of the two members of the IRA who collaborated with the British and then tricked them by returning to the movement, the collaborators were put to death for their original betrayal, and their later efforts to support the movement were not enough to save them.

Ideological collaboration is not given light treatment either, as the case of Robert Brasillach illustrates. A fascist and antisemitic public intellectual, Brasillach embraced the Nazi Occupation, publishing a newspaper containing antisemitic tirades as well as the specific names and whereabouts of Jews and members of the resistance (Kaplan 2000). He received the death penalty after the Liberation for his treasonous 'intellectual crimes', without strong opposition from towering figures such as Jean-Paul Sartre and Simone de Beauvoir (Kruks 2012: 151–81).

---

[8] In the GDR, some IM were the subject of public ire while other denunciators were thrust into oblivion. For instance, Bruce (2010) argues that alongside the IM, who was not a member of the Stasi but did commit, sometimes in writing, to assisting the agency, many contact persons (*Kontaktpersonen*) – such as factory bosses, police officers, teachers, and so on – were also critical in supporting the Stasi, even if they had no regular exchanges with it. Nonetheless, they remained unaccountable in unified Germany.

Other collaborators manage to resist accountability demands even if some pressure does build up against them. On many occasions legal trials against collaborators trigger acrimonious controversies. The famous Kastner trials in Israel are a case in point. As is well known, Rezső Kasztner, also known as Rudolf Israel Kastner, conducted a negotiation with Adolf Eichmann to extend a permit to some 1,600 Jews to leave for Switzerland instead of Auschwitz in what came to be known as the 'Kasztner train'. The fact that a disproportionate number of passengers were Kasztner's friends or relatives tainted the rescue mission in the eyes of many observers. Yet Kasztner managed to transfer another 15,000 Jews to Switzerland without Eichmann's intervention. Kasztner survived the war and moved to Israel. There, his negotiation with Eichmann came to public light, as well as the unsavoury fact that he had testified on behalf of a Nazi genocidaire who avoided prosecution and lived in affluence for the rest of his life. Public opinion and judicial decisions in Israel struggled to judge his acts, finding merit in them but openly expressing perplexity about the compromises they entailed.[9]

Not all collaborators – not even those publicly known as such – face legal punishment. Societies have used alternative forms of accountability to confront their acts, such as public shaming, reparative duties, community work, or public confession: treatment that is explored further in some of the chapters of this book.

Collaboration in This Volume

This chapter has introduced the concepts covered in the volume. Here we summarise the range of case studies and the arguments made in each of the chapters.

The chapters in Part I illustrate how declaring someone a collaborator is a deeply contested act. Such a declaration is not based on a pre-existing and undisputed set of identities (who is an enemy, who is loyal) but may be part of a process to construe such identities; in turn, these identities can be leveraged against the alleged collaborator for purposes that go beyond his or her identification as a traitor. Collaborators are not simply found in the political landscape; they are constructed as such as part of a strategy to accrue legitimacy – to combat an adversary, to influence a political process – or to tell a narrative to explain the past.

---

[9] Two trials in Israel touched on his actions. At the first one, in 1955, the presiding judge characterised his actions as a Faustian pact in which he had sold his soul to the devil; he was represented as negotiating to save a handful of Jews close to him at the cost of yielding to the machinery that exterminated millions more. Just three years later, when Kasztner appealed the judgment, the Supreme Court overturned most of the previous ruling and offered an entirely different interpretation of Kasztner's acts. Finding no moral fault in his action, the court ruled that Kasztner had discharged his duty to rescue fellow Jews to the best of his abilities without in any way facilitating the Shoah, as the first ruling had asserted. The second ruling was rendered posthumously because Kasztner had been assassinated one year earlier at the hands of a right-wing extremist (Ben-Yehuda 2001: 289–93; Drumbl 2019). Kapo trials in Israel were equally contentious. See Ben-Naftali and Tuval (2006).

Jacob Dlamini rightly contends in Chapter 2 that the understanding of collaboration presupposes the existence of a-priori affinities or loyalties between individuals and groups. This understanding, he contends, assumes that for there to be a collaborator, there must be a group from which that collaborator comes, and there must be a community to which the collaborator is nominally loyal. Seen through the prism of this understanding, collaboration then becomes a matter of identity – rather than of choice, context, and politics. Instead of seeing identity as contextual, conflictual, fluid, and always open to negotiation, Dlamini argues, this definition of collaboration fixes identity in place. More than that, it vests identity with reliability and stability. Dlamini challenges these views on collaboration by closely examining the case of police informers in South Africa in the colonial and apartheid regime periods. Along the lines suggested, Dlamini argues that informers may have been motivated to pass information on to colonial authorities for some immediate advantages, but he notes that informing could also be a way to communicate directly with colonial authorities, to alert them about local grievances. More importantly, Dlamini underscores that in the South African context one cannot assume Blackness was an intelligible identity that everyone took for granted. Communities at the time were figuring out what it meant to be Black (especially in multi-lingual communities), and in fact many African activists tried to construct a shared understanding of Blackness, through a discourse infused with Christian moral language and imagery, precisely by denouncing the 'good natives', the Judas Iscariots who assisted colonial authorities. As Dlamini puts it, activists fashioned a moral economy of Blackness by shaming Black 'collaborators'.

In Chapter 3, Ksenija Bilbija explores the literary representations of the Argentine leftist female militant ('montonera') Mercedes Carazo, a high-ranking member of the Montoneros, an urban guerrilla movement that combated the dictatorship in Argentina and was eventually crushed by it. Carazo turned into a collaborator for the military dictatorship, which used the information she provided, and later her services, to conduct counter-insurgency activities leading to the arrest and disappearance of former Montoneros. Carazo eventually maintained an intimate relationship with one of her captors (plausibly to protect her daughter). Her collaboration was not voluntary, obtained instead as the result of torture at the infamous clandestine centre ESMA. Carazo's collaboration was taken up and engaged by several writers in a set of fictionalised works. Bilbija argues in her chapter that the ficitionalised versions of Carazo's collaboration attributed a set of motives to her actions that lacked empathy for the circumstances she faced vis-à-vis her torturer/sexual aggressor. The authors violated her right to tell her own story. Bilbija contrasts these representations with Elsa Osorio's 2017 novel *Doble fondo*, in which the victim is given a voice and a community of compassionate readers to evaluate and judge her complicity.

In his chapter on Euskadi Ta Askatasuna (ETA; Basque Homeland and Liberty), Luis De la Calle (Chapter 4) argues that in the 1980s this terrorist organisation waged a discursive war with the Basque government and its police body, Ertzaintza ('People's Shepherd' in Basque). De la Calle argues that ETA fought – and lost – the battle for public legitimacy. First, it attempted to persuade Basques that Ertzaintza was a collaborationist force on the rhetorical domain. It referred to this force not simply with a pejorative *txakurra* (the Basque word for 'dog', traditionally employed to denigrate Spanish security forces) but as *cipayo* (*zipaio* in Basque), a term that can be traced back to Indian soldiers who joined Imperial forces during the British occupation of India but later rebelled, if unsuccessfully. Symbolically, allusion to a *cipayo* evokes colonial occupation, collaboration with the coloniser, and the need to rebel against occupiers. When propaganda failed, and when Ertzaintza began to take on counter-terrorist duties, ETA made that police body a legitimate target of its terrorist attacks, so as to sever the ties between ordinary Basques and Ertzaintza, discouraging collaboration. The strategy, however, was counterproductive, as it alienated Basque citizens. For De la Calle, this example illustrates that civil wars complicate discussions about collaboration because part of what is at stake in conflicts, especially low-intensity ones, is a battle over political identities.

The second part of the volume focuses on what we call the moments of collaboration. Conventional examinations of the phenomenon commonly trace collaboration to clearly distinctive motivations, such as sheer self-interest or ideology (which the collaborator passively follows and never helps to shape). By the same token, the conventional political mechanism that societies immersed in transitions away from conflict or autocracy design to confront the actions of collaborators take these motivations for granted. The chapters in this section paint a more complex picture of both collaborators' motivations and the prospects of truth-seeking initiative that target these motivations.

In Chapter 5 on the former Czechoslovakia, Mark Drumbl and Barbora Holá focus on collaboration (*kolaborace* in Czech) with Communist authorities and the secret police after the Second World War (1948–89), particularly during the years of Goulash Communism in the 1970s and 1980s. Communism had then reached its peak of stagnation across all domains of life (cultural, scientific, political), and apathy, monotony, and apolitical attitudes prevailed in the nation. Against this background, Drumbl and Holá portray a landscape of collaboration where 'ideology and vapidity' and 'political good and private personal gain' were motivations to collaborate with the secret police. This 'bimodal' rather than 'binary' understanding of collaboration means that people could be at one time social navigators and at other principled collaborators. Collaboration was not a devious outgrowth of an unjust regime, but a routine, a way of muddling through life. Drumbl and Holá convincingly argue that transitional justice initiatives, such as lustration, frequently miss this dimension of collaboration because they frame it as strictly ideological. The authors challenge the validity of this reductionist framing, which might be in the immediate interest of the transitional regime but not in that of understanding the architecture of the authoritarian regime. Instead, they argue, the transitional justice paradigm must find a way to reckon with collaboration as it genuinely is – opportunistic, materialistic, petty. After all, as they show in their chapter, petty informing is in no less need of moral and political repair after transition.

Andrea Dennis's Chapter 6 discusses the role of Black informers during American slavery. This chapter considers whether Blacks who informed during antebellum slavery are worthy of condemnation and blame. During the ante-bellum era, Black informants were vital to the maintenance of the institution of slavery. Multiple factors – some internal and others external – probably influenced whether Blacks informed. Weighing in favour of informing were loyalty to one's owner, preservation of one's life or status, communal self-regulation, attainment of liberty or criminal leniency, and financial reward. In contrast, communal solidarity, resistance ethic, fear of retaliation, and protection of others countenanced not informing. The impact of religious conviction depended on the individual or circumstance. Today, some view these informants as traitors to their race. However, viewing their situation and behaviour through Claudia Card's theory of the 'grey zone' of evils and atrocities complicates a tendency toward strident conclusions. As both victims of slavery and perpetrators, Dennis claims, Black informants operated in a grey zone. In this ethical space in-between and especially in retrospect, it is difficult to label them either as fully responsible moral agents or wholly unaccountable survivors.

Gerson Iván Arias and Carlos Andrés Prieto's Chapter 7 delves into a particular collaboration story about José Miguel Narváez, an adviser and instructor for the Colombian military. For at least 10 years, instead of coordinating the disbanding of paramilitary groups, Narváez served as a go-between for paramilitary commanders, and subsequently became a paramilitary adviser and an active collaborator from within the state itself. Through this study of Narváez, the chapter explores how collaborators should be defined, the context in which they emerge, their incentives and motivations, the different dimensions of collaboration, and its correlation with a lack of trust in institutions. The chapter reveals specific facets about his collaboration with paramilitary groups. Among other actions, he provided ideological and political advice to the paramilitary organisation from the highest level of national decision-making within the Colombian government; and he collaborated – as a public official – with an enemy (illegal) actor through omission and the disclosure of information, in addition to other intelligence-gathering activities. Arias and Prieto's chapter notes two striking aspects of Narváez's collaboration – it was difficult to distinguish whether he was directly part of the organisation or a collaborator, and his contributions were not always beneficial or strategic for the armed organisation; they could in fact be detrimental. In such cases, this type of collaboration was a way for Narváez to 'create the need' for his work and to guide the behaviour of the paramilitary organisation. All of these considerations paint a complex picture of collaboration in the Colombian conflict.

Ron Dudai and Kevin Hearty (Chapter 8) reconstruct and challenge the narrative according to which the work of informers was of the greatest importance (their role being greater than that of politicians or international figures) to peace in Northern Ireland. By infiltrating the IRA and the smaller Irish National Liberation Army, so the narrative goes, informers and their handlers from the Royal Ulster Constabulary Special Branch saved lives and 'defeated' Republican groups, leaving them no alternative but peace negotiations, ultimately contributing to the abatement of violence. The authors argue that the narrative of heroification of informers overlooks the negative consequences of informing, which include the production of what it intended to curb, namely violence. The systematic recruitment of informers has the durable effect of sustaining opposition to peace processes. For one, it provides ammunition to discontented Republicans, who use it to erode the public legitimacy of the peace process, contending that the prevalence and ubiquity of informers shows the process was crafted and directed in their interest. For another, informers are used as an excuse to boycott and set obstacles to negotiations. The legacy of informers also places obstacles to truth-recovery efforts because it enables the state to withhold information related to informers on the grounds (not always justified) of protecting their identity, thus obscuring state action; and on the Republican side, it inhibits members or sympathisers from speaking out, as the Republican code of honour against informing is invoked and those who do come forth are labelled touts. The legacy of informing has also hampered Irish Republican engagement with policing insofar as informing as a whole (even when justified and necessary) is tarnished by deliberately establishing a false equivalence among all kinds of informing; an informer-phobia has been entrenched and is difficult to dislodge. Finally, to the extent that the hostility toward informers has proved durable, it has produced a category of individuals, particularly within Republican communities, who are stigmatised and remain unforgiven.

Oren Gross's Chapter 9 explores the collaboration of law professors with the crimes of the Third Reich. Broadly speaking, academics supported the regimes' project of racial purification, territorial expansion, and its imperialistic goals in general. In particular, law professors conferred a veneer of legality and legitimacy on the actions of the regime by providing the necessary doctrines to support the regime's political, national, and racial passions. The role of legal academics is all the more problematic because, being socially prestigious, they did nothing to oppose Nazi policies, before or during the Third Reich. Gross argues that legal academics were absent from the circles of resistance against the Nazi regime, while other professions were present. It is quite commonly argued on behalf of professors that they complied because of their tradition of obedience (*Obrigkeit*) and neutrality, or because they intended to avoid the wrath of the regime, should they fail to comply. The reality is that the legal establishment in universities was deeply conservative, coming from the social elite. Many law professors had even been quite supportive of the war of 1914, and were deeply critical of the Weimar Republic, which many disparaged as a *Judenrepublik*. None of these professors was held accountable for their complicity, most of them shielded by the 'Heidelberg Myth', according to which the few Nazi professors who supported the regime were an imposition from the outside. Just as in the rest of Germany, where denazification was timid at best, professors who supported the Nazi regime resumed their careers, while those who had been purged by the Nazis faced a steeper hill. One of them, Theodor Maunz (1901–93), who defended a National Socialist conception of the *Rechtsstaat*, compatible with the existence of concentration camps, continued his academic career uninterrupted and became a member of the constitutional convention for West Germany's new Constitution.

Initiatives that seek to punish collaborators in transitional societies, if any are set in place at all, commonly encounter significant obstacles and are likely to fail. This is the topic of the chapters in the third part of the volume, as well as the neglect of national and international law to regulate the use of collaborators, particularly informers, in the context of inter- or intra-state conflict. Together, these chapters show the legal deficit around collaborators – through failure either to punish them if they wrong others, or to punish those who wrong them.

Colleen Murphy's Chapter 10 takes up the question of whether, why, and how to hold informers accountable after the fall of a repressive regime. The starting point is the Hart–Fuller philosophical debate in jurisprudence. In their discussion of how to justify the punishment of Nazi-era grudge informers, Hart and Fuller take up core dilemmas surrounding accountability for acts that were sanctioned by law at the time they occurred, and with which transitional justice scholars continue to grapple. Importantly for this chapter's purposes, the Hart–Fuller debate concentrated on accountability not for the worst perpetrators of human rights violations, but rather for individuals who took advantage of a repressive system to rid themselves of personal enemies. As transitional justice scholars increasingly emphasise, accountability for large-scale wrongdoing should not be restricted to perpetrators. Yet, since the Hart–Fuller debate, little has been written about accountability for collaborators specifically, which is why any discussion of the moral point of holding collaborators to account inevitably must begin with that debate. Despite their prescient focus on informers and recognition of dilemmas associated with the pursuit of accountability for them, Murphy argues that Hart and Fuller's discussion is too narrow.

In Chapter 11 on business collaboration in Argentina, Gabriel Pereira focuses on corporate collaborators who were not in institutional power but 'worked together' with an illegal regime and engaged in the commission of crimes against humanity. Business companies were complicit with the dictatorship by directly supporting the violations of human rights perpetrated by it (what Pereira calls hardline collaboration). The chapter describes how hardline collaborators have been prosecuted in Argentina in legally innovative ways. Pereira contends that the nation has found innovative ways to prosecute collaborators for the dictatorship. But collaborators have been equally innovative and resourceful in finding ways to remain unaccountable. Not only have they conducted extra-legal public campaigns, which they can easily fund, to discredit accountability efforts, they have also found legal ways to do so, most notably through hiring expensive lawyers (beyond reach for victims and even the state) to undertake complex legal battles. A key part of their strategy has been to delay prosecutions, which they have done successfully. As Pereira explains, the judicial circuitry where cases against collaborators navigate give the appearance of progress but they ultimately become mired. This is either because judges invoke internationally discredited standards for the assessment of evidence (e.g. rejecting the possibility of establishing the knowledge and intent of the accused through inferential and contextual evidence) and thereby conclude that the prosecutors' cases 'lack merit', forcing them to collect evidence that it is hard to come by given the dictatorship's clandestine modus operandi, or because judicial cases against collaborators enter an 'appeals spiral', whereby appeals processes move back and forth between courts (Appeals Chambers, Criminal Cassation Chambers, Supreme Court), going nowhere, and failing to reach a conclusion. This illusion of progress in the cases, which Pereira calls the stop-motion effect, allows judges to withhold action while simultaneously avoiding significant public criticism for doing so. It gives collaborators time, which can lead eventually to a suspended trial, or no trial, given the advanced age or severe illnesses of the accused.

In Chapter 12, Shane Darcy contends that, despite its enduring prevalence during wartime and the widespread reliance on informers by police, and security and intelligence authorities, international law has overlooked the phenomenon of collaboration. There is no explicit reference to informers or other collaborators in the treaties of international humanitarian law, and a similar silence is found in international human rights conventions. A closer look reveals, however, that international law consciously tolerates collaboration and permits the recruitment and use of informers and other collaborators by public authorities, while at the same time placing restrictions, often indirectly, on the conduct of recruiters, collaborators, and those who may seek to punish such betrayal. This 'tentative embrace' of collaboration by international law is characterised by its long-standing general permissiveness toward the practice, coupled with a steadily increasing application of key standards of international humanitarian law and human rights to some of collaboration's most harmful aspects. This chapter explores international law applicable to collaboration primarily, but not exclusively, in situations of armed conflict. It considers the emerging expectation of regulation that emanates from international human rights law, which holds the potential for a more forceful engagement of international law with collaboration. The chapter considers the embedding of international law standards in national legislation and military doctrine, with a focus on United Kingdom legislation applicable to informers and their use in the context of armed conflict. The analysis is conducted against the backdrop of an increasingly strident domestic opposition to the application of human rights law during armed conflict.

In the conclusion, Juan Espindola and Leigh A. Payne bring together some of the main insights of the case studies presented in the volume to enrich the conceptual framework presented in this introduction. They do so by returning to the key questions posed here: *who* is a collaborator, *what* is collaboration, *why* and *when* does collaboration occur, and *how* can societies reckon with collaboration?

References

Adorno, T. W., Frenkel-Brunswik, E., Levison, D. J., and Nevitt Sanford, R. (eds) (1950), *The Authoritarian Personality* (New York, Harper and Bros).

Alighieri, D. (1935 [1320]), *The 'Divine Comedy' of Dante Alighieri: 'Inferno', 'Purgatory', 'Paradise'* (New York, Union Library Association).

Apor, P., Horváth, S., and Mark J. (eds) (2017), *Secret Agents and the Memory of Everyday Collaboration in Communist Eastern Europe* (New York, Anthem Press).

Arendt, H. (1994), *Eichmann in Jerusalem: A Report on the Banality of Evil* (New York, Penguin).

Arens, M. (2011), *Flags over Warsaw. The Untold Story of the Warsaw Uprising* (Jerusalem, Gefen).

Assaf, D. (2002), *The Regal Way: The Life and Times of Rabbi Israel of Ruzhin* (Stanford, Stanford University Press).

Ben-Naftali, O. and Tuval, Y. (2006), 'Punishing international crimes committed by the persecuted: The Kapo trials in Israel (1950s–1960s)', *Journal of International Criminal Justice*, 4, 128–78.

Ben-Yehuda, N. (2001), *Betrayals and Treason: Violations of Trust and Loyalty* (Boulder, Westview).

Borges, J. L. (1944), *Ficciones* (Buenos Aires, Sur).

Browning, C. (1992), *Ordinary Men: Reserve Police Battalion 101 and the Final Solution in Poland* (New York, Harper Perennial).

Bruce, G. (2010), *The Firm: The Inside Story of the Stasi* (New York, Oxford University Press).

Card, C. (2002), *The Atrocity Paradigm: A Theory of Evil* (New York, Oxford University Press).

Cohen, H. (2010), *Good Arabs: The Israeli Intelligence and the Israeli Arabs* (Berkeley, University of California Press).

Connelly, J. (2005), 'Why the Poles collaborated so little – and why that is no reason for nationalist hubris', *Slavic Review*, 64, 771-781.

David, R. (2018), *Communists and Their Victims: The Quest for Justice in the Czech Republic* (Philadelphia, University of Pennsylvania Press).

Drumbl, M. (2019), 'Histories of the Jewish "collaborator": Exile, not guilt', in I. Tallgren and T. Skouteris (eds), *The New Histories of International Criminal Law: Retrials* (New York, Oxford University Press), 237–52.

Dudai, R. (2012), 'Informers and the transition in Northern Ireland', *British Journal of Criminology*, 52, 32–54.

Dudai, R. (2018), 'Underground penality: The IRA's punishment of informers', *Punishment & Society*, 20, 375–95.

Dudai, R. (2021), 'Exception, symbolism and compromise: the resilience of treason as a capital offence', *British Journal of Criminology*, 61:6, 1435–51.

Espindola, J. (2015), *Transitional Justice after German Reunification: Exposing Unofficial Collaborators* (New York, Cambridge University Press).

Fabre, C. (2020). 'The Morality of Treason', *Law and Philosophy*, 39 (2020): 427–61.

Finkel, E. (2017), *Ordinary Jews: Choice and Survival during the Holocaust* (Princeton, NJ, Pricneton University Press).

Goldhagen, D. (1996), *Hitler's Willing Executioners: Ordinary Germans and the Holocaust* (London, Little, Brown).

Hoffman, S. (1968), 'Collaborationism in France during World War II', *Journal of Modern History*, 40:3, 375–95.

Joshi, V. (2002), 'The "private" became "public": Wives as denouncers in the Third Reich', *Journal of Contemporary History*, 37:3, 419–35.

Kalyvas, S. (2008), 'Collaboration in comparative perspective', *European Review of History – Revue européenne d'histoire*, 15, 109-111.

Kalyvas, S. (2012) *The Logic of Violence in Civil War*. Cambridge: Cambridge University Press.

Kaplan, A. (2000), *The Collaborator: The Trial and Execution of Robert Brasillach* (Chicago, University of Chicago Press).

Keefe, P. R. (2019), *Say Nothing: A True Story of Murder and Memory in Northern Ireland* (New York, Anchor Books).

Kelly, T. (2010), 'In a treacherous state: The fear of collaboration among West Bank Palestinians', in T. Kelly and S. Thiranagama (eds), *Traitors: Suspicion, Intimacy, and the Ethics of State-Building* (Philadelphia, University of Pennsylvania Press), 169–87.

Kelly, T. and Thiranagama, S. (2010), 'Introduction: Specters of Treason', in T. Kelly and S. Thiranagama (eds), *Traitors: Suspicion, Intimacy, and the Ethics of State-Building*, (Philadelphia, University of Pennsylvania Press), 1–23.

Kruks, S. (2012), *Simone de Beauvoir and the Politics of Ambiguity* (New York, Oxford University Press).

Kutz, C. (2000), *Complicity: Law and Ethics for a Collective Age* (Cambridge, Cambridge University Press).

Lepora, C. and Goodin, R. (2013), *On Complicity and Compromise* (Oxford, Oxford University Press).

Levi, P. (1996), *Survival in Auschwitz*, trans. S. Woolf (New York, Touchstone).

Levi, P. (2017), *The Drowned and the Saved*, trans. R. Rosenthal (New York, Simon & Schuster).

Lifton, R. J. (1993), *The Protean Self* (Chicago, University of Chicago Press).

Margalit, A. (2017), *On Betrayal* (Cambridge, MA, Harvard University Press).

Milgram, S. (1974), *Obedience to Authority: An Experimental View* (New York, Harper and Row).

Nalepa, M. (2010), *Skeletons in the Closet: Transitional Justice in Post-Communist Europe* (Cambridge, Cambridge University Press).

Narvselius, E. and Grinchenko, G. (2018), *Traitors, Collaborators and Deserters in Contemporary European Politics of Memory: Formulas of Betrayal* (Zurich, Palgrave Macmillan).

Natapoff, A. (2009), *Snitching: Criminal Informants and the Erosion of American Justice* (New York: NYU Press).

Oz, A. (2014), *Judas* (London, Chatto & Windus).

Pauw, J. (1997), *Into the Heart of Darkness: Confessions of Apartheid's Assassins* (Johannesburg, Jonathan Bell).

Payne, L. A. (2008), *Unsettling Accounts: Neither Truth nor Reconciliation in Confessions of State Violence* (Durham, NH, Duke University Press).

Rouquet, F. and Virgili, F. (2018), *Les françaises, les français et l'épuration* (Paris, Gallimard).

Sartre, J.-P. (2017 [1976]), *The Aftermath of War* (Chicago, University of Chicago Press).

Shklar, J. (1984), *Ordinary Vices* (Cambridge, MA, Harvard University Press).

Strauss, J. (2010), 'Traitors, terror and regime consolidation on the two sides of the Taiwan Straits: "Revolutionaries" from 1949 to 1956', in S. Thiranagama and T. Kelly (eds),

Traitors: Suspicion, Intimacy and the Ethics of State Building (Philadelphia, University of Pennsylvania Press), 89–109.

Sullam, S. L. (2020), *The Italian Executioners: The Genocide of the Jews of Italy* (Princeton, Princeton University Press).

Thiranagama, S. and Kelly, T. (eds) (2010), *Traitors: Suspicion, Intimacy, and the Ethics of State-Building* (Philadelphia, University of Pennsylvania Press).

United Nations (2010), 'Guidance note of the Secretary-General: United Nations approach to transitional justice', https://www.un.org/ruleoflaw/files/TJ_Guidance_Note_March_2010FINAL.pdf (accessed 21 January 2022).

Van Onselen, C. (2007), 'Jewish police informers in the Atlantic world, 1880–1914', *Historical Journal*, 50:1, 119–44.

Voisin, V. (2018), 'The Soviet punishment of an all-European crime: "Horizontal collaboration"', in E. Narvselius and G. Grinchenko (eds) (2018), *Traitors, Collaborators and Deserters in Contemporary European Politics of Memory: Formulas of Betrayal* (Zurich, Palgrave Macmillan).

Webster, P. (1999), *Petain's Crime: The Complete Story of French Collaboration in the Holocaust* (Chicago, Ivan R. Dee).

Part I

The Politics of Collaboration

2

Native Intelligence: African Detectives and Informers in White South Africa

JACOB DLAMINI

SOMETIME IN JANUARY 1926, a schoolteacher named Thabo Keable Mote sat down to write a report about the 14th annual conference of the African National Congress (ANC), which had just ended after five days of deliberations in Bloemfontein, capital city of the Orange Free State province of South Africa. Mote was a prominent member of the ANC in the city and Provincial Secretary of the Industrial and Commercial Workers' Union (ICU), a radical Black trade union founded in 1919. He was also a police informant, and the three-page report he wrote about that ANC conference was meant for his police handler, a Detective-Sergeant Du Plessis of the Criminal Investigation Department (CID) in Bloemfontein. As a highly regarded radical and an educated African fluent in a number of languages, especially English, Mote not only served as a prominent African activist in the Orange Free State, but acted often as an interpreter during meetings of the ANC and the ICU. This placed him at the centre of these organisations' activities.

As Du Plessis said of Mote in a letter that accompanied Mote's confidential report to the police top brass, 'He [Mote] was the only educated and reliable native I could get.'[1] The five-day conference, held annually since the ANC's founding in the same city in January 1912, was an open and widely advertised event open to the press and attended by, among others, E. R. Grobler, the Administrator of the Orange Free State; Bloemfontein mayor Hermanus Steyn, the city's Resident Magistrate; and J. R. Cooper, the Superintendent of Waaihoek, the Black township in which the conference took place. All four White men were the cream of the White segregationist crop. Why, then, would an open meeting of a legal organisation, and one graced by no less than some of the political elites of segregationist South Africa, require the services of a police informant?

---

[1] Du Plessis, letter to Sub-Inspector R. S. Mitchell, 7 January 1926, records of the South African Police, South African National Archives, Pretoria, JUS: 915–22.

Proceedings of the British Academy, **248**, 29–49, © The British Academy 2022.

Rather than address that question, I intend to use Mote's story to examine what Juan Espindola and Leigh A. Payne call the 'problem of collaboration', meaning the difficulty of defining collaboration (Chapter 1). As Espindola and Payne point out, collaboration has two sides to it: one positive and one negative. Positive collaboration means two or more parties working together to achieve a set goal or to create something; negative collaboration means 'traitorous cooperation with an enemy' (Espindola and Payne, Chapter 1). However, as the various contributors to this volume show, the trouble with the negative definition of collaboration is not just that it dominates both popular and scholarly treatments of the phenomenon, but that it rests on shaky definitional grounds. Put simply, this dominant understanding of collaboration assumes the existence of a-priori affinities or loyalties between individuals and groups. These loyalties might be ethnic, ideological, national, racial, or regional, or fall along class lines.

This understanding assumes that, for there to be a collaborator, there must be a group from which that collaborator comes, there must be a community to which the collaborator is nominally loyal. The understanding holds that, by definition, a collaborator belongs somewhere, and that collaboration happens when an individual betrays the loyalties that come with that belonging. Seen through the prism of this understanding, collaboration then becomes a matter of identity – instead of choice, context, and politics. Rather than see identity as contextual, conflictual, fluid, and always open to negotiation, the negative definition of collaboration fixes identity in place. More than that, it vests identity with reliability and stability. Built into this definition of collaboration is the idea that collaborators emerge in contexts where there are at least two sides to a conflict: an oppressive elite/foreign nation versus a polity/community or nation over which that oppressive elite/foreign nation rules or seeks to rule.

However, the primary sources on which this chapter draws challenge the assumption of a-priori loyalties that lies at the heart of the negative definition of collaboration. More importantly for the South African context, these sources help us avoid the sterile resistance-versus-collaboration theme that was such a dominant feature of the historiography of African history, especially in the 20th century. The sources allow us to track over time the development in early-20th-century South Africa of Blackness as a political category, meaning an identity that some actors could use to mobilise certain communities in pursuit of specific goals. In other words, the incidents depicted in these sources illuminate the complex ways in which Africans working with and against the state came to see what we might call, for lack of a better word, collaboration as an arena in which to work out both the content and limits of Blackness as a political identity.

In that sense, the stories recounted below call to mind Daniel Branch's observation about the Mau Mau insurgency in colonial Kenya in the 1950s, namely that it was no 'simple dispute between colonizer and colonized' (Branch 2007: 294). As Branch says, far from being opposites, resistance and collaboration were co-constitutive and shared 'common intellectual origins and idioms' in Kenya (294).

During the insurgency and the ensuing counter-insurgency, individuals and communities moved back and forth between loyalty to the colonial authorities and support for the Mau Mau. Part of the explanation for this was that these individuals and communities shared what Bruce Berman, Dickson Eyoh, and Will Kymlicka call a moral ethnicity, meaning the 'contested process of defining cultural identity, communal membership and leadership' (Berman *et al.* 2004: 4). Individuals in colonial Kenya served as loyalists to the colonial state for the same reason that others acted as insurgents against that same state – to achieve autonomy. And moral ethnicity was about the power to fashion that autonomy.

In the case of South Africa, rather than assume what Blackness entailed or take for granted the mutual obligations imposed by such an identity, Africans had to fight over what it meant to be Black. The moral economy of Blackness, by which I mean a set of interlocking expectations and obligations between those who saw themselves as belonging to a new and broadly defined Black community, could not be assumed. It had to be forged in conflict and in dialogue. Whereas the nascent South African state sought, through its police force and other apparatuses, to turn Blackness into an object of surveillance, African activists pursued strategies that set out not only to achieve Black unity but to do so using a moralising discourse influenced largely by Christianity. Knowing that they could not assume a commonality of experience, let alone a-priori loyalties among those defined as natives by colonial authorities, African activists took to labelling some of their opponents Judas Iscariot – taking a leaf straight from the Bible. The label came directly from the missionary schooling to which those (like Mote) who led the struggle for Black unity in South Africa had been exposed. By drawing on the stories of these actors, this chapter seeks to do two things. The first is to suggest a new direction in the study of collaboration – one not founded on identity (however defined) as a key determinant of whether an individual is a collaborator or not. The second is to take seriously what these stories teach us: that Blackness is a historical construct that emerged over time in the first half of the 20th century in South Africa. This second point is especially important given the nativism that has taken root in contemporary South Africa, where racial chauvinists and ethnic entrepreneurs have sought to naturalise Blackness as a timeless category that can be used to determine who is a real South African, and who is not, to decide who is authentically Black and who is not, and to use this to figure out who can claim what from the post-apartheid state.

The Only Educated and Reliable Native:
Mote's Ambiguous Biography

Detective-Sergeant Du Plessis had recruited Thabo Keable Mote to keep tabs on the ANC's deliberations, especially its plans for strikes and protests against segregation. For reasons to be explored below, the Orange Free State had become a hotbed of Black political activity by the 1920s. In fact, a series of community protests, notably against heavy-handed policing in 1913 and in 1925, had resulted in the deaths of a number of protesters and the jailing of hundreds. The 1925 demonstrations, which began when two police officers tried to arrest a group of men drinking illegally brewed beer, had caught the local police by surprise. Particularly surprising was the determination with which the locals, armed with nothing more than stones, had jostled with the mounted police and the White vigilantes who had come in support of the police.

Although not organised by the ANC or the ICU, the 1925 riots had been serious enough (with one dead) for the police to worry about a repeat. As Baruch Hirson argued, 'Riots were a frequent occurrence ... and ... could be transformed into political demonstrations, at least partly directed by political leaders' (Hirson 1984: 84): hence Du Plessis's recruitment of Mote to spy on his fellow delegates. Mote did not disappoint. Save for a few sessions held in camera, most of the conference's discussions were open to all attendees, including the local press. Mote, being a key member of the ANC and the ICU, was present at all the pivotal moments of the conference. As he reported to Du Plessis, ANC president Zacharias Mahabane told the delegates: 'We are here in an endeavour to prepare the mind of the Bantu people for the far-reaching events of the next five years or so, to determine the right attitude to be adopted by our people, and finally to discover a common modus vivendi to be followed by our race in this hour of supreme need.'[2] Mote then added his own voice: 'This phraseology was further discussed *in camera* [*sic*] Select Committee *where I was*; that the hour of agony was coming, and the people must appeal secretly to all Chinese, Japanese, Asiatics and send an envoy to Soviet Moscow and a strong campaign be carried throughout the country. This was agreed to by the Select Committee' (emphasis mine). That was not the only secret session about which Mote told his police handler. He also mentioned the following: 'In camera the Congress discussed the whole aspect of ... Segregation, Land, etc.' He summarised speeches delivered by his comrades, including John Gomas, a Communist from Cape Town who told delegates that the 'Government of the white man in South Africa is worse than the Pharaohs of Egypt [and the] despotism of the Tzar'. According to Mote, Gomas said Russia was coming to South Africa. 'They must be ready to challenge the existence of the white capitalists by revolution in South Africa.' Lest we think that Mote spent all his time at the conference compiling his secret report, he also participated actively in conference activities and associated public rallies. For example, on 4 January 1926, he was among five speakers who addressed delegates at an open-air meeting involving members of the community – a fact that he mentioned toward the end of his report, listing himself in the third person. Mote was keen for his police handler to know that he was present at all the key moments in the conference. He used phrases – 'in camera', 'where I was' – intended to show how he had come by his information and to prove that his account was reliable. Tellingly, Mote did not pass judgement on

[2] Ibid.

his colleagues. Save for its verbatim accounts with their strong language, his report reads like a dispassionate story that one might find in a newspaper digest. He refers to John Gomas as a 'brother', and, paraphrasing Gomas, calls wages paid to Black workers a 'diabolical iniquity'. The absence of compromising information about his colleagues is suggestive.

It raises the possibility that, far from seeing his betrayal of his comrades as an act of treachery, Mote saw Du Plessis's request to spy on the conference as an opportunity to make the White authorities aware of African grievances and to expose White elites to what African activists were thinking. It may be asked why Mote would have felt the need to do this when White officials (not to mention the local press) were present at the conference. That would indeed be a fair question. Except it would miss the point that these men's presence at the conference would have been largely ceremonial. They would not have been invited to any of the closed sessions and would probably not have been fluent in all the indigenous languages spoken by the delegates. As Du Plessis himself remarked in his note to his superiors, 'The Press was allowed to be present at the meetings until ... the 3rd instant [meaning January 1926]; thereafter, both reporters of *The Friend* and *Volksblad* were requested to leave the hall, by Rev. Mahabane.'[3] In his own report, Mote mentioned a request by Clements Kadalie, president of the ICU and a delegate, for English to be declared the conference's medium of expression, 'in view of the vital importance of the Convention'. Kadalie – a qualified teacher born in Nyasaland in 1898 and educated there by Scottish missionaries – had immigrated to South Africa in 1915 and could not speak any of its indigenous languages. His request was meant clearly for his benefit. But it also shows that the delegates were communicating in languages other than English, making it more difficult for the White elites to follow all the proceedings. Given all this, it is possible that Mote saw his spying as politics by other means: that he took advantage of his position to act more as an intermediary than a traitor. This did not make Mote pure of heart and pure of motive. He was, as I show below, a complex figure. He did not always act in honourable ways.

To be sure, Mote's report does not say what motivated him to act as a confidential informant for the police. But we know what his handler and the handler's superiors made of it. Du Plessis used it to accuse Kadalie of making 'irresponsible utterances [that] created a corrupt impression on the native mind as well as a feeling of dissatisfaction amongst the White community who read his speeches in the newspapers.' What had Kadalie done at the conference to earn Du Plessis's displeasure? Kadalie had, according to Mote's report, rejected a conference motion to pass a vote of thanks praising Prime Minister John B. Hertzog for his courage. Hertzog had come to power in 1924 after defeating Jan Smuts and the South African Party. Hertzog headed a Pact government made up of an alliance between Afrikaner nationalists and the Labour Party, a racist organisation bent on the protection of White workers at the expense of Black workers.

---

[3] Ibid.

The Pact government had introduced a 'civilised labour policy' that sought to eliminate Black workers (skilled and unskilled) from the workforce and to replace them with White workers, especially poor Afrikaners. Kadalie had in fact supported Hertzog against Smuts, believing that Hertzog would be better for African workers. Hertzog had also donated money to the ICU in 1921, saying 'It is for us by our common endeavours to make this country, that we both love so much, great and good' (Roux 1964: 183). Hertzog had written to Kadalie at a time when he needed all the votes he could get (including Black ones) to win against Smuts. Once in office, how-ever, Hertzog had systematically gone against Africans. So when Kadalie rejected the ANC motion to give Hertzog a vote of thanks, he was expressing his personal disap-pointment in the Prime Minister. As Kadalie told his fellow delegates (according to Mote's report), previous ANC votes of thanks for Louis Botha, South Africa's first Prime Minister in 1910, and Smuts had done nothing but spoil these White politicians. The ANC's accommodationist politics had not worked.

Kadalie said, 'They [the ANC] should call a spade a spade. We have to tell the Prime Minister and the white people emphatically that we cannot and will not accept the proposals of the Prime Minister.' These proposals, known as the Hertzog Bills, included moves to limit further land ownership by Africans and to strip the franchise from the very few Africans who still had the vote (the very thing that had inspired Hertzog to write to Kadalie in 1921). As Kadalie said (again, according to Mote): 'The white people speak of native problems. This is no native problem, but a European problem of weakness, greed and robbery. This is a white problem of robbing the aboriginal races of South Africa of their inheritance, and we cannot congratulate the enemy of our race, our wives, our children. We must fight the white out of Africa.'[4] These are the statements that drew Du Plessis's ire. Kadalie, inspired by the teachings of Marcus Garvey, sought to make the struggle against racial segregation and economic exploitation a movement for Black unity (Vinson 2012). Du Plessis's superior, Sub-Inspector R. S. Mitchell, was also clear about what speeches such as Kadalie's meant. Mitchell said that while most Africans were likely to ignore the 'violent tone' of the speeches delivered at the conference, some would be swayed. 'This may not lead to violence, but forms a fertile soil for the propagation of strikes and other so called "anti capitalistic propaganda". Where natives are concerned, the European represents capital and the propaganda of the African National Congress is clearly calculated to cultivate a feeling of antagonism against all Europeans.'[5] Mitchell, who was also relying on Mote's report, noted that the ANC was organisationally weak. But he said that, as the 1925 protests showed, it only took a few 'hot heads' to disrupt Bloemfontein. 'Close touch is being kept with informants who unfortunately cannot be relied upon entirely', Mitchell wrote.[6]

[4] Ibid.
[5] Ibid.
[6] Ibid.

The Police Informer as a Historical Source

In his essay on the massive strike that swept along the railway network in French West Africa between 1948 and 1949, Frederick Cooper uses reports produced by police spies to show what the colonial authorities knew and what they made of that information. However, Cooper cautions against putting too much faith in these reports. As he says, 'They must of course be used with care, since spies have a tendency to see what their superiors want them to see' (Cooper 1996: 83). Given that the primary sources that serve as the foundation for this chapter come exclusively from South Africa's segregationist archive and are made up of confidential reports by informers and African detectives, we too must reflect seriously on their status as windows into the past and we must consider their reliability as a historical source. As James Campbell says, these sources constitute a 'massive (and still largely unexploited) encyclopaedia of African politics' (Campbell 1995: 315). In exploring this encyclopedia, this chapter pays heed to the advice offered by Cooper and Campbell. But it also pays attention to what the voices of men such as Mote tell us – not just about who they were as individuals but, more importantly, about how they saw their place in segregationist South Africa. This means that, rather than reading Mote's report as irrefutable proof of his spying, the chapter also considers, as stated earlier, the possibility that Mote saw his actions as a form of communication intended to speak directly to the police and, by extension, the White authorities. Taken in that sense, Mote's report can be read as a tainted (by his duplicity) but reliable window into the world of ANC and ICU activists in 1920s South Africa. As William Beinart and Colin Bundy, who have also made use of this massive encyclopedia, say, 'The intention of the police reports was to provide an accurate record of what was taking place, rather than to collect evidence for use in court cases' (Beinart and Bundy 1987: 318).

The official archive is silent on whether this was Mote's one and only stint as an informer. In other words, we have no other record of Mote spying on the ANC and the ICU for the police. But we do know that Detective-Sergeant Du Plessis thought it important to have an informant in place. As Du Plessis said in his letter to Sub-Inspector R. S. Mitchell, 'I have instructed the native staff, C.I.D., to keep in close touch with the general strike movement, and to report to me immediately should anything come to their notice. In this respect, it will be advisable to employ a Private Informer, as it will be difficult for natives of this Department to get information.'[7] Having used Mote so successfully once already, it would be a surprise for Du Plessis to drop him. Mote had produced a report considered reliable enough to pass on to the Secretary for Justice and so there is no reason, based on the sources available to us, to think that Du Plessis stopped using Mote. But who was Mote? What is it about his report that allows us to track over time the making of Blackness as a political category in colonial South Africa?

---

[7] Ibid.

Mote was born in 1898 in Leribe, Basutoland (renamed Lesotho on independence in 1966). He was educated in Pietersburg in the Transvaal, South Africa. He
joined the ICU in 1924, rising to the position of provincial secretary in the Orange
Free State. Mote joined the ICU at a pivotal moment in the history of both the
union and South Africa. When he signed up in 1924, South Africa was at the start
of a period of five years of unbroken prosperity – the longest stretch in 50 years
(Bradford 1988: 8). Hertzog and his White-labour allies had opposed Jan Smuts
on the grounds that his government was too close to the mining cooperatives that
dominated South Africa's economy, and too supportive of British interests in South
Africa. Instead, Hertzog and his allies set about creating what was essentially a generous welfare state for White workers. In the process, they destroyed the educated
class of Africans represented by individuals such as Mote.

As Helen Bradford (1988: 9) explains, when the ICU was founded in 1919, its
leaders were mainly poorly educated but full-time wage earners. However, by the
mid-1920s, when individuals such as Mote joined, the ICU had become a haven for
disillusioned educated Africans who had found their entry into the economy limited
by Hertzog's segregation. In turn, these Africans transformed the ICU into a mass
political movement fighting against White supremacy (Bradford 1988: 9). In her
profile of the social origins of the people of Mote's class, Bradford says:

> In a society where some 66 per cent of Africans were non-Christian, about 75 per cent
> were labourers or rural cultivators, nearly 90 per cent were illiterate, and almost 100
> per cent had no direct voice in Parliament, ICU leaders of this period [meaning the
> 1920s] were predominantly Christian, educated men, drawn from the middle strata
> and including amongst themselves a sprinkling of voters. (Bradford 1988: 64)

Ironically, it was the industrialisation of South Africa – driven by diamond- and
gold-mining – that destroyed the British Imperial promise of social advancement for
these strata. Bradford writes: 'As monopoly capital seized hold of the gold mines,
so economic and political dominance abruptly shifted from white merchants and
rentier landlords, to "Randlords", manufacturers and commercial farmers. In the
process, a vast African labour force was coerced into being on a scale that left little
room for "black Englishmen"' (Bradford 1988: 64). As an educated African and a
schoolteacher, Mote had disdained manual labour (Bradford 1988: 70), but the pay
of African teachers was so paltry that they tended to sport a 'lean and hungry look'
(Bradford 1988: 71). African teachers earned between £2 and £5 a month but their
salaries were irregular, meaning that individuals such as Mote had to find other
ways to make ends meet (Bradford 1988: 71). It also would not have helped Mote's
personal cause that he could not even rely on his status as an educated African to
shield him from the petty indignities of racial segregation.

The government rejected Mote's application for exemption from the so-called
native laws (Bradford 1988: 75). Qualified teachers were entitled to exemption,
meaning they did not have to carry the passes that limited African mobility. More
importantly, they did not need a White overseer's permission to move about. But the
government denied his application. Slights such as this one must have driven Mote

to the ICU; the indignities to which he must have been subjected as an educated but unexempted African may explain his membership. It may also explain his spying. Unlike the ANC, founded in 1912 by African elites who believed in the promise of gradual change, the ICU was committed to a politics of confrontation. This must have appealed to men of thwarted ambitions. It did not take long for Mote to earn a reputation as a radical committed to the destruction of White supremacy in colonial South Africa.

Ironically, his reputation as a radical lives on in accounts and histories of the ICU. Tshepo Moloi describes Mote as a 'firebrand' (Moloi 2015: 189); Charles van Onselen calls him one of Kadalie's 'fiery provincial lieutenants' (Van Onselen 1996: 145), while Edward Roux seems to mock Mote as the ' "Lion" of the Free State' (Roux 1964: 247). These descriptions are not necessarily wrong. But they certainly obscure Mote's past as a police informer. Mote could have been both a radical and a police informer; there is no contradiction there. To be fair, scholars who mention Mote do refer also to what Roux calls Mote's 'chequered history' (Roux 1964: 247). Bradford speaks of Mote's 'reputation for fast living on ICU funds' (Bradford 1988: 163), while Hirson claims that the ICU expelled Mote from its ranks after he appeared in court as a state witness in a criminal case against James Mpinda, a fellow ICU leader in the Orange Free State, following the 1925 demonstrations in Bloemfontein. Mote, then, was more than an educated African nursing thwarted ambitions (Hirson 1984). He was also a complicated man whose circumstances and needs may have driven him to spy.

If Mote was complex, so was the Orange Free State. One of the four provinces that made up the Union of South Africa at the country's formal founding in May 1910, the Orange Free State was a Boer republic founded in 1854. Like its northern counterpart, the South African Republic (founded in 1852 and colloquially known as the Transvaal), the Orange Free State was a White supremacist polity founded on the denial of racial equality in matters of church and state. Uniquely among the four provinces that constituted South Africa, the Orange Free State had a relatively small African population. The province had a Black–White population ratio of two to one, compared to the national average of four to one (Wells 1983: 59). The province's economic base was exclusively agricultural, and this, coupled with the relatively small size of the local African population, meant an acute labour shortage. Provincial authorities responded to this shortage by introducing some of the harshest pass laws in South Africa – all to limit African mobility.

As early as 1913, the Orange Free State was the only province to require African and coloured women to carry residential passes (Wells 1983: 56). Most Black men also had to carry passes, and failure to comply meant harsh punishment (Wells 1983: 59). The South African War (1899–1902), which destroyed the two Boer republics and laid the foundation for the creation of South Africa, resulted in a sharp increase in the province's Black population – from 1,302 in 1890 to 18,382 in 1904 (Wells 1983: 59). However, by 1911 the figure was down to 10,475, a 43 per cent drop over seven years. In the same period, the province's White population declined only by 5 per cent. As Wells notes, 'No other province in the Union of South Africa applied such strict control over Black lives, encouraging many people to leave the Free State altogether and seek better prospects elsewhere' (Wells 1983: 59). However, the province did attract educated Africans, especially after the end of the war in 1902, and they tended to do better than poor Whites at getting jobs (Wells 1983: 60).

The reconstruction that followed the end of the war led to an economic boom that drew men such as Mote to Bloemfontein. Wells writes: 'In Bloemfontein there is clear evidence of a whole class of carpenters, bricklayers, cart owners, taximen, shoemakers, wagonbuilders, owners of rest houses and cafes, teachers, court interpreters, clerks and ministers of religion' (Wells 1983: 64). Tshepo Moloi says that, by the late 1920s, Kroonstad, a town in the northern part of the Orange Free State and one of Mote's stamping grounds, had become a key site of Black education in South Africa. This made teachers an 'obvious choice within the community to represent the residents' (Moloi 2013: 178). These were new communities, with members – both elite and non-elite – working out as they went along what it meant to be a community – a Black community. Despite the predominance of Sotho speakers among the African residents of the province, many residents spoke other African languages. Phyllis Ntantala, who moved to Kroonstad in 1938 to take up a teaching post at the Bantu High School, describes a vibrant town made up of a number of linguistic communities. Among Ntantala's fellow residents was Mote, whom she describes favourably as the 'Lion of the Orange Free State'. Ntantala said that Mote had, together with his comrades in the ICU in the Orange Free State, confronted the 'Boers and the police, exposing themselves to death and danger' (Ntantala 1993: 83). Mote would have been only 40 years old when Ntantala met him in 1938, but he was already considered a struggle veteran. As for the ICU, it had collapsed in 1934 amid leadership squabbles over the misuse of union funds and resources. In its wake, people such as Mote had only the ANC and municipal politics to fall back on. However, long before the ICU's demise, Mote had softened his position. Having taken a 'militant, anti-capitalist stance' in the early 1920s (Kelley 1986: 108), by 1928 he had embraced a 'lack-lustre reformism' (Bradford 1988: 163). Might this change have been due to his precarious class position and social status?

Mote was not the only ANC and ICU leader to spy on his comrades for the police. A. A. Toba, described by the Police Commissioner as a 'Native Detective', was another.[8] James Campbell describes Toba as being 'singularly efficient' and so assiduous in his job that his reports constitute the 'finest extant record of a single ICU branch' (Campbell 1995: 325). We do not have as much biographical information about Toba as we do about Mote. But, based on his role as chief interpreter at ANC and ICU meetings in the Port Elizabeth township of New Brighton, we can guess safely that he, too, was educated, possibly a teacher. At any rate, we know from his reports that he was fluent in both English and Xhosa. On 24 July 1926, Toba reported on a meeting during which two ICU leaders, Charles Matimka and James Dipa, spoke about the recent arrest of an ICU member named Joseph Sonwabo, who had been accused of embezzling union funds. According to Toba, Dipa, who was

---

[8] A. A. Toba Report to Secretary of Justice, 27 July 1926, South African National Archives, JUS: 915–22.

Provincial Secretary of the ICU in the Eastern Cape, expressed surprise 'at the attitude taken by [Matimka]. He [Dipa] did not expect that the matter regarding the arrest of Sonwabo would be discussed at that meeting.'[9] Dipa told the meeting he had uncovered Sonwabo's embezzlement but that when he had brought this to the attention of Matimka, who was chairman of the local ICU branch, Matimka had downplayed the incident. Dipa had then confronted Sonwabo: 'I told him to refund it at once and he promised he would do so. He did nothing for five months and only refunded it after I had taken steps against him criminally. My position is a very serious one. I am entrusted with public funds and it is my duty to protect them from misappropriation.' This is one of the many reports we have in which the union's dirty laundry was brought to police attention. Toba took down every speech spoken at the meeting. For good measure, he noted at the end of each speaker's account: 'He spoke in Sixosa. No interpreter'. This neglected, of course, the fact that Toba was an interpreter – interpreting his comrades' words for his police bosses. On 31 July 1926, Toba reported on an ICU meeting during which Dipa objected to the discussion of the minutes from a previous meeting. According to Toba, Dipa said the meeting 'was only an open-air one to propagate the doctrines of our union, with a view to people joining our union, and not the proper place to divulge the secrets of our organization'.[10] Toba continued, 'After some heated discussions, his [Dipa's] objection was overruled.' Matimka, who chaired the meeting, proceeded to accuse Dipa of official overreach and assuming responsibilities that were not a part of his union brief. This was probably Matimka's attempt to get back at Dipa after the latter had accused Matimka of failing to act against Sonwabo for theft. Dipa did have supporters at the meeting. George Nazo, a committee member of the New Brighton sub-branch of the ICU, said it was 'most unfortunate that the secrets of our affairs, intended only for active members, should be discussed in public in the propaganda meetings'. Asked to defend himself, Joseph Sonwabo, ex-collector of the sub-branch, explained: 'I never stole the money alleged to have been stolen by me. Ever since I was appointed, I was never paid my wages. In spite of all the other collectors having been paid, my case has been an exception, having been time and again … put off by the Provincial Secretary.'[11] Toba concluded his report thus: 'The meeting numbered about three hundred, including both sexes. The meeting was very disorderly. Some of the leading members nearly came to blows. What saved the situation was shouts from the audience to close the meeting, which was closed after the benediction.'

Judas Iscariot and the Making of Black South Africa

In her appraisal of the social origins of men such as Mote, Helen Bradford describes a minuscule class force-fed a mission school diet (Bradford 1988: 65). This diet

[9] Ibid.
[10] A. A. Toba Report to Secretary of Justice, 31 July 1926, South African National Archives, JUS: 915–22.
[11] Ibid.

included instruction in biblical studies and gave African activists a language
through which to talk about belonging and betrayal. In this language, the figure of
Judas Iscariot loomed large. We have no record of Mote himself using either the
figure of Judas or referring to any of his political opponents as a Judas. But we have,
from the police archive, accounts of ICU activists denouncing their opponents as
Judases. As David Johnson points out, Clements Kadalie and his ICU comrades
'reinterpreted the Bible to serve their own ends' (Johnson 2015: 49). On 6 March
1926, Hosea Thagadi, an African detective stationed at the CID's headquarters in
Pretoria, reported on an ICU meeting in the city. According to Thagadi, Thomas
Mbeki, a key leader of the ICU in the Transvaal, accused a member of the audience named Benson Bottoman of being a spy. Mbeki said Bottoman was 'another
Judas Iscariot' and he would 'hang him to the nearest tree'.[12] On 17 March 1926,
Thagadi reported on another ICU speech by Mbeki. Mbeki urged the 30-strong
crowd to join the ICU, saying that, 'God and the Angels will not help them, they
must help themselves.'[13] Mbeki told his audience that 'They must not take notice
of the "Good natives", as they will be treated like Judas and will hang themselves
on the nearest tree when the time arrives.' Thagadi stated in 'another report that
by "good natives", Mbeki meant black supporters of the government who were of
no assistance to the natives'.[14] These included African policemen and detectives.[15]

Mbeki had more than Judas Iscariot as his biblical reference. Here is Thagadi,
whose rank is given as Native Detective Corporal, reporting on an ICU rally in
Pretoria on 31 March 1926. Again, Mbeki was the targeted speaker. Mbeki,
according to Thagadi, told the 20 people gathered 'that natives must wake up and
not remain "Hewers of wood and drawers of water"'.[16] Activists such as Mbeki
were of course aware that they were under police surveillance; they knew that
Black and White police officers (not to mention informers) were keeping watch
over them. On 1 May 1926, an ICU activist named Mrs M. Bhola told a rally in
Potchefstroom, Transvaal:

> I am not satisfied because I see here is a Native detective taking notes. I won't say
> much because the Native Detectives are liars. They always tell the white people things
> we haven't said. Also these Natives who are not members of the [African National]
> Congress go about telling the white people lies. The reason is because the white
> people then give them something extra for their lies.

According to Tenson Maphaga, the 'Plain Clothes Constable' who recorded Bhola's
speech, Bhola went on to say 'that she is not afraid of the Detective and that she
wishes the people in the Hall will not follow the footsteps of the Native Detectives

[12] Hosea Thagadi Report, 6 March 6 1926, South African National Archives, JUS: 915–22.
[13] Hosea Thagadi Report, 17 March 1926, South African National Archives, JUS: 915–22.
[14] Hosea Thagadi Report, 3 March 1926, South African National Archives, JUS: 915–22.
[15] Hosea Thagadi Report, 18 February 1926, South African National Archives, JUS: 915–22.
[16] Hosea Thagadi Report, 31 March 1926, South African National Archives, JUS: 915–22.

to tell the white man everything'.[17] On 23 May 1926, James Thaele, an ICU activist educated in the USA, addressed an ANC meeting in the Orange Free State town of Vrede. According to the policeman who reported on the meeting, attended by about 500 people, Thaele told his audience:

> The constitution [of the African National] Congress gives you the right to hire a local lawyer to defend in troubles arising out of your Congress [activities]. You make a personal friend with the white man, this won't help you. You tell them all what you do [*sic*]. I do not say insult them or disobey them, but don't tell them your Congress and private matters. By doing so you are giving yourselves away and you will be sorry afterwards. The white men will never tell you their secrets.[18]

On 16 June 1926, Native Detective Martin Gwamanda reported on an ICU rally in Port Elizabeth during which an unidentified man said:

> You must be very careful, people of our blackness, in discussing matters of that sort. There are amongst you here Vetfoots [meaning detectives] and they are also people of the black races, and they have only come here to detect our views and feelings and convey same to the Whites, and so matters of that sort should be reserved for our confidential places where we can discuss them and nothing can reach the ears of the Whites.[19]

Another unidentified man added that this 'nuisance of Vetfoots must be stopped, we do not want them here as they are traitors to their own blood and nation. I wonder if they think that this Taxation and Colour Bar Bill will exclude or exempt them from its operation, as they are black and will remain black until they are no more.' However, the very fact that the unidentified speaker had to complain about Africans spying on African activists even though they were all African and were, as such, all subject to racial segregation proved that, despite their best intentions, African activists could not assume that Blackness meant the same thing to every African so identified. These activists had to fight for a shared understanding of Blackness in order for their demands for loyalty to work and for their charges of treachery to stick. They could not assume African loyalty and Black unity. On 8 August 1926, Thagadi reported on a speech by ICU leader Theo Ramoenti in which Ramoenti said that the 'Government was employing natives such as Police boys to help keep the natives down. These police boys when in uniform thought they were demi-Gods, particularly those at the Pass Office.'[20]

African activists sought to use the ANC and the ICU to bring about a shared sense of Blackness. But like many nationalist activists, they also tried to remake Africans in their own image. Sometimes, these attempts tapped right into the eugenicist arguments used to justify White domination over southern Africa.

---

[17] Tenson Maphaga Report, 1 May 1926, South African National Archives, JUS: 915–22.
[18] Report by Police Head Constable, Vrede, 26 May 1926, South African National Archives, JUS: 915–22.
[19] Martin Gwamanda Report, 16 June 1926, South African National Archives, JUS: 915–22.
[20] Hosea Thagadi Report, 8 August 1926, South African National Archives, JUS: 915–22.

On 17 January 1926, a constable identified as B. J. van der Merwe reported Thaele as telling a Pretoria meeting the following:

> The white man [*sic*] had tried their best to ruin the natives but with no result because the natives are not like the Hottentots, who died out by the tobacco and brandy given to them by the whites. But they multiplied and the whites tried their level best to ruin them. But they won't succeed because natives give birth from 12 to 25 children whereas whites only give 2 to 3.[21]

Napthali Mutshese, an African constable tasked to cover an ICU meeting in Middelburg, Transvaal, in April 1926, reported a teacher and ICU activist named Ramonte thus: 'Ramonte told us that he did not want any cowards but brave boys to join the ICU as this country does not belong to the whites. It belongs to us and we must fight for our fathers' land.'[22] Spying on the same meeting, 'Native Constable' James Apidi reported Ramonte as urging Africans to join the ICU in order 'to get this country back again'.[23] Some tried to use the Garveyite slogan of 'Africa for the Africans' to forge unity. As Thaele told a reception hosted by the Transvaal Native Congress on 13 May 1926, 'The natives must therefore unite and to do this, they must all join the Transvaal Native Congress to get their rights.' According to Thagadi, Thaele 'then touched upon the New Immorality Law which he said ... was intended to prevent the growth of the native nation'.[24]

The fact that men such as Thaele connected their struggles to a puritanism that made the ICU sound like a temperance movement should not blind us to the fact that these men also had a complicated relationship to Christianity. On 18 July 1926, an ICU activist named William Dipheko railed against religion. According to a report submitted by Toba, Dipheko said:

> when Europeans came to this country, they brought with them church, heaven and hell. They told us to throw away our forefathers' customs and, if we did that, we would go to Heaven and, if we did not, we would go to hell. They told us also to go to church and, when praying, to look up to heaven with our eyes closed. When we reopened our eyes, we found all our properties gone.[25]

During an ICU meeting in Johannesburg in July 1926, Kadalie castigated Africans for supporting White churches. According to the unnamed police-officer who covered the meeting, Kadalie said he

> could not understand the attitude of the natives of the Transvaal. Instead of coming forward and attending the ICU meetings, they went to church to pray. How they expected this to help them he did not know. The ministers could only tell them to wait for eternal life. But he [Kadalie] warned them that if they never got to heaven, there would be nobody but themselves to blame.[26]

[21] B. J. Van Der Merwe Report, 17 January 1926, South African National Archives, JUS: 915–22.
[22] Napthali Mutshese Report, 19 April 1926, South African National Archives, JUS: 915–22.
[23] James Apidi Report, 19 April 1926, South African National Archives, JUS: 915–22.
[24] Hosea Thagadi Report, 13 May 1926, South African National Archives, JUS: 915–22.
[25] A. A. Toba Report to Secretary of Justice, 18 July 1926, South African National Archives, JUS: 915–22.
[26] Police report, 12 August 1926, South African National Archives, JUS: 915–22.

Addressing an ICU meeting in Benoni, east of Johannesburg, on 8 August 1926, Kadalie blamed the poor attendance at the gathering on religion. Kadalie said that African women and children should always come first:

> The suggestion of the ministers [of religion] that God and the King [of England] should come first was to his mind a ridiculous suggestion ... The damnable hypocrisy practiced by ministers of religion was one of the things he could not put up with. [Kadalie] spoke of the usual ridiculous promise, as he termed it, of eternal life in Paradise, and he asked his hearers to look around the Benoni Location. If the paradise of the ministers was so much to be desired, was it not necessary for them to have in their present life something far better than the locations in which they now resided?[27]

Dipheko and Kadalie were not necessarily dismissive of Christianity as such. After all, Kadalie was the product of mission education and many ICU leaders were, as we know from Bradford, graduates of mission schools. What Dipheko and Kadalie were preaching was a separatism connected to their attempts to fashion a moral economy of Blackness. As Alexander Maduna, the first Provincial Secretary of the ICU in Natal, told a meeting in Bloemfontein on 12 June 1926, Africans 'should leave all the European churches and join churches of the black nations'.[28]

Maduna said European-led churches favoured White congregants at the expense of their Black members:

> A white man would come from England without a blanket, yet six years later he would be a rich man living in a double-storey [house] ... It is through the churches and the Europeans that your children become robbers, thieves, murderers and slaves. We are given some pictures of Dutch people and told that the picture is Jesus Christ, your Saviour. Through this picture, your Africa is going out of your hands. By the name of Almighty Jesus, our land is stolen from us. You are praying from Monday to Sunday and are not doing anything for yourselves in your yards or your homes because you are kept in the white man's service.[29]

As Maduna's speech shows, ICU activists were not above playing the nativist card in their bid to mobilise African support for the union. They also used this card to shame African policemen and informers spying on their activities. In the same speech cited above, Maduna said sarcastically that he was pleased to see African policemen among the 70-odd people at his meeting. But, continued Maduna, he was 'very sorry that they were black and taking notes in long hand and thought that they were poorly-educated'. Fashioning a moral economy of Blackness demanded the deployment of shame and reference to a precolonial past free of White domination. Addressing an ICU gathering in Pretoria on 18 April 1926, activist Douglas Ngana said that 'this country was not Whiteman's land, that it belonged to the natives and had been stolen by the whites. That they must not trust the white man and that they must demand higher wages from the white man ... They must call the whites their friends but, at the same time, they must not trust him but must know

---

[27] Police report, 8 August 1926, South African National Archives, JUS: 915–22.
[28] Police report, 12 June 1926, South African National Archives, JUS: 915–22.
[29] Police report, 1 July 1926, South African National Archives, JUS: 915–22.

him as a thief who has stolen their lands.'[30] On 22 June 1926, an African activist named Moses Mahala told a meeting of the Transvaal Native Congress in White River that 'The white people came to the country and took our land away. Now you people are crying. It's not the time to cry; it's the time to work. You people must try and collect money and have your Congress started. Money is everything today and with money, you can do a lot.'[31] References to a precolonial past free from White domination traded at times on myths of an innocent history. Speaking at an ICU rally in Port Elizabeth on 25 July 1926, ICU leader William Dipheko said 'Today we have murderers, thieves and all classes of desperates among our people, having been contaminated by foreigners after their arrival here. Go back ... to the customs of your forefathers and throw away the customs of the Europeans. All will be well.'[32] On 1 August 1926, ICU leader John Mzaza told his audience 'We are the owners of Africa. The country belongs to us.'[33]

History and the Moral Economy of Blackness

References to a precolonial past did not work. This was for the simple reason that Africans did not share a common history. The ICU could not evoke a shared memory of Africa's past and hope for that memory to work its political magic. Union activists could not demand that Africans see themselves as one and expect that to become the case. On 21 February 1926, policeman English Hlalele reported on a speech by James Thaele during which Thaele discussed the naming of Africans in colonial South Africa. Thaele said Europeans called Africans kaffirs,

> and this word kaffir we don't like because this name is not our name but a name that came from India. It means in India the man that does not read the Bible and so the white people are kaffirs and King George himself is a kaffir, because if he is not Christian he is a kaffir. It is not our name at all. The white people call us Bantu. Bantu means one man or a lot and it is not a native [word]. The real name that a native should be called is a Africander [sic].[34]

However, even among African activists, the notion of what a precolonial past might look like did not enjoy mass support. On 29 March 1926, ICU leader Paulus Mashow said 'it was not good that the natives should always speak against the Europeans', and that they 'should speak to Europeans of their grievances and the laws affecting natives'.[35] Referring to the slogan 'Mayibuy'iAfrica' ('Africa must return'), popular among ANC members, Mashow said that 'he hear[d] natives saying "Africa must come back" but he [did] not know where from as they [were]

[30] Hosiah Thagadi Report, 19 April 1926, South African National Archives, JUS: 915–22.
[31] Sergeant J. C. Kruger Report, 22 June 1926, South African National Archives, JUS: 915–22.
[32] A. A. Toba Report, 25 July 1926, South African National Archives, JUS: 915–22.
[33] Molteno Faku Report, 3 August 1926, South African National Archives, JUS: 915–22.
[34] English Hlalele Report, 21 February 1926, South African National Archives, JUS: 915–22.
[35] Hosiah Thagadi Report, 29 March 29 1926, South African National Archives, JUS: 915–22.

in Africa'. Compared to fellow ICU leaders such as Thaele, Mashow certainly sounded moderate. But that was a function of the ICU's social base and historical context. Given its location in a racially segregated society, the ICU could not help but sound radical.

In South Africa, every challenge to the status quo constituted by definition an existential threat to the prevailing order. For some ICU leaders, this meant that their struggle had, of necessity, to involve imagining a new future. No one expressed this realisation better than James Thaele. He told an ICU meeting on 21 February 1926 that:

> The battle is on and you have to beat the white man at his own table. If the white man cannot agree with us, let him go back to Europe where he originally came from. We will remain in Africa our land. I want the black races to unite and become one race in order to beat the white man. You are not kaffirs, nor natives or Bantus ... do not allow a white man to call you that. You are African.[36]

In a speech that he concluded with the slogan 'Europe for Europeans and South Africa for South Africans', Thaele also offered an expansive understanding of who South Africans were. He began his speech with 'I don't call you natives, Indians or coloured people, but I call you South Africans.'[37] Thaele urged Africans and coloureds to unite with Indians and to support Indian businesses. Speaking at another ICU rally a few days later, activist Hosea Mutha made a similar call: 'The Indians are now joining the ICU and we should no more call ourselves Indians, Native or Cape [coloured]. We should call ourselves South Africans.'[38] However, no amount of pleading could, on its own, bring about Black unity. In April 1926, a 'loyal Griqua named Frank Meyer' told a policeman named W. Mackesy about meetings at which attendees discussed ways whereby the country would 'be taken again with blood and they [Griquas] would drive the white man out of the country'. Meyer made sure to ask Mackesy 'not to make use of his name as he feared personal injury from the followers of Le Fleur', the man who had organised the meetings.[39] On 11 April 1926 a farmworker named Mothla Rokosa attended an ICU meeting during which the organisers distributed propaganda leaflets. According to Rokosa, the organisers said that 'white people must be killed with assegais during the night time'.[40] Rokosa collected some of the leaflets in order to show his 'master', but one of the organisers 'caught hold of me and took the paper away. I don't know what was on the paper as I cannot read. It was not printed matter but written in ink.' The actions of men such as Meyer and Rokosa explain the ICU's fears that fellow Africans were reporting on the union and thereby disrupting its activities. The actions of Meyer and Rokosa also explain why ICU leaders worried constantly

[36] Marthinus Grobbelaar Report, 21 February 1926, South African National Archives, JUS: 915–22.
[37] Sergeant J. F. Bekker Report, 1 March 1926, South African National Archives, JUS: 915–22.
[38] H. J. Redelinghuys Report, 8 March 1926, South African National Archives, JUS: 915–22.
[39] W. Mackesy Report, 7 April 1926, South African National Archives, JUS: 915–22.
[40] Mothla Rokosa Report, 20 April 1926, South African National Archives, JUS: 915–22.

about what spies and African policemen told their bosses. As John Mzaza, an ICU leader, told his audience:

> I know there is [*sic*] some of you people here who do not belong to our ICU. You people must not go and tell your masters what is said here. At some time, these people will be sorry they have not joined us. The time will come when they will be eager to join us, but we shall have something to say to them then.[41]

However, as we know from the cases of Mote and Toba, it was wishful thinking on the part of Mzaza to believe that only non-members spied on the ICU. Sometimes, fear of what informers and African policemen could do to the union resulted in assaults against the police. On 24 April 1926, a man named Willem Philander physically attacked Naphtali Mutshese.[42] The archives do not say what happened to Philander. But it is not hard to imagine that the story did not end well for him. The police were, after all, the representatives of God on earth (Weber 1991: 213).

Conclusion: Rethinking Collaboration

On 23 May 1926, John Mokhahle, a sergeant in the South African Police stationed in Kroonstad, about 133 miles north of Bloemfontein, attended a meeting of about 50 African men and women convened by a local activist named Max Mareka. As Mokhahle reported to his superiors afterwards, Mareka had called the gathering to prepare the attendees for a visit to the town the next day by Alexander Maduna, a leader of the ICU. The attendees were mostly farm labourers and sharecroppers and they had a lot of grievances about land dispossession, especially in the Orange Free State.

> Mareka said to them, 'You know, we live very poorly here; in fact, we live like dogs. We are badly driven and badly treated, but you will see in the end. I shall be very glad if you will think over this poor way we have to live … What I am telling you here is what all members of the ICU say.'[43]

Mareka, speaking Sotho, implored his audience to return the next day to hear Maduna speak. He added: 'When the pot boils, you must add the meal.' This, explained Mokhahle, was a Sotho idiom meaning that 'when the time is right, action must be taken'. According to Mokhahle, Mareka added, 'You, our men, you are very frightened and would rather see us all dead; we should not be trampled on.'[44] The sergeant understood the idiom because, like Mareka and the 50-or-so people at the meeting that day, he was fluent in Sotho; so would have been the

---

[41] Molteno Faku Report, 23 August 1926, South African National Archives, JUS: 915–22.
[42] Naphtali Mutshese Report, 26 April 1926, South African National Archives, JUS: 915–22.
[43] John Mokhahle Report, 23 May 1926, South African National Archives, JUS: 915–22.
[44] *Ibid.*

people at the meeting. By explaining the idiom to his superiors, Mokhahle was doing more than playing native informant. He was alerting his police superiors to potential strife in the area. Those superiors had every reason to send him to that afternoon meeting. Memories of the 1925 demonstrations were still fresh in their minds. The demonstrations had placed the police and other White officials on edge, and led to an increase in police patrols and surveillance.

The authorities worried about a repeat of the riots and so sought to pre-empt the next one by keeping close tabs on political activity among Africans. The police were especially concerned about attempts by the ICU in particular to foment labour strikes. They had reason to be. As Mokhahle said in his report, after Mareka spoke, one David Moshodi, a self-described member of the ICU, told the meeting: 'The members of the ICU at Bloemfontein have a movement afoot that they will no longer work for 2/6 [2s 6d] per diem, they want a wage of 6/6 [6s 6d] per diem in Bloemfontein and they want the natives around Kroonstad to also demand that wage.' These were serious matters and the police wanted to ensure that, should there be protest action planned, they were not caught by surprise.

In what way do this story and the episodes recounted in this chapter allow us to rethink collaboration? If we go by the standard definitions of collaboration, whereby a collaborator is a person who works with an oppressive elite/foreign nation to help it rule over a polity/community/nation from which the person comes, then Mote and Mokhahle were definitely collaborators. After all, they were African men in a society founded on racial segregation and White supremacy. They worked for a police force whose primary goal was the maintenance of the racial order and the protection of the status quo. This is not to say that the two men were similar. Mote was a full-time activist contracted to work as a confidential police informant; Mokhahle was a sergeant in the police force. The one worked in secret; the other worked under cover. Mote's collaboration came out of his betrayal of his political comrades; Mokhahle's issued from his taking advantage of his Black skin to pass as yet another Black person among those who attended Mareka's meeting because he was interested politically in what Mareka and the ICU had to say. However, to call these men collaborators, we have to privilege their racial identity as Africans in segregationist South Africa. We have to assume that Blackness was for them – as for the Black communities in which they operated – an untroubled category. We have to take as given that their understanding of what it meant to be Black in 1920s South Africa would have been the same throughout the country. But as we know from the stories recounted above, Africans had different understandings of what it meant to be Black. They had different reasons for supporting the ANC, the ICU, and the South African Police. We cannot get at these reasons if we limit our enquiry to questions about collaboration and resistance. We cannot hope to under-stand the choices that individuals made in South Africa in the 1920s if our interest is limited only to whether some Africans collaborated with the White authorities or not. But we can grope our way toward some understanding if we start from the humble position that humans do not act simply out of concerns with identity.

That humble position means also acknowledging the fact that we may never know why Mote agreed to spy on his comrades for Du Plessis, why scores of Africans agreed readily to inform on African activists, and why Africans could not agree on what it meant to be Black.

Among scholars of the Bible, there is no agreement over why Judas Iscariot betrayed Jesus (see Chapter 1). For some, Judas betrayed Jesus for 30 pieces of silver; for others, the devil possessed Judas and led him astray; for yet others, Judas was a faithful disciple who did nothing more than follow Jesus's instruction; while others argue that Judas was an instrument through whom God sacrificed his only son all so that humanity might be saved. That, of course, is not the Judas that African activists had in mind when they called others Judas. They had Judas with the 30 pieces of silver in mind. But that is not necessarily how the African detectives and informers subjected to the Judas-as-traitor label saw themselves. We cannot say for certain how they saw themselves, but it is easy to guess that they did not see themselves as traitors.

References

Beinart, W. and Bundy, C. (1987), *Hidden Struggles in Rural South Africa* (Johannesburg, Ravan Press).

Berman, B., Eyoh, D., and Kymlicka, W. (eds) (2004), 'Introduction: Ethnicity and the politics of democratic nation-building in Africa', in *Ethnicity and Democracy in Africa* (Oxford, Oxford University Press), 1–21.

Bradford, H. (1988), *A Taste of Freedom: The ICU in Rural South Africa, 1924–1930* (Johannesburg, Ravan Press).

Branch, D. (2007), 'The enemy within: Loyalists and the war against Mau Mau in Kenya', *Journal of African History*, 48, 291–315.

Campbell, J. (1995), *Songs of Zion: The African Methodist Episcopal Church in the United States and South Africa* (New York, Oxford University Press).

Cooper, F. (1996), '"Our strike": Equality, anticolonial politics and the 1947–48 railway strike in French West Africa', *Journal of African History*, 37, 81–118.

Hirson, B. (1984), *The Bloemfontein Riots 1925: A Study in Community Culture and Class Consciousness*, Collected Seminar Papers (London, Institute of Commonwealth Studies), 82–96.

Johnson, D. (2015), 'Clements Kadalie, the ICU, and the language of freedom', *English in Africa*, 42, 43–69.

Kelley, R. D. G. (1986), 'The Third International and the struggle for liberation in South Africa', *Ufahamu: A Journal of African Studies*, 15, 99–120.

Moloi, T. (2013), 'The emergence and radicalization of black political formations in Kroonstad, 1915 to 1957', *New Contree*, 67, 167–86.

Moloi, T. (2015), *Place of Thorns: Black Political Protest in Kroonstad since 1976* (Johannesburg, Wits University Press).

Ntantala, P. (1993), *A Life's Mosaic: The Autobiography of Phyllis Ntantala* (Berkeley, University of California Press).

Roux, E. (1964), *Time Longer than Rope: A History of the Black Man's Struggle for Freedom in South Africa* (Madison, University of Wisconsin Press).

Van Onselen, C. (1996), *The Seed Is Mine: The Life of Kas Maine, a South African Sharecropper* (New York, Hill and Wang).

Vinson, R. 2012). *The Americans Are Coming: Dreams of African American Liberation in Segregationist South Africa* (Athens, Ohio University Press).

Weber, M. (1991), *From Max Weber: Essays in Sociology*, ed. H. H. Gerth and C. Wright Mills (London, Routledge).

Wells, J. (1983), 'Why women rebel: A comparative study of South African women's resistance in Bloemfontein (1913) and Johannesburg (1958)', *Journal of Southern African Studies*, 10, 55–70.

3

Be My Character: Framing the
Female Collaborator in Postdictatorship
Argentine Novels

KSENIJA BILBIJA

THIS CHAPTER EXPLORES literary representations of the Argentine leftist female militant Mercedes Carazo that emerged right after the transition to democracy through the second decade of the 21st century. Carazo was cast as a collaborator for exhibiting different degrees of complicity with the Argentine military (1976–83), and these representations frame her prison camp survival through her intimate relationship with her torturer. I propose to re-examine that relationship and, more specifically, the lens through which Carazo's interaction with her torturer has been deemed dishonourable and treacherous. I contend that the particular storification of the female Montonera militant led to her re-violation-by-novel(ist) in works such as *Recuerdo de la muerte* by Miguel Bonasso (1984), *El fin de la historia* by Liliana Heker (1996), and *Noche de lobos* by Abel Posse (2011).[1] The identification and even doubling of each novelist with an in-text 'teller' figure implies a further doubling between the novelist/teller – who violates the victim's right to tell her own story eliciting empathy for her difficult circumstances – and the original torturer/sexual aggressor. Bonasso, Heker, and Posse become informants of sorts by presenting an assumed – or, better put, fictional – intimacy, regarding their knowledge of Carazo's story. They provide insider information on Carazo that others do not have, and they do what they accuse her of doing: betrayal of the sacred/secrets that harmed those she allegedly betrayed.[2] It is only in *Doble fondo* by Elsa Osorio (2018) that the victim is given a voice and a community of compassionate readers

---

[1] The Montoneros were an Argentine left-wing Peronist guerrilla organisation mostly active during the 1960s and 1970s.

[2] I would like to thank Leigh Payne for her insightful comments on this chapter.

Proceedings of the British Academy, **248**, 50–67, © The British Academy 2022.

to evaluate and judge her complicity. To this extent, my chapter is not about missing narratives of survival but about the referential status of the novelistic content – textual agents such as narrators and characters used in the process of making sense of the traumatic past.

Carazo, at the time a physics student and a Montonera militant, was abducted on 21 October 1976, and imprisoned at the Naval Academy School, which the military regime had turned into a clandestine torture centre (ESMA). She was the highest-ranking Montonera officer to be captured by the military. According to later testimonies of ESMA survivors such as Susana Jorgelina Ramus (2000: 90) and Graciela Daleo (Di Tella 1998: min. 70), she never broke down under torture, nor did she reveal any information about her comrades. Naval operatives also kidnapped and interrogated Carazo's 10-year-old daughter, later returning the child to her grandparents but keeping her under surveillance in order to control her mother. Eventually, while still in the ESMA, Carazo became part of a group of prisoners assigned to military intelligence gathering, transcribing telephone conversations, and producing press summaries related to the portrayal of the Argentine government in foreign media. By some accounts, she saved and eased the lives of numerous other prisoners in this role (Actis *et al.* 2000: 186–7).

Mercedes Carazo also entered into a sexual relationship with her torturer, Naval Officer Antonio Pernías. Pernías probably saved Carazo's daughter from death. It was under his constant supervision that Carazo went to Paris to work in a newly formed public relations task force called Pilot Centre (Centro Piloto). The task force's goal was to counter hostile international press coverage of Argentina's human rights violations and, when possible, to infiltrate groups of political activists and opponents who tried to oppose Argentina's military government from outside the country. After some months, in 1979, Carazo was returned to the clandestine ESMA torture centre. In 1980 she was allowed to leave Argentina for Peru, where she eventually succeeded in reinitiating her career as a scientist. In 2004 she joined the Centre for Technological Innovation within Peru's Ministry of Production (Centro de Innovación Tecnológica del Ministerio de la Producción de Perú) and is currently directing the Department of Alternative Energy. She now lives with her family in Lima.

Carazo never wrote an autobiography or any other written account of her imprisonment and the day-to-day reality of her violent, traumatic experience. But she did testify in several trials against individuals who perpetrated human rights abuses during Argentina's military dictatorship. Testifying in the Unified ESMA case (*Megacausa ESMA*), she specifically referred to her relationship with her torturer: 'If I had been free I would never have been with him [Antonio Pernías]. In the '80s, when I was no longer under surveillance, that relationship ended' (*Prensa* 2014).

In the absence of a detailed account from Carazo herself, the Argentinian press has engaged in extended speculation, framing the former Montonera's experience as a classic Stockholm syndrome story with sensationalist titles such as 'A Marvellous

Love Story' in *Página/12* (Meyer 1998b) and 'Stockholm Syndrome: The Strange Love of the Executioner' in *Gaceta mercantil* (Devita 2013). The journal *Noticias* even illustrated a series of investigative articles entitled 'Love in ESMA' (14 March 1998) with a heart constructed from barbed wire on the journal cover. The Stockholm syndrome label suggests a strong, positive emotional attachment that victims of abduction develop toward their captors and maintain even after they have been freed. It proposes a narrative model where female prisoners feel empathy, gratitude, and even 'love' toward their male abductors, to the point of accepting their oppressors' norms and views.[3]

Stockholm syndrome has been reified in the popular media, and thus in the popular imagination. The medical profession has yet to recognise Stockholm syndrome as a real affliction, however. It has never been included in the American Psychiatric Association's *Diagnostic and Statistical Manual of Mental Disorders*, the commonly used reference for classifying psychiatric disorders. In Argentinian legal contexts, the syndrome has been weaponised against its supposed victims. In 2007, during the reopened trials of ESMA officials, defence attorneys tried to argue that the raped and sexually harassed female prisoners were, to varying degrees, complicit in and responsible for the actions of the accused, in a systematic effort to disguise the crimes of the dictatorship and exonerate its prison guards and torturers. The defence counsel exploited Stockholm syndrome optics to victimise the prisoners further, suggesting they were actually 'voluntary participants' who benefited from their relationships with military officers (who, in this reading, were seduced from their moral and professional principles by the female prisoners). This attempt to reverse the responsibility from torturers and rapists to the tortured and raped detainees – transferring blame to the prisoners themselves – further humiliated the regime's victims. Assuming that a prisoner is capable of freely establishing a sentimental relationship with her captor within a torture centre denies her victim status and decriminalises the rapist's aggression, transforming it into a consensual relationship.[4] Ultimately, this kind of reasoning implies that there is no one to blame.

---

[3] The term was coined in 1973 during Sweden's first televised bank robbery, in Stockholm, when one of the hostages publicly defended her captor and later, while he was in prison, became engaged to him. Beyond the Swedish case, the best-known historical examples include Patty Hearst, the wealthy heiress kidnapped in 1974, and Natascha Kampusch, who was abducted in 1998 and spent 3,096 days with her captor. Popular-culture accounts of Stockholm syndrome include fictional stories such as *Beauty and the Beast*, the TV series *Veronica Mars*, and the film *Die Hard*. These treatments suggest that women are particularly susceptible to this disorder. For more examples related to the uses of Stockholm syndrome in recent Argentine culture see Bilbija (2018).

[4] The context of the Argentine dictatorship and its kidnapping and torture of political opponents is very different from the cases that brought global attention to Stockholm syndrome. The Swedish hostages repeatedly stated that they felt safer with their captors than with the police – or with Prime Minister Olof Palme, with whom they were in communication – because they feared an attack in which they might be collateral damage. In Argentina, the distinction between captors and security forces did not exist; the state, under President General Videla's control, was the illegal kidnapper. Furthermore, while in the Swedish case the hostages developed positive feelings toward their captors, who treated them well, and

The Stockholm syndrome label, complicit in patriarchal misogyny, has offered an enticing formula of sex and violence activated by female betrayal and collusion. The pathology this syndrome assigns to women suggests they are more prone than men to moral transgression; their integrity is compromised, and they are incapable of autonomous, sovereign action and agency. Miriam Lewin, survivor of the ESMA clandestine torture centre, now a journalist and co-author with Olga Wornat of *Whores and Guerrillas* (*Putas y guerrilleras* (Lewin and Wornat 2014)), presents a contrasting account. Her book examines the invisibility of sexual violence during the dictatorship and refutes the claim that victims collaborated with the military officers who were their captors. She notes the double standard that Argentine society has imposed on female survivors: 'Because if it had been the other way around, people would have said, "He is a badass! He seduced the female guard to get better treatment in the torture centre" ' (Garzón and Romero 2008: 172, my translation).[5] A female victim with agency does not fit easily into the patriarchal imaginary. Argentine leftist militant women such as Mercedes Carazo were not desexualised mothers and wives when they took up arms. As militants, they already challenged the standards of traditional gender values. As captives, their bodies were dehumanised and disciplined through brutal torture and sexual violence, thus undermining their sense of agency and selfhood.[6] By later reducing the (surviving) women to their corporeality, the military attempted to strip away even further their identity as politically engaged militants.

As a society we have been led, not least by some bestselling works of fiction, to condense the survivor story into a simple binary: dead hero–living traitor. If you left the extermination camps alive, it must be because you collaborated with the repressors. If you are female, and you eventually crossed the detention centre's threshold into freedom, the collective doubting of survivors is paired with the classic patriarchal virgin–whore opposition to reinterpret the sexual violence that victimised prisoners as consensual, a collaborationist interaction. Furthermore, the vocabulary the patriarchal system associates with sex distinguishes its role in procreation (coupled with marriage and love) from sex as pleasure (without love) labelled as prostitution. 'Putas y guerrilleras' was the soldiers' insult for the abducted militant women: when they abandoned the private spaces of their homes and entered the public arena of political struggle, they immediately became *public women*, whores. This social stigma carried over to survivors of state terrorism, who were later denied recognition of their real status as victims of sexual violence.

So far, nearly half a century after her abduction and torture, Mercedes Carazo has chosen not to tell – at least not in public – her own story of survival. Like

---

could see the robbers as contemporary Robin Hoods who attacked the institution and not the citizens, in Argentina the torture of individual detainees was institutionalised.

[5] Lewin reiterates this idea in her interview with Natalia Arenas (2014).

[6] Luisa Valenzuela's (1982) short story 'Cambio de armas' ['Other Weapons'] brilliantly portrays such a situation via an amnesiac protagonist with marks of torture on her body who tries to reconstruct her life while caught in a sexual relationship with a person who is pretending to be her husband.

many other victims who managed to stay alive through long imprisonments, she has valued her right to privacy above anything she might gain from publicly denouncing the perpetrator(s) of her own rape, sexual degradation, humiliation, and abuse. Maybe she believed that accounting for the disappeared was a higher priority for post-authoritarian Argentine society. Or perhaps she did not trust the nation's legal system, which at the time failed to recognise sexual violence and rape as crimes against humanity. Maybe Mercedes Carazo, like other survivors, has felt shame and guilt for surviving the clandestine detention centre. It is also possible that she saw victimhood as a trap that would have precluded other forms of identity. And it is imaginable that she wanted to put behind her the violent death of her husband and to try to build a new life with her surviving child in a different country. She did, after all, fulfil her role as witness to others' suffering by testifying in the trials and identifying the disappeared she saw in ESMA, without seeking justice for herself (Meyer 1998b). It could be that the words she might have used to articulate her trauma are themselves now disappeared. Facing an audience now evidently in search of other kinds of survival narratives, she may not have had the strength to trust that those who did not experience her ordeal were ready to face the horror of her story. Maybe she just needed to grieve the loss of the society she had imagined for her child and had fought for when she and her husband decided to take up arms against social injustice. In any case, why some survived and others did not has remained an open public question among Argentines. The survival of numerous prisoners, Mercedes Carazo among them, has been shrouded in shame and doubt. To talk about a traumatic experience, the survivor must believe that representation is possible, that she will not have to adjust her experience to existing narrative patterns but can be heard in her own right. Willingness to speak presupposes belief that some kind of cathartic liberation is achievable. '*We*, the victims', wrote Jean Améry (1980: 80) in relation to the Holocaust, 'will appear as the truly incorrigible, irreconcilable ones, as the antihistorical reactionaries in the exact sense of the word, and in the end it will seem like a technical mishap that some of us still survived'. His words imply that without strangers listening in solidarity, the survivor's story would not be worth telling. It would not unmake her trauma, nor would it bring healing.[7]

The number of novels that claim to embody Mercedes Carazo's experience and engage with narrating her capture and survival, explicitly as well as implicitly, is significant. Some of the bestselling Argentine fiction writers of Carazo's generation seem to have been unable to resist reshaping the contours of her militancy, her imprisonment, and her survival to match the authors' personal literary vision and societal changes associated with ideological shifts – from the *Nunca más* (Never Again) call for the end of human rights abuses, to the consolidation of the *Ni una menos* (Not One [Woman] Less) movement against femicide. Miguel Bonasso, Liliana Heker, and Abel Posse all told the untold story of Carazo's life by casting

---

[7] In her book *The Body in Pain: The Making and Unmaking of the World* the philosopher Elaine Scarry (1987) uses the term 'unmaking the trauma' with regard to the role of language in repairing the survivor.

her in a consensual sexual, and even amorous, relationship with her torturer. They added imagination to rumour; they claimed to relay confidential (yet unauthorised) conversations; they stereotyped, romanticised, imposed their own rhythm, assigned voice, righteousness, and sequence to a story that Carazo herself never spoke aloud.

Some of those novelists eroticised violence, sexualised women's bodies, and pathologised female agency in their literary accounts of atrocities committed during the military dictatorship. Others focused on the ethical dilemmas of betrayal and collaboration. These authors – allegedly comrades, childhood friends, and acquaintances – seem to have been more interested in her story than in her. Bonasso uses Carazo's name explicitly. Heker and Posse used a transparent pseudonym in their novels and relied heavily on paratextual venues such as interviews and marketing to make sure readers would recognise in their protagonist a historical figure known as Mercedes Carazo. These writers intentionally blur the lines between fiction and non-fiction by articulating their alleged first-hand knowledge of Carazo's actions and then overlapping their narrators with the implied figure of the empirical author – thus usurping her voice rather than representing it.

Only Elsa Osorio (2018), in *Doble fondo* (*Double Ground*), stays away from establishing any direct reference to the Montonera militant. Osorio thus allows the reader to examine the larger context of sexual abuse. She also facilitates a less judgemental and more gender-conscious reading of the story of an abducted woman who survives inhuman treatment and saves her child despite an unequal and abusive relationship imposed by a representative of the terrorist state. Osorio's novel, published within the context of the *Ni una menos* feminist commitment to fight all gender-based violence, in that sense reconfigures the representation of the survivor. By looking at the Argentine military repression in the context of femicide, the novel confronts, from a gender-conscious perspective, the cultural myopia of patriarchal society.

Article 27 of the Universal Declaration of Human Rights clearly states that art, and therefore literary fiction, is a human right, thus signalling the importance of fiction writers in documenting the atrocities of the authoritarian regime.[8] On the other hand, Theodor Adorno (1967: 34) warns of dangers associated with literature's power and argues that 'after Auschwitz, to write a poem is barbaric'. Pain, artistically depicted, may 'elicit enjoyment' in the reader, and horror, transfigured into rational chronology, may become meaningful. Language, as an instrument of fiction, is guided by rules. Stories follow a cause-and-effect logic. In the human rights template, stories shape their characters as victims and perpetrators. An author who embarks on the literary project of transmitting pain through words must balance and amend the relationship between the abuser and the abused.

In examining the novels by Bonasso, Heker, Posse, and Osorio, I will focus on how these writers frame the story of the female Montonera prisoner who was in a

---

[8] United Nations, Universal Declaration of Human Rights, https://www.un.org/en/universal-declaration-human-rights/ (accessed 19 April 2021).

sexual relationship with her torturer at ESMA: how does each novelist negotiate the conventions of the literary genre he or she has chosen to render their account and to construct the notion of victimhood in relation to the militant's gender?

In 1984, the same year that *Never Again: The Report of the Argentine National Commission on the Disappeared* detailed human rights abuses of the era, former Montonero press secretary Miguel Bonasso published his 'real novel or novelised reality' ('novela real o realidad novelada'), *Recuerdo de la muerte* (*Memory of Death* (Bonasso 1984: 397)). The book was an immediate bestseller and was received as an official account of the history and ideology of Montonero political activism. Despite claims of rigorous truthfulness and accuracy buttressed partly by the author's reliance on oral testimony from the leftist militant Jaime Dri – the only prisoner ever to escape from ESMA – *Recuerdo de la muerte* wavers in its commitment to truth. The book's genre fluctuates between testimony and fiction. In creating his 'real novel', Bonasso enhanced the material he obtained from his own interviews, from historical and journalistic Montonero documents, and from survivors' testimonies in human rights forums, using techniques and rhetorical strategies typical of novelistic discourse: interior monologues, recreated dialogues, flashbacks, dramatic irony, and character development, among others. Despite framing the work as relating the first-person testimonial account of Jaime Dri, Bonasso constructs his narrative predominantly from the point of view of an omniscient third-person narrator. While the book itself thus uses a narrative technique typical of the realist novel (striving for verisimilitude rather than veracity), the publisher's promotional materials and Bonasso's comments to the media on the publication of the novel emphasised its testimonial value based on the story told by the survivor himself.

Bonasso's well-crafted narrative achieves suspension of disbelief in the reader – to the point that few will pause in reading this fast-paced crime story to ponder how the writer accessed the thoughts of characters who were not interviewed – for example military officers or prisoners such as Carazo – whom the novel portrays as traitors and enemies of the movement. Needless to say, we are only required to engage in the suspension of disbelief when we are first aware that what we are reading is fiction.[9] When presenting a testimonial account, the writer makes a tacit pact with the reader that what is read is the truthful reflection of the survivor's experience. Yet how could one *know* – rather than *imagine* – what was going on in the heads even of protagonists, let alone antagonists? Time after time, Bonasso underscores the veracity of his narrative over its verisimilitude. He explains at the end of his book that everything is 'absolutely true and supported by conclusive and extensive documentation'.[10] Yet while Bonasso (and his publisher) celebrate Jaime

---

[9] In her reading of Bonasso's book in *Traiciones*, Ana Longoni (2007: 63) mentions that it was advertised as a winner of the competition for the best detective novel of the year, *Premio a la novela policial del año*.

[10] 'Todo lo que se dice es rigurosamente cierto y está apoyado sobre una base documental enorme y concluyente' (Bonasso 1984: 404).

Dri as an unquestionable hero in the narrative – and Dri is in theory the survivor telling a story that is merely edited and organised by the author – in practice, the mediator, Bonasso, often slips out of Dri's narration and introjects himself as an ersatz or even superior and usurping witness, thus allowing the empirical author to contest the internal narrator. While this kind of framing is acceptable and common in novels, it becomes questionable when the author asserts that his goal is to give an account of the 'absolute truth' and identifies – or allows his publisher's publicity team to identify – the resulting literary production as a testimonial.

While *Recuerdo de la muerte* maintains ambiguity regarding its narrative form – its 'truth' oscillating between historical fact and the verisimilitude of fiction – the narrative allows for no moral ambiguity. In that sense the book subscribes to the Montoneros' ethical codes, which assumed the only way for detainees to survive torture was by trading information about the organisation. To survive was, *de facto*, to betray. Even simulated collaboration with the military was treason.[11] The articulation of the terms 'hero' and 'traitor' is accordingly explicit and unambiguous. Bonasso's writing, however, feminises the Montonero binary in a telling simile: 'betrayal looks like a seduced woman. The one that gives a kiss, then another, and finally ends up spreading her legs' (134). Through a misogynistic and sexist lens, Bonasso sees women as by nature prone to treachery. A female suspect is thus doubly suspect – condemned once by the Montoneros' expectation that betrayal of the organisation's secrets is a precondition of survival, and a second time by nature of her sex. One of those survivors, fully identified in the narrative by her *nom de guerre* Lucy and directly labelled as a traitor, is Mercedes Carazo (244–5).

Carazo's collaboration and survival are conveyed through a story told to Jaime Dri by a man named Chacho, who, together with Dri, belonged to a group within ESMA that 'simulated collaboration without actually collaborating' (Bonasso 1984: 289). Chacho says he heard the story from Carazo herself, although he was still free when the events took place. In this alleged account Antonio Pernías intervened to save Carazo's 10-year-old daughter because he wanted to seduce Carazo, who had apparently previously rejected the advances of another military officer. 'It's like a novel', says Chacho in Bonasso's book (243), as he describes to Dri how Carazo's husband was mortally wounded in the attack and then transported to the ESMA, where she was allowed to hold him in her arms as he died. In this telling, Pernías, also present, addressed Carazo using a term of endearment ('Lucita'). Hence the agonised husband was first shocked to discover that his wife was still alive, and then to realise she was in a relationship with her captor. The reader is left to imagine the state of mind of Carazo's dying husband as he comprehended that his wife was a traitor not only to the Montonero movement but also to their marriage. Carazo is thus depicted through an image of the betrayal within a betrayal. While Dri's

---

[11] Jaime Dri reflects on these issues as he contemplates his escape from ESMA and weighs the potential usefulness of joining the group of prisoners who reviewed the foreign press and performed other similar activities for the military.

version of the story conveys the unforgiving nature of Carazo's treachery and the depths of her (im)morality, it can be told otherwise. One real-life Montonero militant who worked with Carazo's husband did, indeed, relate the story differently, saying he already knew that his wife was alive and was actually empathetic to the horror and agony she was enduring under torture: 'Poor thing. She must be suffering so much. She has such low pain tolerance' (Longoni 2007: 146).

Apocryphal or not, the story of a mortally wounded husband who realises his wife's ultimate betrayal, which Bonasso first related in his 1984 *Memory of Death*, had sufficient novelistic power that Liliana Heker would retell it in her 1996 metafictional novel *The End of the Story*. Though that novel was published on the 20th anniversary of the military coup, when sufficient time had passed since the end of the dictatorship to allow the post-authoritarian society to move away from the testimonial imperative, the author still maintained the porosity of the genre by declaring it 'document and fiction' (Heker 1999). The treacherous protagonist in Heker's novel is named Leonora, represented as a childhood friend of the intradiegetic novelist Diana Glass, who attempts to narrate her betrayal of the cause and her love relationship with her torturer. All the paratextual venues underline the novel's (auto) biographical value. Promotional reviews, running in parallel with the interviews Heker gave to the Argentine dailies and foreign journals, reiterate numerous past conversations she had had with her close friend who chose militancy: 'Between 1992 and early 1994 I conducted a number of interviews (from which I would return feeling intoxicated) with the person I used as a basis for Leonora's character. In March 1994 I wrote in one breath and without any literary intention the chronicle of events narrated by my interviewee' (André 2002: 145). It is not clear if Heker's friend knew at the time that their intimate conversations would be used as the basis of a novel about betrayal. The novel itself is structured around two authorial voices: a writer friend, Diana Glass, and a professional Jewish-Austrian writer, Hertha Bechofen, who escaped the Holocaust. Throughout the narrative these voices represent Leonora's thinking, so that the militant sees her own lived experience only indirectly, through the novel's intervening exchange between writers.

Heker's narrative represents the Montonera fighter as a promiscuous, narcissistic woman who falls in love with her captor and consequently abandons her leftist political commitment. The protagonist's betrayal is predetermined by her beauty, femininity, promiscuity, and narcissism – all of these traits she allegedly exhibited even before her abduction. Such prefiguration morally condemns the militant in advance of her capture.[12] She is portrayed as capable and determined in her seduction, an active agent who makes her target abandon their path and duty so she can get what she wants. For example, Heker describes in her novel a scene in which her character reacts strongly to a newspaper article suggesting she was seduced by the torturer: 'Nobody ever seduced me ... I was always the one who seduced'

---

[12] Evidenced in accounts that narrate how she got the attention of a teacher, seduced an airport employee during the Montonero action, or cheated on her husband.

(Heker 1996: 235).[13] In the extradiegetic world, fully outside the novel in an interview with *Página/12* journalist Adriana Meyer, Heker ascribes this very statement to a conversation she had with Mercedes 'Lucy' Carazo in which she described her relationship with Pernías: 'It is not true that he seduced me. Nobody seduces me, I am the one who seduces' (Pridgeon 2015: 38). Alleged seduction is not seen as a tactic to gain control of the situation and secure some agency in the torture centre by reversing the usual dynamic between torturer and victim; it serves instead to show that Lucy has no scruples and is morally corrupt. The novel's narrative authority goes even further to portray Carazo's character as morally deficient by depicting her as incapable of feeling 'true' love. The character declares she fell in love with her torturer. The narrative voice then questions that assertion by disparagingly enumerating the many 'loves' of Leonora's life, insinuating that none was special, none was a real love. This representation of love contrasts sharply even with the love the torturer feels. In an interview Heker gave to *La Prensa*, she claims she was horrified to discover that 'this man who was her torturer *really loved* [Leonora]', while she appears to be 'more cunning and it was hard to know how manipulative she was in that love', (Longoni 2007: 95, emphasis in original). By not *really* loving but merely seducing and thus manipulating him, the Montonera militant seems to descend on the scale of morality despite her status as a prisoner in the clandestine torture centre. Her captor, ironically, ends up higher on the moral scale. Heker goes even farther to denigrate her character, and consequently the childhood friend, who she says served as a template. She actually creates in her novel a purely fictional betrayal in which Leonora shows the interrogators where her husband was hiding.[14] While this might be defended as an example of novelistic licence, it is then unclear why the author would have insisted so strenuously, in paratextual venues, on the testimonial value of her narrative.

Abel Posse's rendition of Carazo's life in his 2011 bestselling 'novel without fiction' *Noche de lobos* (*Night of the Wolves*) suggests that only attractive female prisoners survived detention during the dictatorship. He depicts a relationship between a Montonera militant named Greta Carrazco and a male torturer, Armando, as consensual and sadomasochistic. Posse served as a diplomat in a number of posts in Europe during the military dictatorship and was silent on the human rights abuses then perpetrated by the terrorist state. His novel's ideological framing tips the scale of the 'theory of two demons' in favour of the military and against the militant left, which Posse presents as terrorist. The success of Posse's novel indicates that three decades after the transition to democracy, Argentine readers were still sufficiently interested in the story of a captured female militant who has a sexual relationship with her torturer to send the novel to the top of bestseller lists. One may also wonder

---

[13] In an interview with Adriana Meyer, Liliana Heker said that Carazo told her this in one of their conversations (Meyer 1998b).

[14] All testimonial accounts maintain that Mercedes Carazo did not break under torture and did not reveal the whereabouts or identities of any of her comrades (Actis *et al.* 2000).

if the reactionary decade of Carlos Menem's neoliberal 'free-market' economy, and the deep social inequality and economic marginalisation that followed in its wake, has brought Argentine society into a new moral era.

The promotional material for Posse's novel underscores its veracity by stressing its author's direct acquaintance with several of its protagonists. According to Lewin and Wornat, Carazo and Posse met in Lima in 1998, when she testified at the Argentine embassy regarding her ESMA detention. It was the time of Alberto Fujimori's government in Peru, and the Shining Path was active. Since Carazo was then working for the Peruvian Ministry, the press was inundated with articles bringing up her past leftist militancy. Posse, although an ambassador for Argentina at the time, never supported the idea of trials for the military. He defended Carazo's decision to testify by calling his contacts in the Ministry. Lewin and Wornat report that he told them: '[T]his lady was forced to testify and if it were up to her she would never have done it. I trust her completely.' He also added that he knew that 'she was disgusted by the accusations against the military' (Lewin and Wornat 2014: 367). We can imagine that Carazo told Ambassador Posse about her tragic history in ESMA and Centro Piloto, but it is not likely that the sexual fantasies under torture that Posse later gives to his character, Greta Carrazco, were part of those conversations.[15]

Posse's novel has two parts. The first is divided into two sections, suggestively titled 'Inferno' and 'Purgatory'. These are structured around the first-person narrative of a captured militant woman, who relates her experience to an anonymous chronicler. The second part, 'The House of Life', describing Carrazco's time in the Pilot Centre in Paris, her religious conversion, and an eventual pilgrimage to Jerusalem, is narrated by an Argentine writer assigned to a diplomatic post in France, to whom the character entrusts her story. *Noche de lobos* suggests that both characters – the military man who tortures and the militant woman who heroically endures the torture – find refuge in love. That the lovers are in the clandestine torture centre and that she is a detainee whose whereabouts and survival are unknown to the outside world remain unproblematised by the narrative. Furthermore, the torturer-redeemer not only teaches the tortured female guerrilla fighter proper authoritarian political ideology, but also spiritualises her through religious conversion.

The novel finally crests at the Inferno, into which the militant woman is thrown after her capture with sexual fantasies, where she recalls promiscuous sexual encounters with different partners. Through the prism of zoomorphism, she animates the torturous electric prod that 'ejaculates electric semen' when inserted into her orifices by naming it Cobra. The anonymous chronicler articulates his sexist philosophy, reflecting on the role of women: 'woman is the one to whom the pain of childbirth, rape, and beating corresponds. It is the dominator, the male, who is

---

[15] This is further confirmed by Mercedes Carazo's reported reaction of disgust and betrayal after she received a copy of the book (Lewin and Wornat 2014: 367–9).

in charge of the rhythms of tolerated sexual sadomasochism. The female retreats in an ambiguous game of provocation, challenge, and cynical renunciation of her bodily autonomy' (Posse 2011: 41). Later on, the novel postulates a strange theory of survival called 'erotic Darwinism' that proposes that among the female prisoners, 'pretty ones, regardless of how smart or stupid they are', have the greatest likelihood of survival (Posse 2011: 41). Posse's novel features pornographic representations of torture, using exhibitionism and dehumanisation of the victim.

Each one of these novelists – Bonasso, Heker, Posse – offer a particular reading of and commentary on recent Argentine history. Each, in their own way, bears witness to a repressive, traumatic past. All of these authors, as contemporaries of the Montonera Mercedes Carazo, who never publicly told the story of her detention, carve out spaces for themselves as witnesses or storytellers in the novels they shape around her experience. Whether in the character of a righteous Montonero comrade recalling a heroic escape from ESMA, a writer faced with a dilemma of how to tell the story of a friend's betrayal, or a chronicler who lends his ear to the survivor, each novelist fashions a character who serves as a relatively transparent proxy for the author. By fictionalising themselves in the role of a neutral, disinterested teller of the narrative, these novelists suggest to the reader that their female captive character is also real. When they claim to write a 'real novel or novelised reality', a 'document and fiction', or a 'novel without fiction', and even when they disguise the name of their fictionalised versions of Mercedes Carazo, these authors invoke the pact of truth guaranteed by the testimonial genre and make sure their readers know they had first-hand knowledge and direct access to the flesh-and-blood militant. The problem is that their supposed conversations were never corroborated, recorded interviews were never made available to the public, and their incursions into the mind of the survivor-collaborator are purely fictional. While they are driven, as novelists, by the desire to tell the story, these authors, with their uneasy engagement with truth, put the reader in an unsettling position: they ask her to suspend disbelief (a novelistic convention) while at the same time maintaining with their texts a categorical pact of truth regarding the narrated events (a convention of non-fiction). Ultimately, by impersonating the survivor's voice they all appropriate her right to tell her own story and thus perform a kind of rhetorical rape.

In her 2018 novel *Doble fondo* (*Double Ground*), Elsa Osorio takes a different path to an imaginary landscape of female transgression and punishment. Her pact with the reader, paratextual as well as textual, is unambiguous and clear: she is writing a historical detective novel and her characters are fictional. *Doble fondo* is structurally a complicated text, featuring a number of first-person narrators. The text oscillates between the epistolary testimonial of the female ESMA survivor, the progress of a French journalist investigating the mysterious death of a woman who turns out to be a former prisoner, and the victim's estranged son who reads the testimonial without at first knowing that it belongs to his mother. Nevertheless, after following all the protocols of exegesis, it is possible to see numerous parallels that an Argentine reader would draw between the Montonera Mercedes Carazo and

Osorio's main protagonist. Each is a militant mother who after being kidnapped tries to save her child; each is taken to the ESMA detention centre after a broken guerrilla fighter denounces her under torture; Carazo's *nom de guerre* is Lucía, while the novel's protagonist is called Lucy by her comrades; each is a high-ranking Montonera who heroically endures brutal torture and never betrays anyone; in each case the militant woman is also married to a leftist militant; each, during her detention in ESMA, agrees to write a history of her leftist militant movement to show her willingness to be 're-educated' and cooperate with the military; after a stay in the infamous torture centre in Buenos Aires, each is transferred to the Pilot Centre in Paris where, under constant surveillance, she works to improve Argentina's image in Europe, threatened as it then was by the military's abuse of human rights; each has a sexual relationship with the torturer, who takes her out to popular restaurants during her captivity and in some moments protects her from further excessive harm; each manages to leave Argentina and remake her personal and professional life elsewhere; and finally, each is considered a traitor by some of her militant comrades as well as by part of society.

Even while adhering to the *Nunca más* call of human rights organisations, Osorio's novel adds another dimension: she depicts the sexual abuse of victims as a weapon that was systematically used by the terrorist state apparatus. Her story is the one about a homicide that was to be committed for political and ideological reasons during the dictatorship and that ends up being a femicide committed in a free country by an abandoned lover. Osorio thus also firmly situates her narrative within the *Ni una menos* call for justice with regard to sexual and gender violence. Here the novelist 'saves' her militant female character from a death flight in 1978, only so that an embittered perpetrator who considers her his property can later locate her in France and throw her (sedated, but alive), from a chartered plane. He thus, in 2004, completes the revenge of a self-proclaimed proprietor against a woman who dared to leave him. *Doble fondo* clearly connects state terrorism and sexist terrorism by showing that the murderer is not a social deviant but a calculated defender of the patriarchal *machista* paradigm. Osorio portrays the rape and sexual abuse of the protagonist as the repressive practice of the military dictatorship and as a form of human rights violation. In that sense, she elevates the discussion surrounding the detained female militant in a sexual relationship with her torturer. Beyond the betrayal, deception, and religious redemption, she frames the alleged collaboration of the detainee as an act of child- and of self-preservation chosen in exchange for her sexual integrity. Juana, the incarcerated protagonist of *Doble fondo*, has chosen to act, thus demonstrating her agency and claiming for herself an active role in transforming the meaning of her circumstances. In that sense, the narrative is about gender (in)justice and agency.

Osorio's novel was not written and published in a judicial and socio-cultural vacuum. While the 1984 report of the National Commission on Disappeared Persons (CONADEP) had failed to acknowledge and account for sexual aggression, and the 1985 trials against the military junta wrapped sexual violence within the crimes of torture, a number of important legal changes in the international human rights arena have subsequently led to the recognition of rape as a war crime and human rights violation.[16] In Argentina, after the Full Stop Law (1986), the Law of Due Obedience (1987) and Menem's pardon of the officers condemned at the junta trials were declared unconstitutional in June 2005, the Supreme Court reversed the blanket amnesties and justice could again move forward. In 2012, Law 26.791 was adopted into the Argentine criminal code, finally recognising femicide as aggravated homicide.[17] This context empowered some victims to step up and denounce sexual crimes that had been committed against them; others felt that the judicial process could revictimise them. In her article 'Abuse as a crime against humanity and the right to privacy', Argentine sociologist Elizabeth Jelin acknowledges that the 'notions of morality and the definition of the boundary between public and private are slow processes full of conflict and generate new tensions', and urges us to construct 'new notions of morality, [and to] redefine spaces of intimacy and the border between the public and private' (Jelin 2012: 7). *Doble fondo* is a novel that frames its notions of morality in relation to sexual crimes in more humanising terms than we saw in earlier portrayals by Bonasso, Heker, and Posse.

The Argentine military systematically used sexual violence as a tool of discipline and a show of power. Violence was gendered, and women were victims of masculine power. Osorio's character enters into a relationship with her torturer because the officer who tortured her, Raúl Radías, spared her three-year-old son from the trauma associated with the torture centre and possibly saved the son's life after the two were kidnapped and taken to the clandestine ESMA centre.[18] In the letter Juana writes to her son, she tries to justify her decision to accept the relationship with the perpetrator by saying:

> There is a limit to feeling pain and once that limit is reached, I did not feel anything. It was as if I had abandoned my own body. I am not telling you this so that you feel sorry for me or so that you understand me. It is true that I suffered torture, but it could have been worse. They did not break me. I don't understand the relationship with Raúl as being broken. I am not saying that I loved him, but I was grateful to him. He got you out of that place. (Osorio 2018: 231)

The perpetrator's gesture thus shows that, as a proper Argentine Christian, he was prepared to save an innocent family member. Still to come was the re-education of the 'bad' mother who, by taking up arms, had refuted and defied her gender

---

[16] The Declaration on the Elimination of Violence against Women was adopted by the United Nations General Assembly in 1993, and the Inter-American Convention on the Prevention, Punishment, and the Eradication of Violence against Women was adopted by the Organization of American States in 1994.

[17] Gregorio Molina, an officer serving at the Military Air Force Base of Mar del Plata and a torturer, was the first Argentine repressor condemned for sexual crimes as crimes against humanity in June 2010.

[18] Maternity was the Achilles' heel of many female detainees in Argentine torture centres. Many survivors related that they prioritised the rescue or security of their children over their own security and in some cases over the security of the militant group for which they fought.

stereotype and questioned the social order imposed by the patriarchal structure. Some of the captured female militants also presented a challenge to the oppressors, who previously knew women only through their domesticity. They had never before met militants who, like them, were able to talk about politics, discuss intelligence strategies, and use weapons. Osorio's novel presents such a case, as the torturer Raúl Radías admires the bravery and integrity of his victim, who does not break under torture or denounce any of her comrades. Juana uses her sexual subjugation to the torturer to prove her 'recuperation' and her abandonment of previously held ideological positions. Once she manages to assure him that she is no longer his political adversary and now shares his Christian values, he becomes her protector and personal warden in the torture camp and later in the Paris Pilot Centre. Back in Buenos Aires and living in an apartment she shares with Raúl, Juana continues to cement her submissive relationship with him while remaining under constant sur-veillance. The sexual relationship she has with Raúl is marked both by pleasure and by abject humiliation. Their implicit subjugating pact breaks when he decides they should form a 'real' family and have a child. It is at that moment that the protagonist abandons him and escapes to another country. Forced motherhood is a violation that this survivor of the extermination centre is not willing to accept.

Motherhood plays a pivotal role in *Doble fondo*, since it marks the moment of the protagonist's induction into her relationship with the torturer, as well as her subsequent liberation. Juana saves her son Matías by sacrificing her own sexual integrity and by denying herself a life with her son, thus depriving herself of experi-encing motherhood with him (Osorio 2018: 373). Matías grows up far away in another country with his father, who adapts his once-progressive, socialist ideology to the neoliberal prerogative, and she knows Matías is under constant close watch by her former torturer. Any attempt to make contact with her son would make it possible for the former torturer to locate her and thus put her life in danger. Though she knows the risks associated with any communication with her son, after two decades Juana makes a mistake by approaching him anonymously in an online discussion group related to the Argentine dictatorship. Her former lover finds her and executes her exactly as he might have done when she was under the control of the dictatorship, this time for refusing to become the mother of his child and for abandoning him. Juana thus achieves a pyrrhic victory by challenging the perpetrator's masculinity, denying him fatherhood, and denying him possession of the ultimate trophy of his power over her. For that victory, she pays with her life. What she gains through this act, however, is the possibility of explaining to her son the reasons for her apparent abandonment of him and a chance to ask his for-giveness. Unfortunately, Matías receives the letter after her death. Nevertheless, he recognises her ultimate sacrifice and determines to engage with the judicial system, so that this time the perpetrator's crime will not go unpunished.

Osorio situates her novel in a small coastal village in France, a place where those who search for clues into the mysterious death of the local woman need to learn about what happened in Argentina decades before. In that sense, *Doble fondo* teaches its younger readers, as well as those unfamiliar with the history of Argentine dictatorship, the long-lasting legacies of that era. By creating a community of intradiegetic, invested researchers who are determined to find the truth and make sure that criminals are tried both in France and Argentina, Osorio also charges her readers with the responsibility of pursuing social justice. For an individual victim to remember and tell the story of her abuse, she must have a community. Thus, Osorio gives voice to her protagonist, who finally, after so many years of silence, decides to put her experience into words and assign meaning to it. Although her testimonial is destined for her son, circumstances beyond her control make her life story known to several readers, who then work as an empathic collective to contextualise it. Osorio's target audience seems to be the post-dictatorship generation – those born during and after the military held power in Argentina – who are charged with ensuring that the forces of neoliberalism, represented in some of the novel's characters, are not allowed to whitewash and forget the nation's past.

Oppressive environments are coercive and posit challenges for resistance. Beyond obtaining information about a militant's contacts, torture's function was to obliterate the subjectivity of the victim and break her will. At the same time, while shattering the bodily integrity of the victim, the military felt empowered and above the law. After the dictatorship ended, the enacted amnesty laws proved them right. Recognition of sexual violence as a war crime and human rights violation makes us revisit the Stockholm syndrome label and its use as an explanation for female behaviour, not only in the earlier trials of Argentine state perpetrators but also in other narratives.[19] The changing international and Argentine legal structure helps us look at the authoritarian past in which the terrorist state systematically used sexual violence against the rights of its citizens. It is imperative that we refute the Stockholm syndrome myth, given the legal recognition of rape as a weapon against the subjectivity of the victim. Furthermore, rewriting the victim's story can lead to her re-violation by the novelist/teller who, as it happens with Bonasso, Heker, and Posse, doubles with the original aggressor as they manipulate the authenticity of her discourse, impersonate her, or completely silence the victim.

Doble fondo features a character whose torture and rape go beyond solely ideological crime and military punishment. Osorio's Montonera eventually reaches the point at which her action would compromise someone else – her child – and breaks away from the perpetrator. She rebuilds her intimacy through a new relationship in France and eventually, years later, reaches toward her son in order to tell her story. Although she is killed before fully achieving her goal and never reconciles with her son, she is able to tell her story. That testimony becomes her subjective restitution and, thanks to the community of strangers, finds its way toward justice. Her son will start criminal proceedings in Argentina as well as in France, and the

---

[19] I talk more extensively about the implications of the use of Stockholm syndrome with regard to the recent Argentine Netflix series *Stockholm: Lost Identity* (Bilbija 2018).

reporter will write a novel about the case. In that way both legal and poetic justice will be achieved.

Literature, with all its distortions and refractions, not only mirrors reality but also maps the roads that society has travelled. Argentine writers' spectral conjectures regarding an abducted Montonera who had a sexual relationship with her torturer have shaped the way readers in a post-authoritarian society have judged unprecedented circumstances that very few women were able to survive. The sheer number of writers who have engaged so far with the story of Mercedes Carazo's ordeal confirms the symbolic value of her experience. And while previous novels explicitly or implicitly endeavoured to project a claim that they bore witness to and accounted for what happened to Mercedes Carazo (even as they portrayed her as a collaborator), Osorio's writing allows the reader to detach herself from a narrative that constructs the culturally stigmatised militant purely as a traitor and to take a fresh look at the circumstances that a female detainee had to overcome. Fictional worlds can only symbolically repair the damage suffered by the survivors of state terrorism. Elsa Osorio makes her contribution by resignifying the formulations woven by Argentine writers such as Miguel Bonasso, Liliana Heker, and Abel Posse regarding the betrayal of the ESMA survivor. We, the readers who have learnt from the characters of Osorio's novel how to search for the truth, are then entrusted with the ethical and social responsibility to make visible actual crimes of sexual and gender violence, and to hold accountable those who commit them.

References

Actis, M., Aldini, C., Gardella, L., Lewin, M., and Tokar, E. (2000), *Ese infierno: Conversaciones con cinco mujeres sobrevivientes de la ESMA* (Buenos Aires, Sudamericana).

Adorno, T. (1967), 'Cultural criticism and society', in *Prisms* (Cambridge, MA, MIT Press), 17–34.

Améry, J. (1980), *At the Mind's Limits: Contemplations by a Survivor on Auschwitz and Its Realities* (Bloomington, Indiana University Press).

André, M. (2002), 'De principios y fines de la historia: Conversación con Liliana Heker', *Confluencia*, 17, 141–8.

Arenas, N. (2014), 'Miriam Lewin: "La verdad cura siempre"', *Diario popular*, 21 October, https://www.diariopopular.com.ar/libros/miriam-lewin-la-verdad-cura-siempre-n206 644 (accessed 19 April 2021).

Bilbija, K. (2018), 'Argentina, Estocolmo, Netflix y el síndrome de la identidad perdida', *Kamchatka: Revista de análisis cultural*, 11, July, https://ojs.uv.es/index.php/kamcha tka/article/view/12208/11800 (accessed 19 April 2021).

Bonasso, M. (1984), *Recuerdo de la muerte* (Mexico, Ediciones Era).

Devita, M. (2013), 'Síndrome de Estocolmo: El extraño amor al verdugo', *Gaceta Mercantil*, 31 August, https://www.gacetamercantil.com/notas/38414/ (accessed 19 April 2021).

Di Tella, A. (dir.) (1998), *Montoneros, una historia*, film (Cine Ojo).

Garzón, B. and Romero, V. (2008), *El alma de los verdugos* (Buenos Aires, Del Nuevo Extremo).

Heker, L. (1996), *El fin de la historia* (Buenos Aires, Alfaguara).

Heker, L. (ed.) (1999), 'Acerca de *El fin de la historia*', in *Las hermanas de Shakespeare* (Buenos Aires, Alfaguara), 100–3.

Jelin, E. (2012), 'Sexual abuse as a crime against humanity and the right to privacy', *Journal of Latin American Cultural Studies*, 21, 343–50.

Lewin, M. and Wornat, O. (2014), *Putas y guerrilleras: Crímenes sexuales en los centros clandestinos de detención. La perversión de los represores y la controversia en la militancia. Las historias silenciadas. El debate pendiente* (Buenos Aires, Planeta).

Longoni, A. (2007), *La figura del traidor en los relatos acerca de los sobrevivientes de la represión* (Buenos Aires, Grupo Editorial Norma).

Meyer, A. (1998a), 'La ESMA persigue a Massera', *Página/12*, 16 November, https://www.pagina12.com.ar/1998/98-11/98-11-16/pag03.htm (accessed 19 April 2021).

Meyer, A. (1998b), 'Un maravilloso cuento de amor', *Página/12*, 16 November, https://www.angelfire.com/ar/hijosskane/laesmapersigueamaser.html (accessed 19 April 2021).

Osorio, E. (2018), *Doble fondo* (Barcelona, Tusquets).

Posse, A. (2011), *Noche de lobos* (Buenos Aires, Planeta).

Prensa (2014), 'Juicio Esma: La defensa recusó al juez que suplantó a Hergott', 18 June, https://web.archive.org/web/20140714144405/http:/www.prensa.argentina.ar/2010/06/18/9148-juicio-esma-la-defensa-recuso-al-juez-que-suplanto-a-hergott.php (accessed 19 April 2021).

Pridgeon, S. (2015), 'Subverting subversion: Refiguring 1970's revolutionary militancy through recent Argentine novels and films (1996–2012)', doctoral thesis (Emory University), available at https://etd.library.emory.edu/concern/etds/w9505118j?locale=en (accessed 26 January 2022).

Ramus, S. J. (2000), *Sueños sobrevivientes de una montonera a pesar de la ESMA* (Buenos Aires, Ediciones Colihué).

Scarry, E. (1987), *The Body in Pain: The Making and Unmaking of the World* (Oxford, Oxford University Press).

Valenzuela, L. (ed.) (1982), 'Cambio de armas', in *Cambio de armas* (Hanover, Ediciones del Norte), 111–46.

4

Collaborationism in Low-Intensity Conflicts: The Case of the Basque Country

LUIS DE LA CALLE

Introduction

COLLABORATIONISM REFERS TO the existence of local dwellers who help foreign rulers to keep domestic resistance at bay – out of coercion, necessity, or loyalty to the non-native rulers. Thus, collaboration is intrinsically related to the concept of alien rule (Hechter 2013), a predominantly modern concept. It involves a well-defined 'us' that draws a precise line in the sand between natives and foreigners. It would be preposterous to refer to the Tlaxcaltecas as collaborators with the Spanish conquerors in 16th-century North America and against the ruling Mexicas, when no identity in the region at that time linked pre-Colombian peoples to each other. Quite ironically, the colonial period contributed to the production of that common identity, as in many other experiences of colonisation (McFarlane 1998). Similarly, it would not make much sense to talk about the different warrior factions during the Spanish Civil War as collaborators, when that conflict is widely understood as a contest between 'brothers', even when the largest contenders had foreign support and troops fighting on their side (Thomas 2001).

Thus, the act of collaboration is as much about performing specific tasks to favour some side in a conflict as about a battle for defining identity and the morally correct behaviours associated with it. As epitomised by the French citizens accommodating Nazi occupation and sustaining the puppet Vichy, French right-wingers were morally bound to combat a foreign occupier who threatened French regional integrity by accepting the division of the land into two separate political entities. By not doing so, they would be subjected to forced exile from the nation and prosecution for treason. Note that similar pro-fascist sympathies were also widely condemned in other European countries, but without any reference to

Proceedings of the British Academy, **248**, 68–84, © The British Academy 2022.

'collaboration'. Confronted with a foreign challenge, as the argument goes, everybody, regardless of ideology, should come together to stand up for the nation and guarantee its survival against alien encroachment.

The French example is the quintessential illustration of domestic collaboration with a foreign power, as discussed in Chapter 1. Both French and German identities had crystallised for centuries, although there was still some margin for dispute – recall the German-speaking provinces of Alsace and Lorraine reintegrated by France after the First World War, and later annexed by the Nazis during the war. More generally, interstate conflicts, where identity borders may have been in place long enough to cement national identity against rapacious neighbours, offer the least controversial setting to prove ideas about collaboration.

Civil wars, on the other hand, complicate matters. Many domestic conflicts are precisely about the definition of identity, as when a territorially concentrated minority aims for secession, or an excluded ethnic group fights to earn its share of the public budget. In these instances, members of the in-group who keep helping the out-group are publicly debased as collaborators of 'foreign' rulers, although in this case the *foreignness* of the regime is usually a matter of public contention. This accusation is sometimes also applied in ideological civil wars, when radicals of every persuasion try to mock their rivals as foreign satellites, the domestic stooges of the great powers. Granted, these accusations are weaker the less direct foreign intervention there is, given that local support for radical, potentially foreign-bred ideas is probably large enough to counter the collaborationist tag.

Civil wars are high-intensity conflicts where armed control usually secures a level of collaboration, either out of loyalty or coercion (Kalyvas and Kocher 2007). In these settings, the battle for setting the rules of the game – what relevant groups are at play, and how to draw membership boundaries among them – is as much about public discourse as armed capacity, if not clearly more about the latter (see Arias and Prieto's Chapter 7). This is why governments put a lot of effort into setting up militias operated by local dwellers, as a way not only to gain intelligence on the ground but also to challenge the standard rebels' narrative that theirs is a fight against a colonising power (Jentzsch *et al.* 2015). By resorting to local militias, the government is able to counter this narrative, but at the cost of producing a principal-agent problem contingent on sharing counter-insurgent procedures with local groups that may turn against the government at little notice.

One fascinating example of this is the Sepoy Rebellion in 1857 India against British colonisation then led by the British East India Company. The sepoys were local soldiers enrolled in occupation army units. Some of them stood up against British domination, inequalities, and cultural misunderstandings between the alien rulers and the local population. It was a bloody rebellion, but it was eventually toppled by the British, who decided to get rid of the Company and absorb India within the borders of the British Empire (Mukherjee 1990). In this sense, imperial victory was hailed with direct rule and a substitution of more British-friendly local groups (such as the Sikhs and the Gurkhas) for the West Bengalese sepoys that had spearheaded the rebellion. Although the etymology of 'sepoy' seems to refer to an older origin based on the Sipahi, the cavalrymen of the borderland in the Ottoman/Persian empires (Bryant 2000), it is the Indian word that took root in Argentina during the early 20th century, popularised by Arturo Jauretche as a term for its foreign-friendly oligarchy (Doti 2010). Translated into Spanish as *cipayo*, it was broadly used to mock those natives with a general preference for foreign goods over local ones. This is similar to the *malinchista* adjective very common in Mexico. Malinche, a young woman, was offered by Mayan groups as a gift to the Spanish conquerors in exchange for peace. As Malinche had managed to learn several languages, including Spanish, she became instrumental in helping the Spaniards topple the Mexicans and conquer Tenochtitlán (Thomas 2001). Thus, her supposed preference for the foreigners over indigenous populations created the myth of *malinchismo* in Mexico. The word also has ramifications in the Aceh conflict, where Indonesian soldiers were termed *Si Pai*, apparently in reference to the Javanese soldiers who used to team up with the Dutch colonisers (Good 2019). Interestingly, Basque separatists of the late 20th century adopted the word *cipayo*, the Spanish translation for sepoy, as their derisive identifier for Basque police forces.

The last step in the ladder of organised warfare lies in low-intensity conflicts where rebels cannot even dream of seizing territory from the state's hands and holding onto it. In this chapter, I focus on this category. Low-intensity conflicts offer very interesting conditions for the study of collaborationism, as rebels struggle to impose collaboration by coercion alone. Rebel groups in low-intensity conflicts remain clandestine, which means that they have little coercive capacity to force local dwellers to take sides, as governmental cooperation is always an option (De la Calle and Sánchez-Cuenca 2011). Of course, clandestine groups can exert some level of coercion – for instance, raising funds through kidnappings – but they can't simply operate without a certain level of support from their key constituencies. In turn, states facing highly asymmetrical insurgencies have trouble in spotting rebels and will often turn to local dwellers to gain intelligence and legitimacy. Although the former can be fixed through coercion, this rarely grants the latter. Thus, voluntary collaboration seems to be more widespread than coercive compliance in low-intensity conflicts, as both states and rebels need to attract supporters.

The purpose of this chapter is to understand how rebels deal with the existence of local security forces who are the ultimate guardians of foreign rule in the territory and, as such, inimical to the interests of the local population. To succeed at charging co-ethnics as collaborators in conflicts where rebels are not able to control territory is challenging, given that rebels can neither legally enforce this accusation nor coerce entire communities into submission. The best rebels can do is to try to win the narrative battle by identifying those locals working for central institutions as foreign collaborators. In this case, collaboration is less about compliance under duress and more about preferences and the battle for public legitimacy. For rebels, the dilemma is as follows: if efforts to win over collaboration-prone locals with ideas fail, you may have to resort to violence against them to increase the risks associated with collaboration. But at the same time, the sheer threat against co-ethnics may backfire and encourage more locals to side with the state and against the rebels. In other words, the existence of local militias is risky not only for foreign rulers, who face a principal-agent problem, but also for rebels, whose armed strategy depends on cutting the ties between alien rulers and local supporters without alienating the latter.

This is obviously more easily said than done. I show in the following sections that rebel groups in low-intensity conflicts are left to fight for the symbolic dimension of collaborationism, whereas the use of coercion usually backfires in the absence of enough military capacity to make threats credible. If rebels' threats are not credible, the only way they can break the repressive link between foreign security forces and local police bodies is by taunting the latter as illegitimate and encouraging them to break ranks and join the *real* armed representative of the nation.

I test these ideas with evidence from the Basque Country by focusing on Euskadi ta Askatasuna (Basque Country and Freedom, ETA), a terrorist group that pursued the independence of the Basque Country from Spain and France from the 1960s until its ultimate disbandment in 2018. In 1980, after over a decade of ETA terrorist violence, the Basque government was granted the right to set up a Basque police body, the Ertzaintza (literally, 'people's shepherd'). Initially ETA believed that this police force would allow for independence, or at least that it would not get in the way of the independence struggle. But the opposite occurred. During the 1980s and the early 1990s, Ertzaintza took on more policing duties, increased its security role, and adopted a proactive counter-terrorist stance against the ETA. In response, ETA first issued a verbal offensive against the local force and then, when that strategy failed, started using violence targeted at officers of the police force. In line with my expectation, ETA avoided crossing the line of including the Ertzaintza within the full list of potential targets until very late in the conflict, when the group openly declared the Basque police force as a 'legitimate' target. By then, however, ETA had lost the battle for public legitimacy. The risk of suffering even larger losses in public support drove ETA quickly to abandon the targeting strategy just shortly after it began. The ETA story illustrates in brief that in highly asymmetric low-intensity conflicts, the charge of collaborationism is more about establishing legitimacy and defining the in-group than about the dynamics of coercion and warfare.

Theoretical Expectations

There are three interesting questions when dealing with local police aimed at recruiting from local populations. The first one is why central governments would embrace this idea, as it is clear that problems of adverse selection (how to attract members of the community who carry some level of prestige over their kin) and moral hazard (how to make sure that the local police corps do their best to fight the rebels) are pervasive, as aforementioned. Central governments promoting the regionalisation of counterinsurgent policy pursue two broad goals: to regain legitimacy inside local communities – and with it, better fine-grained information – and to reduce their exposure to the conflict. Legitimacy and exposure must overcome the risks of deepening the conflict by yielding power to local allies who prefer secretly shirking their duties to cooperating. The so-called 'Ulsterisation' campaign promoted by the British government during the 1980s, as an attempt to minimise UK intervention in the province, gave the Royal Ulster Constabulary (the local police force) more power to fight IRA terrorism through expanded tasks and patrolling. As long as it dramatically reduced the number of British army casualties and alleviated public pressure to disengage from Northern Ireland, the strategy paid off for Westminster. But sometimes these strategies backfire. Once these militias are empowered, weak central governments will have trouble implementing policies that all local authorities follow. The inability of central governments in Somalia and Afghanistan to rein in militias assumed to be loyal to those regimes provides examples of this failure.

The second interesting question is more sociological and relates to the willingness of locals to join local police units. Security forces are naturally embedded in their communities as long as they recruit from the local population, and this usually happens when the body is more oriented to policing and taking care of minor crimes. In contexts where some fraction of the population challenges the authority of the state in the region, the stakes for being a member of the local police body may be higher. Personal risks in those situations will depend on whether the challenger is openly criticising participation in those institutions or not. Note here that rebel groups in low-intensity conflicts rarely target career-driven public servants, which seems to indicate that risks are manageable if public employees avoid the spotlight. Of course, local police-officers will confront greater risks if the direction of counter-terrorist tasks is within their remit. Such a scenario will probably attract the attention of the local armed group and increase the costs that local members of the police force will bear. There is little research on recruitment in local police forces, but one could easily hint at a combination of material need and ideology as the main driver of police membership.

The final question of interest is under what conditions armed groups take a stance against local police forces that recruit from resident communities. This is the challenging question I try to tackle in this chapter. For separatist armed groups, security forces are usually deemed one of the quintessential legitimate targets. The issue has an interesting twist when local security forces are included in the picture. Should rebels target police corps whose membership is made up of resident members of the ethnic nation? The answer is somehow clearer if the police are already acting against armed rebels, but the question sets out more of a dilemma when repression has not yet begun.

On paper, armed groups have three options. First, they may look the other way. The armed groups may see all members of the local community as inherently worthy of respect, as sharing the goal of secession, and therefore as highly unlikely to act against independence efforts. This is a naive position that has little traction in real-world conflicts. The second, opposite attitude is to adopt a narrow-minded policy of denouncing all collaboration of local residents with police forces. The goal here is to shatter any sense of ease for potential recruits by explicitly stating that police membership automatically involves being a legitimate target. This stance may be attractive for armed groups, because if effective it damages the capacity of the state to manage the conflict locally. Without local recruits, the state would have to seek officers from outside the region, reinforcing the useful narrative for armed rebels of occupation, because outside forces will be considered legitimate targets for the armed rebels. Despite its appeal, this is a risky strategy. It has the potential of jeopardising some segments of the local community who would not sanction violence against fellow residents because of their occupation. They may not see working in the police force as an act of disloyalty or betrayal of local goals, per se.

There is a third strategy, a middle way between the two others. There is the possibility of running a smear campaign, with some intimidation, but short of killing. The goal here is to state clearly that the group has nothing against the local police body as long as its members refrain from openly operating against the clandestine organisation. This requires some credible threat. For instance, the terrorist group could target high-ranking officers in charge of running counter-insurgent task units – especially if they form part of the state-wide security forces. This may be complemented with public warnings for lower rank-and-file members to avoid cooperating with the central government. The stronger the terrorist group, the more credible these threats may be, with no further action necessary from the terrorists' side. In contrast, the perception of weakness within the group is likely to lead to efforts to broaden the symbolic battlefield and identify new targets. However, in order to do so, the terrorist group must prepare the ground for attacks against locals by delegitimising them first.

I theorise that most armed clandestine groups will go for a selective campaign as long as there is little police involvement in counter-insurgency tasks and the group feels relatively strong. That may change once the tables are turned in the balance of power and the police force becomes more involved in the conflict. Mediating the transition between the two scenarios, we should expect to observe a smear campaign against the local police force. In general, killing co-ethnics is costly for any armed group. Just recall the heated exchange between Al Zawahiri (Al Qaeda's military leader) and Al Zarqawi (Iraq's Al Qaeda leader) with regard to the (in)convenience for the jihadist cause of targeting Shia civilians. Thus, before attacking local groups, rebels should increase the costs to new potential targets by defaming their reputation through verbal and low-scale harassment. Before being fully targeted, this group must first have been excluded from the community, at least symbolically, which means that rebels' supporters must have accepted that local police members are no longer honourable representatives of the group, but outcasts who value loyalty to foreigners above their allegiance to the motherland.

In general, this delegitimising transition is carried out through verbal escalation and harassment. A typical pathway is to opt for a tactic of provocation, trying to justify retaliation as a way to compensate for local police repression. This may have been the case of the Provisional IRA after the Ulsterisation strategy was adopted by the UK government. As the army was largely withdrawn from the province, the local police body, the Royal Ulster Constabulary (RUC), took on a more prominent counter-terrorist role, and therefore the IRA started to target its members. Although the IRA was careful to kill mainly Protestants, it also assassinated Catholic police-officers. The logic was distinct for each target: whereas protestant RUC members were legitimate targets by definition, those from Catholic backgrounds made it onto the list only when they cooperated in the counter-terrorist effort. Many Catholic police-officers ended up defecting as a way to avoid being targeted by both the IRA and the protestant paramilitary squads (for a discussion of the RUC's use of informers, see Dudai and Hearty's Chapter 8.)

In the Basque case, as I will discuss in the next section, this strategy played out through street violence. As a convenient low-scale, youth-led, supposedly unorganised tactic, it allowed for the harassment of and threats against previously untouched constituencies, such as the Basque police, local politicians from state-wide parties, journalists, and anti-nationalist intellectuals. In order to become full and legitimate targets, the local constituencies would have to recognise local police-officers as state collaborators – as allied to the foreign occupying power – and not as misguided or desperate members of the local community who deserved pity rather than death. This is not an easy feat, though. The battle for public legitimacy is tougher the less openly repressive the local police body is, and the more socially embedded police members are in their communities.

Evidence from the Basque Conflict

The history of the terrorist group I focus on in this section – ETA – is relatively well known (see De la Calle 2015). It emerged during the late Francoist dictatorship as an instrument to halt Basque assimilation and raise consciousness about Basque identity, and contributed significantly to the acceleration of the end of the regime and increased nationalism in the Basque Country. It coalesced a new nationalist movement around language as the defining core feature and violence as a legitimate means to achieve independence. This movement has always won between 10 and 20 per cent of the vote in the region. The ETA organisation negotiated with the Spanish government three times (1989, 1999, and 2005), but it always miscalculated its odds and ended the ceasefires without significant concessions. After squandering its last chance with the socialist government of José Luis Rodríguez Zapatero (2004–11), ETA's political front leaders, banned from any legal activity, took steps to convince those with the weapons to renounce violence unilaterally in exchange for a return to legality for its political party. When ETA declared the definitive ceasefire in 2010, its consolation prize was political rehabilitation

It is not accidental that the first ETA groups were born in Bilbao (Biscay). This city had also been the original seedbed of nationalism and, consequently, many ETA leaders came from nationalist families (Unzueta 1988). Many of them, however, did not speak Basque, because the city and its outskirts had remained a Spanish-speaking area for some decades (Tejerina 1992). They felt that the only way to save the Basque nation from extinction was to raise awareness about the fate of their language. Given the dictatorial nature of the regime, they believed that only through violence could they tilt power and wrest support away from national control (Garmendia 1996). Finally, university students, the future leaders of the movement, rejected the elder nationalists' clericalism and became involved in the ideological clashes taking place at the time among different Marxist factions. The organisation spent the 1960s trying to formulate an ideological synthesis that attracted Spanish migrants relocating to the Basque Country in search of a better life, without denouncing support from the local bourgeoisie. As it was not an easy mix, ETA was doomed to the same failure as other clandestine anti-Francoist organisations. It was clear for them that the only way to bring the regime down required the cooperation of the working class, which was becoming more and more alienated from Basque culture because of the high proportion of migrants.

Two factors helped to save ETA. On the one hand, industrialisation took off in the late '50s, and thousands of intra-Spain migrants flooded the Basque Provinces – mainly Biscay and Gipuzkoa (Gurrutxaga 1985). The arrival of a massive Spanish-speaking working-class population and the absence of the necessary policy instruments to halt the decrease of the number of Basque speakers boosted the demands for action. In the absence of a Basque university system that would have created some sort of Basque-speaking intelligentsia interested in the language, the Basque clergy took up the task. Evenly divided between Nationalists and Carlists during the Civil War, the Basque clergy started to move overwhelmingly towards nationalism in the early 1950s.

By chastising Gipuzkoa and Biscay as 'traitor' provinces and taking away their fiscal power, Franco began to alienate local populations and catalysed local complaints. The more militant clergy, for example, took issue with the prohibition of using the Basque language in their sermons and the curtailing of their freedom to teach the language. Many priests and members of religious orders in the Basque Country shared a similar extraction: rural Basque-speaking strongholds, where male primogeniture was the convention (Gurrutxaga 1985: 358). In this context, the seminary provided an alternative to out-migration, with the added value of gaining an education. Industrialisation created the propitious environment for those priests and monks to spread their nationalist apostolate against the regime. In 1959, 339 members of the Basque clergy wrote an open letter to their bishops calling for the defence of human rights as well as the rights of the Basque people (De la Calle 2015: 62). Later, the contact of rural priests with the new working-class neighbourhoods that hosted the recently arrived migrants radicalised their message, moving toward left-wing ideologies. From then on, it was usual to have Basque priests fined and arrested under charges of collaboration with clandestine organisations. Given the privileges the Catholic Church enjoyed within the dictatorship, it was easy for the rebel clergy to take advantage of their privileges to promote all types of labour and nationalist initiatives (Iztueta 1981). The contribution of the Basque nationalist clergy to the legitimisation of ETA violence and the spreading of its goals were of key importance (Barroso 1995: 124). Many of them finally opted for secularisation and pursued political careers within the ETA-backed political front. For the Basque case, the secularisation of religiosity consistent with canonising the nation is one of the main engines that led the process of nationalist awareness, as several monographs have well documented (Onaindia 2001; Pérez-Agote 2008).

The second factor contributing to the consolidation of ETA was the start of the action–reaction spiral. By the end of the 1960s, ETA theorists had realised that the only way to attract support for the Basque revolution entailed the use of violence pursued in order to raise nationalist awareness by forcing the state to over-repress. The mechanism was easy: initial attacks carried out by unknown militants would prompt the security forces to gather information by raiding broad segments of potentially suspect groups. The use of indiscriminate repressive methods to collect information affected broad sectors of society, leading to their withdrawal of support for the state. For instance, the failed attempt to derail a train carrying old Civil War combatants to San Sebastian to celebrate the anniversary of the military coup and Franco's rise to power was followed by the arrest of more than 100 mostly innocent suspects (Anasagasti 2003). After the first ETA killing in 1968, a state of emergency was called and more than 1,000 arrests were made, many of them unrelated to the terrorist action (Garmendia 1996). In the absence of good information, the Spanish dictatorship reacted with massive, indiscriminate repression.

Recruitment by ETA increased during this repressive period. It thrived in nationalist environments, such as traditional dance associations, mountaineering groups, Basque language schools, and Catholic-led unions (Gurrutxaga 1985; Lamikiz 2005: 470; Pérez-Agote 2008). The dense network of associative ties, centred around the *cuadrillas* (peer groups), quickened the spread of radical nationalism. The wide use of torture and illegal methods to extract information accelerated the process of state delegitimisation and increased the number of ETA recruits and supporters (Della Porta and Mattina 1986; Irvin 1999). Thus, many Basque-speaking youngsters of non-nationalist family origins were attracted to ETA and linguistic nationalism, owing to a combination of sympathy toward an organisation standing for a language-based nationalism, and the direct effect of repression (De la Calle 2015: 61).

Against this backdrop of repression and nationalist mobilisation, the transition to democracy encouraged the new Spanish government to concede autonomy and regional government to the Basque Country and Catalonia as a way to gain legitimacy and attempt to contain its erosion in those critical regions – together they made up around 25 per cent of the Spanish GDP and housed the most competitive industrial sectors. Soon the moderate Basque Nationalist Party, in charge of the new regional government, claimed to have the right to set up an autochthonous police force, an idea that was received positively in Madrid. As aforementioned, the Spanish government liked the idea because it could ease the pressure on its highly authoritarian and repressive security forces deployed in the region, and at the same time bring into the security matrix the collaboration of local forces. Of course, this could also be a problem should the regional authorities decide to leverage counter-terrorism duties against extracting greater regional concessions. The Spanish solution was to offer a sequencing map of deployment that began with low-level counter-terrorist duties and an emphasis on local policing of petty crime, traffic control, and patrolling institutional buildings, but would move by the early 1990s to more serious counter-terrorism policing once the force was fully trained. Both national and local authorities were content with the scheme: the nationalists aimed to prove that they had local control; the Spanish government aimed to regain legitimacy in the region and emphasise the regional internal divisions behind the conflict. In the late 1970s, even some ETA members, although from a different perspective, considered a Basque police force to be a good idea, because police 'patriots' would look the other way, thereby passively supporting and protecting ETA cells.

It was not long before ETA realised that the Basque police force presented a critical dilemma. On the one hand, it was not going to be easy to denigrate a police body made up mostly of Basques and largely organised by nationalists. On the other, something had to be done if the police force got in the way of the autonomy struggle by taking seriously its anti-terrorism task. The solution that ETA devised to this dilemma was quite thoughtful. Aretxaga (2004) rightly poses that ETA decided to nickname the Basque police force not *txakurra*, the Basque word for dog, which radical nationalists usually employ to mock Spanish security forces. Instead, they adopted a new word, *cipayo* (*zipaio* in Basque) with remarkably interesting connotations, because it combines three layers of blame: (1) for colonialism in the Basque country, since *cipayo* is the term used for Indian soldiers who joined Imperial forces during the British occupation of India (see also Aretxaga (2008)); (2) for collaboration with the enemy, since the *cipayo* belonged to the oppressed nation and also collaborated with the occupiers of that nation; and (3) for supporting occupation, since the *cipayo* advanced the British occupation of India in 1857. But the sepoys also mutinied against the British colonisers, so this act of expiation could guide Basque *cipayos* and encourage them to fight against the Spanish security forces.

By using *cipayo*, ETA identified the Basque police force as a collaborationist body, but it stopped short of making its members legitimate targets for violence. The situation moved slowly during the 1980s, at the same pace as Ertzaintza's deployment and its assumption of counter-terrorist tasks. In autumn 1990, however, ETA made the following declaration:

> There is no doubt about the goal pursued by the government in its assignment of the Ertzaintza to tasks of repression and confrontation that used to be the exclusive jurisdiction of the Spanish Armed Police and the Civil Guard: to try to denaturalise the

true character of the conflict, namely the actual contradiction between Euskadi and the Spanish state, and to try to distort it and limit it within the Basque society alone, seeking confrontation of communities and social confrontation among Basques, between the MLNV [Movimiento de Liberación Nacional Vasco (Basque National Liberation Movement)] and the signatories of the self-styled Reformist Block. It is clear that the recent escalation of the Ertzaintza leadership and its intervention units in its highly publicised intelligence tasks, detention, imprisonment, and even torture of separatist young militants aims to provoke a frontal and irreversible confrontation between the MLNV and the Ertzaintza. (Aguirre 2007: 91, my translation).

A year later, after several rounds of arrests of ETA members, ETA released a new statement, in which it said:

As we have repeatedly stated, ETA is not going to fall into the hateful and contempt-ible trap that the enemies of our people are repeatedly trying to set us: civil confronta-tion, whether among Basques or between Basques and Spaniards … However, those responsible from Ajuria Enea [this refers to the House of the Basque Prime Minister] are mistaken if they believe that our organisation will remain impassive in the face of such actions. We hope you take good note of it. (Aguirre 2007: 96, my translation)

Two years later, in November 1993, ETA would kill the Ertzaintza's intelligence chief. In the aftermath of the attack, ETA submitted a letter to the main Basque police unions in which it lambasted the Basque police by stating that the Ertzaintza 'had become the political police of the Basque government and its armed branch'.[1] Still, ETA declared that low-ranking police officers should not worry about being targeted as long as they stopped persecuting ETA militants. 'Our future attitude will be absolutely conditioned by your behaviour against us, nothing else will influence it.'[2] For ETA, the Basque police force was not a full member of the list of 'legit-imate' targets by 1993, and only those in charge of managing counter-terrorist operations were imperilled.

The years from 1990 to 1995 marked a new turn to the Basque conflict; ETA was unable to keep pace with the state, as its campaign against the 1992 global events held in Spain (the Olympics in Barcelona, the World Expo in Seville, the European City of Culture in Madrid) was halted after the arrest of several high-profile ETA members. At the same time, the passing of the so-called *Ajuria Enea* pact (referring to the official residence of the Basque president, the place where the agreement was signed) also harmed the political position of the terrorist group. In the pact, all parties with the exception of Herri Batasuna, ETA's political front, agreed to refuse negotiations with ETA until the organisation renounced violence as a strategy. The agreement sparked popular mobilisations by social movements challenging Herri Batasuna's monopoly on street actions and, indeed, using those tactics to protest ETA actions, such as the kidnapping of two well-known Basque entrepreneurs in the early 1990s.

---

[1] See https://elpais.com/diario/1993/12/31/espana/757292410_850215.html (accessed 17 May 2021, my translation).

[2] *Ibid.*, my translation.

Forced by its increasing military weakness and a less solid presence in the streets (and in the ballot booths), ETA shifted strategies. It replaced the war of attrition – leveraging a high cost on the government to force it to yield and to bargain – with a strategy aimed at breaking the pact-of-convenience between moderate nationalists and state-wide socialists, thereby forcing a united nationalist coalition behind a new project. This resembled the Northern Irish Nationalist Front, which had proved successful in bringing the Northern Ireland conflict to an end. Called 'the social-isation of suffering', the strategy intended to bring the conflict to every corner of the Basque Country. The idea was to broaden the 'battlefield' to make sure that not only the security forces, but also politicians from state-wide parties, journalists, and even intellectuals who had been vocal against ETA and moderate nationalists alike would become 'legitimate' targets. The key step was the strategic use of *kale borroka* (literally, street fighting) as a weapon to frighten potential enemies, such as politicians and members of the Basque police force. *Kale borroka* consisted of pri-vate and public death threats, including mob actions, and Molotov cocktails thrown at cars and houses, aimed at those local residents deemed by ETA as opponents of the separatist cause. *Kale borroka* had traditionally been used in Basque streets to protest extraditions of ETA militants arrested in France, or in the aftermath of the assassination of ETA members. In a situation of weakness, the ETA leadership incited hundreds of pro-ETA youths to engage in nearly nightly attacks against local targets. Initially, this constant but non-lethal violence attracted little attention. It soon became very clear that the violence was neither random nor meaningless, and instead involved a pattern of violent targeting of local residents that constituted ETA's new strategy (De la Calle 2007).

Table 4.1 reports the numbers of attacks by target during the 1990s. Firms still bore the brunt of street violence during those years – for instance, many cars from French makers were burnt because separatists accused the French govern-ment of unnecessarily collaborating with the Spanish government in prosecuting ETA militants on French soil. But the pressure placed on moderate nationalists highlighted by the attacks against their local charters' sites, as well as against the Basque police, indicates that *kale borroka* was no longer a reactive, spontaneous uprising. Thus, although ETA was still falling short of publicly justifying the killing of any member of the Basque police force, it encouraged its young followers to carry out low-level intimidation attacks against the Ertzaintza.

It is worth noting that during the mid-1990s the Ertzaintza remained a very popular police force. In 1995, a countrywide survey on individual perceptions about police bodies in Spain reported that in the Basque Country 68 per cent of the popu-lation singled out the Ertzaintza as the most prestigious police corps, compared to 10 per cent for Spanish forces, another 10 per cent for the municipal police, and 5 per cent mentioning none (Raldúa 1996). This popularity helps explain why ETA avoided overt confrontations against the Ertzaintza during this period.

The 'socialisation of suffering' strategy rendered success when all nationalist parties agreed in late 1998 on a new pact that annulled the previous *Ajuria Enea* consensus on no negotiations with terrorists. By highlighting synergies between

Table 4.1 Longitudinal data on street violence with geographical aggregation: number of attacks (percentage of annual total)

	1990	1991	1992	1993	1994	1995	1996	1997	1998	1999	2000
Firms		209 (68.5)	383 (69.4)	203 (47.43)	121 (42.16)	470 (50.87)	579 (52.02)			124 (31.79)	228 (39.24)
Transport		64 (20.98)	50 (9.06)	42 (9.81)	42 (14.63)	131 (14.18)	195 (17.52)			19 (4.87)	41 (7.06)
Police forces		17 (5.57)	19 (3.44)	32 (7.48)	52 (18.12)	149 (16.13)	179 (16.08)	130 (13.39)	62 (12.68)	36 (9.23)	43 (7.40)
Parties		15 (4.92)	26 (4.71)	24 (5.61)	32 (11.15)	84 (9.09)	103 (9.25)	97 (9.99)	33 (6.75)	118 (30.26)	101 (17.38)
Others			22 (3.99)	24 (5.61)	40 (13.94)	90 (9.74)	79 (7.10)	693 (71.37)	166 (33.95)	93 (23.85)	162 (27.88)
Basque police force						123 (84.25)	114 (69.94)	92 (70.77)	47 (75.81)	8 (22.22)	20 (46.51)
Spanish police force						23 (15.75)	49 (30.06)	38 (29.23)	15 (24.19)	28 (77.78)	23 (53.48)
Nationalist Party						46 (55.42)	58 (64.44)	64 (65.98)	14 (42.42)	6 (5.09)	9 (9.09)
State-based party						37 (44.58)	32 (35.56)	33 (34.02)	19 (57.58)	112 (94.92)	90 (90.90)
Total	**294**	**305**	**552**	**428**	**287**	**924**	**1,113**	**971**	**489**	**390**	**581**

Note: Totals do not always coincide with their breakdown because different sources were used to collect the data.

Source: De la Calle (2007).

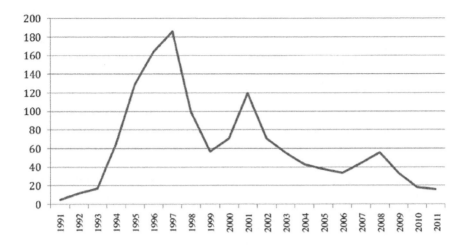

Figure 4.1 *Kale borroka* attacks against Ertzaintza members and their relatives.

different nationalist projects, the so-called *Estella* pact advanced steps toward independence without violence. In participating in the pact, ETA initiated a partial ceasefire, while escalating street violence against the state-wide parties opposed to the pact. After a little more than a year, both the pact and the truce collapsed under mutual accusations of disloyalty between the Partido Nacionalista Vasco (PNV) and ETA.

The ensuing terrorist violence focused largely on state-wide parties and security forces. A new pattern nonetheless was observable: for the first time, ETA included the Ertzaintza on the list of legitimate targets. After assassinating two police officers patrolling traffic in a small town, ETA derided the Ertzaintza as a 'Spanish serf' and a key link in the chain of the Basque Country's oppression by Spain. It accused the Ertzaintza of 'leading traffic today, but tomorrow beating us, killing us, putting us in jail, torturing us, forcing us into exile, as the faithful guardians of Spanish law'.[3] From 2001 onwards, ETA might have fallen into the trap of fully denouncing a police body that still enjoyed broad public support within the community. From 2000 to 2005, five members of the Basque police force were killed and many more were victims of street violence attacks. Figure 4.1 also shows that low-intensity attacks against Basque police members sky-rocketed after being strategically stopped during the 1999 truce.

Yet this strategy ended mid-stream, with ETA reversing its tactics once the 2005 truce came into effect. Attacks against Basque police members dramatically declined. Even after the truce had ended, no member was deliberately targeted.

---

[3] See https://www.lavozdegalicia.es/noticia/espana/2001/12/02/eta-acusa-ertzaintza-sierva-espana-amen aza-atentados/0003_858627.htm (accessed 13 May 2021, my translation).

The leadership who ended up forcing ETA to renounce violence unilaterally anticipated that the Ertzaintza could not be successfully labelled as collaborationist without forcing a rupture with the Nationalist Party. In the end ETA lost the public battle for legitimacy and had to back-pedal on targeting the Basque police force. In brief, one could claim that for the Basque public, the Ertzaintza remained a safe and loyal Basque institution, instead of being considered a collaborationist puppet.

One might wonder what would have happened if ETA had achieved the independence of the Basque Country, or a negotiated settlement à la Northern Ireland's Good Friday Agreement. Independence is improbable. A negotiated agreement, on the other hand, would have put a lot of pressure on members of the Ertzaintza under fire, particularly owing to the mounting accusations of prisoner mistreatment. Indeed, several PNV leaders had observed the lack of nationalist zeal in the new generations of the police body, and warned against the effects of bureaucratisation. On the other hand, the Northern Ireland experience of a peace agreement (see Hearty and Dudai, Chapter 8) shows that full-fledged amnesties, initially adopted as a tool to gain compliance from the rebel side, may end up significantly benefiting those supporting the Loyalist side.

Concluding Remarks

Although ETA's armed fight is over, the battle for public discourse is still ongoing. In 2016, Arnaldo Otegi, long-time separatist leader, declared that 'in the Basque Country, not only did ETA kill people, but so did the Spanish security forces (the Civil Guard, the National Police, the Intelligence Unit), the death squads, and the Spanish Autonomous police in the Basque Country (the Ertzaintza)'.[4] The then (and current) president of the Basque autonomous government, Iñigo Urkullu (of the moderate PNV), quickly responded, rejecting the allegation that the Ertzaintza had 'killed' anybody during the conflict. (Unsurprisingly, perhaps, he did not include in his defence any other security body.) The president may write off other politically charged statements of ETA-friendly sentiments, but not this one: there must be no doubt that the Basque police were always on the right side of the conflict, defending the regional institutions and prosecuting those Basques who violated sacred constitutional rights. Actually, in 2019 the Basque government inaugurated a room named 'Hemen Gaude' ('Here We Are') within the Museum of the Basque Police, specifically dedicated to the 15 officers of the Ertzaintza killed by ETA. In the inauguration, Urkullu said that their killings had been a 'radical and unjustifiable injustice',[5] implying that the assassination of co-ethnics was less justifiable than the assassination of others.

---

[4] https://elpais.com/politica/2016/11/12/actualidad/1478954518_745581.html (accessed 29 January 2022, my translation).
[5] https://www.elmundo.es/pais-vasco/2019/06/02/5cf3b9d4fc6c83c7478b466b.html (accessed 29 January 2022, my translation).

The word *cipayo* is still in use. As late as 17 May 2021, graffiti appeared in Basque towns referring to the Basque police and the PNV with this derogatory word, but without any specific accusations of betrayal. The term seems to have been more cautiously employed by the separatist movement in official speech, an acknowledgement that they have lost the semantic battle.

There are some lessons from the Basque case. First, collaboration in low-intensity conflicts is largely defined in the symbolic space of public legitimacy. Rebels' propaganda rarely sullies the reputation of a specific constituency if the relevant public does not sanction it in some way. The current wave of unrest in the United States driven by police violence against Black citizens shows how difficult it is for those protesting to tip public opinion against the police. Even after the sentencing in George Floyd's murder trial, majorities overwhelmingly reject policies such as defunding the police, with only 34 per cent of Democrats and 28 per cent of Blacks in favour of it.[6]

Second, rebels must be careful when dealing with high-profile local groups backed by local elites. Against the Basque police force, ETA had attempted to use a highly selective campaign. It was only after the end of the 1998 truce that the armed group started openly to kill its rank-and-file officers, as well as non-nationalist politicians – acts that cost ETA's political front dearly in terms of public support (De la Calle and Sánchez-Cuenca 2013). This speaks to the risks of forcing co-ethnics to take sides when the context is not fully polarised. In the end, collaboration allows shades of grey. As such, protesting against it is more likely to succeed by avoiding derogatory terms that will alienate future and fellow travellers.

References

Aguirre, J. (2007), *¿Cipayos? Policía vasca o brazo armado del PNV* (Tafalla, Txalaparta).
Anasagasti, I. (2003), 'José María de Areilza o la variante ovoide de la ocupación del espacio', in I. Anasagasti and J. Erkoreka (eds), *Dos familias vascas: Areilza–Aznar* (Madrid, Foca), 13–332.
Aretxaga, B. (2004), 'Out of their minds? On political madness in the Basque Country', in B. Aretxaga, D. Dworkin, J. Gabilondo, and J. Zulaika (eds), *Empire & Terror: Nationalism/Postnationalism in the New Millennium* (Reno, University of Nevada Press), 163–76.
Aretxaga, B. (2008), 'Madness and the politically real: Reflections on violence in postdictatorial Spain', in M.-J. DelVecchio Good, S. T. Hyde, S. Pinto, and B. J. Good (eds), *Postcolonial Disorders* (Berkeley, University of California Press), 43–61.
Barroso, A. (1995), *Sacerdotes bajo la atenta mirada del régimen franquista* (Bilbao, Desclée de Brouwer).
Bryant, G. J. (2000), 'Indigenous mercenaries in the service of European imperialists: The case of the sepoys in the early British Indian army, 1750–1800', *War in History*, 7, 2–28.
De la Calle, L. (2007), 'Fighting for local control: Street violence in the Basque Country', *International Studies Quarterly*, 51, 431–55.

[6] See a recent *USA Today*/Ipsos poll, https://www.usatoday.com/story/news/politics/2021/03/07/usa-today-ipsos-poll-just-18-support-defund-police-movement/4599232001/ (accessed 14 June 2021).

De la Calle, L. (2015), *Nationalist Violence in Postwar Europe* (New York, Cambridge University Press).

De la Calle, L. and Sánchez-Cuenca, I. (2011), 'What we talk about when we talk about terrorism', *Politics & Society*, 39, 451–72.

De la Calle, L. and Sánchez-Cuenca, I. (2013), 'Killing and voting in the Basque Country: An exploration of the electoral link between ETA and its political branch', *Terrorism and Political Violence*, 25, 94–112.

Della Porta, D. and Mattina, L. (1986), 'Ciclos políticos y movilización étnica: El caso vasco', *REIS*, 35, 123–48.

Doti, M. (2010), *Breve aproximación a Gino Germani y Arturo Jauretche en la historia de la sociología argentina: La clase media y el peronismo desde dos ópticas sociológicas*, VI Jornadas de Sociología de la UNLP, 9 and 10 December (La Plata, Argentina).

Garmendia, J. M. (1996), *Historia de ETA* (San Sebastián, Haramburu).

Good, M.-J. D. (2019), 'Spectral presences of *Si Pai*: Begoña Aretxaga's *cipayo* and uncanny experiences of *Si Pai* in Aceh 2008', *Ethos*, 47, 480–8.

Gurrutxaga, A. (1985), *El código nacionalista vasco durante el franquismo* (Barcelona, Anthropos).

Hechter, M. (2013), *Alien Rule* (Cambridge, Cambridge University Press).

Intxaurbe, J. R., *et al.* (2016), *Informe sobre la injusticia padecida por el colectivo de ertzainas y sus familias a consecuencia de la amenaza de ETA* (Vitoria, Gobierno Vasco).

Irvin, C. (1999), *Militant Nationalism: Between Movement and Party in Ireland and the Basque Country* (Minneapolis, University of Minnesota Press).

Iztueta, P. (1981), *Sociología del fenómeno contestatorio del clero vasco: 1940–1975* (Donostia, Elkar).

Jentzsch, C., S. N. Kalyvas, and L. I. Schubiger (2015), 'Militias in civil wars', *Journal of Conflict Resolution*, 59, 755–69.

Kalyvas, S. and Kocher, M. (2007), 'How "free" is free riding in civil wars? Violence, insurgency, and the collective action problem', *World Politics*, 59, 177–216.

Lamikiz, A. (2005), *Sociability, Culture and Identity: Associations for the Promotions of an Alternative Culture under the Franco Regime (Gipuzkoa, 1960s–1970s)* (Florence, European University Institute).

McFarlane, A. (1998), 'Identity, enlightenment and political dissent in late colonial Spanish America', *Transactions of the Royal Historical Society*, 8, 309–35.

Mukherjee, R. (1990), 'Satan let loose upon earth: The Kanpur massacres in India in the revolt of 1857', *Past & Present*, 128, 92–116.

Onaindia, M. (2001), *El precio de la libertad: Memorias, 1948–1977* (Madrid, Espasa).

Pérez-Agote, A. (2008), *Las raíces sociales del nacionalismo vasco* (Madrid, Siglo XXI).

Raldúa, E. (1996), 'Cambios en la imagen pública de la policía (1980–1995) y situación actual', *Revista española de investigaciones sociológicas*, 74, 327–41.

Tejerina, B. (1992), *Nacionalismo y lengua: Los procesos de cambio lingüístico en el País Vasco* (Madrid, Centro de Investigaciones Sociológicas).

Thomas, H. (2001), *The Spanish Civil War* (New York, Modern Library).

Unzueta, P. (1988), *Los nietos de la ira: Nacionalismo y violencia en el País Vasco* (Madrid, El País-Aguilar).

Part II

Collaboration Moments

5

Collaboration and Opportunism in Communist Czechoslovakia

MARK DRUMBL AND BARBORA HOLÁ

> Big Daddy: What is the smell in this room? Don't you notice it, Brick? Don't you notice
> a powerful and obnoxious odour of mendacity in this room?
> Brick: Yes, sir, I think I do, sir.
>
> Tennessee Williams, Cat on a Hot Tin Roof, Act III (1954)

> Pleased to meet you
> Hope you guessed my name …
> But what's puzzling you
> Is the nature of my game
>
> The Rolling Stones, 'Sympathy for the Devil' (1968)

IN *SECOND-HAND TIME*, literary Nobel Prize winner Svetlana Alexievich delivers oral histories and polyphonic reportages about life in the Soviet Union. She does so powerfully and piercingly, often through the force of repetition, over and again invoking the wrenching imagery of 'butterflies crushed against the pavement' (Alexievich 2013: 73). Among the stories she relates is one of Elena Yurievna S, 49 years old – third secretary of the district Party committee – within a section Alexievich entitles 'Ten Stories in a Red Interior'. This story – Elena's tale of snitching and snagging and snatching – is particularly gutting. It is a story of a neighbour who tattles in order to rattle about in a larger home. Elena recounts:

> A regular communal apartment … Five families live there – twenty-seven people in total. Sharing one kitchen and one bathroom. Two of the neighbors are friends: one of them has a five-year-old daughter and the other one is single with no kids. In communal apartments, people were always spying on one another, listening in on each other's conversations. The people with ten-square meter rooms envied the ones with twenty-five. Life …That's just how it is … And then, one night, a Black Maria, a police van, shows up … They arrest the woman with the five-year-old daughter.

Figure 5.1 Nikola Emma Ryšavá, *Dialogue A*, 2019, Václav Art Exhibition, Prague.

Before they take her away, she has a chance to cry out to her friend. 'If I don't come back, please look after my little girl. Don't let them take her to an orphanage.' So that's what happened. The neighbor took the child in, and the building administration gave her a second room ... The girl started calling her Mama ... Mama Anya ... Seventeen years went by ... And seventeen years later, the real mother returned. She kissed her friend's hands and feet in gratitude. If this were a fairy tale, this is where the story would end, but in real life the ending was very different. Without a 'happily ever after'. When Gorbachev came to power, after they unsealed the archives, they asked the former camp inmate whether she wanted to see her file. She did. So she went down to look at it, opened the folder ... and the very first page was an informant's report. Familiar handwriting ... it was her neighbor's, Mama Anya's ... She'd been the one who'd informed on her ... Do you understand any of this? I don't. And that woman couldn't, either. She went home and hanged herself ... I remember my father's words: 'It's possible to survive the camps, but you can't survive other people.' (Alexievich 2013: 113–14)[1]

Collaboration is a Janus-faced word. On the one hand, as pointed out in Chapter 1, to collaborate is to be functional, to be part of a team, and to produce a sum that is larger than the parts. The 'new shared economy', indeed, covets collaborative skills. Law faculties – we are both law professors after all – increasingly (try to) teach

---

[1] A play on words, perhaps notably on 'L'enfer, c'est les autres', from Jean-Paul Sartre's (2019) *Huis clos*.

students to *work together* rather than *vie apart*: extroversion, buoying, sharing, supporting, rallying, allying, connecting – all these are nowadays taken as virtues and imperatives, in particular, in a modern, inclusive, crowd-sourced workforce.

Yet immediately following that first definition of collaboration in any dictionary is something more nefarious, namely, 'traitorous cooperation with an enemy' during periods of armed conflict, often – but not necessarily – undertaken by a minority of individuals: this is, in other words, Quisling-style collaboration (Darcy 2019).[2] In a sense, though, the dyad is chimerical because 'collaboration' connotes the same behaviour – going along to get along, to build *something* better for oneself or for the whole – which can be attractive or insidious depending on the 'something' (and the 'whole') in question. How about when the 'enemy' lurks within – namely, when one's own state or government is backed while it lasts with considerable (often enthusiastic) public support? In other words, what happens when the 'enemy' is a decent idea that, in hindsight, goes awfully awry?

Unsurprisingly, then, in light of these multiple dynamics, the term 'collaboration' becomes fraught and taut. 'Collaboration' and 'collaborator' are fuzzy concepts that elude an easy definition. Within any specific historical context, those retrospectively condemned as collaborators, and actions or inactions reproached as collaboration, largely vary. Even within one state, within one regime, and one historical epoch, it is challenging clearly to delimit and define 'the collaborator'. What if the whole society is, in one way or another, complicit in sustaining a repressive regime? As Tina Rosenberg notes, discussing eastern European Communist regimes as 'conspiracies of all society':

> Just as almost everyone was a victim of communism by virtue of living under it, almost everyone also participated in repression. Inside a communist regime, lines of complicity ran like veins and arteries inside the human body. Even the most natural responses of self-preservation were also, in a sense, acts of collaboration. The eighth-grade history teacher who taught students of the glorious march of the proletariat and its vanguard, the Communist Party; the journalist who wrote positive articles because she knew she would be fired for writing negative ones; the millions who fooled their leaders into thinking they were beloved by granting them their votes and cheering at party rallies – all were complicit. Their complicity was hidden, even from themselves, by that fact that every ordinary citizens behaved the same way. It seemed normal. But such 'normal' collaboration kept the regime alive. (Rosenberg 1995: 138)

In Czech, *kolaborace* has largely negative connotations and is used primarily in connection with two historical phenomena.[3] First and foremost, it refers to

---

[2] See also Shane Darcy's Chapter 12, where he discusses collaboration during armed conflict by the parties thereto through the lens of international law, noting that the law inadequately addresses this phenomenon despite the prevalence of collaboration and the, at times, fatal consequences that befall individuals who collaborate with an enemy.

[3] According to the *Czech Encyclopedia of Sociology* (Bubeník 2017), *kolaborace* is 'a word used in political life to denote accommodating/friendly/helpful, morally negatively assessed behavior of individuals or groups ... in certain exceptional situations, in particular situations of violent domination of

Czechoslovaks who supported the Nazis. However, it is also regularly employed to refer to those who had supported Communist authorities in the decades after the Second World War, notably those who cooperated with the secret police. And it is this latter group that is the main focus of this chapter. We understand 'collaboration' to mean snitching on others to regime authorities, notably secret police. That regime soured, in the slippery-slope language of Prague's kitschy Museum of Communism, from 'dream' to 'reality' and then to 'nightmare'.[4] We ask: why do people squeal on others to secret police? Even such narrowly delimited collaboration, however, comes in different shades and forms. It can entail action and inaction; collaborators can range from active secret agents, to manipulative informers, to persons blackmailed into coughing up information,[5] to those who provide authorities with false or irrelevant 'fake news', to others who dissent and support all at once.[6] Therefore, in our chapter we opt at times to use a plural 'collaborations' as opposed to a singular 'collaboration' to refer to a plurality of actions and actors with many motives and motivations.

How might transitional justice approach 'collaboration' when there are so many 'types' of 'collaborators' operating in different contexts? As a starting point, the fact remains that the experiential fit between collaborations and normatively 'palatable' transitional justice remains raw. Collaboration, in particular from within – namely, connivance with the internal enemy – does not map well upon the operational desiderata of transitional justice praxis. For example, lustration may have anaemic effects in contexts where the state becomes replaced by private markets (Siklova 1996). Public shaming triggers concerns over vigilantism, accuracy, and humiliation (Espindola 2015). A broader challenge arises, however. Much of the transitional justice imagination fixates on ideologically and politically motivated actions. But what about people, like Mama Anya, whose motivations are presumably not ones of ideology but, rather, involve avarice, convenience, and an extra 15 m² of

---

their own community by another (bigger, stronger) whole'. It denotes a 'knowing cooperation rewarded usually by political or economic privileges from a ruling group, whose aim is to paralyze liberalization or emancipation efforts, or facilitate oppression, or assimilation'. It became synonymous with 'treason', and allegations of collaboration are stigmatising.

[4] Glenn Spicker, a US businessman, opened this museum in 2001. Spicker had arrived in Prague shortly after the fall of Communism. The museum is somewhat directive. The signage about the regime is peppered with plenty of adjectives such as 'oppressive' and 'despotic'. The museum intimates the occupation of Czechoslovakia by a foreign-sourced Communism, which contrasts with the historical record that is more nuanced, in that elements of Communist rule were internally motored and *in situ* in nature. That said, the museum delivers considerable information in an accessible and detailed fashion. Its content aligns with information determined to be mainstream from credible academic and historical sources.

[5] This is not an uncommon reality. See generally Dudai (2012: 40), noting 'the practice of recruiting informers from among criminals or using blackmail based on marital infidelity or other behaviours considered deviant'.

[6] Another example is Roman David's invocation of Milan Kundera. David (2018) introduces reports by and about Kundera, who himself both collaborated and critiqued, then distanced and, after the fact, further obscures, according to David, his collaborative acts while mining his critical resistances. The Kundera case remains tense. See also Třešňák and Hradílek (2008).

living space? How to approach Mama Anya's collaboration? *Should* these people, who indeed hurt others, have that harm redressed or even addressed by a transitional justice paradigm?

In this regard, then, this chapter unwinds the place of collaborators, informants, colluders, and connivers within Communist Czechoslovakia (1948–89), with an eye toward their opportunistic interactions with state security forces focusing in particular on the period of the so-called normalisation (beginning in 1969) that ended with the fall of the Communist regime in the 1989 Velvet Revolution. Additionally, this chapter discusses how and why lustrations adopted in the post-Communist Czech Republic as the main transitional justice mechanism have fallen short in dealing with a variety of collaborative acts and the harms they occasioned.[7] Our goal is to demonstrate the complexity of collaboration while emphasising that many transitional justice efforts excessively simplify collaboration.[8] This chapter's contribution is not to totalise collaboration in any way but to emphasise the motivational, and behavioural, heterogeneity among informants and their actions. This move is key, since, all told, the odour of mendacity – this stench exuded by all forms of collaboration – hangs in the air. It grows thorns and turns people into nettles, rendering embraces – such as those in the *Dialogue A* sculpture that visually opens our chapter – prickly and discomfiting, infected by suspicion.

The chapter proceeds through several parts. First, we provide a brief exposé of the role and standard operating procedures of the state secret police – the Státní bezpečnost (StB) – in Communist Czechoslovakia and the practices of its network of collaborators. Second, we engage in a discussion that presents a narrative review of archival records in the Security Services Archive in Prague and of the *Paměť národa* (*Memory of Nations*) oral history project documenting instances of what we call opportunistic collaboration: namely, snitching that is not per se predominantly political or ideological in nature but, instead, seems motivationally material or personal – to wit, cunning non-partisan exercises in mining, acquisitively, the cracks and crevices of an authoritarian polity.[9] While these categories are not mutually exclusive and, in fact, remain deeply imbricated, we believe that – while the separateness of these categories should never be overdrawn – classing collaboration within opportunistic motivations/actions and ideological motivations/actions is a worthwhile taxonomic or heuristic endeavour. We also believe it helpful to

---

[7] Slovaks played a salient role within Czechoslovakian authoritarianism. Slovakia, moreover, after 1993 when Czechoslovakia was divided into two independent states – the Czech Republic and Slovakia – engaged in transitional justice processes as well. That said, this chapter limits its conversation only to the Czech Republic. This choice is in no way normative.

[8] Here, too, it is important to recognise that certain kinds of informants, tattlers, and squealers may be seen as heroes – breaking ranks to disseminate information about human rights abuses (photographs at Abu Ghraib) or opening a window on alleged corruption and wrongdoing ('Deep Throat' in the case of the Nixon impeachment or the 'whistleblower' in the case of the Trump impeachment).

[9] The oral history project *Paměť národa* is conducted by the non-governmental organisation Post Bellum, in cooperation with Czech Radio and the Institute for Study of Totalitarian Regimes. Available at:= https://www.memoryofnations.eu/en/o-projektu.

talk not of opportunists or ideologues but, rather, of people who in a moment *acted* opportunistically or *acted* ideologically. Third, we give a brief description and critical analysis of the main transitional justice mechanism adopted after the fall of Communism in Czechoslovakia (and, following the division of the country in 1993, in the Czech Republic) to deal with collaborators – namely lustration[10] – recognising that a generation later, as Roman David (2018) notes, the results are disappointing for many Czechs.[11] Finally, we interrogate how and whether transitional justice mechanisms ought to approach acts of collaboration.[12] In the Czech context, this interrogation challenges 'assumptions of the homogeneity of secret collaborators that underpin the lustration and similar laws' (David 2018: 33).

Collaboration with the State Secret Police in Communist Czechoslovakia (1948–1989)

The StB was created in 1945 and was initially dedicated to searching for collaborators with the Nazi Protectorate and Slovak puppet regime (Williams 2001). Throughout its existence, however, it served a catalytic role in stoking and structuring the climate of fear, which more or less characterised the repressive regime in Communist Czechoslovakia while it lasted. The StB's mission was to uphold the spirit of Marxism-Leninism and to fight ostensible enemies of the state (persons suspected of anti-Communist sympathies) – both external and internal – and to prevent leakage of state secrets. The StB is conceptually similar to the KGB in the Soviet Union, the Stasi in the German Democratic Republic, the Securitate in Romania, and other 'political police units' established in other Communist countries that were tasked with 'ideological policing' (Espindola 2015: 42).

For most of its history, the StB exercised coercive surveillance of varying intensity (Williams 2001). During its existence, it was reorganised with remarkable frequency, and its focus, main targets, and standard operating procedures varied over time according to the changing character of the repression. In the immediate aftermath of the Communist take-over in 1948, StB coercion was directed mainly against Communists' immediate opponents. Repressive measures on the part of the StB – including torture and show trials – were also most pronounced in this period. Interrogations were harsh; forced confessions legion; drugs such as scopolamine were routinely injected into people being interrogated so that they would admit

---

[10] Other measures not discussed herein include transparency measures and the opening of the StB archives, restitution of property, rehabilitation of victims, compensation, and declaratory laws regarding the Communist regime.
[11] David (2018) claims that Czechoslovak transitional justice methods across the board fell short of their goals.
[12] See also Dudai (2012: 48),who notes that informants expose several 'blind spots' in transitional justice discourse, notably the binary reductionism of persons into either victim or perpetrator categories and the diffidence in engaging with emotions such as betrayal and resentment.

to practically anything; interrogations went on for many hours, through the night into the following day; and competitions were established among interrogators as to who could interrogate the longest.[13] Afterwards, the StB escalated into a wider repression, which was announced in 1950, and started to mutate in the second half of the 1950s into a less expansive policy of selective surveillance and persecution (Williams 2001).

To fragment society the StB relied not on large-scale, open terror, but on a reputation for omnipresence and ubiquity (Williams 2001). Like its counterparts in the other states of the Soviet bloc, to function effectively and sustain this reputation the StB relied on large armies of informers. It usually employed around 9,000 people in a population of 15 million, and therefore a large informer network was necessary (Williams 2001). Their numbers oscillated, however, depending on different levels of repression and surveillance throughout the years (David 2018). Estimates of the total number of collaborators differ. Williams (2001: 34) notes that by 1968, an estimated 150,000 had passed the informers' ranks. Moran (1994) writes that the Czechoslovak Security Services had 18,000 full-time workers and 140,000 informers. Other reports put the informer figure slightly higher: 150,000 or 160,000 (Hauner 2008: 346). In comparison, the GDR Stasi had 86,000 full-time workers and 2 million informers.[14] Hence, 'while the ratio of security to non-security people in the GDR was 1:8, in Czechoslovakia it was 1:100' (Moran 1994: 104). Moran (1994) also provides comparison with Bulgaria, where the ratio of security- to non-security-associated people stood at 1:33. The secret police, and its web of collaborators, played an indispensable role in Czechoslovak Communist repression, however.[15] Members of the StB, collaborators, and agents 'infiltrated all parts of society – from embassies to schools and sports clubs' (Museum of Communism n. d.).[16] The StB built a dense surveillance network and thereby curried betrayal, broken trust, fear, phlegmatism, and cynicism throughout society. It stewed and brewed unease by turning citizen against citizen. Loyalties frayed and individuals pettily looked out for themselves.

That being said, however, the intensity and forms of collaboration varied amid Communism's different periods. The concrete methods of carrying out intelligence and operational (police) work were continuously being modified according to how Party leadership or top StB officers viewed the international situation, as well as

---

[13] See the website of the Museum of Communism, https://muzeumkomunismu.cz/en/about/ (accessed 14 June 2021).

[14] Espindola (2015) provides different figures for the DDR. He finds that in total nearly 600,000 citizens were informers. Some were very intimate: 'There have also been tales of familial betrayal involving Stasi informers – husbands informing on their wives and brothers or sisters spying on their siblings' (4).

[15] Espindola (2015: 42) finds: 'The ratio of secret police officers for every citizen in the Soviet Union was one for 595; in Czechoslovakia, one for every 867; and in Poland, one for every 1,574. None of these figures comes close to the ration in East Germany of one full-time secret police officer for every 180 East German citizens.'

[16] Museum of Communism website.

the internal stability of the regime. Czech historian Libor Bílek (2016) notes how periods of increased perception of threat were linked to a tightening of repression and intensification of surveillance (e.g. the period of Stalinisation in the 1950s, or following the Soviet-led invasion of 1968),[17] and alternated with times of relative liberalisation and an easing of repression (1968 and preceding years). Similarly, the categories of collaborators and the StB's methods of work and recruiting police informes continuously evolved.[18] According to the 1978 Guidelines (confidential orders issued by the Minister of the Interior, which were in place until 1989), there were two main categories of informers: (1) secret collaborators, and (2) confidants (Obzina 1978). The secret collaborators (including agents, residents, and owners of 'conspiracy flats') were considered the main tool in the fight against subversion and were used by StB members to 'disclose, elaborate on, and document anti-state criminal activities, and prevent such activities' (Obzina 1978: art. 5). Confidants, on the other hand, were an auxiliary category, meant to 'assist [the StB in] fulfilling partial tasks of state security character' (Obzina 1978: art. 17). The secret collaborators usually signed an agreement to cooperate (though this practice was not consistent, especially after 1970) and their cooperation was sometimes remunerated. For confidants no formal agreement or payments were involved, and their cooperation assumed more of an ad hoc character (Williams 2001). Additionally, the StB files, opened in the 2000s to the public, also contain files of the so-called 'candidates for secret collaboration' (Obzina 1978: arts 26–35). These were individuals who were considered by the StB to be 'a potential agent material', and their recruitment was initiated. Many were unsuccessful because of, for example, rejection by the candidate, or upon the conclusion by an StB member that the person was not suitable for collaboration.

The recruitment process of would-be collaborators was also set out in detail for the StB officers by the ministerial guidelines. Each candidate was to be selected based on personal characteristics, including his/her intellectual, psychological, and physical predispositions, and his/her potential to infiltrate 'enemy and emigré circles' (Obzina 1978, arts 27–9). All candidates were subjected to background checks, and had to be approved by StB superior officers. The guidelines envisaged the following motivators to recruitment: ideological reasons, material incentives, and compromising material (Obzina 1978: art. 36). According to the directives, prospective collaborators were to decide 'of their own volition' whether to collaborate, and voluntariness was emphasised as the basic principle in recruiting informers. The StB members were instructed to use compromising material only in reasoned/justified cases. Such material, according to the guidelines, could

---

[17] In 1968, the USSR (together with other countries of the Warsaw Pact) invaded Czechoslovakia and quashed the vacillating but reformist ambitions of Alexander Dubček's 'socialism with a human face'. The invasion abruptly halted the Prague Spring.
[18] The Minister of the Interior issued confidential orders and directives that regulated aims of work with secret collaborators, their recruitment, and methods, and stipulated different categories of collaborators. Such regulations were issued for example in 1948, 1954, 1962, 1972, and 1978 (Žáček 2005).

include information relating to a person's reputation in public life, at work, or in private, or any information that could ordinarily lead to criminal prosecution for misdemeanours (Obzina 1978: arts 40–1).

As the StB focused most of its attention on social groups whose members were openly or secretly hostile to or critical of the regime (or at least indifferent thereto), recruiting collaborators from their ranks was not easy (Bílek 2016). According to Williams (2001), however, the majority of informers were not coerced into signing up. Nevertheless, blackmail was not uncommon, and compromising material was regularly used by the StB, in particular in the early years before it turned out that informers recruited in this way could not be easily motivated to collaborate. Williams (2001) reports that 30 per cent of agents were bullied into cooperation when confronted with evidence of their own criminal activity, their Second World War collaboration, or sexual indiscretions. Alongside compromising materials, other forms of 'persuasion' were deployed, including material or other advantages and 'patriotic inducements' (Bílek 2016: 100). Only a minority of collaborators were recruited from the Communist Party. In 1964–7, Party members accounted for between 7 and 10 per cent, mirroring the proportion of Party membership in the Czechoslovak population (Bílek 2016).[19] Financial benefits and material gains were, in general, limited to minor monetary rewards or material gifts (Williams 2001). Bílek (2016: 100) notes that '[t]he particular motivation … was naturally specific to every collaborator and always stemmed from a particular situation'. He cautions against condemning the collaborators *ex post facto*, as a 'majority of people were "asked" to collaborate (albeit perhaps covertly or ambiguously, as officers acted in such a way as to get the committed person to make the actual proposal) and rejecting such an "offer" was in view of the reputation that accompanied the State Security very difficult and in some cases virtually impossible' (Bílek 2016: 100). Whether the 'offers' by the StB to collaborate could be turned down or not remains a contested question both to ask and to answer. However, many collaborators paved the way to collaboration with their own ambition, desire for a career, or willingness to fulfil the demands that the StB placed on them in order to keep their jobs, social status, or way of living (Bílek 2016). Additionally, David notes an apparent gender imbalance among secret collaborators. He reports that based on his estimates about 85.5 per cent were men and only about 10.2 per cent women (David 2018: 38–9).

The StB was dismantled in 1990. Its members and collaborators were putatively banned from returning to positions of power and influence. The former StB headquarters in Prague have been repurposed as the city's police headquarters: these are located at no. 4 Bartolomějská, a street named for the Church of Saint Bartholomew. The StB had commandeered these premises from their previous use as a convent. The nuns who served the public from within these buildings were removed to a detention camp. Convent cells became interrogation chambers.

[19] Williams (2001), however, also notes that many more party members regularly provided information without a formal agreement with the StB.

The street is lovely, with a gentle curve, belying the terrors that occurred within these architecturally pleasing structures. Today, other than no. 4, the buildings have been restored to the nuns.

Snapshots of Collaboration – Informers' Narratives

'Why do you do it?'
'Because. Why shouldn't I do it?'
'Are you doing it for the world revolution?'
'What?'
'You have a nice blouse.'
'Don't I? It cost seventy dollars.'
'It suits you. The pants too.'

Škvorecký (1977: 58–9)[20]

Our research assesses informant reports from throughout the Communist period, but we focus on the 'Goulash Communism' years (1970s and 1980s), which represented 'normalisation'. Hence, the vignettes that follow date in whole or in part from that period. Kevin McDermott captures the *Zeitgeist*: 'the recurring themes that punctuate the historiography of normalised Czechoslovakia provide an unrelentingly grim picture: alienation, apathy, careerism, collaboration, corruption, disillusionment, informing, manipulation, opportunism, passivity, stagnation, "inner emigration", "civilised violence", a "timeless" era of monotony and ritualised conformity' (McDermott 2015: 154).[21] McDermott indeed chides this discourse as 'hegemonic', suggesting that life then was more complex, but he still concludes that this dominant narrative 'is in many ways historically accurate'(McDermott 2015: 154). These were phlegmatic, resigned, cynical times. 'No one cared about anything', reports a placard at the Museum of Communism, adding that:

> Communist leaders gradually set down the path towards creating a sort of pseudo-consumerist society, in which everyone took care of themselves and their families and spent their free time playing sport, at the cinema, or watching television ... The defining characteristics of normalization included inflexibility, routine, monotony, the total stagnation of cultural, social, economic and scientific life, and the absolute negation of politics.

Why goulash? Well, 'the regime bought the silence of the masses, paying for it with a bit of food – goulash'. Crucially, in the 'goulash' period, McDermott (2015: 158) underscores that 'unlike in the first two decades of communist rule, the vast majority of party members in the 1970s and 1980s almost certainly retained very little, if any, faith in Marxism-Leninism, itself a damning reflection of the "crisis of

---

[20] Smiřický, a Czech writer in exile, is visited by Svobodová, an informant, in Toronto.
[21] See also McDermott (2015: 162).

ideology" that affected the regime and country after 1968'. Yet this vapid, amoral phase lasted for 20 years! An entire tentacled structure of informants persisted despite collective disinterest in ideology or dogma or politics.

While references to actual collaborators and their affirmed or attributed motivations and practices weave throughout this chapter, we set out in what follows two collaborator profiles in narrative form. We believe such a presentation helps to put actual human faces upon the industrialisation of collaboration throughout Czechoslovakia and thereby story-tell motivations and manners. In addition to the two vignettes presented, we have compiled similar profiles about a number of other collaborators that we are glad to share with interested readers. All of these profiles derive from our review of the StB files or the *Paměť národa* oral histories project.[22]

Jiří Imlauf (aka a candidate of secret collaboration 'Hráč' ('Player'), turned into an agent 'Vijan' according to his StB file) was born in 1966.[23] His father was a pilot in the Czechoslovak People's Army. After 1968 his father was forced to leave the army, as he did not express his agreement with the Soviet occupation, and thus ended up as a construction worker. Jiří did not remember ever discussing politics with his parents. He thought that his parents wanted to spare him: 'I was a chubby boy with glasses, who only listened to music and read. That was my world' (*Paměť národa* [n.d.]b). Only at the university did he remember meeting people who were openly voicing their disagreement with the socialist regime. Jiří's hobby was music: he played guitar in a local band and was a big fan of The Beatles. He did not enjoy studies. His contact with the StB started in 1987. In December of that year, 21-year-old Jiří went to Prague to join in a commemoration of John Lennon's death. Together with his friend, he witnessed how the police intervened in this 'illegal gathering of subversive elements' by the Lennon Wall. Jiří and his friend were scared, excited, and took a train back home. A month thereafter, Jiří was summoned for interrogation at the StB. The interrogation 'was done by a bloke in civilian clothes. I zigzagged, said that I was in Prague because I like music, not because I wanted to protest against the regime. He asked from whom I heard about the meeting and to whom I talked about it' (Drda and Kroupa 2017: 83). Sometime thereafter he was summoned for another interrogation. This time around, there were two men, 'the so-called good cop and bad cop. And [the bad one] was tough

---

[22] We acknowledge the limitations of StB files as (historical) sources, as the files are often incomplete (lot of documents in the files were destroyed during and after Communism); they are one-sided and bureaucratic (the reports are drafted by StB officers for their organisational purposes), and it is impossible to verify and triangulate 'facts' reported in the files. The files however still provide a peek into the workings of collaboration, through the official, StB perspective, and as such still reveal a very varied picture of collaborators and their collaborations. For some of these limitations and considerations see Křen (2005) and De Baets (2004).

[23] The story of Jiří Imlauf, including audio and video materials (in Czech), is available at *Paměť národa* ([n.d.]b), and was also published in Drda and Kroupa (2017: 68–95). His StB file is registered under no. 26032.

and directly told me that it could easily happen that the next week I would not go to university' (Drda and Kroupa 2017: 84). Jiří remembered how they explained that he needed to inform them any time he uncovered any anti-regime action, and that compliance was mandatory if he wanted to finish his studies. During the next meeting, he was given 'a paper' to sign. He did not remember where exactly it happened. According to him it was in a flat in one of the high-rise buildings – *paneláky* – so characteristic of communist suburbs in Ústí and Labem.[24] He recalls that on a table there was 'a salami, a bread roll, and a bottle of vodka' (*Paměť národa* [n.d.]b). The StB officers explained that if he signed, everything would be easier. 'They were playing it light, as if nothing was going on' (*Paměť národa* [n.d.]b). And thus he signed the pledge to collaborate with the StB. According to his StB file he unequivocally agreed to further collaboration, and only asked about its duration. Jiří was willing to cooperate during his studies, but did not wish to continue after graduation. His task was to inform on students and people he met at cultural events and at restaurants. His StB file contains information he provided on his fellow students and teachers, and he was also given active tasks by the StB, such as making recordings during concerts. He could not recall if he did so or not. The StB contacted him quite frequently. He was rewarded financially for his 'service'. Later on, Jiří said it was incomprehensible to him to suggest that he complied only to finish his studies, which he did not enjoy at all. 'It was a mix of various influences. Ranging from the fact that my parents insisted that I had to graduate, to my personal characteristics and a naive conviction that I could somehow play the system. All that combined in a perverse dependency on the idea that I had to finish my studies at any price' (Drda and Kroupa 2017: 93). Jiří insists that he did not want to harm anyone, and tried only to provide information he thought the StB already knew. Only after seeing his file did he realise that perhaps this was not always the case.

Ladislav N. (aka a candidate of secret collaboration and later an agent 'Rolf') was born in 1922 to a workers' family.[25] According to his typewritten CV, included in his StB file, his father worked as a shoemaker. After completing basic education right before the start of the Second World War, Ladislav was banned by the Germans from further apprentice education and so started to work. During the war, he also was a member of one of the partisan groups 'Konstantin', operating at the territory of the Protectorate. After the war ended in 1945, Ladislav frequently changed employment, and worked as a labourer or a driver in various industries and firms. He did not have any political affiliation. In 1969 Ladislav responded to an advertisement of the GDR embassy in Prague, which was seeking a driver for its business representation department. He got the job, in which he was required to travel frequently to the GDR and was also often tasked with handling deliveries

---

[24] According to his StB file, however, his pledge to collaborate was signed in a village nearby in a conspiracy house.

[25] This vignette is based solely on the information contained in StB file no. 752665; StB registration no. 2664.

of documents from the airport to the embassy, both of which made him very interesting to the StB. According to one of the first StB reports proposing him as a candidate for secret collaboration, Ladislav is described as an embassy employee who is 'able to create very good conditions for himself and gain the trust of his superiors, as he arranges for them various deals and services, always according to their wishes'. As with other (potential) collaborators, the StB used its large network of informers and its own members to 'profile' Ladislav before personally approaching him. His file contains a number of reports in which he is reprimanded for trading with embassy employees, selling traditional Czech crystal products and bijouterie for profit, smuggling items to the GDR, and having a bank account in the GDR, as well as a report of his being privately critical of the political and economic situation in Czechoslovakia. All this could have provided the StB with potentially compromising material; however, it is not clear from the file whether it was ever used. In contrast, Ladislav is described as an active informant, who, after being contacted by the StB in May 1971, took the initiative and provided 'a number of operationally interesting information items … including photocopies of documents from the embassy, which he procures on his own initiative'. His 'career' as a candidate for secret collaboration was thus launched. Ladislav seems to have approached his cooperation very eagerly. In addition to 'operational information', he provided the StB with copies of various documents, lists of all employees of the GDR embassy, and duplicate keys for closets in its buildings. After only four months and 11 meetings, in September 1971, Ladislav was swiftly 'promoted' to an agent. The StB report notes that 'since he takes initiative and has a good attitude toward members of the StB, it is not appropriate to have him sign a pledge of collaboration'. On the occasion, Ladislav received a monetary reward as appreciation for his 'service'. At first hesitant, in the end Ladislav accepted the reward, and as of then was regularly given money as an appreciation for his active contribution. In the subsequent 13 years until November 1984, when his collaboration ended as a consequence of his retirement and ill health, Ladislav received financial remuneration at least 18 times 'further to promote his initiative and, at the same time, acknowledge his conscientiousness in fulfilling tasks'. As with all the StB files, it is difficult to pinpoint why Ladislav collaborated and what his motivations were. In any case, in addition to providing monetary rewards, the StB was amenable to assisting Ladislav, if needed and considered appropriate, in private life matters. Ladislav actively made use of these new possibilities. For example, in 1972, and a couple of subsequent times during his collaboration, the StB assisted him and members of his family in gaining permission to travel abroad, including a holiday trip to Yugoslavia. In May 1973, during one of the meetings with his handlers, Ladislav asked the StB for help him obtain a permit from the Ministry of Finance to buy an old BMW from one of his colleagues at the embassy. In October 1973 Ladislav shared with the StB the difficulties of his daughter, who wanted to study at a gymnasium, had been told that she would never be admitted because her father worked at the GDR embassy. His StB handler responded that 'he [would] do all in his power so that [the situation] is resolved positively'.

All the StB files and oral histories we have reviewed reveal a kaleidoscopic picture of opportunistic collaborations. One can find files of former (political) prisoners
who were promised release from prison if they signed a pledge of collaboration with
the StB. František Kraus, for example, after being convicted in 1952 and sent to the
Jáchymov uranium mine as a political prisoner, agreed in 1959 to sign a collaboration pact with the StB in exchange for his early release.[26] 'I said to myself, I have
already been here for eight years, so I will give it a try. I could not imagine what
they could possibly want to know from me. The officer called me in three times,
and the third time I signed' (*Paměť národa* [n.d.]a). Kraus collaborated with the StB
increasingly more actively over the subsequent 30 years, well until the 1980s. The
StB archives contain material from secretaries, office workers, and professionals
who informed on their co-workers and were 'awarded' permits to travel abroad or
assisted with professional advancements, for instance Martin K. (aka candidate for
secret collaboration Marcel), who attempted to exchange information for advanta-
geous placement at work.[27] According to the StB, he was motivated by the desire to
'secur[e] a better situation for himself personally' and also to broaden his potential
to travel abroad. There are also files of parents, similar to Ladislav, who wanted to
secure a 'prosperous and successful future' for their children. For example, Jarmila
N. (aka agent 'Inženýr'), complained to the StB in 1958 that because of 'her class
origins, it [was] difficult for her to find a job' and that for the same reason 'her
daughter ha[d] troubles getting into a high school'.[28] Her collaboration from that
point lasted for 22 years, well into the period of normalisation. In the late 1950s the
StB assisted in finding her a job as a translator, and her son was also admitted to
university that year. Whether the StB played any role in getting her son, who had
'an unsuitable cadre profile', into the university is not clear from the file. However,
in 1969 the StB intervened on his behalf in an ongoing criminal investigation for
fraud, and the prosecution was halted. For other individuals in the files, in turn, collaboration brought other possibilities and material advantages. Similarly to Mama
Anya, some collaborators were 'helped' by the StB to get a new apartment, such
as Ivana K., aka an agent Martin. In addition to monetary rewards for her 'good
results', the StB helped her secure a new place residence.[29]

Some collaborators were approached by the StB, some came forward on their
own initiative. Some informants seem to have been reluctant, avoiding contact
with their handlers or providing very cryptic, scattered information; some were
eager, more than willing, and creatively developed ways to gather information.
Regardless, much of the information contained in many of the files we have seen
reads more like a conversation between two close friends over a beer complaining
and gossiping about their families, friends, and foes. An intimacy veneer seems

[26] See *Paměť národa* ([n.d.]a). We were not able to find Kraus's StB file in the digital archives.
[27] StB file no. 796432; StB registration no. 42004.
[28] StB file no. 710172 MV, StB registration no. left blank.
[29] StB file no. 796909; StB registration no. 796909.

to have arisen – the process of informing became one of social bonding. Tedium, ennui, and disillusionment arose as well – along with 'collaboration fatigue' – among informants in certain cases. Many informants ceased informing of their own volition, 'tuning out', so to speak, or (putatively or actually) because of illness: they thereby 'exited' the collaborative role. For example, in the case of informant Jarmila N., her file reveals that during the 1970s her readiness to collaborate waned. In 1976 her StB officer complained about her mediocre results, and two years later it is stated that 'lately she was indifferent and uninterested in meetings with the StB'. In 1979 Jarmila seemed to avoid the StB altogether, claiming to be 'busy' or ill. Informants appear to have exercised some agency. They became uninterested or bored or conflicted about the process of informing, and then deployed their agency and discretion to ween themselves away from informing. Interestingly, therefore, on the one hand the StB forced some citizens to collaborate, and on the other hand, it seemed to flail when informants stalled or retreated.

In sum, based on our explorative research we construe certain acts of informing to police within Communist Czechoslovakia as acts of conversation, expiation, interlocution, social navigation, and opportunism. These collaborative acts were neither in defence or support of an ideology. Rather, they evidence 'complexities of the relationship *between* state and society' (Apor *et al.* 2017: 2–3; emphasis in original) within a given historical epoch and societal context. All those who lived under the socialist regime and strove for social improvement had to work through the official Party political and professional structures. Opportunistic acts of collaboration with the secret police can be seen as one way of navigating possibilities and seizing limited opportunities within Communist society. Similar to collaborators in other Communist regimes of central and eastern Europe, collaborators in Czechoslovakia had variable, sometimes very mundane, reasons to join the ranks of the StB. The StB files demonstrate that collaboration could have also been either a means to retain the status quo in individuals' professional or personal lives, or manipulated as an opportunity for further progress. The secret police could 'provide individuals and their families with prospects for career building, better living conditions, and even the freedom to travel' (Slachta 2017: 310).[30] In some cases, informers had mixed motivations – thereby existing in a place 'in-between' ideology and vapidity, a 'space' between political good and private personal gain. While the ends of the material opportunism and ideological purity continuum attract individual cases, to be sure, these lines also blur and may overlap even in the case of the same individual. As Espindola (2015: 48) notes, 'distinguishing between convinced socialists and reward-seeking opportunists might prove difficult, as one can do things out of conviction but also expect to be compensated for a job well done'.[31] Moreover,

[30] As also illustrated by Krisztina Slachta (2017) in her case study of two collaborators from GDR and Hungary.

[31] Espindola (2015: 49) claims, 'Of course there are clear examples of each of these cases: devout socialists who believed they were contributing to the consolidation of socialism through denunciation, citizens who were blackmailed into collaboration, or opportunists who were willing to denounce fellow

following Aristotle, human beings may intrinsically be political animals (*zoon politikon*), such that all acts of collaboration may be construable as communitarian and political. And, to be sure, snitching and snagging and snatching were rendered officially possible by the politics of Communist Czechoslovakia. Indeed, the politics of the state germinated and encouraged these spaces of distrust – 'engineered the souls', so to speak – to corrode personal bonds and to promote allegiance to the state and state officials (David 2018: 1).[32] Lying and pretending became omnipresent, in particular in the public sphere, outside the relative privacy of the home (Šimečka 1984; Havel (1991 [1979])). So, yes, it might be possible to construct the pettiness of material squealers as political. Still, we underscore the salience of a bimodal, rather than binary, method that approaches ideological denunciation differently than opportunistic grabbing.

Reckoning with Collaborators through Lustration

> ...so I asked him to forgive me, without knowing what for, but that was my lot, asking forgiveness, I even asked forgiveness of myself for being what I was, what it was my nature to be.
>
> Hrabal (1990 [1976]: 46)

In Czechoslovakia, the 1989 Velvet Revolution evidences a relatively peaceful transition from Communism to democracy. David opines that the 1989 transition is somewhat unremarkable for Czechoslovakia in light of the fact that in that single century the country had already transitioned five other times. He pithily notes: 'The Czechs are experts in regime change. The years 1918, 1938, 1945, 1948, 1968, and 1989 are years in which fundamental changes took place in the country's political structure' (David 2018: 52). Secret police, and sycophants, informers, and connivers were present in and embedded throughout all of these regimes. Cycles of snitching and abuse and cleansing, frankly, are not novel. Despite the fact that the kinds (some with the outside enemy, some with the inside regime) and scales of collaborations(s) (numbers of collaborators) differed, a 'regularity' of collaboration with unjust regimes (or regimes that soured into injustice) arises throughout Czech history. This is important, as it shows ubiquity of collaboration: informing and collaboration as routine, as a coping mechanism, as a method of navigation, as a modality of muddling through life – in juxtaposition to the modern transitional

---

citizens for a few coins, or a vacation trip to Finland.' Our purpose in this project is to address, rather than neglect, the opportunists.

[32] The Khmer Rouge proceeded similarly, and far more drastically, through policies of forced marriage, separation of family members, and active propaganda to ensure fealty to the state (Angkar) over affective bonds to friends and family. See also Andrea Dennis's Chapter 6 on how, intentionally or not, slave owners prompted distrust among slaves, and how this was one of the reasons why slaves did not follow through with insurrections on a larger scale.

justice narrative that casts collaborations as pathological and anomalous, disjunctive rather than continuous.

The main transitional justice mechanisms adopted by the nascent democratic government after 1989 to deal with the StB collaborators were large-scale lustrations.[33] Only a very limited number of criminal prosecutions have been conducted, in part because of a policy determination and in part also because of the technical realities (implicated state officials being dead, aged), or the crimes themselves became statute-barred (a 50-year period had elapsed).[34]

Lustration (from Latin *lustratio*, 'purification by sacrifice') was 'the systematic vetting of public officials for links to the communist-era security services' (Williams *et al.*, 2005: 23) and links with higher echelons of the regime, amongst others.[35] Lustration effectively institutionalised political exclusion of groups of people based on their affiliation with the repressive state apparatus. The 1991 lustration legislation 'targeted former secret policemen and their agents, former communist officials (from the district level up), members of the Peoples' Militia, and members of the National Front Action committees' who 'would be barred ... from holding jobs in high-level governmental/administrative posts, the military, the intelligence services, the police corps, state radio and television organisations, news agencies, state-owned enterprises (including foreign trade companies), railways, banks, high academic positions, the judicial bench, and other positions connected with the courts' (Moran 1994: 103).[36]

According to David (2018), official lustrations effectively concerned over 23,000 StB members who were under 65 (i.e. not retired) in 1989. Czech pursuit of lustration has been branded as 'radical' in its systematisation; it 'combined elements of both vetting and exclusion from certain public offices for secret service functionaries and Communist Party officials' (Williams *et al.* 2005: 24).[37] Lustration activists succeeded in implementing this policy even though the 'urge

[33] Law no. 451/1991, 'Setting certain further requirements for execution of certain functions in state organs and organisations of the Czech and Slovak Federative Republic, Czech Republic, and Slovak Republic' (Prague), effective as of 5 November 1991; Law no. 279/92, 'Setting certain further requirements for execution of certain functions filled by appointment of members of the Police of the Czech Republic and members of the prison service' (Prague), effective as of 1 July 1992. See also generally Williams *et al.* (2005).

[34] See generally Hauner (2008); Williams *et al.* (2005); Moran (1994).

[35] Lustration was not at all new to the Czechoslovak political context. In 1958 and 1969 the Communist government also issued governmental orders aimed at getting rid of 'politically unreliable elements' and preventing them from getting important posts.

[36] Lustration Law no. 451/1991 has been amended 12 times since, most recently in 2017.

[37] Williams *et al.* (2005: 24–5) additionally noted that 'All those who served as officers and agents of the communist security services or as party officials from district level upwards (except in 1968) were automatically excluded from around 9,000 posts in government and public administration, the military, the security services, the state media, state-owned enterprises, senior academic posts and the judiciary. The lustration law was applied subsequently in the Czech Republic (but not Slovakia) following the break-up of the Czechoslovak State in 1993, extended for a further five years in 1995 and then indefinitely in 2000.'

to purge ... could easily be deplored as retribution for bygones', (Williams *et al.*, 2005: 27, 38):

> In the Czech Republic, a survey conducted in July 1991 (three months before the lustration law was enacted) found that 54 per cent of respondents concurred that lustration was necessary for the development of a democracy, and a full 80 per cent welcomed the prospect of a public sector rid of StB collaborators. Equally noteworthy, however, was that two-thirds of respondents felt lustration to be a means of political competition between parties and a distraction from more pressing matters. (Williams *et al.*, 2005: 34)

Compared to other post-Communist countries, in the Czech Republic the attempted scale of lustrations was unprecedented – certainly initially. As of 2005, according to Stan (2010), the Czech Ministry of the Interior issued 451,000 lustration certificates, of which, however, only approximately 2 per cent were *positive*, meaning that it was found that the individual was in fact registered under one of the law's 'prohibited' categories. In 870 cases such decisions were contested in court, and in most of these cases courts found that the StB's registration of the person was unjustified. Similarly, the validity of some *negative* lustration certificates has been challenged (Nedelsky 2009).

David lumps lustration into the box of retributive justice mechanisms. Indeed, lustration served to condemn individuals and endeavour to expiate the anger of those who had been wronged, especially political prisoners, torture victims, and others who suffered immensely from the acts of snitches. Moran (1994: 101) observes, similarly, how in the early days of post-Communist transition in Czechoslovakia, 'calls for punishment have overwhelmed those for forgiveness'. The lustration laws might also be constructed as 'cleansing' the new regime by permitting certain individuals who were disfavoured by that regime to be 'cancelled', so to speak, while giving others, who may have become useful to that regime, a pass. It aimed to get rid of those whose 'morals, values and commitments to the new democracy [might have been] compromised by their previous beliefs, affiliations and actions' (Horne 2014: 503). Therefore, lustration was not just about accountability and political exclusion. It also included explicit streaks of moral cleansing and symbolic change (Horne 2014). According to the Czech Constitutional Court, which reviewed the lustration laws twice (in 1992 and 2001), the main goal of the measures has been to *protect and promote democracy, secure political loyalty* to democratic principles, and shore up the *trustworthiness* of state administration among citizens.[38] Lustrations are thus considered as also largely expressive

---

[38] Finding of the Czech Constitutional Court no. 35/2002 from 5 December 2001 regarding the revocation of the Law 451/1991, setting certain further requirements for execution of certain functions in state organs and organisations of the Czech and Slovak Federative Republic, Czech Republic, and Slovak Republic, as amended; the Law no. 279/92 setting certain further requirements for execution of certain functions filled by appointment of members of Police of the Czech Republic and members of prison service, the Kaw 422/2000, which modified the law 451/1991, as amended; and the Law no. 424/2000, which modified the Law 279/1992, as amended (published in 2002).

measures aimed at 'restoring the social order' and 'transforming the moral culture of citizens' (Cepl 1997: 229).

Nevertheless, both within the new private market and even within the public sector, concerns have arisen that many former security agents have insinuated themselves back into senior roles in Czech society – notably in business, but also in the police[39] and even government.[40] The effects of lustration purges on occupational presence are particularly unclear in light of the rapidly growing private neo-liberal market sector that supplanted the state and the official public sector in terms of economic and social importance. Hence, while officially the Czechoslovak transition eschewed a Heidelberg Myth,[41] in practice, many previously involved in the former regime continue to exercise influence amid post-Communist neo-liberal marketism. This phenomenon assuredly is not unique to Czechoslovakia.

In essence, lustrations, as adopted and constructed in the Czech context, flattened the myriad motivations of informants into one dominant explanatory category. That is, informants are largely animated by *devotion* to the Communist cause and *allegiance* to ideology, and thus are 'dangerous' to the emerging democracy. Other behavioural motivations, including opportunism, grudge-holding, and loneliness – for example – were underplayed rationales. Transitional justice in the Czech Republic did not entirely ignore these sentiments, but reframed informants as 'believers', so that ideological commitment remained the dominant image of the 'informant'. We argue that the construction of informants and collaborators as devotees to the cause is one that assuages, soothes, and comforts. Collaboration becomes inordinately revised into an ideological box because it is *easier to see it that way*. Ideology is the illness, and purging it is the vaccine. Instead of being constructed as the taint of the soul, collaboration is constructed as the brainwashing of the mind. That makes it possible for informants to be easily purged or repurposed – and connected to a particular, and now voided, ideological moment. Ignoring differences among types of collaborators, or inordinately focusing only on ideological collaboration, presents an incomplete picture of what actually happened in Communist Czechoslovakia and, moreover, hobbles the deracinatory effects of transitional justice initiatives.

In the end, to be sure, all collaborators, including gripers and grifters and loners, can cause great harms by their actions. These harms, however, may be banal, not

---

[39] Czech newspapers still refer to the 'StB past' of police agents and officers today. See Horák (2019).

[40] For instance, the current Prime Minister of the Czech Republic at time of writing, Andrej Babiš, has been listed as an StB collaborator, and challenged the listing in a court claiming that he never knowingly collaborated with the secret police. The litigation is still ongoing.

[41] Oren Gross in Chapter 9 invokes the 'Heidelberg Myth' in his discussion of German legal academia during and after the Nazi period, in which elaborate narratives served to shield all but a few law professors connected to National Socialism from purging and lustration ('This "Heidelberg Myth" consisted in the claims that the number of "genuine Nazis" on faculties was very small and that they had been imposed on the universities by the Nazi regime against the opposition of the professoriate' (193).

because they are widespread or committed mechanically with indifference, but rather because in certain instances they are *afterthoughts* to other petty motivations: assuaging loneliness, getting a better job, controlling a lover, isolating a rival, winning a lost argument, moving into a larger apartment, spite following a rebuke. When accreted, these acts build a sum of terror that is much larger than its individual parts. Networks of informers are often an indispensable tool in order for repressive regimes to take hold and keep on going. Can transitional frameworks, especially punitive and retributive measures, ever reflect and properly address this conduct? How, then, to speak about blasé, non-ideological collaboration? Should it be cast as such in transitional justice mechanisms? Should transitional justice even concern itself with this kind of conduct? Is the moralising nature of transitional justice an appropriate frame? If not, then another shortcoming arises, namely, that the violence and betrayal associated with these forms of collaborationism remain under-appreciated and thinly theorised such that the place of opportunistic social navigators within the transitional justice process finds itself neglected and under-conceptualised.[42]

Whither Transitional Justice?

Modern transitional justice initiatives, for the most part, hinge on the assumption that collaboration is somehow politically motivated, ideologically animated. Hence, to purge these individuals cleanses the stain of the ugly prior regime that ended up on the wrong side of history. This was also the case of post-Communist Czechoslovakia, where all collaborators were in a way assumed to have been ideologically motivated and all were, irrespective of their real motivations and actions, lustrated from public service functions as 'dangerous' to democratic society. Transitional justice separates and suborns ideological motivations from material or private ones. In South Africa, for example, an amnesty was only available to those who disclosed information to the Truth and Reconciliation Commission related to political crimes, whether in support of the state or of the African National Congress. Disclosures involving crimes that were not political in nature were ineligible for amnesty because they were constructed as 'only' materialistic, ordinary common crimes. The transitional justice community isn't much interested in petty informers. Is that a legitimate reluctance, however, and a justifiable omission? Petty informants acting non-ideologically, after all, create nettles and thorns, actualise vendettas, and embrace perilously just like the prickly 'friends' in the *Dialogue A* sculpture – they, too, emit 'odour(s) of mendacity'.

---

[42] For discussion of informing as a form of betrayal, see Dudai (2012: 34, 48), where he notes also that 'human rights advocates are not sensitive to betrayal'. On the under-appreciated place of intimacy within the phenomenon of collaboration, see Thiranagama and Kelly (2012), where they argue that treachery is a constant, essential, and normal part of the processes through which social and political order is produced.

Politically or ideologically motivated informants may be seen as sharing the same purpose as the delegitimised regime, and hence can be retrospectively cast as more blameworthy.[43] Perhaps opportunists, then, are less blameworthy because they lack this shared purpose. They may be more capable of rehabilitation once offered different incentives. They are in a sense amoral, so can adhere to whatever is the convenience *du jour*. Hence, they are less 'bad' because, in a *utilitarian* sense, they pose less of a threat. They are nimble when it comes to readjusting to new technocracies through the same old skills of cosying up and agile manipulation. The persons they hurt along the way, then, still have to reconcile themselves with the fact that the hurt they suffered isn't really cognisable.

On the other hand, those deluded into failed orthodoxies and willing sacrificially to snitch out others for these delusions may well be seen *deontologically* as more honourable and principled – they are not sell-outs or Judas Iscariots craving nothing more than 30 pieces of silver, after all. Like Brutus in Shakespeare's *Julius Caesar* – shattered by Caesar's final words 'Et tu Brute?', as Brutus betrayingly stabs Caesar – the collaborator, the quisling, and the snitch fits within Mark Antony's extemporaneous eulogy to Brutus, who slew himself upon his own sword, and whose principled political virtue Mark Antony praises as unique among the assassins since the rest of them evinced greedy ulterior motivations:

> This was the noblest Roman of them all:
> All the conspirators save only he,
> Did that they did in envy of great Caesar;
> He only, in a general honest thought
> And common good to all, made one of them.
> His life was gentle, and the elements
> So mix'd in him that Nature might stand up
> And say to all the world 'This was a man!'[44]

Should transitional justice intervene? If so, who should transitional justice mechanisms capture? Should individuals who snitched for materialist or personal reasons be treated like those who collaborated for ideological and 'good faith' reasons? And of course, there is yet another dimension: to wit, those who were compelled to snitch. But the focus of this chapter is not that vector, but rather the *motivational one* in cases of the exercise of agency in informing.[45] If many collaborators acted out of convenience and greed then what is the moral basis to lustrate them? Is it that 'we' don't want squealers and tattlers in public service?

---

[43] See generally Colleen Murphy, Chapter 10 in this volume.
[44] William Shakespeare, *The Life and Death of Julius Caesar*, V.v.73–80, http://shakespeare.mit.edu/julius_caesar/full.html (accessed 21 February 2022).
[45] Some informers and collaborators indeed were *blackmailed and forced into it*. These pressures, to be sure, operate on a continuum: from direct physical threats (beatings, jail, abuse of loved ones), to threats of losing one's job, or that one's children will not be able to attend university. While recognising that the line between opportunism and constraint is gauzy, the focus of this specific chapter, however, is not oriented toward 'duressed' informants.

What about the partial tattler, namely, he or she who gives up friends to get stuff, but doesn't fully give them up, or still hides information thereby demonstrating some restraint while snitching? What about persons badgered into informing who then report irrelevancies and fabrications? What about secret police, like the GDR's Hauptmann Gerd Wiesler in *The Lives of Others*, who manufactures grandiose stories and obscure seditious conduct to shield a target from state sanction because of an equally personal and private motivation, namely, amity and adoration?

As David (2018: 203) remarks, in the Czech Republic 'The predominantly collective character of the [transitional justice] measures suppressed the complexity of each individual's life story under the weight of the totalitarian regime.' The heart of resistance is cast as those individuals who contested the regime ideologically and politically, not those who ethically chose not to snitch on others, and thereby who declined, or were never asked, to use the system for materialistic private gain. This frame further sustains our question, namely, what to do with opportunists, squealers, tattlers, rats – these 'little Czechs' (David 2018: 43) – or with their mendacity, with the broken relationships bereft of trust that are *ex post facto* collateral damage to their informing? If transitional justice is to promote social repair, it should also tend to these kinds of collaborations. The question is: how?

Expressive value arises in sensitively presenting all of these stories of connivance and collusion. The tattlings of all these informants each contributed to the architecture of authoritarianism. Privileging some of their stories while obfuscating or dismissing others results in an incomplete portrait. Acknowledging the petty informant, then, *as* petty informant, helps clarify the realities of what people do and how they act within the repression of an authoritarian state – thereby contributing to what one of us has elsewhere described as a historiography of *etiological expressivism* (Drumbl 2016). Maybe it looks better – is simply *easier on the eyes* and *less taxing on the sensibilities* – to cast collaborators as political, and ideological, rather than petty? Such a framing means that by getting rid of those 'morally deficient individuals' – all those alleged 'zealots' who embody the bad ideology dangerous for the new democracy – society is not pathological, but instead a pathogen (ideology) was ideationally introduced (from outside, hence the outsized emphasis on Stalin and the Russians in Czech transitional narratives) and, once that pathogen is purged, all is better (and vaccinated). It is far easier to assign blame for an idea and to purge it than to recognise the 'souls' of people as part of the problem. Tainted souls cannot so readily be weeded out. And 'tainted souls' may be adroit and agile and may come to serve the interests of the transitional regime quite well.

How do opportunists interface with transitional justice? Do they do so (once again) opportunistically? Some manage quite well. Transitional justice cleanses them, for a variety of reasons, even if their hands are stained. If so, then, the collaborator is a shape-shifter – a chameleon – the cleverly bumbling survivalist

Good Soldier Švejk character of classic Czech literature (Hašek 1993 [1917]).[46] Interestingly, one informant, František Kraus (*Paměť národa* [n.d.]a),[47] directly invokes *Švejk* as he looked back at his own collaboration in the oral histories project, saying that he does not regret anything: 'For me it was a way out of misery. One wants to go home. Life is too short. I did not know that there would be an amnesty in two years. This is how life went and how it was. I am not ashamed ... My whole life credo is Švejk, with it I survived everything.'[48]

Conclusion

In the end, collaboration may be more continuous than discontinuous: acts of 'problematic' collaborative support of authoritarian regimes may hinge upon similar techniques of social navigation (including by the very same individuals). So do subsequent acts of 'salutary' collaborative support of transitional justice frameworks, paradoxically within often destructive and punitive neo-liberal market regimes. Informing really might just be nothing special, going along to get along, as Czechs now collaborate post-transition in destructive neo-liberal impulses, environmental peril, an uptick in authoritarianism compounded by COVID-19 fears, and shabby-chic imperatives. Snitching, tattling, ratting out, and collaboration seem ubiquitous and entangled with the human condition. This, then, presents a distinct challenge to 'transitional justice' as a discipline: to wit, that its interventions when it comes to informing would embed themselves more within contexts of continuities than of discontinuities.

References

Alexievich, S. (2013), *Second-Hand Time* (New York, Random House).

Apor, P., Horváth, S., and Mark, J. (2017), 'Introduction: Collaboration, cooperation, and political participation in the Communist regimes', in P. Apor, S. Horváth, and J. Mark (eds), *Secret Agents and the Memory of Everyday Collaboration in Communist Eastern Europe* (London, Anthem Press), 1–20.

Bílek, L. (2016), 'I undertake voluntarily ... – Residents, agents, informers and others: The State Security's secret collaborators, 1945–1989', in A. Medková (ed.), *Behind the Iron Curtain (4)* (Prague, Ústav pro studium totalitních režimů).

Bubeník, J. (2017), 'Kolaborace', in *Czech Encyclopedia of Sociology*, https://encyklopedie.soc.cas.cz/w/Kolaborace (accessed 14 June 2021).

---

[46] While no 'collaborator' with the Austrians, Švejk is certainly an adept social navigator, somewhat like Danny in Škvorecký's (1977) *The Engineer of Human Souls*.

[47] We were not able to find Kraus's StB file in the digital archives.

[48] In 1960 there was a general amnesty, and the majority of political prisoners convicted during the 1950s trials were to be rehabilitated and released from prisons and forced labour camps.

Cepl, V. (1997), 'The transformation of hearts and minds in eastern Europe', *Cato Journal*, 17, 229–234.

Darcy, S. (2019), *To Serve the Enemy: Informers, Collaborators, and the Laws of Armed Conflict* (Oxford, Oxford University Press).

David, R. (2018), *Communists and Their Victims* (Philadelphia, University of Pennsylvania Press).

De Baets, A. (2004), 'The dictator's secret zrchives: Rationales for their creation, destruction, and disclosure', in A. MacDonald and A. H. Hussen (eds), *Scholarly Environments: Centres of Learning and Institutional Contexts, 1560–1960* (Leuven/Paris/Dudley, Peeters), 181–96.

Drda, A. and Kroupa, M. (2017), *Normalizované životy* (Prague, Post Bellum).

Drumbl, M. (2016), 'Victims who victimise', *London Review of International Law*, 4, 217–46.

Dudai, R. (2012), 'Informers and the transition in Northern Ireland', *British Journal of Criminology*, 52, 32–54.

Espindola, J. (2015), *Transitional Justice after German Reunification: Exposing Unofficial Collaborators* (New York, Cambridge University Press).

Hašek, J. (1993 [1917]), *The Good Soldier Švejk*, trans. C. Parrott ([n.p.], Everyman).

Hauner, M. (2008), 'Crime and punishment in Communist Czechoslovakia: The case of General Heliodor Pika and his prosecutor Karel Vas', *Totalitarian Movements and Political Religions*, 9, 335–54.

Havel, V. (1991 [1979]), 'The power of the powerless', in V. Havel, *Open Letters* (London, Faber and Faber), 125–214.

Horák, J. (2019), 'Inspektoři pražské městské policie: Dva byli u StB, další studoval pod KGB v Moskvě', Aktualne.cz, https://zpravy.aktualne.cz/domaci/vlivni-muzi-praz ske-mestske-policie-jeden-byl-u-stb-dalsi-st/r~7fdbe078c11eaac60ac1f6b220ee8/ (accessed 20 November 2019).

Horne, C. (2014), 'The impact of lustration on democratization in postcommunist countries', *International Journal of Transitional Justice*, 8, 496–521.

Hrabal, B. (1990 [1976]), *Too Loud a Solitude*, trans. M. H. Heim (London, Abacus, 1993)

Křen, J. (2005), 'Dokumenty StB jako pramen poznání minulosti', *Soudobé dějiny*, 3–4, 708–33.

McDermott, K. (2015), *Communist Czechoslovakia, 1945-89: A Political and Social History* (London, Macmillan Education).

Moran, J. (1994), 'The Communist torturers of eastern Europe: Prosecute and punish or forgive and forget?', *Communist and Post-Communist Studies*, 27, 95–109.

Nedelsky, N. (2009), 'Czechoslovakia, and the Czech and Slovak Republics', in L. Stan (ed.), *Transitional Justice in Eastern Europe and the Former Soviet Union: Reckoning with the Communist Past* (London, Routledge), 37–76.

Obzina, J. (1978), *Guidelines for Work with the Collaborators of Counterintelligence: Order of Minister of Interior* (Prague, Czech Socialist Republic).

Paměť národa ([n.d.]a), 'František Kraus 1925, †2014', https://www.pametnaroda.cz/cs/kraus-frantisek-1925 (accessed 28 March 2020).

Paměť národa ([n.d.]b), 'Jiří Imlauf 1966', https://www.pametnaroda.cz/cs/imlauf-jiri-1966 (accessed 28 March 2020).

Rosenberg, T. (1995), 'Overcoming the Legacies of Dictatorship', *Foreign Affairs*, 74:3, 134–52.

Sartre, J. P. (2019), *Huis clos* (Paris, Gallimard).

Siklova, J. (1996), 'Lustration or the Czech way of screening', *East European Constitutional Review*, 5, 57–62.

Šimečka, M. (1984), *Obnovení pořádku* (London, Edice Rozmluvy).

Škvorecký, J. (1977), *The Engineer of Human Souls* (Dallas, Dalkey Archive Press, 1999).

Slachta, K. (2017), 'Unofficial collaborators in the tourism sector (GDR and Hungary)', in P. Apor, S. Horváth, and J. Mark (eds), *Secret Agents and the Memory of Everyday Collaboration in Communist Eastern Europe* (London, Anthem Press), 309–29.

Stan, L. (ed.) (2010), *Transitional Justice in Eastern Europe and the Former Soviet Union: Reckoning with the Communist Past* (Abingdon, Routledge).

Thiranagama, S., and Kelly, T. (2012), *Traitors: Suspicion, Intimacy, and the Ethics of State-Building* (Philadelphia, University of Pennsylvania Press).

Třešňák, P. and Hradílek, A. (2008), 'Milan Kundera's denunciation', Respekt cz, https://www.respekt.cz/respekt-in-english/milan-kundera-s-denunciation (accessed 23 December 2019).

Williams, K. (2001), 'The StB in Czechoslovakia, 1954–89', in K. Williams and D. Deletant (eds), *Security Intelligence Services in New Democracies: The Czech Republic, Slovakia and Romania* (London, Palgrave).

Williams K., Fowler, B., and Szczerbiak, A. (2005), 'Explaining lustration in central Europe: A "post-Communist politics" approach', *Democratization*, 12:1, 22–43.

Žáček, P. (2005), 'Ostrá zbraň Státní bezpečnosti: Spolupracovníci StB ve směrnicích pro agenturně operativní práci 1947–1989', https://www.ustrcr.cz/data/pdf/clanky/ostra-zbran-stb.pdf (accessed 31 January 2022).

6

Black Collaboration during American Slavery

ANDREA L. DENNIS*

Introduction

FROM THE MOMENT the first enslaved Africans arrived on the shores of what would become America, Blacks in the colonies and later America have been legally subjugated, socially marginalised, and viewed as disposable. Through 400 years spanning slavery, Reconstruction, Jim Crow, the Civil Rights and Black Power Movements, mass incarceration, and Black Lives Matter, Black people have continually lived with insecurity in every aspect of daily life concerning physical, emotional, social, and financial health. In addition to focusing on meeting basic needs for survival, Black people have also lived under the ever-present spectre of physical violence and death. Whether looking at the innumerable physical and sexual atrocities suffered by Blacks during slavery, the thousands of Blacks lynched by Whites post-Emancipation into the mid-20th century, the untold numbers of Blacks who have died slowly in the grip of mass incarceration, or all the Black lives lost as a consequence of police violence and White citizen 'justice', Black lives in America have been and continue to be devalued.

No matter the era or context, White society has relied on Black informing or snitching to regulate the Black community and carry out these cruelties. During slavery, White slaveholders and Whites more broadly looked to enslaved and free Blacks to provide information on all manner of Black behavior that potentially undermined the interests of Whites and White society. During the Civil Rights and Black Power Movements of the 1950s through the 1970s, J. Edgar Hoover's Federal

* This chapter is adapted from an earlier work: A. L. Dennis, 'A snitch in time: Black informing during slavery', *Marquette Law Review*, 97 (2013), 279–334.

Bureau of Investigation (FBI) created the Counter Intelligence Program aimed at infiltrating, surveilling, undermining, extinguishing, and ultimately bringing down movement leaders (such as the Revd Dr Martin Luther King, Jr, Malcolm X, Huey P. Newton, and Fred Hampton, to name a few) and the movements themselves. Mass incarceration of Black people, particularly young Black men, has relied extensively on snitching and cooperation, i.e. providing information about the alleged criminal activities of others who in turn are prosecuted and incarcerated. Most recently, the FBI and local police forces have used informants to monitor and infiltrate Black Lives Matter activities.

Whether in popular consciousness or everyday conversation, Black cooperators are routinely reviled in the Black community. Labelled house slave, Uncle Tom, Mammy, sellout, Oreo, snitch, informant, cooperator, or collaborator, their loyalty to the Black community is questioned. At the extreme, they are deemed traitors to their race. Often, all manner of cooperation is lumped together indiscriminately and unfavourably characterised.

American scholars and policy-makers grapple with the implications of these perspectives. From a normative stance, academics enquire: have Black informants committed a wrongful act? Are they morally condemnable? Should they inform or not? Policy-makers, confronted with Black community members who are categorically resistant to informing and disdainful of informants, seek to disentangle and destigmatise particular types of cooperation that might be viewed as productive.

As with collaboration in other contexts, these perceptions and the resulting struggles may be rooted in history. As Ron Dudai and Kevin Hearty explain in Chapter 8, informerphobia, a result of centuries-long Irish Republicanism, is deeply entrenched in Northern Ireland, producing violence, interfering with policing, and permanently stigmatising individuals. Similarly, the existence of an anti-snitching ethos in the Black community may be rooted in historical experiences during antebellum slavery.

This chapter considers whether Black informants are worthy of the condemnation and hatred heaped upon them, and it does so through the context of antebellum slavery, the point of departure for the Black experience in America.

Answers to these questions may be found by reference to theoretical principles concerning evil and 'grey zones'. Claudia Card's theory of a 'grey zone' is that people 'who are simultaneously victims and perpetrators' in atrocities find themselves 'complicit with the very evils they have suffered' (Card 2004: 11, 26). Voluntary and calculated choices of victims that maximise survival 'seem justifiable' (216). On the other hand, a victim's decisions that are made out of sympathy or attachment are 'problematic', i.e. potentially evil (216–17). As Card articulates, victim status does not immunise one from doing evil or equate to innocence in the grey zone, and victims still have moral agency and can resist engaging in echoing oppression (217–18).

A necessary antecedent to applying Card's theory to Black collaboration during slavery is unearthing information about the potential motivations of enslaved and free Blacks during slavery with respect to informing. This chapter gathers that information, drawing on primary archival sources, such as legislative enactments and records, autobiographies and memoirs, and oral history projects, as well as secondary sources. Particular attention is paid to potential collaboration by 'house slaves', often the subject of vitriol and about whom many myths exist, as well as informing in connection with insurrections.

Recreating accounts based on ancient documents and reporter memories may present concerns of accuracy, reliability, and bias. Additionally, the identity of the storyteller or involvement of an intermediary in narrating events raises, as Ksenija Bilbija details in Chapter 3, questions of who is permitted to tell the story and who determines whether someone is a collaborator. However, confidence in the information collected herein ideally derives from the similar or same chronicling in other sources.

Finally, the chapter filters this information through Card's theoretical lens of 'grey zones'.

Motivating Collaboration

This section catalogues and exemplifies significant internal and external factors, though surely not all factors, conceivably influencing the decision of whether to inform. The factors are broadly grouped into three categories – pro-informing, anti-informing, and wafflers – although this taxonomy is probably imperfect.

Two points are worth noting. First, determination of the actual motive or motives animating a potential informant is elusive, given that ascertainment of an individual's actual mindset is often unknowable, even in the face of expressed positions or apparent behaviour. Second, the subcategories of plausible motivations set forth herein are not necessarily mutually exclusive. As Drumbl and Hola likewise explain in their Chapter 5 on informers in Communist Czechoslovakia, for any particular individual or circumstance, multiple or mixed motives may apply.

Pro-Informing

Owner loyalty and favour. Discussions of snitching invariably raise questions of loyalty (Rich 2012: 1518–23). To whom does the informant owe their loyalty? Themself? Their community? Which community? The state? Whose loyalty are they betraying by informing? Is that betrayal acceptable?

Some who were enslaved viewed their interests as being aligned with those of their owners (Aptheker 1983: 62). Thus, fidelity to their owners caused some of these persons to inform. For example, Scipio, the 'body servant' of his owner, revealed a potential uprising in Camden, South Carolina, in 1816 in order to save his owner (Jones 1990: 190; Cornish 2007: 97–8). Scipio was freed as a result of his efforts but continued to work for his owner, although it is unclear whether he was paid or unpaid for his work (Jones 1990: 190).

Jim, an enslaved person, presents another example of the extent to which the enslaved might go to protect an owner's interest. Jim killed another enslaved person who was attacking property that Jim's owner had entrusted to Jim. The same man owned both Jim and the victim. Jim was charged with murder. His owner, the Revd Richard Johnson, petitioned the legislature for Jim's release (Jones 1990: 190–1, 128).

Akin to those who informed because of owner loyalty are those Blacks who did so because of a poor self-image and in an effort to earn White recognition and respect (Jacobs 1861: 181; Jones 1990: 190). Harriet Jacobs, as she hid from her owner in her grandmother's attic, observed: 'I was warned to keep extremely quiet, because two guests had been invited. One was the town constable, and the other was a free colored man, who tried to pass himself off for white, and who was always ready to do any mean work for the sake of currying favor with white people' (Jacobs 1861: 181).

Lew Cheney, a man enslaved in Louisiana who organised a party of enslaved Blacks to escape to Mexico, betrayed his group when he became 'convinced of the ultimate failure of his project, in order to curry favor with his master'. Cheney was apparently successful in this pivot, as he was eventually rewarded for his betrayal. Many of those from his group, on the other hand, were captured and hurriedly executed (Lester 1968: 118).

Self-preservation. When investigating alleged misconduct by an enslaved person, an owner might have given the enslaved person a choice between dying or providing information about another slave's misconduct (Stowe 2011 [1852]: 514–15). Quite naturally, some chose to live (Jones 1990: 127). In a similar vein, some enslaved people informed in order to prevent or stop Whites from torturing them (Jones 1990: 168, 179; Brophy 2013: 1864–5).

The fallout from Nat Turner's rebellion represents such a scenario. After learning of Turner's planned insurrection, Whites in Harriet Jacobs's South Carolina town were in fear for their lives (Jacobs 1861: 97). So, they set about squelching any such plans in their town by calling in poor, non-slaveholding Whites to search the houses of and torture both enslaved and free Blacks (Jacobs 1861: 97–8). Jacobs wrote: 'Poor creatures! They thought it was going to be a holiday. I was informed of the true state of affairs, and imparted it to the few I could trust. Most gladly would I have proclaimed it to every slave; but I dared not. All could not be relied on. Mighty is the power of the torturing lash' (97).

Recognising the choice between withstanding torture and informing, Jacobs further commented: 'One black man, who had not fortitude to endure scourging, promised to give information about the conspiracy. But it turned out that he knew nothing at all. He had not even heard the name of Nat Turner. The poor fellow had, however, made up a story, which augmented his own sufferings and those of the colored people' (103).

Self-protection also focused on avoiding responsibility for alleged misconduct. Thus, someone who was enslaved might inform in order to divert or deflect blame from himself (Jones 1990: 128). Lew Cheney, who earlier served as an exemplar of a 'house slave' seeking to curry favour with Whites (Northup 1975 [1853]: 188–9), was also self-interested. He organised a group of slaves to run away to Mexico. However, when he became 'convinced of the ultimate failure of his project', he sought to avoid the negative consequences that would naturally follow if it were learnt that he had organised the mass escape (Lester 1968: 118): 'Departing secretly from the encampment, he proclaimed among the planters the number[s] collected in the swamp, and, instead of stating truly the object they had in view, asserted their intention was to emerge from their seclusion the first favorable opportunity, and murder every white person along the bayou.' Cheney was rewarded while his campmates were captured and executed.

New York City's Negro Plot Trials of 1741 tell the story of northern enslaved people who informed – sometimes falsely – to deflect criminal attention, as Whites were vigorously investigating and prosecuting slaves for a perceived insurrection (Hoffer 2003). In 1741, a series of fires started throughout New York City (Hoffer 2003: 71–3). Whites began to believe that enslaved Blacks – and possibly some Whites – were starting the fires. Hysteria reigned, and Whites targeted Blacks to round up and arrest (2, 73–4). A grand jury was impaneled to investigate (74–80). Trials lacking due process – though granting more process than normally accorded the enslaved – were quickly held, resulting in many convictions and executions (81–129).

In the course of investigating and adjudicating the fires and alleged conspiracy, monetary rewards and pardons were offered to Whites and Blacks for informa-tion: a free non-Black could receive £100 for information; a free Black could receive £45 and be pardoned; and an enslaved Black could be freed, receive £20, and be pardoned, while his owner could receive £25 (Hoffer 2003: 75).

Additionally, slaves who came under suspicion informed to protect themselves from harsh punishment by diverting attention to others who were also enslaved (Hoffer 2003: 125–8). For example, Sandy – the first slave to confess to the grand jury – was able to save his life through informing (8–89, 91, 116). Quaco and Cuffee, however, who were both convicted after trial, were still executed after confessing at the last moment (102–3).

Scholars today debate whether there was an actual concerted plot by slaves to burn New York City, a hoax, or something in-between (Hoffer 2003: 1–9). Nonetheless, the available evidence confirms that slaves were motivated by self-preservation to inform on other slaves.

Criminal leniency. Enslaved persons who were involved in unlawful conspir-acies obtained sentencing leniency, such as the avoidance of execution, by testifying against other enslaved individuals (Cobb 1858: 3, 226, 230). For example, John was convicted of conspiracy and attempted insurrection after he confessed and pleaded guilty. Having testified against others who were enslaved, he was sentenced to be sold out of the United States rather than executed, which was the usual punishment for his crime (Enslow 1831). In another instance, Paul, also known as Figaro, was involved in an insurrection plot in Charleston, South Carolina. He testified against others who were convicted and executed. Paul's sentence, however, was also reduced from execution to sale out of the country (Delaire 1798). Similarly, Moses, one of the early participants in the Nat Turner rebellion in Southampton, Virginia, was caught and charged with murder and conspiracy (Brophy 2013: 1825). He, however, provided important testimony against other enslaved persons (Brophy 2013: 1825n45). Though he was convicted and sentenced to death in spite of his cooperation, the court 'recommended that the governor commute his sentence to transportation out of the state' (1825). Finally, a Louisiana court expressly held that a jury had the discretion to commute a capital sentence, presumably for informing, if it so desired.[1]

Because enslaved people might attack or kill their owners, owners viewed awareness of what was happening among their slaves as a vital preventive measure. Some owners were desperate for information to protect their personal safety (Aptheker 1983: 63). For example, Martha L. Nelson, a slave owner, wrote to her state Governor seeking a pardon for a valuable informant: '[He] would inform on the negroes, as soon as any white person would, if he knew or suspected anything wrong was plan[n]ing among them ... I write, beseeching you to pardon my servant ... such a servant ought not to be sent away particularly in these perilous times of insurrection' (Aptheker 1983: 63).

Manumission. The prospect of manumission was a strong motivator for informing (Jones 1990: 127). In the early years of slavery, owners could free enslaved persons by will as a private matter (Friedman 1985: 219). Over time, legislatures began to regulate manumission: freeing people became illegal except with government approval, whether executive or legislative (McCord 1840: 459; Finkelman 1988: 59–60).

Only the most helpful of informants were eligible for manumission. In Louisiana as of 1831, with legislative approval, an owner could emancipate an enslaved individual 'for long, faithful or important services rendered to himself or family' (Finkelman 1988: 73). Similarly, the Louisiana Code provided in 1851 that governors could free, as well as pardon or commute the sentences of, Black informants.[2] The Virginia legislature permitted freedom for 'meritorious services, to be judged of by the Governor and Council'. Revelation of a slave conspiracy constituted '[m]eritorious services' (Ritchie 1819: 433–434n; Higginbotham 1978: 48).

In South Carolina, an enslaved Black person could be emancipated if 'in actual invasion, [he] kill[s] or take[s] one or more of our enemies', the Act going on to say that 'the same [on proving], by any white person, [that this was] done by him, shall, for his reward, at the charge of the public, have and enjoy his freedom, for such his taking or killing, as aforesaid' (McCord 1840: 349, 350). Finally, in North

---

[1] *State v. Slave Jack* (1859) 14 La. Ann. 385.
[2] *McDowell v. Couch* (1851) 6 La. Ann. 365, 370.

Carolina, emancipation could be sought for informants who revealed the where-abouts of runaways (Banks 1792). Toney, owned by Samuel White, learnt of a plan by slaves and the owner of a ship to convey the slaves north. Toney revealed the plan and some of the participants were thwarted. To reward his revelation, a group of 16 White community members petitioned the court to free Toney (Banks 1792).

White communities sought state-based rewards for slaves whose informing efforts protected the White community's safety by preventing slave insurrection. The following are descriptions from three legislative or judicial petitions filed by Whites seeking rewards for slave informing. First, a slave named Abram, owned by William Kirk, revealed an alleged plot by Blacks to 'massacre' Whites in the community, thereby preventing the insurrection and resulting in punishment of those (allegedly) involved. For his efforts, 92 community members petitioned the South Carolina Senate to reward Abram for his 'highly meritorious conduct', 'fidelity and services'. Additionally, if the Senate determined to emancipate Abram, the petitioners asked that Kirk be compensated 'handsome[ly]' for the loss of Abram's labor (McCumbee 1803).

Second, a slave named Henrietta overheard an enslaved man named Charles conspiring to start an insurrection. Henrietta reported what she heard to her owner, Ann Paisley. Charles was thus arrested, and upon being confronted with Henrietta's information, he confessed, implicating other Blacks. Because of her informing, '[B]lacks were very generally excited' against Henrietta and one even attacked her, leading to his execution. Because of her 'fealty' and need for protection, six members of the community petitioned the legislature to free Henrietta and her child, provide Paisley a stipend, and indemnify Paisley for the loss of Henrietta (Wilson 1829).

Third, a slave named Monday, several other enslaved people, and three White men, who were selling the slaves as part of an estate sale, were travelling in Georgia. Some of the slaves conspired to kill the White men and anyone who would not join the conspiracy. Having armed themselves to carry out the plan, they awakened Monday to enlist his involvement. He refused to join, whereupon the conspirators tried to silence him. They were unsuccessful, and Monday managed to run and tell of the plot, saving the White men's lives. As a result, the petitioner – one of the saved men – asked the court to emancipate Monday (Rogers and Moring 1812).

Monetary reward. Surprisingly, monetary rewards to enslaved informants – either in conjunction with or distinct from emancipation – were available (Aptheker 1983: 143; Hoffer 2003: 75). Blacks as a class were prevented by law from both personal freedom and possession of property, thereby ensuring and fortifying their complete marginalisation (Cobb 1858: 3, 235, 237). The permissibility of a monetary reward for informing thus reveals the lengths to which Whites were willing to go in order to obtain highly valuable information. Monetary rewards could also serve as a strong motivator to enslaved individuals (Jones 1990: 127).

As with manumission, an enslaved person entitled to a monetary reward had to have performed exceptional acts (McCord 1840: 352, 362).

In recognition of the concern for personal safety, legislatures – such as those in Georgia and South Carolina – enacted statutory provisions rewarding slaves who provided information regarding poisonings by slaves. South Carolina's 1751 Code provided a £4 reward for information regarding the attempt to poison an owner that resulted in conviction (McCord 1840: 420, 423). In the 1770 and 1848 Georgia Codes, a slave who informed about the poisoning of another received 20s per year till death, and on the day he received the reward was excused from work (Hotchkiss 1848: 841; Aptheker 1983: 143).

States also rewarded slaves for turning in runaways. For example, in South Carolina, a slave who informed on a runaway received money (McCord 1840: 343, 345, 352, 362).

Slaves who assisted slaveholders in capturing runaways received monetary rewards (Jones 1990: 168). As Georgia and South Carolina provided monetary rewards to slaves who revealed poisonings (McCord 1840: 420, 423; Aptheker 1983: 143), so too did South Carolina for slaves who disclosed stolen property (McCord 1840: 365, 367).

Slaves who betrayed insurrections received monetary rewards (Jones 1990: 179). In 1822, the South Carolina legislature emancipated Peter Desverneys, who revealed the Denmark Vesey insurrection plot (see later in the chapter, 126–7). In addition to his freedom, Desverneys was awarded $50 per year (Desverneys 1857). In 1857, he petitioned the legislature for an increase in his annuity on account of old age and poor health. He was supported by multiple members of the community (Desverneys 1857).

Anti-Informing

Communal solidarity and resistance. If a slave viewed loyalty to the Black commu-nity as being of prime importance, they might also take the position that refusing to inform constituted evidence of and reinforced communal solidarity and resistance against oppression. Professor Norrece T. Jones contends that historical sources in South Carolina overwhelmingly support the conclusion that slaves who helped runaways did so voluntarily and revelled in doing so (Jones 1990: 168). His pos-ition stands in stark contrast to Professor Eugene Genovese's claim that 'slaves often refused to betray organized runaways not because of a sense of solidarity but because of fear of ghastly reprisals' (Jones 1990: 168). Both are probably correct.

In his narrative, Frederick Douglass (1845: 19) opined that a slave who refused to inform was demonstrating fidelity to both the Black community and humanity at large:

> The slaveholders have been known to send in spies among their slaves, to ascertain their views and feelings in regard to their condition. The frequency of this has had the effect to establish among the slaves the maxim, that a still tongue makes a wise head. They suppress the truth rather than take the consequences of telling it, and in so doing prove themselves a part of the human family.

Further, Douglass related a story he heard when he was a free man in the North (Douglass 1845: 114–15). As he writes it, Douglass's tone indicates pleasant surprise at the lengths to which escaped slaves would go to protect each other from being sold back into slavery:

> I found the colored people much more spirited than I had supposed they would be. I found among them a determination to protect each other from the blood-thirsty kidnapper, at all hazards. Soon after my arrival, I was told of a circumstance which illustrated their spirit. A colored man and a fugitive slave were on unfriendly terms. The former was heard to threaten the latter with informing his master of his whereabouts. Straightaway a meeting was called among the colored people, under the stereotyped notice, 'Business of importance!' The betrayer was invited to attend. The people came at the appointed hour, and organized the meeting by appointing a very religious old gentleman as president, who, I believe, made a prayer, after which he addressed the meeting as follows: 'Friends, we have got him here, and I would recommend that you young men just take him outside the door, and kill him!' With this, a number of them bolted at him; but they were intercepted by some more timid than themselves, and the betrayer escaped their vengeance, and has not been seen in New Bedford since. I believe there have been no more such threats, and should there be hereafter, I doubt not that death would be the consequence. (Douglass 1845: 115).

Protection of others. Closely related to communal solidarity was the desire of a slave to protect another by not informing. Again, Frederick Douglass's autobiographical writings are informative. Before narrating how he escaped to freedom, Douglass sets forth a caveat regarding his storytelling:

> I deem it proper to make known my intention not to state all the facts connected with the transaction. My reasons for pursuing this course may be understood from the following: First, were I to give a minute statement of all the facts, it is not only possible, but quite probable, that others would thereby be involved in the most embarrassing difficulties. Secondly, such a statement would most undoubtedly induce greater vigilance on the part of the slaveholders than has existed heretofore among them; which would, of course, be the means of guarding a door whereby some dear brother bondsman might escape his galling chains. (Douglas 1845: 100)

Communal ostracism and retaliation. As mentioned, Professor Eugene Genovese claimed that 'slaves often refused to betray organized runaways ... because of fear of ghastly reprisals' (Jones 1990: 168). Plenty of evidence exists from a variety of sources that slaves who informed on others were stigmatised by the Black community and faced violent physical retaliation (Jones 1990: 118). According to Jones, all slaves knew that revealing slave misconduct, with limited exceptions, would be viewed as 'sacrilegious and sinful'. Even Whites were aware of this viewpoint (125).

A justice of the Tennessee Supreme Court – undoubtedly White – confirmed both the non-violent and violent repercussions in a case in which an enslaved informant – Isaac – was allegedly killed by another slave – Jim. In an opinion, the justice wrote reviewing Jim's conviction:

> The truth seems to be that Isaac had not only excited the enmity of George and Jim, but he seems to have lost caste with the other negroes in the neighborhood. He had

combined with the white folks to betray George to the sheriff, and it was thought he
was also engaged to apprehend Jim. – This was no slight offence in their eyes: that
one of their own color, subject to a like servitude, should abandon the interests of his
caste, and, for hire, betray black folks to the white people, rendered him an object
of general aversion. Hence it was, that George and Jim felt so little hesitation in the
utterance of their threats; and hence it was, that Cindy did not wish to destroy Jim for
such a fellow.[3]

Slave owners too were aware that slaves suspected of or found to be collaborating
were subject to being ostracised, assaulted, or killed. Petitions formally filed on
behalf of slaves by Whites hinted that those who informed on slaves faced or feared
retaliation by Blacks (Bolah 1824; Wilson 1829). For these reasons, slave owners
would protect the identities of their informants (Jones 1990: 118–19). For example,
in Camden, South Carolina, in 1816, a slave revealed a conspiracy scheduled for 4
July 1816 (Aptheker 1983: 257). Ultimately, the legislature freed him, awarded him
a life pension of $50, and paid his owner $1,100 (258). The enslaved person asked
his owner never to reveal his name because he did not want to have 'to leave this
country, and he knew the negroes would not let him live here' (257).

Wafflers

Communal regulation. While enslaved people may have refused to cooperate as a
measure of communal solidarity and resistance, at times they found it necessary
to inform in order to ensure the security of the community. Most times, enslaved
communities internally controlled miscreants – so called 'bad' men (Genovese
1974: 625) – in order to protect each other and because slave owners ignored
the negative behaviour of slaves unless it affected owners' property and financial
interests. However, when internal communal strife reached a level that was beyond
their ability to control, or desire to control, slaves turned to their White owners to
regulate communal behaviour. To initiate the involvement of an owner, a slave had
to reveal the offending conduct (Genovese 1974: 625–7, 629).

What type of behaviour or person merited this tactic? Bully slaves who
assaulted other slaves would be revealed. Those who taught slave children immoral
behaviour, such as how to gamble, were subject to outing (Genovese 1974: 627).
A slave who shirked responsibilities, thus forcing others to do more work, and a
slave whose behaviour might cause an owner to exact penalty upon the entire community, could be handed over to an owner. In all these instances, the 'bad' slave
would force the normally silent slave into invoking White protection by telling on
their caste mate (Genovese 1974: 629).

Religion. In the early days of slavery, Whites did not expose slaves to religion for
a variety of reasons, including the belief that slaves did not need religion and the fear

---

[3] *Jim v. State* (1844) 24 Tenn. (5 Hum.) 145, 151.

that they would learn to read and write (Jones 1990: 131). Eventually, Whites believed that slaves who learnt religion would be more subservient and that religion could be a useful tool in maintaining the institution of slavery (131–2). White religious leaders strictly controlled Blacks' access to religion, and cultivated and enlisted Black religious leaders to assist in detecting and investigating slave misconduct (143–44).

Slaves who embraced a religious life told church authorities about formerly private matters handled within the enslaved community (Jones 1990: 144–5). Some religious slaves would reveal both moral crimes (e.g. adultery, theft) and political crimes (e.g. not working, being rebellious, running away) (143, 145–6). For example, according to records of the Salem Presbyterian Church dated 28 August 1831, 'Cato Servant of John Shaw, was suspended for Six months for an assault made upon one of the Church members. Jack servant of R. Witherspoon, was suspended for six months for charging the above named Cato with theft and Causing the assault' (143).

Others, though religious, distinguished between moral and political crimes, with the latter not being subject to revelation (Jones 1990: 146). Interestingly, for those who refused to betray political crimes, religion also provided the justification. Some slaves believed it a deific decree not to reveal the whereabouts of runaways, among other 'transgressions' (137).

House Slaves

Slaves who worked in the owner's household or performed in domestic roles were known as 'house slaves' (aka Mammies and Uncle Toms) (Jones 1990: 113). House slaves were known or reputed to be willing to do the bidding of White owners, including informing, to the detriment of other slaves (Aptheker 1983: 61–3). Today, house slaves are still vilified in the Black community, and being called a house slave is a serious insult (Zeitchik 2012).

Historian Herbert Aptheker (1983: 61) opined that spies and traitors primarily came from the domestic class. He contended that owners encouraged domestics to maintain distance from field workers (62). Presumably, the lack of connection to other slaves promoted owner loyalty over allegiance to community, and thus a willingness to protect an owner's interests (62–3). Aptheker's position finds support in both the reporting of unsuccessful slave rebellions and first-person slave accounts (62, 328; Bibb 2001 [1849]: 136).

Some house workers did reveal rebellion plots beforehand, allowing the plans to be quashed before getting underway. In South Carolina and Georgia in October 1835, '[a]n old domestic slave revealed … a plan for rebellion' (Aptheker 1983: 328). In East Feliciana, Louisiana, in December 1835, a 'confidential servant' revealed a 'serious' plot that was being undertaken by two Whites and 'a great many of the most favorite confidential servants', making 'it all the more disturbing' (329). Denmark Vesey's plot in Charleston, South Carolina, was undone in whole or part by a domestic slave. Beck, a young enslaved girl who considered herself a house slave, testified against alleged members of Nat Turner's rebellion in Virginia, although she did not betray the rebellion beforehand (French 2004: 37–40).

Likewise, some house slaves betrayed runaway slaves. Harriet Jacobs, who was secreted from her owner in the house of her grandmother, was twice almost betrayed by a domestic servant (Jacobs 1861: 168, 231–3):

> In stepped Jenny, the mischievous housemaid, who had tried to enter my room, when I was concealed in the house of my white benefactress ... I had slunk down behind a barrel, which entirely screened me, but I imagined that Jenny was looking directly at the spot
>
> ...
>
> Uncle Phillip was sent for, and he agreed with his mother in thinking that Jenny would inform Dr. Flint in less than twenty-four hours.
>
> ...
>
> Of course, the day was an anxious one for us all. But we concluded that if Jenny had seen me, she would be too wise to let her mistress know of it; and that she probably would not get a chance to see Dr. Flint's family till evening, for I knew very well what were the rules in that household. I afterwards believe that she did not see me; for nothing ever came of it, and she was one of those base characters that would have jumped to betray a suffering fellow being for the sake of thirty pieces of silver.

Henry Bibb, after escaping to freedom and writing his story, claimed: '[T]he domestic slaves are often found to be traitors to their own people, for the purpose of gaining favor with their masters; and they are encouraged and trained up by them to report every plot they know of being formed about stealing [anything], or running away, or [anything] of the kind; and for which they are paid' (Bibb 2001 [1849]: 146).

Similarly, ex-slave Austin Steward offered much criticism regarding house slaves (Lester 1968: 90–1). He claimed:

> [M]any of them are the most despicable tale-bearers and mischief-makers, who will, for the sake of the favor of his master or mistress, frequently betray his fellow slave, and by tattling, get him severely whipped; and for these acts ... he is often rewarded by his master, who knows it is for his interest to keep such ones about him; though he is sometimes obliged, in addition to a reward, to send him away, for fear of the ven-geance of the betrayed slaves. (Steward 1857: 32; Aptheker 1983: 62–3).

The quotes from Bibb and Steward indicate that they, and probably other enslaved people, believed Whites purposely cultivated informant behaviour among domestic slaves, rewarded betrayals by house slaves, and believed what their trusted servants told them. A domestic slave confirmed their beliefs: 'They taught us [domestics] to be against one another and no matter where you would go you would always find one that would be tattling and would have the white folks pecking on you. They would be trying to make it soft for themselves' (anon. 1958: 45, 47; Lester 1968: 90).

On the other hand, Jones has observed that the conclusion that domestic slaves would 'betray a fellow slave for little more than a hand-me-down garment or a flattering remark' is overblown (1990: 114, 118). The story of William Hayden, an enslaved domestic worker, supports Jones's proposition (Hayden 1969 [1846]: 77–8; Lester 1968: 91). Hayden acknowledged informing on his brethren. His motivation, though, was more significant than the mere receipt of prized clothing or owner favour: the rebellious slaves on whom he informed planned to kill him along with all present Whites (Hayden 1969 [1846]: 77–8):

> Sleeping in a room adjacent to the slaves, who were ironed, I discerned enough from their conversation to enable me to know that a mutiny was abroad, and that it was the intention of the slaves, in order to effect their freedom, to put to death all the whites on board, – and that I, too, was included, – owing to the attention that was paid me, – with the doomed. By jests and cheerfulness with them, however, I gathered from their detached hints, their every movement. That they had even then provided themselves with a file from the lot of Blacksmith tools on board, and that many were at that moment, free from their chains. This information I immediately carried to my master; and after ascertaining the truth of my statement, he had them again bound more firmly than ever.

Notwithstanding the first-hand accounts of slaves, without more data it is arguably either speculative or erroneous to conclude that most Black informants were domestic slaves or that overwhelmingly domestic slaves were informants. Undoubtedly, domestic slaves may have had special or greater incentives to inform than other slaves (e.g. owner loyalty, preservation of status). They may also have had more opportunity and faced great pressure to betray their fellow slaves because of proximity to owners who sought to use them as informants.

As a class, however, it is unclear that they were actually more likely to inform or more likely to be informants than other Blacks. All enslaved people – including domestics – had to be cognisant of the repercussions from other slaves if they informed. At a minimum, they faced ostracism, and at worst, death, and their owner might have been unwilling or unable to protect them from either. Further, at some point all slaves probably needed the benefit of a slave code of silence, for much behaviour could be deemed misconduct by owners. And while some domestic slaves might have had few close relationships with other slaves, others probably had relationships worth prioritising. Thus, many domestics who could have informed on another slave would have had strong incentives not to do so.

Insurrections

White efforts to promote informing and Black informants contributed to division and distrust within, and inaction by, the Black community during slavery. Escaped slave Frederick Douglass emphatically proclaimed: 'The motto which I adopted when I started from slavery was this – "Trust no man!" I saw in every white man an enemy, and in almost every colored man cause for distrust' (Douglass 1845: 98).

Douglass was probably not alone in his perspective, although he may have been the most public voice on the topic.

If slaves distrusted each other, then Jones's claim that the potential for betrayals did more to deter rebellions than the lack of weapons, information, or organisation is not surprising (1990: 182, 191). According to Jones, as far as slaves were concerned, it appeared true that rebellions were always betrayed beforehand (191).

The many infamous and less well-known rebellions that were squelched because of Black informants support this contention. Consequently, it is understandable if many slaves completely avoided rebellious efforts because they reasonably expected their efforts to be unsuccessful.

Even for those slaves willing to contemplate organised resistance, the few rebellions that were successful, in whole or part, reveal how difficult it was to keep a rebellion-in-waiting from being betrayed and forestalled. Such difficulty could serve as a strong disincentive to act. The Nat Turner Rebellion in 1831 in Southampton, Virginia, is the most well-known, successful slave-led rebellion (Larson [n.d.]; Tragle 1973). Ultimately, Turner was captured alive, and before his execution, he recounted the events to Thomas Gray, who officially recorded Turner's confession (Turner and Gray 1832: 3–4). Assuming the credibility of Turner's confession to Gray and the accuracy of Gray's work, Turner's version of events reveals the great lengths he went to in order to keep his plans secret, and how luck was sometimes necessary to avoid other slaves pre-emptively revealing information to Whites (Turner and Gray 1832: 10–11).

Turner believed God had commanded him to rebel and that he was not to tell anyone until he received a sign. When he received the sign, he told 'four in whom [he] had the greatest confidence, (Henry, Hark, Nelson, and Sam)'. They worked together to come up with plans but rejected them all. Turner then received another sign that told him they could wait no longer. So, the group agreed on 20 August 1831 to meet the next evening over dinner to finalise a plan. When the five met, they were joined by Will and Jack (Turner and Gray 1832; Larson [n.d.]). Turner provided no explanation as to how Will and Jack came to be invited, except that Jack 'was only a tool in the hands of Hark' (Turner and Gray 1832: 10–11). They all agreed to start the insurrection that night – Sunday – at the house of Turner's master and in fact did so (10–11). Their killing spree began and spread (11–14). Other slaves joined as they went along; the group numbered 15 men, then about 40, then 50 or 60 members (12–14).

Eventually the group encountered White resistance that forced them to separate (Turner and Gray 1832: 14–15). Turner sent two men (Jacob and Nat) to find Henry, Sam, Nelson, and Hark and tell them to meet him where they had had dinner the Sunday before (16–17). By Wednesday, when no one had joined him and he saw White men riding around looking as though they were searching for someone, Turner 'concluded Jacob and Nat had been taken, and compelled to betray' him. He hid in the woods for six weeks and was only discovered because a dog came across his cave, where Turner had a piece of meat. When the dog passed by the cave again, this time accompanied by two slaves, the dog alerted them to the cave.

Turner thought he was discovered and so made himself known. The two slaves ran off and Turner knew 'they would betray' him. So he left that hiding place and was free for two more weeks before being discovered (17).

Slave owners and Whites more generally placed high value on the willingness of Blacks to inform on rebels. Evidence of such high value can be found in the granting of freedom to some slaves who revealed insurrections.

Researchers have substantiated numerous instances in which planned rebellions were betrayed beforehand by slaves (Aptheker 1983: 170, 173–4, 189, 222; Jones 1990: 179). Indeed, as indicated earlier, Jones (1990: 191) has noted that many enslaved Blacks believed rebellions were always betrayed beforehand. Two well-known rebellions that were betrayed before they got under way include the Gabriel Prosser rebellion in Richmond, Virginia, in 1800 and the aforementioned Denmark Vesey rebellion in Charleston, South Carolina, in 1822 (Bennett 1993: 125–31).

During the spring and summer of 1800, Prosser planned his rebellion (Bennett 1993: 125). By August, several thousand enslaved people had been enlisted (126). On the day it was to begin, 30 August 1800, Tom and Pharaoh betrayed the plot to their White owner, who in turn told authorities (Aptheker 1983: 221; Bennett 1993: 126). The governor called out the militia. Prosser did not know of the betrayal, and that night approximately 1,000 slaves gathered. A thunderstorm prevented them from attacking when the storm washed out points of entry into the city. So, Prosser postponed the attack (Bennett 1993: 126). He fled by boat but was located in Norfolk, Virginia, on 25 September 1800, by 'two Negroes' who ultimately betrayed him (Aptheker 1983: 222). Prosser and many co-conspirators were arrested before they could reassemble to carry out the insurrection (Bennett 1993: 126).

As we have seen, Denmark Vesey sought to strike Charleston, South Carolina, in 1822 (Bennett 1993: 127–31). Peter Poyas was Vesey's second-in-command (128). Poyas identified house slaves as the most likely betrayers (129). 'He told one of his recruiting agents to "take care and don't mention it to those waiting men who receive presents of old coats, etc., from their masters, or they'll betray us: I will speak to them" ' (129; Aptheker 1983: 270–1). Notwithstanding Poyas's command, some slaves ignored his instruction because they knew of house slaves 'willing to poison their masters' wells' (Jones 1990: 178; Aptheker 1983: 270–1). The attack was planned for 16 July 1822 (Bennett 1993: 130). An estimated 9,000 slaves had been enlisted (Bennett 1993: 129).

Authorities detected the plan in the last week of May when an enslaved man named William Paul tried to recruit Peter Devaney, a house slave (Bennett 1993: 130; Jones 1990: 179). Devaney betrayed the group by consulting a free Black named William Pencil who advised Devaney to tell his master, which he did (Jones 1990: 179; Aptheker 1983: 271). However, Devaney was only able to give the authorities a barebones plan (Bennett 1993: 130). Recruits knew only the name of their assigned leader and general plans. Only leaders of the plot knew details, in order to prevent the arrest or betrayal of one person from resulting in the collapse of the entire plan (Bennett 1993:129).

For two weeks, Vesey continued to plan and the government authorities investigated (Bennett 1993: 130). He moved up the date of attack (131). On the Friday before the new scheduled day, the group was betrayed again, this time by an enslaved person who knew plans and some names (131). George Wilson, an enslaved leader in the African church, also provided information (Jones 1990: 179).

Vesey and five leaders were tried, convicted, and executed on 2 July 1822. 'Only one leader confessed', while all others 'remained silent' (Bennett 1993: 131). Devaney and Wilson were emancipated by the legislature and given lifetime pensions (Jones 1990: 179). Pencil received $1,000 and a tax exemption (Aptheker 1983: 271n21; Jones 1990: 179).

Both before and after the planned Prosser and Vesey rebellions, slaves betrayed in advance many lesser-known insurrections. An early instance is the betrayal by Will of a conspiracy by slaves in Surrey and James City Counties, Virginia, in 1710 (Aptheker 1983: 170). A few years later, in 1713 in Goose Creek, South Carolina, a slave named Job revealed a conspiracy (173–4). In Charles Town, South Carolina in 1740, a slave named Peter revealed a conspiracy 24 hours before it was to be initiated, allowing slaveholders to capture the rebels and execute them (189).

In 1835 in South Carolina, Georgia, and Louisiana, domestic slaves revealed slave plots against Whites (Aptheker 1983: 328). In October 1837, in Rapides Parish, Louisiana, an enslaved man named Lewis revealed a conspiracy of slaves and free Blacks that was set to begin in Alexandria, Louisiana. His revelation led the conspiracy to be squelched. The state freed Lewis and rewarded him with $500 to 'establish himself in some distant community where he would be safe' (330).

In June 1853, in New Orleans, Louisiana, Albert, enslaved, asked George Wright, a free Black, to join a rebellion in the planning. Wright expressed interest and Albert took him to meet Dyson, a White teacher from Jamaica (Aptheker 1983: 343). Dyson, trusting Wright, urged him to join. Wright seemed committed, but immediately revealed the plot, leading police to Albert (343–4). Years later and further north, in July 1859, in Clarksburg, Virginia (now West Virginia), a female slave revealed a plot (351).

Condemnable?

Having compiled a taxonomy of the conceivable motivations of Black informants during slavery, let us now revisit the questions presented at the outset of the chapter. Have Black cooperators who cooperated with Whites during slavery committed a wrongful act? Are they morally condemnable?

As mentioned at the outset, Claudia Card's (2004) work on atrocities and evil offers a helpful perspective. Card explores 'grey zones', drawn from the experiences of Primo Levi (1988). A Holocaust death camp survivor, Levi coined the concept to describe spaces in which camp prisoners were given authority over other prisoners and rewarded for perpetrating evil upon their own people (Card 2004: 212). Card's work is an effort to understand the evil done to victims by perpetrators and 'the moral positions and responsibilities of those who inhabit gray zones' (Card 2004: 213).

Card identifies three features of grey zones:

> First, its inhabitants are victims of evil. Second, these inhabitants are implicated through their choices in perpetrating some of the same or similar evils on others who are already victims like themselves. And third, inhabitants of the gray zone act under extraordinary stress. Many of them have lost everything and everyone, and they face the threat of imminent and horrible death. (2004: 224)

The third feature – what Card calls the 'stress feature' – is necessary to 'distinguish gray zones from other mixtures of good and evil in our lives' (Card 2004: 224). For example, Card distinguishes 'gray areas' from 'gray zones'. Grey areas involve stress less than that of 'imminent and horrible death', such as 'when agents must choose under such conditions as intense or prolonged fear for basic security or their very lives or for the lives or basic security of loved ones' (224).

Victims occupying grey zones are innocent, undeserving of their suffering or situation with little or no ability to exercise discretion or exit the situation. They operate with a lack of clarity, making it unclear to what extent they may avoid harms and at what cost. They 'may have to make difficult, irreversible decisions quickly and in the absence of relevant information' (Card 2004: 225). They may appear to collaborate in order to resist. It may be difficult to assess threat level, ability to resist, or willingness to compromise (225–6).

Although oppression creates an inhospitable environment for developing or maintaining morality, Card is clear that victims in grey zones do not abandon morality, cease acting morally, or fail to hold others responsible (Card 2004: 213, 227). In fact, victims who are complicit with their oppressors may feel shame (213).

In terms of judging the complicit behaviour of victims, Card remarks that voluntary and calculated choices of victims that maximise survival 'seem justifiable' (Card 2004: 216). On the other hand, a victim's decisions that are made because of sympathy or attachment are 'problematic', i.e. potentially evil (216–17).

Unquestionably, antebellum slavery was a 'grey zone' occupied by innocent African or Black people – enslaved and free – who were daily forced to make morally perilous decisions concerning individual or communal concerns.

However, in this fraught context, it is difficult to gauge whether collaboration by victims – generally or in a particular instance – is condemnable. Involuntarily forced into lifelong servitude, completely disenfranchised, and continually faced with life-or-death circumstances, potential Black collaborators, in addition to practical considerations, confronted many ethical dilemmas. For example, was a Black person's individual life worth more or less than, or the same as, a White person's? Should the Black community's interest carry more weight than a single Black person's interest? How should freedom be measured if it comes at the cost of another's life? Do Black collaborators bear responsibility for the physical or psychic harm they may, or do, cause within the victim group? How should they be viewed when their decisions and actions undermine the collective action of the Black community?

Although Whites may have strongly incentivised Blacks to cooperate with their oppressors during slavery, not all Blacks became complicit. Seemingly, plenty of

Blacks did not inform despite the extremely stressful circumstances under which they lived. They protected runaways by helping them escape and not revealing their whereabouts. They maintained silence in order to prevent retaliation against community members. They refused to reveal rebellion plans in order to promote the greater cause of freedom.

Examples of non-complicit behaviour demonstrate victim autonomy and frustrate determinations as to whether Black informing can be forced into a right–wrong binary. If some refused to inform under extreme circumstances and their decisions are deemed right, should others be held to the same standard and their failures labelled wrong?

Conclusion

This chapter has explored whether Black informants during slavery – viewed by some, in retrospect, as traitors to their race – were condemnable.

During the American antebellum era, Black collaborators were vital to maintenance of the institution of slavery. They helped detect, investigate, and prosecute myriad and diverse behaviours by Blacks deemed antithetical to the interests of slaveholders and Whites more generally. Multiple factors probably influenced whether Blacks informed. Weighing in favour of informing were loyalty to Whites, preservation of one's life or status, communal self-regulation, attainment of liberty or criminal leniency, and financial reward. In contrast, communal solidarity, resistance ethic, fear of retaliation, and protection of others countenanced not informing. The impact of religious conviction seems to have depended on the individual or circumstance.

Should Black informants during slavery be damned as collaborationists, or freed from moral condemnation and allegations of disloyalty? The answer defies clear categorisation. Informing to survive the transatlantic slave trade and American slavery, two dark stains on the world and America, was arguably a necessary evil – neither moral nor immoral. Without question, victims and survivors of slavery existed in a space that was ethically grey. On one hand, and despite the dehumanising efforts of White society, they continued to be moral agents responsible for their acts that harmed their brethren. On the other hand, in light of the extreme circumstances, they might be forgiven or viewed as blameless for their injurious actions. Perhaps, adjudication of their behaviour in retrospect is an unnecessary and unfair exercise.

References

Anon. (1958), 'Unwritten history', in L. Hughes and A. Bontemps (eds), *The Book of Negro Folklore* (New York, Dodd, Mead), 45–52.
Aptheker, H. (1983), 'American negro slave revolts', in H. Marbury and W. H. Crawford (eds), *Digest of the Laws of the State of Georgia, from its Settlement as a British*

Province, in 1775, to the Session of the General Assembly in 1880, Inclusive (Savannah, Seymour, Woolhopter, & Stebbins), 61–3, 143, 170, 173–4, 189, 221–2, 257, 270–1, 273, 328, 330, 334, 343.

Banks, J. (1792), 'Petition to the County Court of Quarter Sessions for the County of Pasquotank, North Carolina from J. Banks et al.', in *Race, Slavery, and Free Blacks: Petitions to Southern Legislatures, 1775–1867*, Series 2, Part D, Reel 1, Frame 0138, PAR 21279202, microform (Lanham, MD, University Publications of America).

Bennett L., Jr (1993), *Before the Mayflower: A History of Black America* (New York, Penguin).

Bibb, H. (2001 [1849]), *Narrative of the Life and Adventures of Henry Bibb: An American Slave*, ed. C. J. Hegler (Madison, University of Wisconsin Press).

Bolah, L. (1824), 'Legislative petition from Lewis Bolah to the Senate and the House of Delegates of the Commonwealth of Virginia', in *Race, Slavery, and Free Blacks: Petitions to Southern Legislatures, 1777–1867*, at Series 1, Reel 18, Frame 0450, PAR 11682404, microform (Lanham, MD, University Publications of America).

Brophy, A. (2013), 'The Nat Turner trials', *North Carolina Law Review*, 91, 1817–80.

Card, C. (2004), *The Atrocity Paradigm: A Theory of Evil* (Oxford, Oxford University Press).

Cobb, T. (ed.) (1858), *An Inquiry into the Law of Negro Slavery in the United States of America* (Philadelphia, T. & J. W. Johnson).

Cornish, R. T. (2007), 'Camden, South Carolina, Plot (1816)', in J. Rodriguez (ed.), *Encyclopedia of Slave Resistance and Rebellion*, Vol. I, *A–N* (Westport, CT, Greenwood Press), 97–8.

Delaire, J. (1798), 'Legislative petition from James Delaire to President John Ward and the members of the Senate of South Carolina', in *Race, Slavery, and Free Blacks: Petitions to Southern Legislatures, 1777–1867*, at Series 1, Reel 8, Frame 0482, microform (Lanham, MD, University Publications of America).

Desverneys, P. (1857), 'Legislative petition from Peter Desverneys to the state of South Carolina, the Senate and House of Representatives sitting in general assembly', in *Race, Slavery, and Free Blacks: Petitions to Southern Legislatures, 1777–1867*, at Series 1, Reel 11, Frame 0617, microform (Lanham, MD, University Publications of America).

Douglass, F. (1845), 'Narrative of the life of Frederick Douglass, an American Slave', repr. in A. Appiah (ed.), *Early African-American Classics* (London, Bantam Classics, 1990).

Enslow, J. (1831), 'Legislative petition from Joseph Enslow to the President and members of the Senate of South Carolina', in *Race, Slavery, and Free Blacks: Petitions to Southern Legislatures, 1777–1867*, at Series 1, Reel 11, Frame 0007, microform (Lanham, MD, University Publications of America).

Finkelman, P. (ed.) (1988), *Statutes on Slavery: Slavery, Race, and the American Legal System 1700–1872* (New York/London, Garland).

French, S. (2004), *The Rebellious Slave: Nat Turner in American Memory* (New York, Houghton Mifflin Harcourt).

Friedman, L. (1985), *A History of American Law* (New York, Simon & Schuster)

Genovese, E. D. (1974), *Roll, Jordan, Roll: The World the Slaves Made* (New York, Pantheon).

Hayden, W. (1969 [1846]), *Narrative of William Hayden, Containing a Faithful Account of His Travels for a Number of Years, whilst a Slave, in the South* ([Philadelphia], [Rhistoric Publications]), 77–8.

Higginbotham. A., Jr (1978), *In the Matter of Color: Race and the American Legal Process: The Colonial Period* (Oxford, Oxford University Press).

Hoffer, P. C. (2003), *The Great New York Conspiracy of 1741: Slavery, Crime, and Colonial Law* (Lawrence, University Press of Kansas).

Hotchkiss, W. A. (ed.) (1848), *A Codification of the Statute Law of Georgia*, 2nd edn (Augusta, GA, Charles E. Grenville).

Jacobs, H. A. (1861), *Incidents in the Life of a Slave Girl*, ed. L. M. Child (Boston, MA, published for the author).

Jones, N. T., Jr (1990), *Born a Child of Freedom, yet a Slave* (Middletown, CT, Wesleyan University Press).

Larson, J. L. ([n.d.]), 'A rebellion to remember: The legacy of Nat Turner', *Documenting the American South, University of North Carolina*, http://docsouth.unc.edu/highlights/turner.html (accessed 14 June 2021).

Lester, J. (1968), *To Be a Slave* (New York, Dial Books for Young Children).

Levi, P. (1988), *The Drowned and the Saved* (New York, Simon & Schuster).

McCord, D. J. (ed.) (1840), *The Statutes at Large of South Carolina*, Vol. VII, *Acts Relating to Charleston (1685–2848), Courts (1721–1837), Slaves (1690–1835), and Rivers (1714–1817)*.

McCumbee, J. (1803), 'Legislative petition from John McCumbee et al. to the President and members of the Senate of South Carolina', in *Race, Slavery, and Free Blacks: Petitions to Southern Legislatures, 1777–1867*, at Series 1, Reel 9, Frame 0019, microform (University Publications of America).

Northup, S. (1975 [1853]), *Twelve Years a Slave*, ed. S. L. Eakin and J. Logsdon (Baton Rouge, Louisiana University Press).

Rich, M. L. (2012), 'Lessons of disloyalty in the world of criminal informants', *American Criminal Law Review*, 49, 1493–1539.

Ritchie, T. (1819), *The Revised Code of the Laws of Virginia: Being a Collection of All Such Acts of the General Assembly, of a Public and Permanent Nature, as Now Are in Force; with a General Index*, Vol. I (Richmond, VA, Thomas Ritchie).

Rogers, A. and Moring, H. (1812), 'Petition to the Court of Pleas for Wake County, North Carolina from Allen Rogers & Henry Moring', in *Race, Slavery, and Free Blacks: Petitions to Southern County Courts, 1775–1867*, at Series 2, Part D, Reel 1, Frame 0043, PAR 21200014, microform (University Publications of America).

Steward, A. (1857), *Twenty-Two Years a Slave, and Forty Years a Freeman: Embracing a Correspondence of Several Years, while President of Wilberforce Colony, London, Canada West* (Rochester, William Alling).

Stowe, H. B. (2011 [1852]), *Uncle Tom's Cabin; or, Life among the Lowly*, ed. D. S. Reynolds (Oxford, Oxford University Press).

Tragle, H. I. (1973), *The Southampton Slave Revolt of 1831: A Compilation of Source Material* (New York, Vintage).

Turner, N. and Gray, T. R. (1832), *The Confessions of Nat Turner, the Leader of the Late Insurrection in Southampton, VA. as Fully and Voluntarily Made to Thomas R. Gray* (Richmond, VA, Thomas R. Gray), 3–4.

Wilson, J. (1829), 'Legislative petition from John Wilson et al. to the President and members of the Senate of South Carolina', in *Race, Slavery, and Free Blacks: Petitions to Southern Legislatures, 1777–1867*, at Series 1, Reel 10, Frame 0527, microform (University Publications of America).

Zeitchik, S. (2012), 'Samuel L. Jackson on slavery, entertainment, guns in "Django"', *Los Angeles Times*, https://www.latimes.com/entertainment/envelope/la-xpm-2012-dec-27-la-en-samuel-jackson-django-unchained-20121227-story.html (accessed 14 June 2021).

7

Third-Party Collaborators in the Colombian Armed Conflict: A Paramilitary Case Study

GERSON IVÁN ARIAS AND CARLOS ANDRÉS PRIETO*

> Stop going around killing in secret as if no one knows who you are!
>
> . . . the commander did not like to kill without knowing why: he did not like to kill for the sake of killing
>
> (Silva Romero 2020: 120, 125)

Introduction

AFTER COLOMBIAN PARAMILITARY groups demobilised in 2006, and as a result of the Justice and Peace process and the ordinary Colombian justice system, the country learnt countless stories about paramilitary connections, relationships, and links to the state and other social sectors. This chapter delves into a particular story of collaboration concerning José Miguel Narváez, a military forces adviser and instructor who became deputy director of the main state intelligence apparatus in Colombia. Judicial files and journalistic investigations indicate that for at least 10 years, instead of coordinating the prosecution of paramilitary groups, Narváez served as a go-between for paramilitary commanders and subsequently became a paramilitary adviser and an active collaborator from within the state itself. Through this study of Narváez's case, the chapter explores how collaborators should be defined, the context in which they emerge, their incentives and motivations, the different dimensions of collaboration, and its association with a lack of trust in institutions.

---

* We are grateful to Kiran Stallone for the English translations from Spanish sources in this chapter. All translations are by her unless otherwise stated.

Proceedings of the British Academy, **248**, 132–156, © The British Academy 2022.

It considers the complex and unique context of an internal armed conflict occurring within a democracy still in the making, but one that also differs from typical cases of an oppressive regime or total occupation.

Narváez, an economist and business administrator, currently stands convicted for the murder of a comedian and political analyst, as well as for ordering communications to be illegally intercepted and for unlawfully conducting surveillance of social leaders, journalists, magistrates, and members of opposition political parties. Because of these offences, Narváez himself has requested that his case be considered by the Special Jurisdiction for Peace (JEP), a transitional justice mechanism created after the 2016 Final Agreement between the government of Juan Manuel Santos and the Revolutionary Armed Forces of Colombia (FARC) guerrillas, which would entitle him to a conditional amnesty in exchange for truth and accountability.

Narváez's relationship with Colombian paramilitary groups has been labelled in several different ways: he has been seen as an indoctrinator, an ideologist, an instructor, an active paramilitary, and a high-level adviser (*Semana* 2019). The set of facts about Narváez reveal the extent of his collaboration and involvement with paramilitary groups. First, he provided ideological and political advice to the paramilitary national organisation from the highest level of national decision-making within the Colombian government. Second, he collaborated – as a public official – with an illegal actor through omission and the disclosure of information, in addition to other intelligence-gathering activities. Third, his links were so close to the paramilitaries that it was difficult to distinguish whether he was directly part of the organisation or a collaborator. Fourth, he contributed to outcomes that were neither beneficial nor strategic for the military forces that employed him and even constituted organisational mistakes. His type of collaboration provided Narváez with a way to 'create the need' for his work and to guide the behaviour of the paramilitary organisation.

Relationships between armed organisations and civilians have been a recurrent variable of analysis in existing studies on violence and armed conflict at the international level and within Colombia. Recent work has prioritised the systematic collection and detailed examination of information at the subnational level, focusing on the behaviour of armed actors in specific regions, their interactions with the civilian population, and the consequences of their actions, among other variables. Such studies have been conducted using a variety of research questions on conflict patterns (dynamics of violence, logics of recruitment, displacement and demobilisation); units of analysis (individuals, organisations, situations, and events); contexts and geographical settings (countries, municipalities, or other population or political-administrative units); disciplines (economics, sociology, political science); and different quantitative and qualitative methods (Kalyvas 2008: 397–8). As Leigh A. Payne and Juan Espindola outline in Chapter 1, the specific context in which a collaborative action begins is essential to understanding the act of collaboration itself.

However, analyses of collaborative interactions have not always led to in-depth explanations, for example, on the different types of collaborative activities encountered within the same geographical context, on the subjective elements that define the nature and scope of the relationship between armed actors and civilians, or on collaborations between military or other institutions and illegal armed groups (pro-systemic and anti-systemic groups). Within this universe of potential interactions, the notion of 'collaboration' tends to appear frequently even though it is not well conceptualised or comparatively analysed, especially with regard to other types of interactions.

Collaborative activities have been identified in both conventional and irregular warfare situations, in international and internal conflicts, in authoritarian and democratic regimes (or any variation between these two), in weak or failed states, and even in separate analyses of the actors involved in such conflicts. Although the term 'collaborator' refers specifically to individuals who, within the aforementioned contexts, decide to collaborate with an enemy as a form of betrayal (Payne 2001), a more in-depth explanation of collaboration requires a review of the contextual, collective, and individual variables that lead to such behaviour. It also requires a specific discussion of the multiple and varied characteristics of collaboration and the possible consequences and impacts of such behaviour.[1]

Conceptualising collaboration faces several challenges. These include the blurred boundary between collaboration and other terms commonly used to define the same phenomenon or similar actions such as desertion, coordination, association, complicity, alliances, and co-optation, among others. Additionally, as various experts have explained, in protracted war contexts, and particularly within internal armed conflicts, often featuring horizontal confrontations, it is crucial to understand the grey areas and instances in which the roles of the victimiser and victim are not clean-cut (Orozco Abad 2009; Sánchez *et al*. 2016). This is why, in certain cases, a singular armed apparatus tends to be held responsible also for all forms of collaboration. An additional challenge derives from the need to distinguish between circumstantial, coerced, non-coerced, locally isolated, and atypical variations of collaboration. All of these categories offer nuanced understandings about the types of interactions within a conflict or violent setting, and shed light on some of the more systematic patterns of collaboration. Ultimately, these contribute to a broader and more in-depth explanation about the nature and characteristics of a conflict and the actors involved.

In the Colombian case, more than five decades of armed conflict have resulted in the rise, continuation, and decline of different armed actors and, consequently, of different approaches to relations between these actors and the state, local communities, and other types of social actors. These have varied depending on the specific interests of the armed actors (often changing over time) as well as the different

[1] Collaboration can be broadly understood as any action that is aimed at supporting a rival party and that implies a rupture of ties with a specific community or actor (Fichtl 2004; Kalyvas 2008; Ortega 2014; Payne 2001). This encompasses both specific forms of civilian collaboration and also more institutionalised forms, such as militias.

contexts that have influenced and brought about different types of collaboration for different reasons and with varying outcomes. Similarities and differences can be identified, for example, between guerrilla and paramilitary collaborators; some types of collaboration may be very specific to certain geographical contexts and particular moments of the armed struggle, while other types of collaboration seem to have taken root in various regions of the country as a result of the armed groups' deployment and their structures of territorial control. In many cases, the historical presence of an armed group in a specific region has translated into long-standing legacies of violence and power.

This chapter takes a detailed look at collaborators in the context of the Colombian armed conflict, with special emphasis on those who were involved with the paramilitary groups that demobilised between 2003 and 2006. The focus on paramilitarism supports already existing analyses on the nature of this armed group, on the different forms of social order resulting from its occupation and control in specific contexts and periods of Colombia's recent history, and on extensive existing evidence (testimonials, journalistic reports, judicial cases, and academic work) about cases of civilian/paramilitary collaboration more than 14 years after demobilisation (2003–6). Paradoxically, despite the abundant existing information, there are still several questions and pending public debates about the different levels and degrees of collaboration that the paramilitaries managed to secure from institutional and non-institutional actors. An analysis of collaboration with guerrilla groups is beyond the scope of this chapter, although some of the conclusions and analytical criteria explained in the next section can be applied to these groups.

The chapter is divided into four parts. The first two sections introduce the case of Narváez, his professional and personal background, and activities in connection with paramilitary groups according to evidence and existing judicial rulings. The third section develops some reflections on third-party collaborators, using Narváez's case as an example and his current position within transitional justice mechanisms (the Truth Commission and the JEP) operating in Colombia after the Final Accord was signed. Finally, some conclusions are offered about Narváez's case with regard to paramilitarism and the study of the phenomenon of collaboration in the context of armed conflicts and other violent situations.

José Miguel Narváez: Messenger, Intermediary, Collaborator, and Ideologist

Background

As described in a recent publication by the Military Forces Colombia, and in particular the public forces, faced overwhelming challenges in the mid-1990s, and public order deteriorated in alarming ways (Pizarro Leóngomez 2018: 137–48).

After failed attempts to negotiate, the FARC and National Liberation Army (ELN) guerrillas were on the rise militarily and were more determined than ever to seize power through the use of force. Likewise, a new generation of more coordinated paramilitaries (with a stronger presence throughout the country) justified themselves based on the actions of the guerrilla groups and the inability of the state to stop them. These paramilitaries carried out massacres, disappearances, and displacements and, like the guerrilla groups, used drug trafficking as a means to finance their operations.

Colombian paramilitary groups date back to the mid-1960s, when the Colombian state itself issued a decree about 'Self-Defence Groups' (*Grupos de Autodefensas*),[2] which, under the protection and control of the Colombian armed forces, allowed civilians to carry weapons for private use and to work with the authorities to combat increasing crime, especially in rural areas. However, at the end of the 1970s and the beginning of the 1980s, the state's inability to control them and its failure to combat the guerrillas led these groups to go on the offensive and to become private armies at the service of the drug cartels (who sponsored them), as well as landowners and politicians. Often, they worked in collusion with members of the public forces.

This first phase (the first generation of paramilitaries) concluded with the criminalisation of these groups. In 1987 the Minister of Government denounced the existence of at least 140 'Self-Defence Groups', and in 1989 the Colombian Intelligence Service (DAS) made public a report detailing the actions of these groups in the Magdalena Medio area. That same year President Virgilio Barco criminalised the creation and promotion of these groups and the Supreme Court of Justice declared the previously mentioned legislation that enabled them to be unconstitutional.[3]

After 1989, and following a failed justice process in the early 1990s, a second generation of more coordinated paramilitaries emerged. They expanded nationally, became more mobile, were financed by drug trafficking, and managed to infiltrate the state. They grouped themselves under the abbreviation AUC – Autodefensas Unidas de Colombia (United Self-Defense Forces of Colombia) – and were led by brothers Fidel, Vicente, and Carlos Castaño. This second generation of paramilitaries moved from Magdalena Medio to Urabá in Antioquia and southern Córdoba, where the AUC set up its main camps and training sites.

As mentioned, by the end of the 1990s, guerrilla and paramilitary groups were expanding and consolidating, and public order was spiralling dangerously out of control. In addition to the creation of the AUC, paramilitarism grew thanks to the governments of Presidents César Gaviria (1990–4) and Ernesto Samper (1994–8).

---

[2] Decreto Legislativo 3398 de 1965 (24 December) – 'by which the National Defence is organised'. This was converted into permanent legislation with Law 48 of 1968 (16 December), which in art. 33, para. 3, stated: 'The Ministry of National Defence, through authorised orders, may protect as private property, when it deems it appropriate, weapons that are considered to be for the exclusive use of the Armed Forces.'

[3] G. Arias Ortiz, 'Las "generaciones" del paramilitarismo: de las "autodefensas" a la "confederación paramilitar"' (unpublished, 2006).

Ignoring history, they created the Special Services of Surveillance and Private Security, later known as Convivir (literally 'co-existence' in Spanish), which served as a façade for the creation of more than 400 surveillance organisations in different regions of the country (FIP 2008), many of which were used by the paramilitaries to arm themselves, expand their scope, and act with impunity. Very few of these organisations accomplished their objectives legally, which was revealed during the Justice and Peace transitional process.

This second generation of paramilitarism reached its peak during the 1997–2002 period – that is, just before its demobilisation. In terms of the number of combatants, the paramilitaries went from 3,800 to 12,275 during this period, and from impacting 283 municipalities to 592 (more than half of the country). The number of victims of massacres, mostly committed by paramilitary groups, went from 2,066 in 1997 to 3,778 in 2001.[4]

In 2001, the AUC was included in the list of terrorist organisations by the United States and its main commanders were requested for extradition. Moreover, within the AUC itself, discussions were brewing about the decision to finance its activities with drug trafficking resources, its responsibility for massacres and massive forced displacements throughout the country, the inevitable failure of the peace process with the FARC, and the possible election of a new government that would prioritise dismantling the paramilitaries. All this deepened the fractures within the network of paramilitary groups, ultimately leading them to agree on a disarmament and demo-bilisation process at the beginning of Álvaro Uribe's administration (2002–10). In addition, and as Iván Orozco Abad has noted, with the arrival of a president such as Uribe, whose main agenda was to restore security using the public armed forces, negotiations with the paramilitaries can also be explained as an act 'based on the determination of the Colombian democratic state to restore itself as a monopoly of offensive force and to re-legitimise itself' and, in this way, to advance towards ending the state's involvement with the paramilitaries.[5]

Between 2003 and 2006 more than 31,000 combatants demobilised. In the process, they handed over more than 18,000 weapons and accepted the first transitional justice mechanism implemented in Colombia, known as the Justice and Peace Law, or Law 975, of 2005. This legal framework created a set of incentives that encouraged paramilitaries to comply with the law and confess to crimes. In return they received a maximum sentence of eight years in prison. The main paramilitary commanders also benefited from this transitional mechanism and gave their testi-monies in free version (*versión libre*) hearings.

Today there is some consensus on the distinct features of paramilitarism: its anti-guerrilla discourse; its long-term interactions and alliances with government

---

[4] R. Escobedo, 'Apreciación sobre la segunda mitad de los años noventa e inicios del nuevo milenio en Colombia con énfasis en los paramilitares'. Analysis created for this chapter based on data from the Observatorio Nacional de Memoria y Conflicto del Centro Nacional de Memoria Histórica (unpub-lished, 2020).

[5] I. Orozco Abad, comments to a draft of this text sent by email.

actors and security forces to guarantee its impunity (a phenomenon known as 'parapolitics'); its punitive nature (the strategy of 'taking the water from the fish', and using violence to punish communities or anyone suspected of helping guerrilla groups); its networked organisational structure (Gutiérrez Sanín and Vargas 2016); and its strong links to drug trafficking (Arias Ortiz and Prieto 2011). All of these factors are key to understanding the nature of paramilitarism and the ways in which it operated.

One of the main features of paramilitarism was the collusion of members of the security forces and state security agencies with these illegal groups. These ties have been reported since the 1980s and early 1990s by state agencies, academic researchers, and non-governmental organisations (NGOs)[6] (well before the Justice and Peace process began) (Human Rights Watch 2001). Despite many simplistic approaches about this relationship, the collusion was not a myth; these linkages were even developed with members of the armed forces. A recent study commissioned by the Colombian armed forces notes that in the mid-1990s there were internal orders stating that members of the forces should neither 'have any contemplations nor be indifferent to their [paramilitary] criminal actions', and that it was necessary to 'avoid personal or institutional links' with paramilitary groups (Ugarriza and Pabón 2017: 283).

It is in this context that the figure of José Miguel Narváez emerges: someone who, according to one of his judicial proceedings, began to collaborate actively with the main paramilitary commanders as early as 1994 and became an adviser to Carlos Castaño at a time when he was also an adviser and instructor for the armed forces.[7] At that time, paradoxically, he used to defend publicly the authority and effectiveness of the armed forces in their confrontation with illegal organisations.

The Story of José Miguel Narváez

In 2009, we (the authors) worked for the website Verdadabierta.com, which was created to document Colombia's Justice and Peace process. We had the opportunity to conduct in-depth interviews with several paramilitary commanders who had been actively participating in the Justice and Peace *versión libre* hearings for nearly two years. During this process, they exposed the untold story of paramilitarism, and its associated crimes and relations with the state and society. In one of those

---

[6] See, for example, Procuraduría General de la Nación, 'Informe sobre el MAS: Lista de integrantes y la conexión MAS-Militares', 20 February 1983; Departamento Administrativo de Seguridad (DAS), 'Testimonio sobre el narcotráfico y justicia privada', 16 March 1989; Medina Gallego (1990); World Organisation against Torture *et al.* (1992); Americas Watch (1994); NCOS (1995); ASFADDES (1996).
[7] Seventh Specialised Criminal Circuit Court of Bogotá, D.C., sentence against José Miguel Narváez, 13 August 2018. A judge sentenced him to 30 years in prison for the murder of comedian and political analyst Jaime Garzón. This sentence was upheld by the Superior Court of Bogotá, even though it reduced his sentence to 26 years. Subsequently, on 3 February 2021, the Criminal Cassation Chamber of the Supreme Court of Justice affirmed the 26-year prison sentence as the court of last instance.

interviews, when asked about the role of José Miguel Narváez, who was already beginning to be mentioned in the *versión libre* hearings, one of the commanders who was responsible for massacres, displacements, and the recruitment of minors declared without hesitation: 'that man was a real danger, he brought us lists of people he wanted us to kill, he was a madman, a terrorist'.[8]

Narváez began to be mentioned in these hearings by paramilitary commanders when prosecutors investigated several high-profile murders involving human rights defenders, journalists, and political leaders. In particular, since 2007, his name had been linked to the murder of comedian and journalist Jaime Garzón, which occurred on 13 August 1999 in Bogotá. During the judicial proceedings about Garzón, which took place within Colombia's ordinary justice system, Narváez was exposed as a collaborator and political adviser for the AUC and its main commander, Carlos Castaño. His name was also mentioned in the murder case of Senator Manuel Cepeda, a member of the Communist Party and the Patriotic Union, who was assassinated on 9 August 1994 by the paramilitaries. However, Narváez's story begins even earlier.

Narváez was born in 1959 into a middle-class family in Bogotá, and later graduated as an economist and business administrator from the Universidad Santo Tomás de Bogotá. In 1987 he graduated as a professional officer from the reserve of the armed forces, and he later became a National Defence Course student at the Escuela Superior de Guerra (War College). He then worked for a small family business and combined this with professorships at several universities in Bogotá, such as the Universidad Javeriana, La Sabana, and Sergio Arboleda, where he taught business administration. From 1994 he was also linked in various ways (as a professor, lecturer, instructor, etc.) to the Army Intelligence School, the War College (in Bogotá), and later other institutions. He taught courses such as 'Political Warfare of Subversion against the State', which, according to his own court statements, 'had to do more with the history of the Chinese political war and not with the national security doctrine that has been distorted in the media'.[9] This was indeed true, but he did not limit himself to these topics.[10] He also gave talks at military units on the clandestine Colombian Communist Party (the illegal party created by the FARC guerrillas) on the *Nunca más* (Never Again) project, and he was invited by several Convivir units to provide training and education courses.[11]

According to several interviews with retired military officers, during the period 1994–97 Narváez, through several of his military students who were part of the XIth Brigade located in Montería (Córdoba) and others who would later

---

[8] Interviews by Gerson Iván Arias with several paramilitary commanders in the Itagüí prison (Antioquia), 2009.
[9] See statements made by José Miguel Narváez before the Attorney General's Office, Bogotá: 19, 21, 29, and 30 October, and 5 November 2009. Case 1942 on the homicide of Jaime Garzón Forero.
[10] Interviews with two retired army colonels who attended these courses and conferences, December 2020.
[11] The Colombian *Nunca más* project was an initiative led by various non-governmental human rights and social organisations, which since the mid-1990s had been working on reports to document the memories of victims of the last stage of political violence, especially victims of the state.

be in the XVIIth Brigade in Carepa (Urabá Antioqueño), met and established contact with paramilitary groups and especially with military officers who were working in collusion with these groups. The argument given by these military officers was that this was the best way to defeat the guerrilla groups, although there was also an economic interest as the paramilitary groups used bribery as well. It was at this time that Narváez met Carlos Castaño and, according to the judicial file, that Castaño made the decision to assassinate the comedian and journalist Jaime Garzón.

As described by Gutiérrez Sanín (2019: 16), 'Colombian paramilitarism was a new form of (coercive) mediation, which appeared in the midst of the counter-insurgency war and brought together the proverbial mix of 'followers and friends', [and] added to it a large-scale component of security and coercion'. In this process, characters such as Narváez and others acted as middlemen, helping paramilitary commanders to access key information in Bogotá; grasp how the military forces understood the armed conflict; and, in a certain way, justify their actions with ideological arguments based on anti-Communism and the notion of 'taking the water from the fish'. Many former members of the armed forces provided additional support to the paramilitaries. For various reasons and motivations, many officials left the institution and joined the AUC as instructors (Verdabierta.com 2011). They quickly became paramilitary commanders and helped expand the paramilitary presence across the country (CITPAX 2012). In the interviews, many of these commanders acknowledged Narváez's involvement in the armed conflict.

In 2002, Narváez reappeared as part of the defence sector's commission for the transition between the outgoing government of Andrés Pastrana (1998–2002) and the incoming government of Álvaro Uribe (2002–10). Later that year, he was appointed as external adviser for anti-kidnapping and -extortion policies by Martha Lucía Ramírez, who at the time had been designated as Minister of Defence (Publimetro 2020).

Between 2003 and 2004, Narváez began to provide advisory services to the DAS, the main intelligence agency attached to the presidency, even serving as an adviser to the leaders of this agency. During this period, he taught courses to DAS intelligence analysts. It later became known – first in 2009 and then in 2016 through a court ruling – that between 2004 and 2005 Narváez had established the so-called G3 within the General Intelligence Directorate of the DAS. The G3 was a group in charge of carrying out intelligence, monitoring, and illegal interceptions of NGOs, political opponents, and journalists.[12]

Narváez's actions at the DAS have been well documented (Sánchez-Moreno 2018; Martínez 2021). The G3 unit even illegally intercepted communications and had officials of the Constitutional Court and Supreme Court of Justice followed. As stated by one of those involved, 'He went two or three times a week to the

---

[12] Attorney General's Office, National Unit to the Supreme Court of Justice, Office 11, Judicial Archives, document nos 12753 an 12495.

office to define the target groups and oversee the actions that were being taken.'[13] As mentioned by Laverde (2014: 48–9), Narváez's job at the DAS 'was not about the traditional National Security doctrine implemented against communism during the dictatorships of the Southern Cone, but a more refined model, in which repression and espionage took place in a democratic environment and against a new enemy: terrorism'.

For the above, Narváez was sentenced to 8 years in prison in 2016, and was also dismissed and disqualified for 20 years by the Attorney General's Office in 2010.[14] Between 1 June and 25 October 2005, Narváez served as deputy director of the DAS, but was removed along with then director Jorge Noguera.[15] He was removed on account of accusations regarding paramilitary infiltration inside the DAS, specifically by paramilitaries such as alias 'Macaco', 'Jorge 40', the Autodefensas de Cundinamarca, and the Autodefensas del Casanare.[16] As a result of these events, a new director was appointed and a special commission was created to decide what to do with the DAS (FIP 2005).

After his departure from the DAS, Narváez was appointed as a security adviser to the Colombian Cattle Ranchers Federation (Fedegan), a business association that, according to the statements of former paramilitary group commanders in the Justice and Peace process, included some individuals who had strongly supported the paramilitaries since the 1980s.

In 2010 Narváez was captured and taken to prison as the alleged perpetrator of the homicide of comedian and journalist Jaime Garzón. This chapter is based on procedural evidence from this case and allows us to delve deeper into the different aspects of Narváez's collaboration with paramilitary groups, particularly those related to his membership in and advice to institutions that had a constitutional obligation to combat them.[17] In the judicial proceedings that followed, Narváez based his defence on a denialist and dissuasive strategy that included his anti-Communist discourse.[18]

---

[13] Statement by Jaime Fernando Ovalle, coordinator of the G3 within the DAS, 1 July 2009, cited in Martínez (2021: 37).

[14] Sixth Specialised Criminal Circuit Court of Bogotá, D.C., verdict against José Miguel Narváez, 18 July 2016. He was sentenced for conspiracy to commit aggravated felony, in his capacity as a promoter and organiser of the illegal G3 group.

[15] Noguera was sentenced by the Supreme Court of Justice to 16 years in prison for conspiracy to commit a crime and as an indirect perpetrator of the homicide of university professor Alfredo Correa de Andreis, among other crimes. Supreme Court of Justice – Criminal Cassation Chamber, ruling on 14 September 2011.

[16] These incidents were also denounced by the magazine *Semana* and its investigative director Ricardo Calderón, who through several investigations uncovered the relations between the paramilitaries and the DAS and the creation of illegal groups within the DAS to persecute, threaten, and illegally intercept journalists, opposition politicians, and even the magistrates of the Supreme Court of Justice (see *Semana* 2006).

[17] See the judicial case file, Office of the Attorney General of the Nation, Case 1942 on the homicide of Jaime Garzón Forero.

[18] See excerpts from the trial for the crimes committed during his time at the DAS at https://www.youtube.com/watch?v=3Z6L684vchs (accessed 3 February 2022).

José Miguel Narváez: Ties to Paramilitarism and the Murder of Jaime Garzón

The death of Jaime Garzón in 1999 sent shockwaves throughout the country and put the AUC in the spotlight as responsible for this murder. Facing sharp public criticism, AUC commander Carlos Castaño denied any responsibility for this homicide and instructed his entire inner circle not to talk about it and to keep silent.[19] He maintained this position until his death in 2004 at the hands of his own brother, also a paramilitary commander.

The AUC's first strategy to evade responsibility was to use its contacts within the DAS to divert the investigation. In the year 2000, two alleged hitmen were captured on the basis of their responsibility for Garzón's murder. The DAS searched for and prepared witnesses who indicated the two captured were fully responsible. This became evident throughout the judicial proceedings, especially thanks to the legal work done by the captured family's lawyers and the journalist Claudia Julieta Duque, who was also illegally followed by the DAS and had to go into exile.

The next strategy was to silence the criminal gang La Terraza and its leader, nicknamed 'El Negro Elkin', who had carried out Garzón's murder. The gang was linked to the drug trafficker and paramilitary known as 'Don Berna', and was used by the AUC to outsource murders such as that of Jaime Garzón. The gang also progressively became involved in the drug trafficking business and began to cause discomfort within the AUC. For this last reason, but above all to eliminate evidence about Garzón's death, in August 2000, according to the judicial file, an AUC commando ordered the murders of most of the members of this gang, thus eliminating Castaño's links with those directly responsible for the death of the comedian and journalist.

However, at the end of that same year, some survivors of La Terraza in Medellín took responsibility for the murder of Garzón, admitting that they had been supported by members of the armed forces and had received instructions from Carlos Castaño to carry out the murder, as well as other killings (*El Tiempo* 2001).[20] In March 2002, the Attorney General's Office accused Carlos Castaño as a co-perpetrator of the comedian's murder together with the two hitmen who had already been captured.[21] Two years later, a judge convicted Carlos Castaño and acquitted the two hitmen, revealing the attempts to divert the investigation.

The proceedings continued, and in September 2009 the Prosecutor's Office ordered the investigation to be opened up again. Narváez, captured in June 2010, was formally accused of his association with the crime in June 2011. Years later, in

---

[19] 'I had nothing to do with the death of the comedian Jaime Garzón' (see Aranguren 2001: 296).

[20] Public letter from La Terraza, Medellín, 20 November 2000. Case 1942 on the homicide of Jaime Garzón Forero.

[21] Attorney General's Office, National Unit for Human Rights and International Law, document no. 561, indictment against Carlos Castaño, Juan Pablo Ortiz, and Edilberto Antonio Sierra, Bogotá, 12 March 2002.

August 2018 (19 years after the crime), he was sentenced to 30 years in prison as a perpetrator of aggravated homicide.

During the trial, Narváez and several witnesses, including several former paramilitary commanders, were heard. About 20 AUC members testified and confirmed Narváez's relationship with these groups, testifying, some by hearsay and others as direct witnesses, that they had seen Narváez in the AUC camps, and acknowledging that it was Narváez who had suggested the murder of Jaime Garzón. The accusations against Narváez were threefold. First, since at least 1994 he had regularly visited the paramilitary camps, taught courses, and given political talks to upper- and mid-level commanders.

Second, he had contacts with high-ranking members of the armed forces, which gave him access to first-hand information (e.g. interceptions and intelligence reports) regarding possible links of journalists, politicians, and human rights defenders with the FARC and ELN guerrillas. At the same time, through this connection, the paramilitaries ensured their existence and actions were well regarded by some authorities at the central level.[22]

Third, Narváez had proposed the death of Jaime Garzón because of his supposed mediation in a process to release hostages held by the guerrillas in exchange for economic benefits, and because of his repeated criticisms and public mockery of the paramilitary groups.[23] It was not by chance that Narváez had suggested the name of Jaime Garzón to the paramilitary leader. Garzón was a much-loved comedian and a sharp critic of Colombian politics who had mocked not only the economic and political elite, but also the guerrilla and paramilitary groups. Moreover, because of his relevance as a public figure and his commitment to peace he had become a facilitator, with the government's authorisation, for the release of kidnapped individuals, and had in his youth a brief stint as part of the ELN.[24] According to one of the testimonies collected during the judicial proceedings:

> He [Narváez] arrived with information that Jaime Garzón was not only a facilitator of kidnappings but was also part of the FARC structure. He even arrived with a photo, in which Garzón is with a fiyak [sic], that is to say with a camouflaged jacket, in an area of Sumapaz. Carlos told me to call the black guy Elkin and to send [Elkin] to talk to him. We met with him ... Narváez left and Carlos said that he was going to have him killed ... Carlos explained the need to have Jaime Garzón killed, [and] in a

---

[22] 'This meant that our struggle was being heard at an important level within the armed forces and it was further proof for us that the armed forces at that time, due to their limited capacity to combat the guerrillas in our country, did not want to look at us as an enemy and fight us head-on and have to run after two targets at the same time.' Statement made by José Efraín Pérez, alias 'Eduardo 400', to the Attorney General's Office, Bogotá, 17 January 2011. Case 1942 on the homicide of Jaime Garzón Forero.

[23] 'He had ordered the death because friends, high-ranking army commanders, had asked him to do it as a favour; they were annoyed because every time they were investigating a kidnapping, Jaime Garzón appeared as a mediator.' Statement made by Hebert Veloza Garcia, alias 'HH', to the Attorney General's Office, Medellín, 21 August 2008.

[24] For more background on Jaime Garzón, see Ronderos (2007: 321–2).

folder left by Mr Narváez there [was] lots of information about him: that he worked for a well-known radio station, that he had a programme in the morning. Then they travelled to Bogotá and with the help of military intelligence they followed him until they killed him.[25]

It is also important to note that prior to his murder, as was confirmed by various statements made during the judicial proceedings by some of Garzón's friends and relatives, the comedian had stated that he was on a list of those 'sentenced' by the paramilitaries. During the week of his death, Garzón visited Colombia's national prison (La Modelo) in Bogotá, in an attempt to reach out to Castaño through some of the AUC members who were imprisoned, but he was unable to get in touch with him before his murder. The proceedings also revealed that Garzón was the target of threats and surveillance related to his humanitarian activities, which were not well perceived by the armed forces. According to the proceedings, these perceptions were even held by the army's commander at the time, General Jorge Enrique Mora.[26]

In his statements before the Attorney General's Office, Narváez's defence was based on three arguments. The first, which was particularly clear in many of the Justice and Peace proceedings, was that the accusations were made by criminals and were always against honourable people. Likewise, Narváez argued that his professional qualifications were not so outstanding as to qualify him to serve as an adviser to paramilitary leadership. He also pointed to the inaccuracies of some paramilitary statements, and finally, he argued that everything had to do with the revenge of many former paramilitary commanders against President Uribe for having extradited them to the USA in 2008. He used phrases such as 'the guide to slander José Miguel Narváez' or 'the plan for this conspiracy', and 'the thirst for revenge against President Uribe'.[27]

The judge who analysed the evidence concluded it was clear that Narváez had been present in the AUC camps and that he was the main instigator of Garzón's murder, which was carried out by La Terraza on the orders of paramilitary commander Carlos Castaño. This sentence was confirmed by the Superior Court of Bogota and ultimately by the Supreme Court of Justice in 2021. The participation of other members of the armed forces who supported the paramilitary organisation in the assassination of Garzón has yet to be clarified.[28]

---

[25] Statement given by Diego Fernando Murillo, alias 'Don Berna', to the Attorney General's Office, Miami, 13 February 2012. Case file 1942 on the homicide of Jaime Garzón Forero.

[26] Attorney General's Office, pre-classificatory arguments, Case 1942, 1 June 2011. Case file 1942 on the homicide of Jaime Garzón Forero.

[27] See statements made by Narváez before the Attorney General's Office, Bogotá, 19, 21, 29, and 30 October, and 5 November 2009.

[28] 'Jaime Garzón was killed by the extreme right-wing of the military … a radical sector that still exists in the Armed Forces and that in spite of all the efforts to eliminate it is still alive and kicking' (Santos 1999). In addition, 'Garzón was killed by paramilitaries acting in concert with "loose bullets", active or retired, from the security forces' (National Security Archive 2011).

Narváez and the Motivations of a Paramilitary Collaborator

Several of the people interviewed for this chapter who knew Narváez described him as an avid reader of books and documents on war and armed conflict. They said he always carried a suitcase full of them and that, when making any claim in a talk, conference, or class, he had a quote or an extract from a book or document to support his arguments, and always did so in a passionate and dramatic manner.

Likewise, in his public remarks he developed his own anti-Communist expressions, which, according to some analysts, became the ideological basis of the actions of the armed forces during the last decades (Borrero 1990: 191). For one of the former officers interviewed, characters such as Narváez appeared at a time when there was an absence of leadership within the armed forces and when arguments to confront anti-Communism and give the armed forces a more modern appearance were twisted and applied in the opposite way. Although different in magnitude, we find discursive patterns similar to those highlighted by Oren Gross in Chapter 9 of this book on the ideological dimension of collaboration (the case of the teachers during the Nazi dictatorship). Such discursive remarks provided a 'cloak of legality' for oppressive regimes during judicial assessments of the afore-mentioned type of collaboration.

For example, General Álvaro Valencia Tovar, a prominent figure within the Colombian military institution and a key proponent of military thought, made the following observation during the peak of paramilitarism at the end of the 1980s: 'Faced with this guerrilla and revolutionary conglomerate, the Colombian state has maintained a changing attitude with a common core approach: to dele-gate the role of combating it [the guerrillas] to the armed forces and security agencies, without accounting for the fact that the revolution is a political one'. He later called this 'the problem of the ideological insurgency', stating that 'the Colombian state has not given the ideological insurgency problem the priority that the threat requires' (Valencia Tovar 1990: 353). These arguments were stretched and distorted by people such as Narváez who suggested that civilian collaborators with the guerrillas should also be attacked in order to improve the effectiveness of the counterinsurgency struggle.

At the end of the 1990s, Narváez wrote in the magazines of the armed forces and military intelligence that 'the unarmed subversion has achieved more results in the Colombian internal conflict against the state … than the work of the subver-sive entity equipped with rifles and machine guns …. The key to the subversion consists in infiltrating high levels of the political class, the media, [and] academic and social circles. In our milieu, the help received from top jurists, politicians, writers, [and] novelists has been combined with non-governmental organisations that have presented to the country and the world studies on the Colombian conflict that do not reflect the realities of the criminal actions of the FARC and the ELN' (Narváez 1997). This kind of discourse was increasingly communicated to army officers who took his courses.

Other sources agree that what happened in the 1980s helps to explain Narváez's positions, which in turn were echoed by some members of the military and the AUC leadership. For C. A. Velásquez, with the rise of drug trafficking and asset laundering through land purchases, military officers located in difficult areas such as the Magdalena Medio made the mistake of forming a very close relationship with these new regional powers, which, once threatened by the guerrilla groups, found in the military forces and private armies a very efficient response to the problem, although later the fault lines became less clear.[29] Maria Teresa Ronderos agrees that 'the military never understood who their allies were in the regions', and this progressively allowed the paramilitary groups to establish themselves as allies with the same goal: attacking the guerrilla groups.[30]

For many of those interviewed, the emergence of people such as Narváez was not so much about money, but about the desire for recognition, and social status. This subjective motivation, combined with the anti-Communist spirit (the ideological dimension), contributed to the emergence of people such as Narváez in this context.[31] He is a good example of someone who, paradoxically, recognised the military forces' shortcomings with respect to their capabilities at the time.[32] He believed in strengthening the public forces to combat illegal armed groups, but at the same time he was convincing people within the armed forces to accept the paramilitaries as a solution, especially because of the work they could do to combat what he called 'the unarmed subversion'. As one of the ex-military personnel interviewed stated, 'with three or five officers each year who came out convinced of this story – a minority – it was enough for the military units in the field to come to believe that the paramilitaries were a lesser evil'.

Former officers and analysts, such as Ronderos, agree that people such as Narváez were necessary for the emergence of paramilitarism,[33] which was shaped by the central government's arrangement of delegating the provision of security and the resolution of social conflicts to local elites in exchange for votes.[34]

---

[29] C. A. Velásquez, unpublished interview with the authors, 6 November 2020. The testimony of paramilitary commander 'Rodrigo Doble Cero' is very telling in this regard: 'at that time no one saw the narcos as a threat to the stability of the rural areas or as creators of social problems and inequities and injustices, but rather as prosperous cattle ranchers, businessmen and investors who had come to the region to help eliminate communists and provide employment and help the regions to prosper' (Cívico 2009: 143).

[30] Maria Teresa Ronderos, unpublished interview with the authors, 23 November 2020.

[31] Paramilitary commander alias 'Huevo e Pisca' said the following about Narváez: 'I don't think he was part of it, but I do think he had an *autodefensa* [self-defence] ideology, more so than us, because they are from the extreme right'. Statement given by Jesús Emiro Pereira, alias 'Huevo e Pisca', before the Attorney General's Office, Bogotá, 14 September 2010. Case 1942 on the homicide of Jaime Garzón Forero.

[32] See, for example, some interesting interviews with army commanders who analysed that period of history in Nova (2020).

[33] Ronderos, unpublished interview with the authors, 23 November 2020.

[34] 'The national elites in Bogotá never set out to control or regulate vast areas of the country, and instead delegated that task to local elites in exchange for votes in elections. This resulted in a particular

For some interviewees the relevance of characters such as Narváez should not be overestimated, since for the paramilitary groups he was just someone who facilitated communication with the political centre of the country, or a sort of hidden messenger who on occasion 'touted' or claimed to be much more than what he really was and could do. For others, Narváez was the best demonstration of the organised collusion between the armed forces and the paramilitaries during this period, and therefore he was not an isolated actor nor was he detached from the anti-Communist spirit that prevailed within the military. For the latter, he was a fundamental figure within the paramilitary structure, acting as an ideological teacher and trainer of the main paramilitary commanders, as well as an informant and instigator of crimes such as the murder of Jaime Garzón.

According to a former paramilitary leader, 'the self-defence groups could be called paramilitaries, since members of the army had a lot of influence, and they used Mr Narváez as an intermediary, since he boasted of being a professor at the War College, an adviser to the army, and he gave a lot of information about operations against the self-defence groups or people who had links with the guerrillas or the Left'.[35]

Third-Party Collaborators, Transitional Justice, and the Atypical Case

Although there have been studies and systematic investigations of the paramilitaries for nearly 15 years at time of writing, studies on the phenomenon of the collaborator are very new and, therefore, we are far from true methods of accountability through justice with respect to collaborators. In general, paramilitary groups in Colombia used collaborators to achieve political influence, facilitate military and economic expansion, obtain immunity, and establish *de facto* local orders. The different attitudes, motivations, or incentives identified in collaboration cases point to several conclusions, but in particular, they show how the emergence of collaborators responded to particular armed conflict dynamics. It can be explained, on one hand, by low levels of trust in institutions to enforce justice or provide security and, on the other hand, by individual incentives tied to economic, political, or ideological factors.

Just as systems of governance and control imposed by illegal armed groups determine the nature of interactions with institutional and non-institutional actors and the roles that these actors adopt in such environments, it is also important to

---

geographical structuring of the state, state services and development. There is a center of the country where the state is more present, laws and norms are better executed and where there is less poverty; and there is a large periphery where the opposite is true' (Robinson 2014).

[35] Statement given by Diego Fernando Murillo, alias 'Don Berna', New York, 17 September 2009 before Office 26 of the National Unit for Human Rights and International Humanitarian Law, Attorney General's Office, document no. 329.

understand how such interactions shape the construction and maintenance of certain systems of power (and their legitimacy claims); the fulfilment of armed groups' long-term goals; and, in general, their capacity to influence the behaviour of such groups, whether from organised or non-organised sectors such as those of local leaders, businessmen, or religious groups (Arjona *et al*. 2015: 293).

In order to advance our theory of collaboration, it is essential to deepen the analysis of third-party cases that participated in the armed conflict, particularly those cases that have been presented to the transitional justice mechanisms that exist to date in Colombia. On one hand, between 2006 and 2014, more than 4,400 paramilitary groups gave their testimonies within the framework of the Justice and Peace Law, which to date has produced more than 60 macro sentences by judges. These have revealed many violations that were unknown or that the state denied. In addition to the sheer barbarity of the violence, these cases also revealed a network of social, political, and economic collusion that allowed paramilitary expansion, and that, as Ronderos (2014) points out, took place within a formally established democracy.

After 16 years (2005–21) of Colombia's transitional justice process, the Colombian Attorney General's Office has identified 16,980 cases in which the names of civilian third parties and state agent combatants and non-combatants appear.[36] These were brought to the justice system following the confessions of a considerable number of upper- and mid-level commanders and patrol members who belonged to different paramilitary groups.[37] However, despite this progress, recent work by the National Centre for Historical Memory (CNMH) shows that studies on paramilitarism in Colombia require a 'contextualised analysis on how civilians and paramilitary groups interacted, in the sense of identifying the differentiated legacies of paramilitary intervention' (Vásquez and Barrera 2018: 199). In other words, further knowledge of collaborators, even for an advanced and long-standing process such as this one, is required in order to comprehend fully the dynamics of the Colombian armed conflict.

A substantive reflection on why the Colombian justice system has not made progress in clarifying and sanctioning a large number of these third-party collaborators with illegal groups is still needed: the participation of different social, economic, political, and institutional actors in these interactions, most of them with interests that persist to this day, is among the possible reasons for this deficit. There are also challenges regarding the collection of evidence and the limited capacities of the justice administration in certain regional contexts. Additional factors have to do as

---

[36] These cases relate to 311 civilian third parties, 835 non-combatant state agents, and 417 combatant state agents. See *Fiscalía General de la Nación* (2019).

[37] In the framework of this process, 4,981 people applied under the Law, including 4,410 paramilitaries who had demobilised collectively or individually, or who were imprisoned. Between 2006 and 2016, 15,431 *versiones libres* were recorded, during which 66,226 incidents were documented, involving close to 100,000 victims. Contraloría General de la República, 'Análisis sobre los resultados y costos de la Ley de Justicia y Paz', Bogotá, 2017.

well with the lack of sufficient social rejection of these interactions, the persistence of institutional and social explanations that reduce the problem of collaboration to an issue of 'bad apples', and the fear or inability of various social sectors to break the silence about the past or at least accept that there is disagreement about the interpretation of that past.[38]

After the peace agreement between the Colombian government and the FARC in 2016, a new opportunity opened up to uncover the truth about the participation of third parties in the Colombian armed conflict through the implementation of the Comprehensive System of Truth, Justice, Reparation, and Non-Repetition (SIVJRNR, for its initials in Spanish). This system includes, among other things, a Truth Commission, understood as a temporary and extrajudicial mechanism to establish and clarify the truth about what happened in the context of the armed conflict, and the JEP to investigate the most serious and emblematic crimes committed in the context of the armed conflict and to administer justice.

Once the Final Agreement was signed, and after some subsequent procedural developments, in 2017 the Constitutional Court ruled that third parties only had to comply with the SIVJRNR on a voluntary basis, even if there was evidence of their participation in the armed conflict. Therefore, although the System, and particularly the JEP, was left without the power to initiate proceedings against third parties, there was still an expectation that collaborators would approach the System once their proceedings in the ordinary justice system had moved forward in some way (Gómez Pinilla 2020). Those who, by June 2019, were formally linked to an investigation by the Prosecutor General's Office had until September of the same year to comply with the JEP. By that date 659 third parties had complied, but by the end of the year (and despite the deadline), a total of 916 cases were registered for inclusion (Gómez Pinilla 2020). This is a relatively small figure if one takes into account the number of third parties mentioned in the Justice and Peace process (16,980 cases).

In February 2020, the Constitutional Court ruled again on the issue of third parties' compliance with the SIVJRNR. At that time, the Court acknowledged all crimes committed by third parties in the context of the armed conflict and not only those related to the financing and sponsorship of armed groups, which had been the focus of its previous ruling. In August 2020, the JEP reported that a total of 766 third-party submission requests were being processed and that four cases had already been accepted (JEP 2020). In the case of the Truth Commission (as an extrajudicial mechanism), the same standard of voluntary participation by third parties is required (whether they comply with the JEP or not). The Truth Commission focuses on actions that contribute to clarification, acknowledgement of responsibilities, peaceful coexistence, and non-repetition of the conflict, even though, according to publicly available information, there is no precise report on how many and to what extent third parties have participated in Truth Commission activities.

---

[38] As Uprimny *et al.* (2006) stated, 'Colombia is going through a process of transitional justice without transition.'

In the case of Narváez, in addition to his conviction and the other judicial proceedings currently underway in the ordinary justice system, in August 2019 his defence led a request with the Superior Court of Bogotá for his case and all his proceedings to be reviewed by the JEP. This transfer took place, and by the time this chapter was written, the JEP had provisionally decided not to accept Narváez's application to comply with the special jurisdiction as a third-party collaborator considering his application did not offer additional information to what he had already given through his ordinary process (*El Tiempo* 2022). In his application for the case to be transferred, Narváez claimed his role as a third party and that he was not an active paramilitary group member (*El Tiempo* 2019). Now Narváez has one last chance to present to JEP a 'clear and detailed' contribution to truth, reparation, and non repetition; depending on how much he contributes to the truth and how much he acknowledges responsibility, he might be eligible for certain benefits, including exemption from criminal prosecution. In the event that he definitely does not make a true confession or gives false statements, he risks being expelled from the JEP and will have to serve the sentence imposed by the ordinary justice system (Michalowski *et al*. 2020).

In contrast to what he stated in his application to the JEP, according to the testimony of several paramilitary leaders, Narváez was part of the paramilitary groups: 'I would like to begin by saying that Dr Miguel Narváez was an active member of the Autodefensas Unidas de Colombia and I had the opportunity to meet him personally in 1997 ... The only thing that Dr Narváez lacked was an armband.'[39] Likewise, while some paramilitary leaders considered Narváez to be highly respected within the armed forces, others considered Narváez to be very radical: 'he believes that they are all guerrillas' (*Semana* 2019).

There are at least four additional points to make about the case of Narváez and how it sheds light on the phenomenon of collaboration. First, it highlights, as do other chapters in this book such as that of Gabriel Pereira (Chapter 11), the grey areas of collaboration: in this case, it is unclear who was an official part of the paramilitary group and who provided support to the organisation, especially taking into account the impact of these groups on different sectors of society and the extent of the collaboration that different actors (institutional and non-institutional) provided to them. In the case of Narváez, there are different opinions on his affiliation to the paramilitary organisation, despite abundant evidence about his direct relationship with paramilitary commanders. In other cases, such as those of some members of the security forces, political leaders, and businessmen, there were those who ended up 'switching sides' and demobilising from these groups; in other cases, the distinction between the paramilitaries and their collaborators was clearly maintained despite their collaboration (for example, in several of the 'parapolitics' cases).

Second, the Narváez case allows us to identify a wide range of nuanced reasons for collaboration that seem to oscillate between individual (selective) interests, the ideological leanings of the collaborator, and the need to respond to the strategic plans

---

[39] Statement given by Diego Fernando Murillo, alias 'Don Berna', New York, 17 September 2009.

of the paramilitary group. It is possible to conclude that, in specific circumstances or situations, collaboration tends to be actively sought by the collaborator, while in others, collaboration is explained by the armed group's strategy of bringing about a given social order, guaranteeing impunity for its actions, ensuring and expanding its economic power, and influencing decision-making processes at the national or local levels, among other strategic objectives (Saffon 2006: 47).

Third, the Narváez case reveals four distinctive features, particularly in light of the existing judicial, academic, and journalistic evidence:

- His collaboration profile includes an important ideological component that explains some of his incentives for collaboration. He combined this with the use of his responsibilities as a public official to contribute to the (political) objectives set by the paramilitary groups.
- The collaboration was not by a random third-party civilian, nor was it merely incidental. It was by a state official who ended up betraying the constitutional and legal order that he pretended to defend, and he was responsible for specific violent crimes.
- This is one of the few cases that the Colombian justice system has been able to prove regarding the complicity between high-level state security individuals and paramilitary groups. It is probably not the only case of this nature, particularly given existing testimonies and our understanding of the reach of these paramilitary groups; however, determining the systemic nature of this type of collaboration is difficult because there have been no further judicial rulings.
- Despite the progress made on this particular case, there is still a great deal of denial that prevents a complete understanding of the paramilitaries, their accomplices, and the extent of their involvement in Colombia. Likewise, Narváez is also a unique case in that he was what many analyses would refer to as a 'pro-systemic armed actor', and he violated his government and military ties in a very specific way.

Finally, the failure to acknowledge the responsibility (denialist posture) of figures such as Narváez not only represents an obstacle to uncovering what happened and to understanding the complicities, protagonists, patterns, and contexts that form an integral part of the history of Colombia's armed conflict, but also poses an additional challenge for contexts such as that of Colombia, which require better mechanisms socially to sanction those responsible for what happened and more substantive measures that can contribute to coexistence and reconciliation after decades of violence. For now, regarding collaboration and accountability for it, the transition that the country is seeking remains incomplete because only a few third parties have provided information and confessed their responsibility. Furthermore, the present environment is not very conducive to such confessions, given that the ongoing armed conflict poses security risks and associated costs for those who wish to come forward and make genuine contributions to the truth about the conflict in Colombia.

Conclusion

The case of José Miguel Narváez allows for some general reflections on the phenomenon of collaboration in internal armed conflicts in general and in the specific
case of paramilitary groups in Colombia. In the first place, the phenomenon of
collaboration is anything but constant or fixed: it responds to a specific moment
of armed conflict; a specific phase within the evolutionary development of a given
armed group, its interests, and capacities; and other contextual variables that end
up shaping, over time, the terms and conditions under which collaboration takes
place. The nature of Narváez's collaboration, therefore, was subject to, and evolved
during, specific phases of the emergence, expansion, and institutionalisation of
paramilitarism.

This collaboration, according to the information gathered, (i) began with
Narváez's ideological position, which resonated in sectors of the security forces
and the paramilitaries; (ii) evolved when Narváez was used both by paramilitary commanders, who wanted to connect with the central government, guarantee
impunity for their actions, and consolidate their political and economic power, and
by the military, who recognised him as a useful asset for aligning their interests and
actions with the paramilitary groups; and (iii) was consolidated through the use of
the Colombian state apparatus (the DAS, for example) to fulfil strategic and tactical
objectives set by different paramilitary commanders working to institutionalise
paramilitarism. Opinions remain divided to this day as to whether Narváez was an
integral part of the paramilitaries or a collaborator, a discussion that complicates
our understanding (even though there is abundant evidence in the case of Narváez)
of the grey areas of collaboration in internal armed conflicts, and of issues that have
required extensive analysis, such as paramilitarism in Colombia.

Second, the institutional variable plays a fundamental role in explaining this
type of collaboration. At the contextual level, it is clear that institutional weaknesses
and shortcomings are exploited by armed groups to impose social order at the local
level, consolidate their economic and political power, and influence decision-
making processes and the operation of institutions in favour of their interests, all
of which are supported by diverse forms of collaboration at different levels and
from a variety of civilian actors. Likewise, at the discursive level, a classic paradox
becomes evident: Narváez's fierce defence of the rule of law ended up transforming
into a *de facto* recognition of the country's institutional weaknesses in its fight
against insurgent groups, and ultimately justified the actions of illegal armed groups
such as the paramilitaries. In this case, the state (and its defence) becomes the cause
(discourse), instrument (for its expansion and impunity), and ultimate objective
(co-optation) of paramilitary commanders and their power structures, with all of
the aforementioned functions carried out with the collaboration of civilian actors
such as Narváez.

Third, in addition to the contextual variables, and without the intention of sim-
plifying the problem of collaboration (in line with the arguments of Payne and

Espindola), the testimonies collected for this case suggest that the individual incentives are based more on a desire for personal recognition and stability during a time of anti-Communist discourse, rather than on economic and political benefits. Such incentives typically lead to voluntary and consistent collaboration over time. In this case, these incentives translated into different forms of collaboration that included the delivery/exchange of information and political and strategic support to commanders and various paramilitary structures at different moments during their existence.

In addition to direct involvement in acts of violence, this form of collaboration also has a strong ideological component. The systematic nature of such collaboration is in the process of being corroborated by the justice system, but challenges regarding the true history of collaborators continue to prevent a comprehensive understanding of the paramilitary phenomenon, limit the possibility of holding those responsible accountable, and make it difficult socially to sanction paramilitarism and all of its expressions. For now, the Narváez case is one of the few of this type of collaboration that is backed by sufficient evidence and related judicial proceedings, making it an emblematic case.

In this analysis of Narváez's public life, multiple interpretations arise as to whether, in the end, his collaboration with paramilitary groups explains why he was involved in different high-level institutional sectors (a calculated collaboration) or whether the collaboration was the result of specific circumstances of the armed conflict, in which Narváez's strategic position in high-level sectors was of interest to the paramilitaries (fortuitous collaboration). Given how institutionalised paramilitarism had become, the first scenario is more likely to be true, meaning high-level public officials (in this case, with security responsibilities) were assigned to serve the specific interests of armed groups.

A review of other cases may provide further evidence as to how this type of institutional collaboration works at the local level, how it developed in other state agencies (members of the military, police, judicial officials, and elected officials, among others), and the limitations of this collaboration between armed groups and individuals located within the institutional framework. According to Gutiérrez Sanín (2019: 216):

> At the local level the paramilitaries were linked with the state security agencies in ways which were complex and difficult to administer, at several levels: institutional, coalitional, individual .... Even in the face of severely weakened institutional controls the collusion and connivance with the paramilitaries also ran into constraints that neither the army nor the police could possibly override. This does not imply the end of collusion, but rather its transformation and multiple ramifications.

The analysis of these shifts and the many consequences of collaboration represent, without a doubt, the biggest challenge for transitional justice bodies such as the JEP and the Truth Commission in their mission to determine the truth about past violence and explain the continuous repetition of the armed conflict in Colombia.

References

Americas Watch (1994), *Estado de guerra: Violencia política y contrainsurgencia en Colombia* (Bogotá, TM Editores).

Aranguren, M. (2001), *Mi confesión: Carlos Castaño revela sus secretos* (Bogotá, Editorial Oveja Negra).

Arias Ortiz, G. and Prieto, C. (2011), 'El Bloque Central Bolívar: Caso de paramilitarismo y narcotráfico en Colombia', in E. M. Restrepo and B. Bagley, *La desmovilización de los paramilitares en Colombia* (Bogotá: Universidad de los Andes), 327–71.

Arjona, A., Kasfir, N., and Mampilly, Z. (2015), *Rebel Governance in Civil War* (Cambridge, Cambridge University Press).

ASFADDES [Asociación de Familiares de Detenidos Desaparecidos] *et al.* (2000), Colombia nunca más: Crímenes de lesa humanidad zona 14a ([n.p.], ASFADDES).

Borrero, A. (1990), 'Militares, política y sociedad', in F. Leal Buitrago and L. Zamosc (eds), *Al filo del caos: Crisis política en la Colombia de los años 80* (Bogotá, IEPRI Universidad Nacional–Tercer Mundo Editores).

CITPAX (2012), 'Relatorías de la audiencia temática de entrenamiento para actividades paramilitares y terrorismo', *Tribunal Superior de Justicia y Paz de Bogotá*, 13–16 November.

Cruz, M. (2020), 'Los comandantes paramilitares están ad portas de la JEP', *UN Digital Periodical*, https://unperiodico.unal.edu.co/pages/blog/detail/los-comandantes-parami litares-estan-ad-portas-de-la-jep/ (accessed 30 April 2021).

El Tiempo (2001), 'Historia de una vendetta', *El Tiempo*, 21 January, https://www.eltiempo. com/archivo/documento/MAM-638035 (accessed 15 August 2020).

El Tiempo (2019), 'Condena por asesinato de Garzón pasaría a la justicia para la paz', *El Tiempo*, 20 August, https://www.eltiempo.com/justicia/jep-colombia/jose-miguel-narv aez-condenado-por-crimen-de-garzon-pedira-cupo-en-la-jep-402560 (accessed 12 August 2020).

El Tiempo (2022), 'Narváez, condenado por crimen de Jaime Garzón, no entrará por ahora a la JEP', *El Tiempo*, March, https://www.eltiempo.com/justicia/jep-colombia/jep-rechazan-sometimiento-de-condenado-por-crimen-de-jaime-garzon-655175 (accessed 17 March 2022).

Fichtl, E. (2004), 'The ambiguous nature of "collaboration" in Colombia', 29 March, https://ericfichtl.org/articles/ambiguous-nature-collaboration-colombia (accessed 19 February 2022).

FIP [Fundación Ideas para la Paz] (2005), '¿Qué hacer con el DAS?', *La Paz*, 7 April, 42, http:// archive.ideaspaz.org/images/boletin_conflicto42.pdf (accessed 12 December 2020).

FIP [Fundación Ideas para la Paz] (2008), 'Respuesta a derecho de petición del Superintendente de Vigilancia y Seguridad Privada sobre las empresas de servicios especiales de vigilancia y seguridad privada, creadas bajo la Vigencia del Decreto 356 de 1994, posteriormente llamadas "Convivir"'.

Fiscalía General de la Nación (2019), 'Fiscalía concluye estudio sobre terceros civiles vinculados al conflicto armado', 23 May, https://www.fiscalia.gov.co/colombia/notic ias/fiscalia-concluye-estudio-sobre-terceros-civiles-vinculados-al-conflicto-armado/ (accessed 3 February 2022).

Gómez Pinilla, P. (2020), 'A dos años de apertura de la JEP, los terceros van a medio camino', *De justicia*, 13 March 2020, https://www.dejusticia.org/a-dos-anos-de-apertura-de-la-jep-los-terceros-van-a-medio-camino/ (accessed 7 November 2020).

Gutiérrez Sanín, F. (2019), *Clientelistic Warfare: Paramilitaries and the State in Colombia (1982–2007)* (New York, Peter Lang).

Gutiérrez Sanín, F. and Vargas, J. (2016), 'Introducción', in F. Gutiérrez and J. Vargas (eds), *El despojo paramilitar y su variación: Quiénes, cómo, por qué* (Bogotá, Editorial Universidad del Rosario).

Human Rights Watch (2001), 'La "sexta división": Relaciones militares–paramilitares y la política estadounidense en Colombia', https://www.hrw.org/es/report/2001/10/04/la-sexta-division/relaciones-militares-paramilitares-y-la-politica-estadounidense (accessed 15 August 2020).

JEP [Jurisdicción Especial para la Paz] (2020), 'La JEP en cifras', report of August 2020, https://www.jep.gov.co/jepcifras/JEP%20en%20cifras%20%20julio%2031%20de%202020.pdf#search=terceros (accessed 19 January 2021).

Kalyvas, S. N. (2008), 'Promises and pitfalls of an emerging research program: The microdynamics of civil war', in S. N. Kalyvas, I. Shapiro, and T. Masoud (eds) *Order, Conflict and Violence* (Cambridge, Cambridge University Press), 397–421.

Laverde, J. D. (2014), 'Un sistema de inteligencia torcido: El DAS como instrumento de un proyecto presidencialista autoritario' (Bogotá, Universidad Nacional de Colombia-IEPRI), https://repositorio.unal.edu.co/bitstream/handle/unal/47125/75098085.2014.pdf?sequence=1&isAllowed=y (accessed 5 April 2021).

Martínez, J. F. (2021), *Chuzadas*, 2nd edn (Bogotá, Penguin).

Medina Gallego, C. (1990), *Autodefensas, paramilitarismo y narcotráfico en Colombia: Origen, desarrollo y consolidación. El caso Puerto Boyacá* (Bogotá: Editorial Documentos Periodísticos).

Michalowski, S., M. C. Rodríguez, A. O. Ruiz, and L. G. Batancur (2020), *Guía de orientación jurídica: Terceros civiles ante la Jurisdicción Especial para la Paz (JEP)* (Bogotá, DeJusticia).

Narváez, J. M. (1997), 'Guerra política como concepto de guerra integral', *Revista de las Fuerzas Armadas*, 162, https://issuu.com/esdeguecol/docs/162 (accessed 4 April 2021).

National Security Archive (2011), 'Who Killed Jaime Garzón?', https://nsarchive2.gwu.edu/NSAEBB/NSAEBB360/index.htm (accessed 2 February 2022).

NCOS [Nationaal Centrum voor Ontwikkelingssamenwerking] (1995), *Tras los pasos perdidos de la guerra sucia: Paramilitarismo y operaciones encubiertas en Colombia* (Brussels, NCOS).

Nova, M. (2020), *Memorias militares: Conversaciones con los comandantes del Ejército 1989–2019* (Bogotá, Editorial Planeta).

Orozco Abad, I. (2009), *Justicia transicional en tiempos del deber de memoria* (Bogotá, Editorial Temis).

Ortega, P. (2014), 'Colaboradores, boicoteadores y riesgos: Aproximación teórica al impacto del conflicto armado en la movilización social', *Análisis político*, 27, 191–209.

Payne, L. A. (2001), 'Collaborators and the politics of memory in Chile', *Human Rights Review*, 2, 8–26.

Pizarro Leongómez, E. (2018), *De la guerra a la paz: Las Fuerzas Militares entre 1996 y 2018* (Bogotá, Planeta).

Publimetro (2020), 'Marta Lucía y el asesino de Jaime Garzón', *Publimetro*, 15 June, https://www.publimetro.co/co/opinion/2020/06/15/marta-lucia-asesino-jaime-garzon.html (accessed 2 February 2022).

Robinson, J. (2014), 'La realidad colombiana', in M. Ronderos (ed.), *Guerras recicladas: Una historia periodística del paramilitarismo en Colombia* (Bogotá, Aguilar), 15–21.

Ronderos, M. T. (2007), *5 en humor: Rendón, Klim, Osuna, Garzón, Vlado* (Bogotá, Aguilar).

Ronderos, M. T. (2014), *Guerras recicladas: Una historia periodística del paramilitarismo en Colombia* (Bogotá, Aguilar).

Saffon, M. P. (2006), 'Poder paramilitar y debilidad institucional. El paramilitarismo en Colombia: Un caso complejo de incumplimiento de normas', master's thesis (Universidad de los Andes, Bogotá).

Sánchez, N. C., García-Godos, J., and Vallejo, C. (2016), 'Colombia: Transitional justice before transition', in E. Skaar, J. Garcia-Godos, and C. Collins (eds), *Transitional Justice in Latin America: The Uneven Road from Impunity towards Accountability* (New York, Routledge), 252–74.

Sánchez-Moreno, M. M. C. (2018), *Aquí no ha habido muertos: Una historia de asesinato y negación en Colombia* (Bogotá, Editorial Planeta).

Santos, F. (1999), 'Guerra sucia', *Diario el tiempo*, 15 August.

Semana (2006), 'El DAS y los paras', 12 February, https://www.semana.com/portada/artic ulo/el-das-paras/75769-3/ (accessed 22 August 2020).

Semana (2019), 'Narváez, lo que había en la mente del asesino de Jaime Garzón', *Semana*, 13 August, https://www.semana.com/nacion/articulo/perfil-de-jose-miguel-narvaez-el-asesino-de-jaime-garzon/579623 (accessed 31 October 2020).

Silva Romero, R. (2020), *Rio muerto* (Bogotá, Editorial Alfaguara).

Ugarriza, J. E. and Pabón, N. (2017), *Militares y guerrilla: La memoria histórica del conflicto armado en Colombia desde los archivos militares, 1958–2016*, 2nd edn (Bogotá, Editorial Universidad del Rosario).

Uprimny R., Saffon Sanín, M. P., Botero Marino, C., and Restrepo Saldarriaga, E. (2006), *¿Justicia transicional sin transición? Verdad, justicia y reparación para Colombia* (Bogotá, DeJusticia).

Valencia Tovar, A. (1990), 'Las debilidades estructurales del Estado y la solución de conflictos en cuanto a la justicia y el monopolio de la fuerza en el caso colombiano', in J. A. Bejarano (ed.), *Construir la paz: Memorias del Seminario Paz, Democracia y Desarrollo* (Bogotá, Centro de Estudios de la Realidad Colombiana).

Vásquez, T. and Barrera, V. (2018), *Paramilitarismo: Balance de la contribución del CNMH al esclarecimiento histórico* (Bogotá, Centro Nacional de Memoria Histórica).

Verdabierta.com (2011), 'De militares a "paras"', 24 November, https://verdadabierta.com/ de-militares-a-paramilitares/ (accessed 8 August 2020).

World Organisation against Torture *et al.* (1992), *El terrorismo de estado en Colombia* (Brussels, NCOS).

8

Informing, Intelligence, and Public Policy in Northern Ireland: Some Overlooked Negative Consequences of Deploying Informers against Political Violence

RON DUDAI AND KEVIN HEARTY

THE TERM 'INFORMERS' connotes different images depending on context. For many now it is firmly connected with the experience of eastern and central European societies under Communism, and the mass recruitment of ordinary citizens as informers by security services such as the KGB, the Stasi, or the Czechoslovakian Státni bezpečnost (StB). Films such as *The Lives of Others* (Donnersmarck 2006); books such as *The File* (Garton Ash 2009); and the constant stream of revelations, rumours, and 'outings' of alleged former secret informers – targeting people from academic Julia Kristeva to Polish leader Lech Wałęsa – made 'informing' synonymous with despicable betrayal of friends, neighbours, and comrades in the aid of unjust regimes. In this context, informing is considered axiomatically as a moral wrong – though there may be empathy for some informers blackmailed by the regime – and there is much scholarly attention to the legacy of the practice and its long-term effects on society after transitions (Espindola 2015). For others, on the other hand, 'informers' connote ordinary law enforcement in democracies – using criminals-turned-informers as a classic tool of police forces – indeed, a necessary method to prosecute organised crime and other forms of widespread criminality successfully. In this context, informers are generally seen as unsavoury figures, neither victims nor heroes. Much of recent scholarly discussion, however, tends to question the ethics of the practice (Billingsley 2009) – especially its affinity with police corruption – and its corrosive effects on the criminal justice system (Natapoff 2009).

In contrast to these familiar tropes, this chapter examines the images of informing in another setting: the struggle against political violence by armed groups (the neutral term to describe groups known otherwise as 'terrorists' or 'rebels'). We argue that in this context there is an emerging narrative that posits informing as an

Proceedings of the British Academy, **248**, 157–178, © The British Academy 2022.

effective, indispensable tool that states should employ against such groups. Here the image of informing is bound up with the heroics of intelligence services, and the practice is presented as the most shrewd way to beat 'terrorism', more efficient and less problematic than the deployment of military force or methods such as torturing suspects. In this chapter we present and challenge this view, demonstrating how enthusiastic assessments of the role of informing are based on wilfully ignoring many of its darkest features and effects, and disregarding its long-term negative effects on transitions out of violence. Our case study is the Northern Ireland (NI) conflict and transition. This has long been one of the most studied cases of polit-ical violence and conflict-transformation, and has generated an entire 'industry' of 'lessons from Northern Ireland' (Dixon 2012). It has at times involved policy transfers and even direct 'exporting' of methods and strategies by former security personnel (Ellison and O'Reilly 2008). As the experience of NI is often cited in support of claims about the effectiveness of informers, the discussion of their role in this context is of particular significance.

The recruitment and operation by governments of informers from the ranks of armed groups has of course been a global feature of counter-terrorism and counter-insurgency for decades and indeed centuries. As both states and rebels have long recognised, being members of insurgent groups and communities means informers have access to information not easily available by other means of intelligence gathering (Cohen and Dudai 2005: 230; Bamford 2005: 590), and their operation is indispensable for the pursuit of wartime objectives (Darcy 2019: 1). Nevertheless, the 9/11 attacks and the ensuing 'War on Terror' have renewed interest in informing as a counter-terrorist tool. American and British governments adopted policies that placed a premium on recruiting informers from Muslim groups and communities, as part of the effort to reduce the threat from Islamist violence, with informers recruited both at home (Hewitt 2010: 121–46; Ross 2008: 263–5) and in operations abroad, for example in Iraq or Afghanistan (Urban 2010; Sengupta 2016).

Three reasons in particular appear to have made informing seem attractive in the eyes of commentators. First, human intelligence is considered the most effective tool in the case of fighting guerrilla or terrorist tactics: where the state's military strength can be almost immaterial; where the enemy does not move armoured divisions or air forces; and where, therefore, technological surveillance often cannot detect strategic threat. 'In the fight against Al-Qaida we need people, not tanks', Max Hastings, prominent British military historian and journalist, summed up (2005). Second, infiltration of the enemy by western agents, which may have been possible in Cold War Berlin, is not plausible in cases such as that of Al-Qaeda's outposts in Afghanistan. Thus, recruiting informers from within armed groups' ranks – 'spies unlike us', in former CIA officer Robert Baer's (2005) phrasing – becomes imperative. Third, and crucially for this chapter's discussion, informing has been often seen as a 'softer' alternative to abusive and inherently unlawful methods such as the torture or prolonged detentions without trials that the 'War on Terror' has unleashed, as well as an alternative to mass sweeping surveillance.

For example, Conor Gearty, who has offered perhaps the most high-profile and sustained human rights critique of contemporary British counter-terrorism policies, advocated the use of informers, defining it as 'proper police practice', as opposed to preventive detention (2006: 10). Dru Stevenson (2008) similarly argued that the use of informers can substitute for more pervasive forms of surveillance that can threaten civil liberties.

Several authors have pointed out legal and ethical problems arising from the use of informers by security agencies in the 'War on Terror', most notably the placing of illegitimate pressure on individuals to become informers, the risks of 'entrapment', and the unreliability of evidence from informers (e.g. Said 2010). Such assessments tend, however, to focus on isolated features of the system. In this chapter we now turn to a more comprehensive evaluation of our case study. In the next section we present the narrative in favour of informing. The following sections criticise the use of informers, first by demonstrating how the practice generates and not only reduces violence; second, by exploring its negative long-term effects on transition to peace; and third by arguing that systematic recruitment of paid informers can actually harm the flow of voluntary information from the general public.

It should be emphasised that there is no doubt the use of informers can be an effective tactic: a well-placed informer can certainly foil violent plots, and often do it more effectively than other methods, and with fewer human rights abuses. There are three questions, however. First, does this *tactic* translate to an overall effective *strategy*, rendering political negotiations with armed groups unnecessary? Second, what are the costs and risks of relying on such strategy? And, third, can this effective tactical tool actually become counterproductive when turned into a widespread systematic strategy?

Informers as 'Heroes' of the Northern Ireland Peace Process

Tripartite political violence involving (non-state) Irish Republican, Ulster Loyalist, and (state) security force actors in NI claimed approximately 3,600 lives as a low-intensity conflict raged there from 1968/9 onwards (McKittrick *et al.* 2008). After decades of this violence, 'back channel' peace negotiations instigated in the late 1980s eventually bore fruit as a peace process slowly emerged into the public eye by the mid-1990s. The process of moving out of everyday political violence and into a context of largely peaceful coexistence – residual low-level spoiler violence by Irish Republican splinter groups aside – was a protracted and choreographed affair necessitating a certain degree of compromise on all sides (Darby and McGinty 2001). Not without internal discontent that would eventually give way to factionalising into new political and (much smaller) armed groups (Bean 2007; McGlinchey 2019), the process saw a remarkable chain of events that ultimately led the majority of Irish Republicans to replace armed struggle with constitutional politics: ceasefires by the Irish Republican Army (IRA) – and the much smaller

Irish National Liberation Army (INLA) – in 1994 and again in 1997, the acceptance of the consociational Good Friday Agreement (GFA) peace accord in 1998, the placing of weapons 'beyond use' in the early 2000s, the formal disbandment of the IRA in 2005, Sinn Féin's 'critical engagement' with policing in 2008, and a position for Sinn Féin as joint partners in a power-sharing administration at Stormont (Hearty 2017).

While a significant body of scholarship has long discussed the 'meta-conflict' emerging from continued political disagreement over the causes and consequences of conflict in the north of Ireland (Alvarez Berastegi 2017; Hearty 2017), the issue of *what* – or even *who* – created the climate for an end to political violence by non-state armed groups has become of more recent scholarly and public interest. The conventional understandings of the peace process frame it as the logical conclusion to a 'mutually hurting stalemate' whereby no party to the conflict could secure outright victory even if they did not succumb to military defeat, or, conversely, as the natural product of a politically 'ripe moment' where changed local, national, and global constellations made a negotiated settlement of the conflict inevitable (Tonge *et al*. 2011; Connolly and Doyle 2015). Yet a critical counter-narrative began challenging this orthodoxy: according to this narrative the peace process has been the result of the ultimate 'defeat' of the IRA; and this defeat was a result of the work of state intelligence agencies that operated informers in the IRA's ranks. This interpretation, then, rejects that description of the embrace of constitutional politics by the Republican leadership of Gerry Adams and Martin McGuinness as seizing the political initiative through a tactical switch from armed struggle to political struggle in the face of being in a never-going-to-win-but-never-going-to-lose bind, as the common explanations suggest (Hearty 2017). Rather, it poses the final triumph of the forces of 'law and order' over the 'terrorist', yet not so much through direct military conformation as through the cunning secret work of informers and their handlers, which, the argument goes, effectively incapacitated the IRA by the mid-1990s.

Sensationalist media 'exposés', robust investigative journalism, formal truth recovery, and the memoirs of former conflict protagonists have all introduced the figure of the informer to this equation. In the NI context, an 'informer' refers to a person who covertly passed on information about an armed group to the security forces.[1] This could be anyone, for example a local petty criminal who passes on information about local IRA suspects in return for non-prosecution for 'ordinary' crime offences, a nosy neighbour who – perhaps even unwittingly – alerts the security forces to armed activity by reporting suspicious behaviour in their street, a sympathiser on the periphery of the group who passes on information they pick up through the loose talk of others, an active member of the IRA 'turned' by the security

---

[1] The term 'collaborator', on the other hand, was at times used by the IRA and INLA for people, such as civilian contractors working on security installations, who publicly rendered a material service to the 'British war machine' (Hearty 2019), though it was much less prominent than the informer label.

forces upon arrest, or even a community member inserted into underground groups by the intelligence services. They might pass on information reluctantly or willingly, and do so out of spite (like the 'grudge' informers Colleen Murphy discusses in Chapter 10), desperation, ideology, or for self-gain or self-preservation. It is therefore difficult to categorise NI informers, as Darcy (2019; Chapter 12 of this volume) argues, in terms of international law's dominant metrics, and also hard to decipher their actions on moral terms during transitional justice processes, as Mark Drumbl and Barbara Hola further point out in Chapter 5. Although, as the report of the Consultative Group on the Past (CGP) (2009: 71) readily acknowledged, the exact scale of informing within armed groups remains unknown, a steady stream of new revelations has recalibrated how some people interpret the transition from armed conflict to (admittedly imperfect) peace in NI.

Some commentators have been suggesting that the use of informers against the IRA in NI was so successful that it should be replicated elsewhere. The former head of the Royal Ulster Constabulary (RUC) Special Branch (SB), for example, said that informing and intelligence-gathering methods used in NI should be a 'beacon of good practice' in 'mainland' Britain (Clark 2009). In another typical illustration, the *Guardian*'s veteran NI correspondent complained, when people involved in the NI peace process went to advise the political actors in the Basque Country in relation to the peace process there, 'the extent to which all branches of the security forces had successfully penetrated the Provisional IRA' was not prominently on the agenda. He argued that British officials and others mislead when they present 'dialogue' as the key to persuading the IRA to move from armed struggle to politics, and decried how 'in the passing caravan of peace-process tourism there is normally no mention of the secret war conducted by the state and its impact in convincing republicans they could not win the war' (McDonald 2011).

It is very interesting that those who subscribe to – and propagate – this narrative, come from diverse, and at times opposing, camps: they include conservative commentators (Frampton 2008, 2009) and former security force personnel (Matchett 2016; Southern 2018), as well as Republican hardliners who oppose the peace process or are disillusioned by the turn from underground to mainstream politics by the Republican movement (Moloney 2011; Bradley and Feeney 2012; Conway 2014). They also include ex-informers (O'Callaghan 2017); it is perhaps not surprising that they will attribute such effects to their own activities, though the public prominence of the voice of ex-informers in commentating on NI is in itself exceptional (Dudai 2012).

Perhaps the most vocal proponent of the informers-brought-the-peace view is former RUC SB officer William Matchett. Indeed, Matchett's 2016 book (developed from his Ph.D. thesis on the RUC SB) is not only entitled *Secret Victory*, but is premised on the core notion that the RUC SB 'defeated' the IRA (Matchett 2016). Matchett has further propagated this triumphalism through his frequent media commentary and through his academic writings (Matchett 2015, 2017). He argues against the 'mutually hurting stalemate' thesis and that the contribution of intelligence-led policing is left out of the 'Northern Ireland model' and its 'lessons learnt' (Matchett 2015). For Matchett, the omission of the security dimension in preference for a narrative about political negotiation emerging out of stalemate was a deliberate political calculation by the British government to enable the Sinn Féin leadership to save face over having been 'defeated' by the RUC SB's intelligence-led policing (Matchett 2017: 42).

Rather than being in response to politico-military stalemate, Matchett asserts that the Irish Republican move into constitutional politics was an enforced decision brought about by the policing effectiveness of the RUC SB. In short, he believes that through recruiting agents, running sources, and effecting arrests, the RUC SB (along with other intelligence agencies) forced the IRA to sue for peace when the possibility arose in the 1990s, as many activists were jailed and other operatives had become demoralised and paranoid as a result of security successes (Matchett 2015) – and all this, he maintains, in a manner that was much more human-rights-compliant than intelligence-led policing in other conflicts (Matchett 2015, 2016). Even if the RUC SB are not duly acknowledged in the prevailing 'peace process' discourse for their heroics in 'defeating' the IRA, Matchett argues that the hands-on involvement of many former RUC SB officers in assisting Coalition forces in Iraq and Afghanistan with their counterinsurgency efforts provides evidence of their success in the field (Matchett 2017).

This view has, unsurprisingly, been shared by others involved in the intelligence war against the IRA. Former informer Sean O'Callaghan (2017: 71), for instance, asserts that while politicians such as Tony Blair, Gerry Adams, and Bill Clinton take credit for the peace process, these figures simply 'reaped the harvest of peace that others had sown in a long intelligence war'. For O'Callaghan, the RUC SB, and not politicians, had 'won the peace by careful detective work': 'I make absolutely no apology for saluting the brave men and women of RUC Special Branch. It was they who, more than any politician, forced the IRA to stop killing and bombing. They provided the opportunity for glory-hunting politicians to feel the hand of history on their shoulder and to conclude a squalid deal' (O'Callaghan 2017: 73).

And like Matchett, O'Callaghan asserts that one of the most remarkable aspects of the RUC SB 'victory' over the 'terrorist' was that officers 'had to operate under the rules of the civil law and in spite of all the provocation, they behaved, mostly, with impeccable restraint' (72).

This heroification of intelligence agencies and informers as the people who 'won' peace for the north of Ireland also pervades the memoirs of informers and/or their handlers. While there are, of course, moral, political, commercial, and legal considerations at play when these individuals choose to record their activities (Dudai 2012; Hopkins 2017), these accounts have largely echoed, without inflection, Matchett's belief that the IRA were 'defeated' in the intelligence war thanks to the courage and dedication of intelligence agencies and the sources they handled.

These memoirs naturally sanitise and sensationalise the practice of informing (and informer-handling) during the conflict (Dudai 2012); the motives of informers are idealised as wanting to 'save lives' and to defeat the 'terrorist', while at the same time the informer's status within the group, their ability to sabotage planned 'spectaculars', and the extent to which the group was both demoralised and disrupted through this subterfuge are all inflated (McGartland 1997; O'Callaghan 1998; Gilmour 1998; Fulton 2006). Martin McGartland (1997), for example, claims to have saved at least 50 lives during his time as an agent within the Belfast IRA, while informer-later-turned-supergrass Raymond Gilmour (1998) claims that his information led to the arrest of several leading IRA and INLA operatives in Derry. Indeed, Gilmour's former SB handler portrays his prize agent as someone who was not only a highly effective informer dealing a serious blow to the IRA and INLA but was driven primarily by his desire to save innocent lives (Barker 2006). Some disillusioned former IRA operatives, particularly from Belfast, have ruefully acknowledged the success that intelligence agencies had in infiltrating the organisation by the 1990s (Moloney 2011; Bradley and Feeney 2012), with former senior IRA member Brendan Hughes going so far as to state that 'Belfast was rotten' by the time of the IRA ceasefire (Moloney 2011: 284). While all the relevant information needed for a precise picture of how successful or otherwise state intelligence agencies were in infiltrating the IRA and influencing the Sinn Féin peace strategy remains siloed off in locked state archives (Leahy 2020: 14), these memoirs have become the proxy means of framing the emergence of the peace process in accordance with jaundiced perspectives (Hopkins 2013).

This narrative of heroic agents and their handlers defeating the IRA has not, however, gone unchallenged. The notion that intelligence agencies and informers 'won' the peace has been increasingly called into question. For example, former Republican prisoner Danny Morrison, himself imprisoned through the actions of informers, repudiates the theory of the RUC SB 'defeating' the IRA as evinced by those such as Matchett. With his trademark acerbic wit, Morrison (2018) commented 'that theory … would explain why the RUC *is* no longer, and why Matchett's new "beat" is the corridors of Maynooth College where he now lectures'.

Yet the most important critique is that this narrative simply exaggerates the role of informers and downplays other factors. Informers undoubtedly damaged the IRA's campaign, but that did not, for example, foil many of its high-profile operations – e.g. the near-miss assassination attempts on Prime Ministers Margaret Thatcher in 1984 and John Major in 1991, or the mid-1990s bombings of central Manchester and Canary Wharf in London, which costs hundreds of millions of pounds in damages. If the IRA had been as heavily penetrated as described, it would simply not have been possible to carry out such attacks.[2] The narrative of informing as the main cause of the peace process is heavy on anecdotes where planned IRA 'spectaculars' were allegedly averted or disrupted by informers, yet remarkably short on concrete explanations as to why informers failed to stop these actual attacks.

---

[2] The IRA has been a centralised and disciplined organisation, and attacks of this nature would have been approved by the collective decision-making body known as the Army Council.

Moreover, it is clear that a host of factors influenced the decision to engage with the peace process – the end of the Cold War, the further integration of the European Union, the 9/11 attacks, and other such factors (O'Leary 2005). It is somewhat parochial to ignore all of these developments and attribute the peace process only to the actions of the local intelligence services. In short, as Leahy (2020) recently argued, that the IRA did not win militarily does not mean that the intelligence services did win, and no compelling evidence has been presented by those who argue that informers, rather than a stalemate fashioned by multiple political and military factors, led to the Irish Republican engagement with the peace process.

Moreover, we argue not only that the positive (from the state perspective) impact of informing is exaggerated, but that its negative effects are played down, as the next sections explore. Here we echo the critique of the Da Silva report into the killing of human rights lawyer Pat Finucane found in Shane Darcy's Chapter 12; the running of agents within armed groups was defended as a legitimate and effective means of tackling political violence in NI, yet at the same time the report also contained a catalogue of wrongdoing by informers and their handlers that led to the taking, rather than preservation, of life during the conflict.

The Recruitment of Informers as a Policy Generating Violence

Given the premise that the use of informers is effective in the fight against non-state political violence, the first point we emphasise is that the systematic recruitment of informers generates – and not just reduces – political violence. This is, first, because mass recruitment of informers inevitably triggers reprisals by the armed groups, which target real, suspected, and wrongly accused informers.

While exact numbers are still hard to come by, during the conflict the IRA killed over 70 people it alleged were informers, and adding those killed by other Republican groups and Loyalist organisations, the number of alleged informers who were killed during the NI conflict is over 100. Conceivably, if a policy of recruiting informers was not in place, these 100 people would not have been killed. Of course, it may be that the use of informers saved more than 100 lives, but this will be hard to measure, and it is of course morally questionable whether sacrificing dozens of people in order potentially to save others ought to be a legitimate government policy.[3] Many more alleged informers were forcibly 'exiled';[4] others were beaten, injured, or tortured; and the effects on informers' families have also been damaging (Dudai 2018). This amount of violence and

---

[3] As a seasoned human rights activist told one of the authors: 'it's always hard to quantify a negative; we don't know how many lives were saved, but we certainly know a lot of lives were lost' (interview with a human rights activist, London, June 2012).

[4] Forced to leave the area by the IRA with the threat that if they fail to do so – or return later on – they will be killed by the organisation, as indeed happened several times (Dudai 2022).

suffering generated by informing remains largely unmentioned in the glorifying accounts described above. This may be as this kind of violence remains politically and socially invisible to state agencies and others, in a form of what Cohen (2001) termed cultural denial. Put differently, violence affecting those who engage with unlawful organisations or come from an 'enemy' community does not register in the equations offered in the accounts sketched in the previous section.

The reactions engendered by informing also had other effects contributing to violence. The immunity given to criminals in exchange for informing, and the reluctance of victims and witnesses to report crime to the police (both because of ideological reasons and because of fear of being targeted as informers by the IRA) contributed to the under-policing of violent crime as well as to the phenomenon of 'punishment violence' against suspected criminals by armed groups (McEvoy and Mika 2002). A related illustration is that women who were victims of domestic violence were reluctant to report it to the RUC out of fear that they or their partners would be pressured to become informers (McWilliams 1995: 19; Garret 1999: 43) and might end up targeted by the IRA. This, again, remains outside the equation in many narratives. In short, a view of the use of informers as simply reducing violence is not tenable – or is tenable only if commentators choose wilfully to ignore such effects.

Moreover, perhaps the clearest illustration of how recruitment and operation of informers generates violence is that informers themselves were involved in violence; indeed, they had to carry it out in order to maintain their cover. It is a truism of any police handling of long-term informers that it must involve a measure of turning a blind eye to some criminal dealings. Police may, for example, allow their source to carry out some minor drug dealing in exchange for information about massive drug smuggling. But where can the line be drawn in relation to political violence? Laws and guidelines remain deliberately obscure (Darcy 2019). In NI it appears clear that informers and the agencies they worked for involved themselves in the *taking* of life. As in other cases, hard evidence is hard to come by, but more and more revelations point toward such assessments.

For example, the brother of RUC officer John Larmour who was shot dead by the IRA in October 1988 believes that the killer was a 'super tout', protected from prosecution by the intelligence agencies and allowed to progress through the highest echelons of the IRA in furtherance of the intelligence war (Larmour 2016). Former agent handler-turned-whistleblower Marin Ingram frankly admitted in his memoir that intelligence agencies were 'playing God' with people's lives: security force lives, agent lives, *and* civilian lives (Ingram and Harkin 2004). Former informer Kevin Fulton (2006: 139) admits to being involved in certain attacks, albeit offering the proviso that this was for the 'greater good' in enabling him to progress within the IRA where he could 'save more lives than I helped to take'.[5]

---

[5] Although, Raymond Gilmour (1998) maintained that he was never directly involved in the taking of human life, a position supported by his handler (Barker 2006).

We need of course to ask whether that kind of calculation is ever legitimate, and who, if so, should make it, and how – all questions that remained unanswered, and indeed unasked, in many such accounts.

The spectre of state agents taking lives during the 'dirty war' has not been confined to memoirs, but has also featured periodically in formal attempts to 'deal with the past' in NI. Formal efforts at truth recovery have addressed the issue of informer complicity in particular conflict-related deaths. One notable example of this is the Police Ombudsman report into the killing by the IRA of Newry man Eoin Morley. A former member of the IRA, Morley had defected to the Irish People's Liberation Organisation (IPLO) splinter group before being shot by the IRA who later claimed that he was an informer (an allegation subsequently withdrawn years later). The report found that during the investigation into his death the RUC had not pursued a number of lines of enquiry relevant to a number of prominent suspects (OPONI 2005), subsequently believed to be informers protected by the RUC SB. Indeed, the Morley family believe that Kevin Fulton was centrally involved in the attack (Erwin 2019), while Fulton himself does little to dispel such suspicions when he discusses the killing in his memoir.

Yet, concerns in the Morley case are just the tip of the iceberg, given the revelations that a senior member of the IRA's internal security unit (the unit tasked with identifying and eliminating informers within the organisation) was seemingly a high-level state agent codenamed Stakeknife. While Stakeknife's outing as an agent has provided plentiful grist to the tabloid mill, claims that the individual concerned was involved in taking the lives of dozens of people, including other agents, has sparked the largest criminal investigation in UK history. The ongoing Operation Kenova investigation is querying claims that Stakeknife was involved in 'kidnap, torture and murder by the Provisional IRA' in their role as an agent, while also examining 'whether there is evidence of criminal offences having been committed by members of the British Army, the Security Services or other government personnel'.[6] And, as Shane Darcy notes in his discussion of the Da Silva report (Chapter 12), similar concerns about agent – and handler – wrongdoing are to be found when the role of state agents within Loyalist armed groups comes under scrutiny.

This paints a much more troublesome picture of agent handling during the conflict than that created through the herofication of the intelligence agencies and their agents. The clear involvement of informers, often with the knowledge, if not tacit approval, of their handlers in deliberate harms, even against other informers, is incongruous with the notion that intelligence-led policing was human-rights-compliant and simply helped to 'save lives'. Despite this more complex reality, Matchett (2018) has seen fit only to concede that 'security policy was not perfect', before caveating this with the assertion that 'some soldiers and police committed criminal acts, as distinct from immediate reaction to events in a high-risk environment, or honest mistake'.

---

[6] See the investigation's website, www.opkenova.co.uk (accessed 6 February 2022).

In short, the phenomenon of informing during political conflicts clearly generates violence, in the host of direct and indirect ways we have identified.[7] This at the very least should make us rethink the claims about the effectiveness of using informers to quell political violence. Moreover, in the next section we turn to long-term effects that illustrate how, as a long-standing strategy, the use of informers can actually become counterproductive to the goals of ending violence and bringing about peace.

How Informing Hinders the Transition to Peace

As we have mentioned, there has been much attention given to the long-term legacy of informing in the eastern European context (see Mark Drumbl and Barbara Hola's Chapter 5, for instance), but it is less usually discussed in the Northern Irish and similar cases. Our argument is that informing complicated the transition out of violence, and its long-term effects must be taken into account as well in assessing the practice. Informing, even if effective in the short-term, can have an unintended lasting consequence of helping to sustain opposition to peace processes and support for continuing violence.[8]

First, the legacy of informing helped dissident Republicans discredit the leadership's decision to end the armed struggle by portraying it as a product of manipulation by informers. Such erosion of the public legitimacy of the peace process, at least in the eyes of some audiences, is a problematic long-term consequence of the pervasive use of informers during the conflict.[9] A toxic culture of 'informer setting' has percolated into internal political disagreement within modern Irish Republicanism.[10] On the one hand, Republican rivals of Sinn Féin have suggested that its peace strategy was only brought about through the machinations of state intelligence agencies and their informers, while on the other hand, Sinn Féin

---

[7] In other contexts, security agencies have also operated 'agent provocateurs' who often had the ironic effect of sustaining defunct subversive organisations (Marx 1988), though this remains outside our remit here.

[8] Cohen and Dudai (2005) made a similar argument in the Israeli–Palestinian context, where the pervasive recruitment of Palestinian collaborators and informers by Israeli security services hampered the support for and legitimacy of Palestinian groups and individuals who genuinely advocated non-violent agendas, as they were immediately suspected and branded as collaborators and informers by other Palestinians. Therefore, while the systematic use of informers has very probably foiled many attacks by Palestinians, it ultimately also sustained the violence by inhibiting the impact of internal Palestinian opposition to it (2005: 239).

[9] Larkin (2012) aptly argued that 'The repeated (and incorrect) assertion that MI5 was running the IRA and pushing the peace process feeds the ire of armed groups in Ireland who oppose the Good Friday agreement.'

[10] In the Irish context there has long been a practice locally known as 'felon-setting', which means arguing that political actions are actually a disguise for criminal activities. The term 'informer-setting' offered in Dudai (2022), describes an analogous practice whereby political factions blame each other as actually being controlled by informers.

leaders have branded their rivals as 'micro groups' heavily penetrated by informers, working to a 'securocrat' agenda (Hearty 2016).

Media speculation has fuelled this. In its most extreme form, tabloids have carried sensationalist and unsubstantiated stories from unnamed 'intelligence sources' claiming that Republican leaders Gerry Adams (McCallion 2020) or Martin McGuinness (McDonald 2006) were agents of British intelligence services.[11] These kinds of claims are undoubtedly disruptive to the peace process, denying the agency of the Republican embrace of peaceful politics. Yet such claims are generated, and are considered plausible by some sectors, because of the reality of the pervasive use of informers during the conflict, and the toxic mix of formal secrecy and persistent rumours (Dudai 2012). Rumours, claims, and counter-claims regarding the identity of alleged informers have not only been targeting leaders but have been periodically surfacing regarding many former conflict protagonists. As Denis Bradley, co-chair of the government-appointed CGP, said, 'the constant pressure now exerted for information about informers to be revealed only serves to further undermine the well-being of communities to a degree that could be poisonous'.[12]

Revelations that figures close to the Adams–McGuinness leadership, such as former senior Sinn Féin official Denis Donaldson or Stakeknife, were informers have provided further opportunity for such charges to be made. Donaldson has been pinpointed as an 'agent of influence' who allegedly helped to silence any internal dissension within the Republican movement in the prelude to the peace process (Hopkins 2017; Leahy 2020), while Stakeknife has recently been linked to the removal of a number of hardline IRA figures (BBC 2019). Although based on conjecture, rumour, and supposition, rather than objective analysis of cold, hard facts, this media circus has created unhelpful background noise. The result of this, as Hopkins (2017) points out, is that some rank-and-file Republicans today retrospectively question just whose strategy the peace process actually was and in whose interest the movement away from armed struggle was ultimately made.

Second, the problematic figure of the informer continues to be a destabilising factor in the attempt to build a new and healthy political culture in a country still facing sectarianism, fragile political institutions, and sporadic violence. The legacy of informing has reverberated throughout post-GFA NI to generate political crisis and frustrate peacebuilding. The spectre of the informer has been ever present during moments of discomfiting political crisis in the north of Ireland. These involve, for example, a break-in at police intelligence headquarters in 2002, which almost derailed the peace process and was blamed on an IRA operation to retrieve files containing informers' identities; the 'Stormontgate' scandal of an alleged IRA spy ring at government offices (bizarrely led by Denis Donaldson) that provided

---

[11] Others, such as self-confessed informer Willie Carlin (2019), have been more measured in their synopsis, suggesting that while McGuinness himself was probably not an informer he was nonetheless 'protected' by MI5, who saw the ascension of the Adams–McGuinness leadership as the Republican movement coming into the hands of people with whom MI5 could 'do business'.

[12] Cited in BBC (2008).

sceptical Unionists with an exit point from power-sharing later that year; and an allegation made by an unnamed informer in 2016 that the Sinn Féin leadership had sanctioned the killing of Donaldson (BBC 2016).[13] Throughout this period, then, allegations relating to informers have been a useful platform when Unionists have needed an excuse to disengage from power-sharing with Sinn Féin.

Third, informing has also been an obstacle for truth recovery and dealing with the past. On the one hand, this reflects, from the state's perspective at least, the need to protect the identities of informers, an argument since used to justify withholding certain information in inquiries and other truth recovery processes (Bowcott 2007). The state has thus sought to withhold relevant files relating to informer involvement in certain incidents on 'national security' grounds, while those impacted by informer-related violence have legally challenged this lack of disclosure (Erwin 2019). Such a restrictive approach to truth recovery flies in the face of the argument that a full truth recovery process is essential for stabilising the transition out of violence.

On the other hand, the legacy of informing has also caused a chill factor against post-conflict 'speaking out' to resonate within the Irish Republican constituency. Take, for example, the 2014 arrest of the then Sinn Féin president Gerry Adams in connection with the disappearance of alleged informer Jean McConville in 1972. Although Adams has long been publicly accused of complicity in the McConville case by disillusioned former associate Brendan Hughes (Moloney 2011), he was formally arrested in connection with the case after being linked to the killing in interviews given by former IRA members to Boston College's oral history project. Although no charges were ever made against Adams, his arrest opened a pro-verbial can of worms for Irish Republican approaches to 'dealing with the past'. Those who had given interviews to the project were criticised for breaking the Republican 'code of honour' by disclosing incriminating information about the role that others had allegedly played during the conflict. Indeed, the Adams arrest was later followed by that of Sinn Féin's Bobby Storey and the protracted trial of former IRA commander Ivor Bell on the basis of the same interviews. This led to interviewees (and the researchers) being labelled the 'Boston College touts' (McIntyre 2016). The 'informer' label also limited – or served as an excuse for limiting – Republican engagement with formal inquiries about the past. Martin McGuiness refused to provide full details about the IRA to the Saville Inquiry into Bloody Sunday, citing the Republican 'code of honour' against informing (*Irish Republican News* 2003), though the relevancy of such a code of honour to peace-time inquiries is not necessarily fully clear. This 'code of honour' has also placed certain limitations on former IRA members during their engagements with other truth recovery processes, such as the Smithwick Inquiry into allegations of Garda Siochana collusion in the IRA killing of two RUC officers (*An Phoblacht* 2014). The continued pull of the Republican 'code of honour' means that some things must

---

[13] Sinn Féin's leaders condemned the killing at the time, and the dissident organisation the Real IRA have claimed responsibility.

remain unsaid, even during post-conflict truth recovery processes, lest one wants to risk being labelled a 'tout'.

Fourth, the legacy of informing also complicated the devolution of policing powers to NI, based on a UK government decision that Sinn Féin (which became a party in government) should not have access to files on informers (McDonald 2008). Yet, more fundamentally, it has also placed unhelpful limitations on Irish Republican engagement with post-reform policing. Internal politicking over informing has framed contestation between pro- and anti-policing factions within the wider Irish Republican community. This has been most notable in terms of competing discourses on 'spoiler violence' and the policing of anti-GFA Republican political activity. Sinn Féin's 'critical engagement' with policing in NI is predicated on empowering those in favour of progressive change via community-based policing and disempowering those seeking to retain regressive 'political policing'. This has birthed a policing narrative of rupture that distinguishes between the 'good' community policing of the present and the 'bad' 'political policing' of the past (Hearty 2017). As part of this process, the Sinn Féin leadership, after initially managing to avoid the issue, has openly called for its supporters to provide information to the Police Service of Northern Ireland (PSNI) about spoiler violence, yet community uptake has been underwhelming.

Several reasons may explain this disengagement. Culturally, informing has always been a taboo practice within Irish Republican communities. The act is also physically dangerous. The 'underground penalty' (Dudai 2018) of punishing informers with death and/or exile has been adopted by spoiler groups post-GFA, with a number of people (mainly members) being killed by such groups for alleged informing (Hearty 2017). A sense of 'informerphobia' (Johnson and Soeters 2015) continues to pervade the post-GFA psyche of Irish Republican communities, whereby even those who support the peace process and are opposed to ongoing spoiler violence are reticent to cooperate with the PSNI – not just out of fear but because of lingering social and cultural norms inculcated through the conflict.[14] Those who oppose the peace process have used the continued efforts to recruit and operate informers within armed groups' ranks to draw a line of continuity between pre-reform and post-reform policing. Anti-policing Republicans have also leveraged the continued role of MI5 in 'national security' in NI to blur the lines between new 'good' and conflict-era 'bad' policing

The most instructive example of this can be seen in the fallout that followed recent arrests of a number of persons allegedly involved in spoiler violence, as part of what was termed Operation Arbacia. The arrests were prompted by the involvement of an MI5 agent in the anti-GFA political group Saoradh (which is a legal political party, albeit one linked in the media to the New IRA) who had apparently entrapped a number of prominent Republicans. The nature of the case naturally invited comparisons with Denis Donaldson's role in the Stormontgate affair (*Irish*

---

[14] Dudai (2022).

Republican News 2020). Under Operation Arbacia, a number of Saoradh offices were raided by PSNI officers. In condemning these raids, one Saoradh spokes-person simultaneously referred to the operation as being carried out by the 'RUC/ PSNI', 'MI5/RUC' and 'Crown Forces' (O'Hare 2020). Far from being a flippant remark made in the heat of the moment, the comment draws a clear line of connect-ivity between past and present policing, and in doing so disrupts the demarcation between the conflict era and the peace process era, feeding off the prevalent sense of 'informerphobia' that still resonates today.

Fifth, the enduring hostility to informers, expressed most vividly in the refusal to countenance the return of exiled informers, is a clear open wound from the past conflict. The report of the CGP (2009: 186) readily acknowledged that 'the use of informers throughout the conflict corroded the fabric of our communities', with the consequence of this being that even today informers remain the 'last unfor-given' (Dudai 2012) within the communities they are estranged from. Just like the 'turned' members of the Montoneros that Ksenija Bilbija discusses in Chapter 3 on Argentina, informers in NI have an inherently irredeemable quality from the per-spective of the movements and communities that they betrayed, regardless of the passage of time or the harms they may have endured. Smyth argued that, in order to complete and stabilise the transition out of conflict, NI requires also a 'demilitar-isation at a cultural and ideological level' (2004: 548), and the issue of informers is one of the main obstacles to such cultural demilitarisation.

Unsurprisingly, the legacy of informing has been most 'poisonous', to use the CGP terminology, within the Irish Republican community. Because informing involves the 'intimacy of betrayal' (Dudai 2012), its legacy has continued to be pol-itically and socially deleterious. Socially, many of those exiled from their communi-ties during the conflict remain as outcasts (CGP 2009), with Raymond Gilmour, for example, dying a lonely alcoholic estranged from his hometown (Monaghan 2016). Politically, too, the legacy of informing has had a palpable impact on contestation over the Sinn Féin peace strategy and contestation over 'critical engagement' with reformed policing (Hearty 2017). In short, the policy of recruiting informers can have damaging long-term implications for the ultimate goals of counter-terrorism and counterinsurgency: to reach a completely peaceful society with 'normal' pol-itical life and citizen–state relationships. These may be unintended consequences, not meant and perhaps not foreseen by those devising conflict-era policies, but this only underlines the importance of identifying and discussing such effects. In the final section we turn to another set of unintended consequences of informing.

The Scale of Informing: How More Informers Can Produce Less Information

So far we have identified a range of negative consequences stemming from the operation of informers, undermining – we hope – the simplistic image that portrays informing as a panacea in the context of political violence. Nevertheless, it remains the fact that the recruitment and operation of an informer can be carried out in a perfectly lawful manner (in clear distinction from practices such as torturing suspects), and it can undoubtedly lead to the interception and prosecution of a violent plot. The key is perhaps one of scale: the difference between a situation whereby security agencies recruit informers in very specific circumstances, in a sporadic and regulated manner, resulting in few, short-term cases, and a policy of systematic, widespread, proactive recruitment, where large numbers of long-term informers operate. We argue that this is one of the cases where quantitative differences lead to qualitatively different phenomena. Pervasive, large-scale, long-term recruitment of informers – as was the case in NI, or in the Israeli–Palestinian case – generates the negative political and social effects sketched above, which targeted, small-scale, ad hoc recruitments may avoid.

Moreover, a pervasive and systematic policy of recruiting long-term informers may eventually lead to the authorities receiving less, not more, relevant information on impeding political violence. There is no doubt that authorities require information from the public in order better to address the threat of political violence. However, such information can come not just from long-term 'proper' informers but also from one-off voluntary 'tip-offs' from members of the public. As Greer (1995) elaborates in his typology of informers, and as has been further shown in many of the contexts discussed in the various contributions to this collection, people passing information to the authorities belong to many categories. They can have long-term, often paid (in money or in kind), relationships with the authorities or engage in a single ad hoc interaction; and they can be inside members of an unlawful enterprise or outsiders in relation to the unlawful acts in question. The 'proper' informer, from inside underground groups, cultivated and handled for long periods, is the figure prominent in the accounts we have surveyed. But voluntary one-off tips from the public can be as important. Willing members of the public, who trust their government, are a crucial source of intelligence, which can also be more reliable than information passed by coerced informers (Rejali 2004). For example, a UK Parliament report on lessons from the 7 July 2005 London bombings found that 'The awareness and vigilance of the public, families and local communities is a significant tool in the fight against terrorism – as important as the resources, manpower, technology and capabilities of our intelligence and security agencies' (ISC 2009: para. 208). We would like to argue that there is potentially a tension between gaining information from these two types of sources: if governments rely too heavily on cultivating long-term informers they can inhibit the equally, if not more important, flow of information from the public.

Creating a widespread and long-lasting *system* of informing, in which informers are *proactively* recruited, can trigger a vicious circle that ultimately results in the reluctance of members of the public to volunteer information to the authorities. This can be sketched as follows. Widespread recruitment of informers inevitably relies on offering reduced penalties to individuals involved in violence and crime, who have to betray close friends or comrades. It thus creates the social stigma of the hated 'informer' within the target communities. This stigma legitimises threats of retaliation, and in turn makes voluntary passing of information from 'ordinary' members of the public less likely. In order to continue to recruit informers the authorities are forced to rely more heavily on ever increasing inducements, both financial rewards and more generous immunities from prosecutions, as well as on various forms of pressure and blackmail. This further exacerbates the social stigma of the 'informer', and anti-state groups will now intensify their efforts in publicly denigrating informers as well as attacking them. By this stage, given the prominence of the hated long-term paid informer, all passing of information to the authorities, no matter the level, context, or motive, comes to be seen as betrayal in the eyes of the relevant communities and is socially proscribed. This leads to a further downward spiral, in which the consequent dearth of voluntary tip-offs from the public forces the authorities to rely even more on coerced and paid informers, and the need to protect them necessitates turning a blind eye to their involvement in crime or violence, an aspect of which the community is well aware, leading to even fewer voluntary tip-offs – and so on and so forth. The result, then, is that over time the goal of influencing most members of society to volunteer information to the authorities about impending crimes can be undermined by the extensive cultivation and use of 'professional' informers.

A few other factors contribute to the development of this vicious circle. The frequent use of inducements and immunities to encourage people who violate the law to turn informer erodes the community's trust in the police and the legal system (Hillyard and Percy-Smith 1984: 353; Frampton 2008: 86). More specifically, the fact that the RUC cultivated informers among suspected criminals and offered them immunities in exchange for information on Republican groups reduced the willingness of people from nationalist communities to cooperate with it (Mulcahy 2006: 81). Crucially, when there is a policy of systematic recruitment of informers the police and security services proactively 'trawl' targeted communities for potential informers, inevitably deploying threats and exploiting vulnerabilities.[15] This practice causes resentment and alienation among members of these communities, and makes a willing voluntary passing of information less likely than it could have been without constant trawling (McGovern and Tobin 2009: 19–20).

The trawling for informers is also tied to other forms in which the law enforcement system treats collectivities as 'suspect communities' and discriminates against them. This results in a view of the legal system as unfair, and makes people less likely to turn in friends or relatives whom they suspect of possible involvement in planning violent attacks. As an interviewee observed to one of the authors:

> The more you strengthen the human rights regime in your country, rather than undermining it with hundreds of counter-terrorism laws, the more likely a parent is to come forward and say 'my son is behaving very oddly and I think he might be planning

---

[15] Such 'trawling' occurs when police do not have a specific person whom they seek to turn informer on account of special information they may possess, but rather target whole groups of people.

something', and that might really save lives. People won't have this confidence if you demonise a whole community.[16]

Similarly, members of the public may see little use in reporting their suspicions about individuals to the police if the perception in the community is that many armed groups' members are in fact informers, or that if suspects are pointed out to the authorities the police are likely to recruit them as informers rather than prosecute them.

From another direction, a proactive policy of recruiting as many informers as possible can create internal organisational pressure within security agencies, with an ever increasing number of recruitments, stemming from the needs of state agencies to perpetuate and justify themselves (Marx 1974: 432). Path dependence, inertia, competition between rival agencies, and financial and other rewards for those who recruit more informers – all can lead to a 'tunnel vision' in which the number of registered informers becomes a target in and of itself, while the broader effects of informing are neglected. The recruitment of informers may thus become, in practice, an end in itself rather than a means. These organisational tendencies are mutually reinforcing with the unreflective belief that informing provides pure benefit against political violence. It is telling, in both these contexts, that in the security services' parlance, informers are termed 'assets'. This reflects the axiomatic thinking that informers equal benefit to security, and that the more informers are on agencies' payrolls the better – these assumptions, as this chapter has shown, are unwarranted.

Marx (1988: 233) concluded that, in some cases, the use of undercover operations is the 'least bad' alternative available: 'Used with great care, they may be a necessary evil. The challenge is to prevent them from becoming an intolerable one.' As long as the recruitment of informers is considered a necessary evil its scope will be limited, regulated, checked – and this means that the widespread long-term politically and socially negative consequences may be much reduced. But as long as informers are treated as 'assets' the phenomenon will generate the effects surveyed here. This does not mean that the use of informers should be outlawed. It should be regulated under effective laws (Darcy 2019) and discussed in honest ways, taking into account the full range of consequences, rather than in simplistic, self-serving accounts.

We conclude that informing – a practice justified by its ability to reduce political violence – may end up *generating* violence, both directly and indirectly; it can complicate and undermine processes of transition out of violence; and it can ultimately even reduce the flow of relevant information to the authorities. In short, the policy of recruiting informers is undoubtedly an effective short-term tactic from a governmental perspective, but as a long-term strategy against political violence it has potential flaws that thus far have not been adequately recognised, and that this research has hopefully helped to identify.

[16] Interview with a human rights activist, London, June 2012.

References

Alvarez Berastegi, A. (2017), 'Transitional justice in settled democracies: Northern Ireland and the Basque Country in comparative perspective', *Critical Studies on Terrorism*, 10, 542–61.

An Phoblacht (2014), 'Smithwick tribunal investigator rejects findings', *An Phoblacht*, 12 January, https://www.anphoblacht.com/contents/23670 (accessed 21 February 2022).

BBC (2008), 'State "let innocent people die"', 29 May , BBC News Channel, http://news.bbc.co.uk/1/hi/northern_ireland/7424668.stm (accessed 6 February 2022).

BBC (2016), 'Gerry Adams "sanctioned Denis Donaldson killing"', *BBC News NI*, 21 September, https://www.bbc.co.uk/news/uk-northern-ireland-37425809 (accessed 21 February 2022).

BBC (2019), 'Stakeknife" Top British spy "helped SAS kill IRA men"', *BBC News NI*, 1 October, https://www.bbc.co.uk/news/uk-northern-ireland-49895529 (accessed 21 February 2022).

Baer R. (2005), 'Wanted: Spies unlike us', *Foreign Policy*, March/April.

Bamford, B. (2005), 'The role and effectiveness of intelligence in Northern Ireland', *Intelligence and National Security*, 20, 581–607.

Barker, A. (2006), *Shadows: Inside Northern Ireland's Special Branch* (Edinburgh, Mainstream).

Bean, K. (2007), *The New Politics of Sinn Féin* (Liverpool, Liverpool University Press).

Billingsley, R. (2009), *Covert Human Intelligence Sources: The 'Unlovely' Face of Police Work* (Hook, Waterside Press).

Bowcott, O. (2007), 'Ulster police chief: Don't make me name informers', *Guardian*, 4 September.

Bradley, G. and Feeney, B. (2012), *Insider: Gerry Bradley's life in the IRA* (Dublin, O'Brien Press).

Carlin, W. (2019), *Thatcher's Spy: My Life as an MI5 Agent inside Sinn Féin* (Newbridge, Merrion).

CGP [Consultative Group on the Past] (2009), *Report of the Consultative Group on the Past* (Belfast, CGP).

Clark, L. (2009), 'Spies, lies and ways to quell terrorism', *Sunday Times*, 2 August.

Cohen, H. and Dudai, R. (2005), 'Human rights dilemmas in using informers to combat terrorism: The Israeli–Palestinian case', *Terrorism and Political Violence*, 17, 229–43.

Cohen, S. (2001), *States of Denial: Knowing about Atrocities and Suffering* (Cambridge, Polity Press).

Connolly, E. and Doyle, J. (2015), 'Ripe moments for exiting political violence: An analysis of the Northern Ireland case', *Irish Studies in International Affairs*, 26, 147–62.

Conway, K. (2014), *Southside Provisional: From Freedom Fighter to the Four Courts* (Dublin, Orpen Press).

Darby, J. and MacGinty, R. (2001), *Guns and Government: The Management of the Northern Ireland Peace Process* (Basingstoke, Palgrave).

Darcy, S. (2019), *To Serve the Enemy: Informers, Collaborators, and the Laws of Armed Conflict* (Oxford, Oxford University Press).

Dixon, P. (2012), 'Was the IRA defeated?', *Journal of Imperial and Commonwealth History*, 40, 303–20.

Donnersmarck, F. H. von (dir.) (2006), *The Lives of Others*, film (Wiedemann & Berg).

Dudai, R. (2012), 'Informers and the transition in Northern Ireland', *British Journal of Criminology*, 52, 32–54.

Dudai, R. (2018), 'Underground penalty: The IRA's punishment of informers', *Punishment & Society*, 20, 375–95.

Dudai, R. (2022). *Penality in the Underground: The IRA's Pursuit of Informers* (Oxford, Oxford University Press).

Ellison, G. and O'Reilly, C. (2008), 'From Empire to Iraq and the "War on Terror": The transplantation and commodification of the (Northern) Irish policing experience', *Police Quarterly*, 11, 395–426.

Erwin, A. (2019), 'Mum calls for "unlocking" of sensitive documents over IPLO man Eoin Morley 1990 killing', *Belfast Telegraph*, 10 September.

Espindola, J. (2015), *Transitional Justice after German Reunification* (Cambridge, Cambridge University Press).

Frampton, M. (2008), 'Agents and ambushes: Britain's 'dirty war' in Northern Ireland', in S. Cohen (ed.), *Democracies at War against Terrorism: A Comparative Perspective* (London, Palgrave Macmillan), 77–100.

Frampton, M. (2009), *The Long March: The Political Strategy of Sinn Féin, 1981–2007* (London, Macmillan).

Fulton, K. (2006), *Unsung Hero: How I Saved Dozens of Lives as a Secret Agent inside the IRA* (London, Blake).

Garret, P. (1999), 'The pretence of normality: Intra-family violence and the response of state agencies in Northern Ireland', *Critical Social Policy*, 19:1, 31–55.

Garton Ash, T. (2009), *The File: A Personal History* (London, Atlantic Books).

Gearty, C. (2006), *Can Human Rights Survive?* (Cambridge, Cambridge University Press).

Gilmour, R. (1998), *Dead Ground: Infiltrating the IRA* (London, Warner).

Greer, S. (1995), 'Towards a sociological model of the police informant', *British Journal of Sociology*, 46, 509–27.

Hastings, M. (2005), 'In the fight against Al-Qaida we need people, not tanks', *Guardian*, 17 October.

Hearty, K. (2016), 'From "former comrades" to "near enemy": The narrative template of "armed struggle" and conflicting discourses on violent dissident Irish Republican activity (VDR)', *Critical Studies on Terrorism*, 9, 269–91.

Hearty, K. (2017), *Critical Engagement: Irish Republicanism, Memory Politics and Policing* (Liverpool, Liverpool University Press).

Hearty, K. (2019), 'Victims who have done nothing or victims who have done nothing wrong: Contesting blame and "innocent victim" status in transitioning societies', *British Journal of Criminology*, 55, 1119–38.

Hewitt, S. (2010), *Snitch! A History of the Modern Intelligence Informer* (New York, Continuum).

Hillyard, P. and Percy-Smith, J. (1984), 'Converting terrorists: The use of supergrasses in Northern Ireland', *Journal of Law and Society*, 11, 335–55.

Hopkins, S. (2013), *The Politics of Memoir and the Northern Ireland Conflict* (Liverpool, Liverpool University Press).

Hopkins, S. (2017), 'The "informer" and the political and organisational culture of the Irish Republican movement: Old and new interpretations', *Irish Studies Review*, 25, 1–23.

Ingram, M. and Harkin, G. (2004), *Stakeknife: Britain's Secret Agents in Ireland* (Dublin, O'Brien Press).

Irish Republican News (2003), 'No contempt charges seen despite IRA honour code', *Irish Republican News*, 11 November, https://republican-news-org/current/news/2003/11/no_contempt_charges_seen_despi.html (accessed 21 February 2022).

Irish Republican News (2020), 'Entrapment alleged as top Saoradh official named as MI5 agent', *Irish Republican News*, 24 August, https://republican-news.org/current/news/2020/08/entrapment_alleged_as_top_saor.html (accessed 21 February).

ISC [Intelligence and Security Committee of UK Parliament] (2009), Could 7/7 Have Been Prevented? Review of the Intelligence on the London Terrorist Attacks on 7 July 2005 (London, ISC).

Johnson, H. N. and Soeters, J. L. (2015), 'See and blind, hear and deaf': Informerphobia in Jamaican garrisons', *Crime Prevention and Community Safety*, 17, 47–66.

Larkin, P. (2012), 'How spooks are undermining peace in Northern Ireland', *Guardian*, 13 February.

Larmour, G. (2016), *They Killed the Ice Cream Man: My Search for the Truth behind My Brother John's Murder* (Newtownards, Colourpoint).

Leahy, T. (2020), *The Intelligence War against the IRA* (Cambridge, Cambridge University Press).

Marx, G. (1974), 'Thoughts on a neglected category of social movement participant: The agent provocateur and the informant', *American Journal of Sociology*, 80, 402–40.

Marx, G. (1988), *Under Cover* (Berkeley, University of California Press).

Matchett, W. (2015), 'Security: Missing from the Northern Ireland model', *Democracy & Security*, 11, 1–43.

Matchett, W. (2016), *Secret Victory: The Intelligence War that Beat the IRA* (Armagh, William Matchett).

Matchett, W. (2017), 'Terrorism and counterterrorism: The criticality of context', in S. N. Romaniuk, F. Grice, D. Irrera, and S. Webb (eds), *The Palgrave Handbook of Global Counterterrorism Policy* (London, Palgrave Macmillan), 39–71.

Matchett, W. (2018), 'Legacy scandal', *News Letter*, 21 August.

McCallion, H. (2020), 'Was Gerry Adams an MI5 informer?', *Mail Online*, 7 August, https://www.dailymail.co.uk/debate/article-8606037/Was-Gerry-Adams-MI5-informer-Harry-Mccallion-tells-senior-IRA-men-died-army-ambushes.html (accessed 21 February 2022).

McDonald, H. (2006), 'IRA searches for proof that agent J118 existed', *Guardian*, 4 June, https://www.theguardian.com/politics/2006/jun/04/uk.northernireland (accessed 21 February 2022).

McDonald, H. (2008), 'Informer files to be kept from Sinn Féin', *Guardian*, 20 October.

McDonald, H. (2011), 'Unspoken lessons from Northern Ireland's peace process', *Guardian*, 18 October.

McEvoy, K., and Mika, H. (2002), 'Restorative justice and the critique of informalism in Northern Ireland', *British Journal of Criminology*, 42, 534–62.

McGartland, M. (1997), *Fifty Dead Men Walking* (London, Blake).

McGlinchey, M. (2019), *Unfinished Business: The Politics of Dissident Irish Republicanism* (Manchester, Manchester University Press).

McGovern, M. and Tobin, A. (2010), *Countering Terror or Counter-Productive: Comparing Irish and British Muslim Experiences of Counter-Insurgency Law and Policy* (Ormskirk, Edge Hill University).

McIntyre, A. (2016), 'BC touts', *The Pensive Quill*, 22 February, https://www.thepensivequill.com/2016/02/bc-touts.html (accessed 21 February 2022).

McKittrick, D., Kelters, S., Feeney, B., Thornton, C., and McVea, D. (1999), *Lost Lives: The Stories of the Men, Women and Children who Died as a Result of the Northern Ireland Troubles* (Edinburgh, Mainstream).

McWilliams, M. (1995), 'Masculinity and violence: A gender perspective on policing and crime in Northern Ireland', in L. Kennedy (ed.), *Crime and Punishment in West Belfast* (Belfast, West Belfast Summer School),

Moloney, E. (2011), *Voices from the Grave: Two Men's War in Ireland* (London, Faber & Faber).

Monaghan, J. (2016), 'IRA informer Raymond Gilmour found dead at his home in Kent by teenage son', *Irish News*, 30 October, https://www.irishnews.com/news/uknews/2016/10/30/news/ira-informer-raymond-gilmour-found-dead-at-his-home-in-kent-by-teen age-son-761484 (accessed 21 February 2022).

Morrison, D. (2018), 'Behind the mask', 6 July, https://www.dannymorrison.com/behind-the-mask/ (accessed 3 December 2020).

Mulcahy, A. (2006), *Policing Northern Ireland: Conflict, Legitimacy and Reform* (Cullompton, Willan).

Natapoff, A. (2009), *Snitching: Criminal Informants and the Erosion of American Justice* (New York, New York University Press).

O'Callaghan, S. (1998), *The Informer* (London, Transworld).

O'Callaghan, S. (2017), 'Heroes of a dirty war', *Quadrant*, April, 71–3.

O'Hare, C. (2020), 'Saoradh's Newry office raided', Newry.ie, 21 August, https://www.newry.ie/news/saoradh-s-newry-office-raided (accessed 21 February 2022).

O'Leary, B. (2005), 'Mission accomplished? Looking back at the IRA', *Field Day Review*, 1, 217–46.

OPONI [Office of the Police Ombudsman for Northern Ireland] (2005), *The Investigation by Police of the Murder of Eoin David Morley on 15 April 1990* (Belfast, OPONI).

Rejali, D. (2004), 'Torture's dark allure', *Salon*, 18 June, https://www.salon.com/2004/06/18/torture_1/ (accessed 21 February 2022).

Ross, J. (2008), 'Undercover policing and the shifting terms of scholarly debate: The United States and Europe in comparison', *Annual Review of Law and Social Science*, 4, 239–73.

Said, W. E. (2010), 'The terrorist informant', *Washington Law Review*, 85, 687–738.

Sengupta, K. (2016), 'Inside Isis: How UK spies infiltrated terrorist leadership', *Independent*, 19 October.

Smyth, M. (2004), 'The process of demilitarization and the reversibilty of the peace process in Northern Ireland', *Terrorism and Political Violence*, 16:3, 544–66.

Southern, N. (2018), *Policing and combating terrorism in Northern Ireland* (London, Palgrave Macmillan).

Stevenson, D. (2008), 'Entrapment and terrorism', *Boston College Law Review*, 49, 125–215.

Tonge, J., P. Shirlow, and J. McAuley (2011), 'So why did the guns fall silent? How interplay, not stalemate, explains the Northern Ireland peace process', *Irish Political Studies*, 26, 1–18.

Urban, M. (2010), *Task Force Black: The Explosive True Story of the SAS and the Secret War in Iraq* (New York, Little, Brown).

9

The Collaboration of the Intellectuals:
Legal Academia and the Third Reich

OREN GROSS

If one day the situation were reversed and the fate of the vanquished lay in my hands,
then I would let all the ordinary folk go and even some of the leaders ... but I would
have all the intellectuals strung up, and the professors three feet higher than the rest; they
would be left hanging from the lampposts for as long as was compatible with hygiene.

(Klemperer 1999: 184)

All will be judged. Master of nuance and scruple,
Pray for me and for all writers living or dead;
Because there are many whose works
Are in better taste than their lives, because there is no end
To the vanity of our calling: make intercession
For the treason of all clerks.

(Auden 1991: 312)

The Treason of the Intellectuals

IN HIS CLASSIC book *La trahison des clercs*, originally published in 1927, Julien
Benda identifies a significant shift in the role played in society by intellectuals. If,
in the past, those whom he calls 'clerks' lived and acted 'in direct opposition to the
realism of the multitudes', by the end of the 19th century the intellectuals 'began
to play the game of political passions' (Benda 1928: 44), harnessing the 'tremen-
dous influence of [their] sensibility ... persuasive power ... [and] moral prestige'
(47) to the promotion of racial, class, and national passions (3). Those intellectual
elites 'who had acted as a check on the realism of the people began to act as its

Proceedings of the British Academy, **248**, 179–200, © The British Academy 2022.

stimulators' (45), becoming, in effect, 'the spiritual militia of the material' (75).[1]
They have done so by supplying the political passion with 'a whole network of
strongly woven doctrines, the sole object of which is to show the supreme value of
its action from every point of view while the result is a redoubling of its strength as
a passion .... Our age is indeed the age of the *intellectual organisation of political
hatreds*' (26–7; italics in original). Benda was particularly struck by the docility,
absence of disgust, enthusiasm, and joy with which the modern intellectual had been
playing his role (139).[2] Moreover, he contended, modern intellectuals were not content simply to act on political passions alongside their intellectual activities. Rather,
they had 'introduced these passions into those activities. They permit, they desire
them to be mingled with their work as artists, as men of learning, as philosophers,
to colour the essence of their work and to mark all its productions' (67). As a result,
declared Benda, 'the game is over. Humanity is national .... The [intellectual] is not
only conquered, he is assimilated. The man of science, the artist, the philosopher are
attached to their nations as much as the day-labourer and the merchant. Those who
make the world's values, make them for a nation .... All humanity including the
[intellectuals] have become laymen. All Europe, including Erasmus, has followed
Luther' (182). Written 12 years before the Second World War, Benda's prediction is
chilling and prescient: '[I]f we ask ourselves what will happen to a humanity where
every group is striving more eagerly than ever to feel conscious of its own particular
interests, and makes its moralists tell it that it is sublime to the extent that it knows
no law but this interest – a child can give the answer. This humanity is heading for
the greatest and most perfect war ever seen in the world' – a war that will cause 'far
more woes than have yet been endured' (183, 194).

While Benda's criticism of the intellectuals is not limited to any particular
country or nation, he does point out the unique role of German intellectuals, in the
trends that he identifies and particularly in their 'adhesion ... to patriotic fanati-
cism .... The nationalist [intellectual] is essentially a German invention' (Benda
1928: 57–8). Indeed, he writes, 'most of the moral and political attitudes adopted
by the [intellectuals] of Europe in the past 50 years are of German origin, and ... in
the world of spiritual things the victory of Germany is now complete' (58).[3]

Writing between 1924 and 1927, Benda did not imagine – and perhaps could
not have – the full extent of the future treason of German intellectuals. Once the

---

[1] According to Benda, the intellectual has made himself 'Minister of War' (Benda 1928: 107). Indeed,
'For half a century, such has been the attitude of men whose function is to thwart the realism of nations,
and who have labored to excite it with all their power and with complete decision of purpose. For this
reason I dare to call this attitude "The Treason of the Intellectuals"' (Benda 1928: 158).

[2] Benda also suggests that 'we see [the intellectuals] joyfully carrying out this realism; we see them
believing that they are rendered greater by their nationalist fury, that it is a service to civilization, an
embellishment to humanity .... Then one [is] faced with a cataclysm of moral notions in those who edu-
cate the world' (Benda 1928: 59).

[3] See also Benda's discussion of the turn away from Greco-Roman universalism to Prussian national,
racial, and class particularism (Benda 1928: 79–103).

National Socialist Party seized power over Germany, six years after Benda's book had been published, German academia turned with great enthusiasm to the projects of substantiating the authoritative bases for National Socialism as well as of justifying and legitimating the actions of the regime (Hilgendorf 2017: 165). Professors from all faculties made 'tangible contributions' to the 'policies of "racial purification" and territorial expansion ... the "*Volksgemeinschaft*" (community of the people) and the "German spirit" in scholarship' (Remy 2002: 239).[4] Indeed, the willing participation of the academic elite 'was of vital importance to the regime's project of "racial" purification at home, the concomitant war of expansion, and its imperialist economic and cultural offensives in occupied Europe' (Remy 2002: 1). As Max Weinreich notes, 'German scholarship provided the ideas and techniques which led to and justified [the Holocaust] ... there was participation of German scholarship in every single phase of the crime ... German scholars from the beginning to the end of the Hitler era worked hand in glove with the murderers of the Jewish people' (Weinreich 1999: 6–9). Indeed, a great number of both professors and students in German universities supported National Socialism well before the Nazi seizure of power in 1933 (Gellately 2020: 249). As a contemporary scholar observed in 1933, 'The National Socialist revolution in Germany is most deeply founded, [and] has its most bigoted and best organised support in the German universities' (Giles 1983: 49).

This chapter focuses on the collaboration of one group of German academics – law professors – in the crimes perpetrated by the Third Reich. While a number of legally trained individuals did belong to the 'annihilationist core' of the Nazi apparatus (Jarausch 2013: 23–5),[5] most law professors facilitated the crimes committed by the Nazis by enthusiastically conferring a veneer of legality and legitimacy on the actions of the regime and by providing the necessary doctrines to support the regime's political, national, and racial passions. This made it possible for the Nazi leadership to proclaim, and for ordinary Germans to accept the claim, that theirs was, when all was said and done, a rule-of-law state, a *Rechtsstaat*.

Several reasons underlie this author's decision to focus on the role of law professors as collaborators. First, there exists some literature focusing on the role of judges and lawyers (as well as others, such as doctors and philosophers) during the Third Reich (for a recent example see Fountaine (2020)). However, a scholarly treatment of law professors' contributions in the support of National Socialism is still lacking (Ladwig-Winters 2018: 67; DeCoste 1999: 792–3). This is particularly troubling because law professors, much more than lawyers or even judges, fulfilled a critical role in providing legitimacy and a cloak of legality to the regime's actions, and their academic writings and publications served as guidelines for the judges sitting in the courts of the Third Reich. Second, German

---

[4] For a detailed discussion of the contributions of jurists to the development of National Socialist law in various fields of law, see Stolleis (2007).
[5] For additional examples see, e.g., Taylor 2011: 357–8 and Hilberg 1993: 73–4.

academics in general, and German law professors in particular, were revered by their compatriots. Their position in that respect was unparalleled anywhere outside Germany (Grüttner 2005: 77). They 'commanded a great deal of respect and easily could have assumed leadership positions had they so desired' (Sims 1978: 247). That position conferred on them a unique opportunity to resist the new regime. Yet, law professors expressed little, if any, opposition to National Socialism, not only during the dark years of the Third Reich, but even before the seizure of power by the Nazis (Kaufmann 1988: 1634). In fact, the vast majority of them supported National Socialism and its goals, with varying degrees of enthusiasm. This is all the more odious when we consider that 'no one could document a single case in which Germans who refused to carry out the killing of unarmed civilians suffered dire consequences' (Browning 1993: 192). For law professors the requisite level of required resistance and the risks entailed in such dissent were clearly lower. As Amos Elon notes, '[p]rotest was still possible. There was none' (Elon 2002: 395). Finally, once Germany was defeated one would have expected the collaborators to be removed from their lucrative positions and made personally accountable. This, too, did not happen. Not only did the academic careers of almost all the former collaborators and perpetrators continue uninterrupted, but after 1945 almost none of them was called to account for their actions and collaboration with the Nazis. German law faculties continued to consist 'almost exclusively of professors who had served in the previous period. This meant, virtually by definition, that they were either favourably inclined to National Socialism, or indifferent, or at least not strongly opposed' (Reimann 1988: 1656; Remy 2002: 3, 5). Despite the failure of legal academics to protect and defend the very basic values of democracy, liberty, and civilisation and, indeed, their active role in dismantling those and substituting them with National Socialist values, none was held accountable. Contrary to W. H. Auden's 'At the grave of Henry James', none was judged.

Purging the Academia

On 7 April 1933, just over two months after Adolf Hitler was appointed Chancellor, two new laws were promulgated. The Law on the Admission to the Bar targeted lawyers, decreeing that attorneys of non-Aryan descent could be excluded from the bar (Gross 2022). The second, the Law for the Restoration of the Professional Civil Service (*Gesetz zur Wiederherstellung des Berufsbeamtentums*), decreed that 'unreliable elements' and non-Aryans were to be dismissed from public service. In accordance with that law, Jewish judges had to retire (Ledford 2013: 167), and Jewish law professors were dismissed from their university positions. Nearly 1,700 faculty members, making up 15 per cent of the universities' teaching staff, lost their jobs (Hartshorne 1937: 99; Demuth 1936). Of those fired, 80 per cent were Jewish (Sims 1978: 254; Grüttner 2005: 91). Thus, for example, '[a] few weeks in spring 1933 sufficed to reduce the University of Göttingen, a world-renowned center of advanced physics and mathematics, to the level of a provincial college' (Elon 2002: 395).[6] In the case of faculties of law, the situation was even worse (Hartshorne 1937: 100). Almost a third of those teaching – 120 out of 378 (Müller 1991: 69; Hartshorne 1937: 98–9) – were removed from their positions, the vast majority on racial grounds. Non-Aryans, who constituted 17. 5 per cent of the total staff of pre-Nazi law faculties, made up 78.5 per cent of the dismissals (Hartshorne 1937: 100). And when their Jewish colleagues were fired, no German professor publicly protested (Friedländer 2009: 22). Six weeks later, on 25 April, the Law against the Overcrowding of German Schools and Universities was enacted. This law limited the enrolment of new Jewish students at any German university to 1.5 per cent of all new applicants, as well as restricting the total number of Jewish students at any university to a maximum of 5 per cent (Friedländer 2009: 13–14).

While protest was still possible, German scholars chose either to remain silent or affirmatively to support the National Socialists. As Robert Gellately (2020: 249) notes:

> In July 1933, when the distinguished physicist Max Planck was asked whether he would like to get involved in a meeting to discuss the treatment of Jewish professors, he answered meekly that if 30 professors did that, there would be '150 people ready to declare their solidarity with Hitler tomorrow, because they want to have those jobs'. Indeed, with a large body of well-educated, unemployed academics, he might have been right, though in their silence the establishment professoriate might be viewed as coming close to complicity. Far from protesting, numerous professors joined the Nazi Party and their support for the regime went well beyond memberships.

The academic positions made vacant were filled in short order by 'promising untenured faculty colleagues with a "nationalistic orientation"' (Müller 1991: 69). By 1939, 45 per cent of German university professors had been appointed during the Third Reich, and by 1945, about two-thirds of university teachers belonged to the Nationalsozialistische Deutsche Arbeiter Partei (NSDAP) (Grüttner 2005: 93). In law faculties the number was even higher, with 60 per cent of professors appointed in or since 1933 (Müller 1991: 235). In December 1933, all professors hired after 1918 had to take a new oath of loyalty to *Volk* and Fatherland (Sims 1978: 255). The universities 'ha[d] been brought thoroughly into line with the sentiments and ambitions of the national government' (Hartshorne 1937: 169).

German universities had been 'infested with militant anti-Semitic student fraternities' (Elon 2002: 371; Friedländer 2009: 22) long before the rise of National Socialism. In 1881 the antisemitic League of German Student Organisations was established, *inter alia*, in opposition to the perceived 'overrepresentation

---

[6] Describing an exchange in 1934 between the Nazi Minister of Education, Bernhard Rust, and famous mathematician David Hilbert, in which the former asked Hilbert if the institute had suffered from the expulsion of the 'Jews and their friends'. Hilbert answered: 'Suffered? It hasn't suffered, Herr Minister. It no longer exists.'

of Jewish students' in departments such as medicine and law (Aly 2014: 129; Jarausch 1983: 270). During the Weimar years, most student fraternities joined the German University League (Deutscher Akademiker Bund), which openly espoused antisemitic and *völkisch* (ethno-nationalist) goals and was later replaced by the National Socialist Students' Association (Friedländer 2009: 22). As the ranks of the professoriate swelled with supporters of National Socialism, so too did the ranks of their students. Great efforts were made to inculcate law students with Nazi ideology, such as the creation of specialised training camps. By 1938, more than 90 per cent of students in German universities were organised in the National Socialist Students' Association (Neumann 1942: 399; Weber 1986). These trends, both among professoriate and students, resulted in the once fiercely independent, apolitical, and revered German universities embracing their new role as political institutions fully coordinated and regulated by the regime (Rein 1933; Weinreich 1999: 68).

Once the National Socialist Party seized power over Germany, German academia turned with great enthusiasm to the projects of both substantiating the authoritative bases for National Socialism and justifying and legitimating the actions of the regime. Looking at the record of one of the most renowned German universities – the Ruprecht Karls University in Heidelberg – Steven Remy finds that the engagement of its professoriate with National Socialism had been 'extensive' (Remy 2002: 1). Professors from all faculties made 'tangible contributions' to the 'policies of "racial purification" and territorial expansion … the "*Volksgemeinschaft*," and the "German spirit" in scholarship' (Remy 2002: 239). In turn, '[t]he willing participation of the academic elite at Heidelberg and other universities was of vital importance to the regime's project of "racial" purification at home, the concomitant war of expansion, and its imperialist economic and cultural offensives in occupied Europe' (Remy 2002: 1).

German legal academics responded with at least as much fervour and gusto in support of the Nazi cause as their colleagues in other disciplines (Kaufmann 1988: 1630). As Max Weinreich (1999: 17) notes, '[t]wo groups deserve the place of honour among those who made their scholarship subservient to Nazi ends: the physical anthropologists and biologists, and the jurists … the jurists distinguished themselves. They spared no effort in moulding the abstruse ideas of the new rulers into clear-cut articles of law and directives and in defending the legality of the measures taken' (see also Stolleis (2004): 364). Professors of law were 'astoundingly productive' in creating and establishing a 'National Socialist legal system. They saw it as their task to bring about a "coordination" of the legal profession's thinking parallel to the "coordination" of legal institutions which had already occurred' (Müller 1991: 70). Much like members of the German judiciary and bar, law professors threw themselves into the task of providing legitimacy and a cloak of legality to the regime's actions, their writings and publications serving as guidelines for the judges sitting in the courts of the Third Reich (Müller 1991: 68). Julien Benda would not have been surprised in the least to read Ingo Müller's scathing assessment of the role played by German law professors in the decline of law during the Third Reich: 'They provided a philosophical cloak for the Nazis' arbitrary acts and crimes .... There was virtually no outrage perpetrated by the Nazis which was not praised during the regime as "supremely just" and defended after the war by the same scholars, with equally dubious arguments, as "justifiable" or even "advisable" from a legal point of view' (Müller 1991: 68).

German legal academia, like German higher education generally, accepted the notion that scholarship was impossible without a foundation of values that were, of course, those of National Socialism. 'The whole of German law today', declared Carl Schmitt, 'must be governed solely and exclusively by the spirit of National Socialism .... Every interpretation must be an interpretation according to National Socialism' (Kaufmann 1988: 1644). Similarly, '[a]ll vague concepts, all so-called omnibus clauses, are to be made absolute and unconditional in accordance with National Socialism' (1645). The tradition of 'neutral research' was displaced by the notion of research as 'the institutional reality of the spiritual realm' (Weinreich 1999: 37; Remy 2002: 6–7) leading to the ominous conclusion that since 'the national goal is to be considered without further ceremony a motive for excluding guilt ... [e]xterminating without remainder the inner enemy is doubtlessly part of restituting German honor' (Weinreich 1999: 37). The guiding theme of academic research became the 'German spirit', which 'encompassed streams of *völkisch* nationalism, anti-Semitism, and biological and cultural racism and entailed an antipositivist conception of scholarship that placed all research and teaching in the service of the "people's community", defined in racist terms' (Remy 2002: 6). The racially homogeneous *Volksgemeinschaft* did not merely inform and define the purpose for scholarship. It had become the exclusive focal point of the law and the legal point of origin as well as law's terminus. It was the source of all legal validity and the purpose in whose guiding light all laws (whether enacted before 1933 or later) were to be construed and interpreted. Law was regarded to be a live order closely connected with the moral life of the community as a whole to whom individuals were subservient (Larenz 1934: 5). It was with the mores of the *Volk*, with the 'healthy popular sentiment' (*gesundes Volksempfinden*) of the German people, that all positive legal norms needed to align (Larenz 1934: 9). In turn, the people's justice and mores were encapsulated in, and reflected through, the will of the Führer, whose 'historic greatness' ensured that he, as the mediator of the people's will, would 'unfailingly always identify the "true" will of the people' (Curran 2001: 174). And since 'Der Führer hat immer recht' ('The Führer is always right'), everything he wishes becomes law.[7] The intrinsic link between Führer and *Volk* also allowed Nazi ideologues to deny claims that the former's will amounted

---

[7] As Gustav Radbruch notes in the second of his 'Five minutes': '[A]rbitrariness, breach of contract, and illegality – provided only that they benefit the people – are law. Practically speaking, this means that whatever state authorities deem to be of benefit to the people is law, including every despotic whim and caprice, punishment unsanctioned by statute or judicial decision, the lawless murder of the sick ... it was the equating of the law with supposed or ostensible benefits to the people that transformed a Rechtsstaat into an outlaw state. No, this tenet does not mean: Everything that benefits the people is law. Rather, it is the other way around: Only what law is benefits the people' (Radbruch 2006 [1945]: 13–14).

to nothing more than arbitrary exercise of power, since the Führer's decisions were seen as but an expression and reflection of the communal will of the *Volk* (Neumann 1942: 83). Thus it was possible to proclaim that 'the National Socialist *Rechtsstaat* is a just state as well as an order-based one' (Koellreutter 1938: 56). Indeed, the National Socialist *Rechtsstaat* was the purest form of *Rechtsstaat* (Schmitt 1993 [1928]: 138).[8] After 1933:

> we find the most abundant adjuration of law and justice by the legal philosophers, an ecstasy of values in face of the German legal state of Adolf Hitler. Instead of defenselessness we find efforts to ingratiate themselves in the form of declarations of loyalty .... Instead of defenselessness, one should rather speak of lack of contradiction – on the ground of inclination, agreement or 'to prevent something worse'. (Rottleuthner 2011: 108)

The fusion of law and morality served the German jurists as 'a welcome means to extend the authority and power of the Nazi regime' (Pauer-Studer 2014: 236; 2012: 373). Such ethicisation of law, fusing it together with, and indistinguishably from, morality, meant that the former could not exist independent of the latter (Ambos 2019: 62–3). National Socialism rejected positivism and, instead, embraced its own unique and particularistic, distorted, and depraved variant of 'irrational and communal natural law, founded in biology' (Fraenkel 2017: 134; Curran 2001: 171; Ambos 2019: 64-65). Hans Schemm, the chief of the National Socialist Teachers' League – membership of which stood at 220,000 by late 1933 – captured the shift when he proclaimed that '[f]rom now on, it is not up to you to decide the truth of anything, but to determine whether it conforms to the meaning of the National Socialist Revolution' (Koonz 2003: 136–7). That same German spirit, and the meaning of the National Socialist revolution, expressed through and reflected in German 'common law', entailed the exclusion of 'non-German' elements from all legal spheres (Remy 2002: 43).

Vom Recht zum Unrecht

'We look in vain', writes Michael Stolleis, 'for the members of the Association of Constitutional Lawyers in the circles of active resistance. Officers, clergy, students, and workers were represented, but as far as we know not a single professor of constitutional and administrative law' (Stolleis 1998: 99; Ladwig-Winters 2018: 57). Apologists point to the fact that, as civil servants, German university professors have had a long tradition of deference to the state – that '[a]s state employees, professors were traditionally apolitical men .... They tended to respect and obey authority, or *Obrigkeit*: Luther had lent the term a quasi-religious aura' (Elon 2002: 317–18). Others claimed that they had associated with the Nazi Party and

---

[8] On the debate as to whether *Rechtsstaat* was an inescapably liberal term or could have been applied to the National Socialist state see, e.g., Caldwell (1994b).

continued their academic work primarily to protect higher education against the possible wrath of the regime. Lawyers, judges, and legal scholars have also argued that under the jurisprudential attitude that had been prevalent in Germany before 1933, they were compelled to recognise even the most unjust statute as law and could not have objected to laws and regulations promulgated by the Nazi state. Of course, fear of Nazi retaliation against any expression of dissent was also quoted in defence of the continued silence. However, while few emigrated or withdrew into the so-called 'inner emigration' (Kaufmann 1988: 1633; Morris 2013: 124; Beatson and Zimmermann 2004; Tuori 2020), a larger number voluntarily coordinated with the Nazi machine,[9] and an even larger number yet actively and enthusiastically supported the new regime. This was all the more odious where university professors were concerned, since German professors had been revered by their compatriots. Their position in that respect was unparalleled anywhere outside Germany (Grüttner 2005: 77). That position conferred on them a unique opportunity to resist the new regime. They 'commanded a great deal of respect and easily could have assumed leadership positions had they so desired' (Sims 1978: 247). They simply did not 'so desire'.

The road *vom Recht zum Unrecht* ('from justice to injustice'; Schorn 1959: 6) of German universities and professors began before Hitler's rise to power. For most German professors, the period after January 1933 saw merely 'the intensification of tendencies which already were pronounced before the advent of the Nazi regime' (Hammen 1941: 188; Ambos 2019: 23–35). The interwar Weimar Republic has often been described as a 'republic without republicans'. Others described it not as a republic but rather as a 'negative monarchy', lacking the monarchy's instinct for self-preservation (Elon 2002: 365–6). Its main institutions remained 'citadels of authoritarianism' (Elon 2002: 366). This was true for the state bureaucracy, the army, and the judiciary. It was also true for German universities (Elon 2002: 344–5).

The 'Mandarin intellectuals', as Fritz Ringer referred to university professors (Ringer 1969), mostly held conservative, nationalist, anti-republican and antisemitic views long before 1933 (Remy 2002: 7-10; Weinreich 1999: 10; Friedländer 2009: 21). Only in one German institute of higher learning, the University of Frankfurt, which was founded after the war, were republican professors not outnumbered by conservatives 'pining for the old order' (Elon 2002: 362). Weimar, with its levelling consequences of democratisation, did not sit well with the intellectual and social elitism that characterised German academia. Most professors came from the nationalistically minded, conservative-leaning middle and upper classes of German society, and rejected the November revolution (Stolleis 2004: 23; Rottleuthner 2011: 105). Political instability, with constantly changing governments and petty party politicking, personal and financial insecurity, high inflation, coup attempts and a mounting crime rate, and even the perceived role of Weimar in promoting 'sexual degeneracy' (Weitz 2007: 297–330; Gross 2013), resulted in the

---

[9] For the medical establishment see, similarly, Kater (1989): 19.

republic's having very few supporters and many more vocal opponents among legal academics (Stolleis 2004: 65). Many of the latter rejected the popular sovereignty at the foundation of the republic and either hoped to replace it entirely with a sort of monarchical sovereignty like the one that existed before the war or sought to inject the Weimar constitution with attributes and features derived from that competing notion of sovereignty.

German intellectuals, including university professors, enthusiastically supported the war of 1914 (Elon 2002: 248; Weinreich 1999: 11). In that 'war of intellectuals', university professors 'were especially diligent in fanning the jingoist fires' (Elon 2002: 317). In 1916, for example, 352 university professors joined 948 other 'notables' in endorsing a memorandum calling for the enemy's unconditional surrender with annexation and reparation payments (Elon 2002: 336). University professors and other intellectuals remained, by and large, supportive of the military and its leaders throughout the war (Elon 2002: 334). For them, Germany's victory in the war was not only just and moral but also militarily inevitable. And so, with Germany's eventual defeat and the subsequent harsh peace terms imposed on it in the Treaty of Versailles, they were especially receptive to the 'stab in the back' legend: Germany's push for *Siegfrieden* was undermined during the war by the *Judenpresse* – the liberal press, which was largely Jewish-owned – clamouring for negotiated peace. Jews were seen as leading an international Bolshevik conspiracy to undermine Germany while, at the same time, they were cast as capitalists profiteering from the war. The ' "weak" and "un-German" Weimer Republic' (Gellately 2020: 249) was disparaged as a *Judenrepublik*, with such claims facilitated, *inter alia*, by the prominent role played in it by the likes of Hugo Preuss (who drafted the republican constitution) and Walther Rathenau (who served as the Foreign Minister). A quarter of a century after expressing their unwavering support for the First World War, German scholars once again mobilised, practically unanimously, in support of Hitler's war. Thus, for example, Paul Ritterbusch, the Rector of Kiel University and a legal scholar, spearheaded the 'Aktion Ritterbusch', which led to the publication of 67 books and brochures, including 24 edited collections containing 299 different contributions by university professors from a wide array of disciplines, all dealing (positively) with war-related issues (Remy 2002: 96; Stolleis 2004: 293). For them, the German Reich, 'through species and origin, blood and soil', was destined to constitute not only a new internal, domestic order, but also a new political reality and a new order of international law (Schmitt 2011: 111). That new reality, centred around *Großräume*, would replace the 'universalistic-humanitarian', i.e. 'Jewish' existing world law (Schmitt 2011: 121–2). Under this new world order, the Reich's *völkisch* order would finally be freed from 'the interference of spatially alien and un*völkisch* powers' (Schmitt 2011: 111).

The Weimar Republic, which accepted the peace terms dictated to defeated Germany in the Treaty of Versailles, not only including harsh reparations but also establishing Germany's responsibility for the war, stood in stark contrast to Germany's grandeur under the Iron Chancellor, Otto von Bismarck. The republican culture and politics of endless debate, discussion, and indecision failed to measure up to the image of the man of action and decision. This was especially the case for the generation of young scholars who ascended the ranks of academia as the First World War came to an end and during the interwar years. Much like many of their generation, these young jurists were shaped by the war and by its disastrous outcomes (Stolleis 2004: 24; Jarausch 2013: 18). For them, the capacity to decide was prized above Weimar's culture of discussion and debate. Weimar's 'effeminate passivity' (Schmitt 1986: 128) was contrasted with the 'masculine cult of action and will' (Herf 1984: 118). The republican focus on legislators and judges was cast aside in favour of the sovereign dictator. The liberal insistence on individual rights was to be replaced by the national, racially based community of the people (*Volksgemeinschaft*), its pluralism and 'emotional pantheism' (Schmitt 1986: 128) substituted by coordination and racial homogeneity (*Artgleichheit*). Its 'cosmic tolerance', which meant that 'there [was] no longer anything that one could love and honestly hate' (Schmitt 1986: 128), gave way to the dichotomy between friend and foe (Schmitt 1976: 26) with the inescapable necessity of the 'physical killing' and the 'existential negation' of the latter (Schmitt 1976: 33, 35).

The intense nationalist views of that generation of legal scholars found an easy companion in individual opportunism. The tumultuous years of economic upheaval in the final years of Weimar, and especially the crisis of the Great Depression, meant that for the younger generation of scholars, finding a job in academia (or, indeed, in their selected profession) would be questionable (Jarausch 2013: 18–19). Thus, for example, in 1931, some 150,000 college graduates were waiting for adequate positions (Aly 2014: 173). The envy of the 'rosy career prospects of their Jewish peers' that Christian students had led them to retreat into 'anachronistic fantasies about Germanic superiority' to which those Jewish peers could not belong (Aly 2014: 128–9), and eventually strongly to support National Socialism (Aly 2014: 174). This sentiment was shared by their professors, as well as by those aspiring to hold academic positions. Both sought, even before 1933, to impose anti-Jewish discriminatory rules and practices in order to protect German academics, proclaiming that otherwise 'all university lectureships and professorships would be held by Jews or Jewish converts to Christianity' (Aly 2014: 130). Indeed, since the legal measures adopted to discriminate against Jews in the legal profession and push them out seemed, to some, to lag behind general economic discrimination, Nazi academics resorted to increasingly virulent rhetoric (Morris 2013: 121). Thus, for example, the University Instructors' Group of the National Socialist Lawyers' Union (Reichsgruppe Hochschullehrer des Nationalsozialistischen Rechtswahrerbundes) convened a conference on 'Jewry in Jurisprudence' on 3–4 October 1936 that highlighted the 'genuine battle of principles' between Jews' 'cruelty and impudence' and Germans' 'ethnic honour' (Sherratt 2014: 101). The jurists in attendance, who exceeded 100 in number, were reminded that 'year after year, semester after semester, for almost 100 years thousands of young Germans, future judges and lawyers, have been schooled by Jewish legal teachers, that standard texts and commentaries in the most important legal disciplines are by Jews, that influential legal journals were dominated by them' (Morris 2013: 121). The Nazis' seizure of power in 1933 brought opportunities not only to find a much-coveted academic position, but also to be promoted practically overnight. With almost a third of those teaching at law faculties removed from their positions, mostly on racial grounds, the vacant positions were filled, in short order, by untenured faculty demonstrating nationalistic orientation (Jarausch 1990: 156–66). By 1939, 60 per cent of professors teaching in German law faculties had been appointed in or since 1933, with a majority of those belonging to the NSDAP. The swift purge of the legal profession – students, lawyers, judges, and professors – left practically no dissenting voices within it. Furthermore, as academic promotion was inexorably tied to support for the National Socialist cause, the newly promoted professors were at great pains to demonstrate their allegiance.

The nationalist, conservative, and *völkisch* views of the vast majority of German university professors (Mosse 1998: 191–203) aligned with their antisemitic views. The 'demise in Germany of liberal law, the transformation of the German legal system, and the creation of a new anti-liberal Nazi legal order' (Morris 2013: 107) had all been entangled 'like vines' with the elimination of Jewish lawyers, who, in addition to being considered the ultimate foreign 'Other' (*Artfremde*), were mostly liberals. 'National' and 'German' were posited in contradistinction to 'international' and 'other', both of which were identified first and foremost as 'Jewish'. As was true for the masses, so too with the intellectual elites: old religious prejudices were, for the most part, replaced by social and economic ones, followed, in short order, by racial antisemitism. Thus, for example, the 19th-century Jewish emancipation introduced increasing social and economic competition to all segments of German society and the marketplace, including the academic job market and the free professions. It led to the perception that 'once you admit the first Jewish full professor, you'll have five of them or more in ten years' time!', and that 'every Jewish professor and every Jewish civil servant keeps down a descendant of the German people' (Aly 2014: 132, 137).

Hitler's Professors

It is tempting to describe the professors who flocked to the Nazi cause as 'nobodies elevated in rank by their Nazi friends and protectors'. Yet, as Max Weinreich correctly notes (Weinreich 1999: 7), many of them were 'people of long and high standing, university professors and academy members, some of them world famous, authors with familiar names and guest lecturers abroad, the kind of people Allied scholars used to meet and fraternise with at international congresses'. Consider the examples of two administrative and constitutional law scholars: Theodor Maunz (1901–93) and Ernst Forsthoff (1902–74).[10]

---

[10] For additional examples see Gross (2022).

Maunz's academic career began in 1932 with his appointment as a lecturer at the law faculty of the Ludwig-Maximilians University in Munich. Three years later he was appointed an associate professor at the University of Freiburg. Posthumously eulogised as a 'kind and reclusive' man (Stolleis 1998: 185), Maunz had also been 'one of the most ardent supporters of National Socialism' (Reimann 1988: 1652). Michael Stolleis's assessment of Maunz is a bit more benign:

> Maunz was a *Vernunftrepublikaner* and supporter of the *Rechtsstaat* when that was still part of the traditional code of conduct at the end of the Weimar Republic; he was a National Socialist as long as the others were, and a little bit more so and for a little longer; then he was once again a legal positivist with a touch of natural law. It all depended on the time and circumstances, like a chameleon that has the ability to adjust its colour and temperature to the environment. (Stolleis 1998: 189)

Yet, there is no disputing that Maunz fully immersed himself in, and supported, National Socialism. In his 1934 work on the New Foundations of Administrative Law (*Neue Grundlagen des Verwaltungsrechts*), Maunz explained that '[t]he central legal structure, behind which all other legal structures have to follow, is the political Führer ... any judicial activity in the field of administrative law is impossible. It follows that the administration of justice can never hinder the political decisions of the Führer' (Maunz 1934: 48, 55).[11] Following that logic, Maunz pronounced arrests by the Gestapo to constitute 'sovereign acts' that fall outside any possible judicial scrutiny and review (Stolleis 1998: 187). After all, he claimed, the source of legality for any police action was none other than the will of the Führer, which served as the exclusive source of all legal authority. Maunz argued that notions such as individual rights and separation of powers belonged in the liberal state, and he decried them as guarantors of the bourgeois concept of freedom and, as such, incompatible with the National Socialist state where the powers are united in the person of the Führer. Similarly to the expropriation of a person's liberty, Maunz expounded on a 'National Socialist right of expropriation' of property that hinged on the national community and the proclaimed will of the Führer (Kaufmann 1988: 1635). Maunz's legalistic contortions in the service of National Socialism can also be seen in his treatment of the principle of equality. According to Maunz, German law did contain this principle, but it was based on race rather than relating to all human beings as such. Thus, the foreign-other could be excluded from, for example, local swimming pools, without such an exclusion violating the law; indeed, such exclusion would be considered as upholding the law (Kaufmann 1988: 1637). In the infamous 1936 conference on 'Jewry in Jurisprudence', Maunz emphasised the 'fatal predilection of Jewish theorists of administrative law for the liberal doctrine of the *Rechtsstaat*' (Stolleis 1998: 187).

Ernst Forsthoff, too, benefited from the dismissal of Jews and unreliable professors from German universities. He began his teaching career in Frankfurt

---

[11] On Maunz's contribution to the creation of a National Socialist administrative law see Stolleis (2004): 382–3.

in 1933, succeeding to the chair previously held by Herman Heller before moving to Hamburg, Königsberg, Vienna, and Heidelberg between 1935 and 1945. In his 1933 essay 'Der total Staat' ('The total state'), Forsthoff developed the argument that a total state was superior to a liberal democracy. Declaring that liberalism was finished (Forsthoff 1933: 7), he stated that the Weimar Republic would be replaced by a national state in which every individual would be placed under complete obligation to the nation (Forsthoff 1933: 42; Stolleis 1998: 374). Individuals were to alienate their autonomy and be subordinate to race, the *Volk*, and the state (Caldwell 1994a: 616), and be prepared 'to give oneself up to society' (Caldwell 1994a: 619). It was the decision-making realm of the state that served as the ultimate source of public order (Caldwell 1994a: 618). This 'kind, learned, and cultivated human being' (Kaufmann 1988: 1642) – who also 'happened' to be a member of the Nazi Party, the SA, and the National Socialist German Lecturers' League (*Dozentenbund*) – then embraced National Socialist authoritarianism and expressed openly his antisemitic views, including the statement that the 'essentially different Jew' had become an enemy that had to be rendered harmless (Caldwell 2016: 269). In similar vein, his *Deutsche Geschichte in Dokumenten seit 1918* (*German History in Documents since 1918*) was described as a work that 'could not have been a stronger propaganda tract had it been written by Joseph Goebbels himself' (Remy 2002: 191), and one in which Forsthoff 'justifie[d] every major public policy of the regime up to 1938' (Remy 2002: 88). Unlike Maunz's perverse insistence that the principle of equality still prevailed under National Socialism, Forsthoff openly challenged the 'horrendous' notions of egalitarianism and egalitarian democracy (Kaufmann 1988: 1637). He argued that concentration camps were compatible with the National Socialist conception of the *Rechtsstaat* (Stolleis 2004: 355) and that 'individualistic liberalism must no longer be allowed to enjoy the privilege of publicity in Germany' (Kaufmann 1988: 1634).

Crime and *No* Punishment

The victorious Allies' denazification and lustration efforts after the war notwithstanding, the West German civil service, including the legal profession, remained overwhelmingly staffed with former members of the Nazi Party and its sympathisers. In 1951–2, 94 per cent of judges and prosecutors in Bavaria, 77 per cent of employees of the Finance Ministry, and 60 per cent of civil servants in the Agriculture Ministry of that state were ex-Nazis; one in three officials of the Federal Foreign Ministry was a former member of the Nazi Party; 43 per cent of the Diplomatic Corps were former members of the SS; and an additional 17 per cent had served in the SD or the Gestapo (Judt 2005: 57–8; Wittmann 2008: 211–17; Biddiscombe 2007: 210–12; *Legal Tribune Online* 2016). With the establishment of the Federal Republic of Germany in 1949, whatever little appetite remained for prosecuting former Nazis and war criminals quickly dissipated, leading to a sharp decline in such prosecutions. Even those relatively few trials actually held 'mostly deal[t] with crimes committed by Nazis against Germans, frequently ending with acquittal. Sensing an opportunity, many former Nazis were coming back to public life, their ideological agenda barely changed to fit into a new political framework' (Petrović 2018: 553; Ambos 2019: 35). By 1958 all German war criminals in the Federal Republic of Germany were out of prison (Taylor 2011: 357). It is also worth noting that in 1951, only 5 per cent of Germans admitted feeling guilty for the fate of Europe's Jews, with 21 per cent stating that 'the Jews themselves were partly responsible for what happened to them during the Third Reich' (Judt 2005: 271).

This state of affairs was no different with respect to German universities and German faculties of law. As Judt (2005: 58) notes, '[u]niversities and the legal profession were the *least* affected by denazification, despite their notorious sympathy for Hitler's regime'. But while such lack of accountability could have been, and was, explained, for example in the context of judges, by reference to the needs of postwar governance of German society and the German nation, no similar explanation was provided regarding the German professoriate. Rather, their lack of accountability was facilitated, to a significant degree, by the evolution in postwar Germany of a myth erected on the foundations of a collective 'culture of forgetting' (Remy 2002: 218–33; Taylor 2011: 374). A network of elaborate narratives was developed that served to absolve all but a few professors of connection to National Socialism and served as a shield against (mostly) American denazification policies after the war (Remy 2002: 240–1). This 'Heidelberg Myth' consisted in the claims that the number of 'genuine Nazis' on faculties was very small and that they had been imposed on the universities by the Nazi regime in opposition to the professoriate (Remy 2002: 241; Ritter 1945). Others, such as Martin Heidegger – appointed in May 1933 as Rector of the University of Freiburg, and later that year appointed 'Führer of the university' – claimed that they had associated with the Nazi Party and continued their academic work primarily in order to protect higher education against the possible wrath of the regime (Fried 2014: 159). At most they would concede that their actions and words – such as speaking out against the 'Judaisation' of German universities (Elon 2002: 390) or publishing a Vow of Allegiance to Adolf Hitler and the National Socialistic State[12] – amounted to a mere blunder ('Dummheit'), as Heidegger put it after the war (Sharpe 2018: 199). Such attitudes, which extended not only to members of German academia but to ordinary Germans as well, served the political purposes of both postwar Germany and also the Allies. It enabled the Allies to find 'good Germans' to govern and run their respective zones of occupation, even where these individuals had formerly

---

[12] The *Bekenntnis der Professoren an den Universitäten und Hochschulen zu Adolf Hitler und dem nationalsozialistischen Staat*, published in November 1933, contained statements by leading university professors and rectors, including Heidegger, and was signed by 900 individuals, most of them professors and academics (NLDS 1933).

been aligned with the Nazi state. It facilitated the decision by the government of Chancellor Adenauer to 'put the past behind' (Taylor 2011: 352); adopt a clean-slate policy; end denazification, first practically and then, in May 1951, formally; enact amnesty laws; allow former members of the Nazi Party to keep or regain positions in the civil service; and to administer 'the sleep cure' to a willing and receptive German public (Taylor 2011: 345–83; Art 2006: 53–5; Frei 2002: 1–91). It enabled German lawyers, judges, and law professors to argue that their engagement with the Nazis 'was not ... a crime of conviction .... Their participation became a crime of mere compliance' (Maier 2019: 1075; Jarausch 2013: 26–7; Foljanty 2013: 35–6). It also enabled the western powers to embrace West Germany as a key ally against Communist expansionism.

The Heidelberg Myth, which was neither limited to that one university nor to any particular department or field of study, facilitated a 'stunning continuity' after 1945, in that '[German] law professors teach, students study, lawyers cite, and judges rely on the views of many of the scholars that [were] enthusiastic supporters of the Nazi regime' (Reimann 1988: 1652).[13] Continuity of academic careers was the rule rather than the exception (Reimann 1988: 1654). Former Nazi supporters were able to maintain or to return to their academic positions relatively easily, while those fired for racial or ideological reasons, or the very few who resigned for similar reasons, 'were much less welcome' (Reimann 1988: 1656–7; Tuori 2020: 29). As Michael Stolleis comments, 'the attitude was that anybody who had not been "excessively" National Socialist, who had merely commented on the prevailing law, could soon return, perhaps clutching a democratic textbook on constitutional theory under his arm' (Stolleis 1998: 88).[14] As a result, after 1945, the law faculties consisted 'almost exclusively' of professors who had served in the Third Reich and were 'either favorably inclined to National Socialism, or indifferent, or at least not strongly opposed' (Reimann 1988: 1656; Remy 2002: 3, 5). Those professors continued, in turn, to influence generations of German scholars, academics, judges, and lawyers.

---

[13] One cannot, and must not, ignore the role that German scientists and engineers, many of whom had been members and leaders of the Nazi Party, played in the US military and governmental agencies during the Cold War. More than 1,600 scientists and engineers, most notably Wernher von Braun – the father of the V-2 rocket – were brought to the United States as part of Operation Paperclip, which was conducted by the Joint Intelligence Objectives Agency (JIOA). Whilst President Truman forbade the agency from recruiting any Nazi members or active Nazi supporters, the JIOA and the Office of Strategic Services – the forerunner to the CIA – bypassed this directive by eliminating incriminating evidence of possible war crimes from the scientists' records. See Jacobsen (2014). The Soviet Union had its own plans to put German scientists to work as part of Operation Osoaviakhim. See Naimark (1995): 220–8.

[14] This should also be considered against the background of the prevailing attitudes in postwar (West) German society. Between the years 1945 and 1949, 'a consistent majority' of Germans believed that 'Nazism was a good idea, badly applied'; a poll conducted in November 1946 showed that 37 per cent of Germans questioned in the American zone regarded the extermination of Jews, Poles, and other non-Aryans as 'necessary for the security of Germans'; and in a poll conducted in 1952, a similar percentage of those surveyed responded that it was better for Germany to have no Jews in its territory while 25 per cent of West Germans held a 'good opinion' of Hitler. See Judt (2005): 58.

Ernst Forsthoff had initially been removed from the Heidelberg faculty in 1946 at the insistence of the Americans (and despite support by the university senate for his retention), after being charged by the Heidelberg Spruchkammer in November of that year. However, he resumed his teaching career four years later and soon thereafter was reappointed to his former full professorship (Remy 2002: 191–4).

Theodor Maunz's teaching career at the University of Freiburg remained uninterrupted until 1952, when he moved to the Ludwig-Maximilians University in Munich, teaching there until his retirement. The high esteem in which he had been held was evident when he was elected, in 1948, to be a member of the constitutional convention that drafted the new constitution for West Germany. This, together with the publication of his authoritative commentary on the constitution (published in 1958), established Maunz as a leading expert on the West German constitution and earned him the moniker of 'der Kronjurist des Grundgesetzes' (Mauz 1993). In addition, from 1957 to 1964, Maunz served as Minister of Education for Bavaria. And while he was eventually forced to resign the position after his pro-Nazi publications were brought to light, he held on to his position at the university (Redeker 1964: 1098). It was only three decades later, in 1993, that his image was tarnished posthumously. This occurred not because of his pro-Nazi writings before 1945, but because of the discovery that Maunz had written hundreds of anonymous articles for a right-radical postwar newspaper. He had also prepared scores of legal opinions for the party – the German People's Union (DVU) – with which that paper was associated, and whose leader described Maunz as 'a quarter-century ... wonderful [and] loyal companion and authoritative adviser' (Mauz 1993; Stolleis 1998: 185–92).

Conclusion

Rather than being exceptional, the stories of Theodor Maunz and Ernst Forsthoff are emblematic of the stories of the vast majority of German law professors before the seizure of power by the National Socialists, during the 12 years of the Third Reich, and after the Second World War. The vast majority of German law professors expressed little, if any, opposition to National Socialism, not only during the dark years of the Third Reich, but even before the seizure of power by the Nazis. Indeed, most affirmatively supported National Socialism and its goals and enthusiastically substantiated the authoritative bases for National Socialism as well as justifying and legitimating the actions of the regime. University professors in general, and law professors in particular, collaborated with, and gave the veneer of legitimacy and legality to, the Nazis' genocidal crimes and depraved policies of racial purification and territorial expansion in the name of the *Volksgemeinschaft* and the German spirit. Yet, when the war was over, hardly any of them were called to account for their actions and collaboration with the Nazis. For the most part, the very same law professors who had thrown their support behind Hitler continued their academic careers uninterrupted.

References

Ambos, K. (2019), *National Socialist Criminal Law: Continuity and Radicalization*, trans M. Hiley (Oxford, Hart).

Aly, G. (2014), *Why the Germans? Why the Jews?: Enfy, Race Hatred, and the Prehistory of the Holocaust*, trans. J. S. Chase (New York, Picador).

Art, D. (2006), *The Politics of the Nazi Past in Germany and Austria* (Cambridge, Cambridge University Press).

Auden, W. H. (1991), 'At the grave of Henry James', in *Collected Poems*, ed. E. Mendelson (New York, Vintage), 310.

Beatson, J. and Zimmermann, R. (eds) (2004), *Jurists Uprooted: German-Speaking Emigré Lawyers in Twentieth-Century Britain* (Oxford, Oxford University Press).

Benda, J. (1928), *The Treason of the Intellectuals/La trahison des clercs*, trans. R. Aldington (New York, William Morrow).

Biddiscombe, A. P. (2007), *The Denazification of Germany: A History 1945–1950* (Stroud, Tempus).

Browning, C. R. (1993), *Ordinary Men: Reserve Police Battalion 101 and the Final Solution in Poland* (New York, Harper Perennial).

Caldwell, P. (1994a), 'Ernst Forsthoff and the legacy of radical conservative state theory in the Federal Republic of Germany', *History of Political Thought*, 15, 615.

Caldwell, P. (1994b), 'National Socialism and constitutional law: Carl Schmitt, Otto Koellruetter and the debate over the nature of the Nazi state, 1933–1937', *Cardozo Law Review*, 16, 339.

Caldwell, P. (2016), 'Ernst Forsthoff in Frankfurt: Political mobilization and the abandonment of scholarly responsibility', in M. Epple (ed.), *'Politisierung der Wissenschaft': Jüdische Wissenschaftler und ihre Gegner an der Universität Frankfurt am Main vor und nach 1933* (Göttingen, Wallstein), 249.

Curran, V. G. (2001), 'Fear of formalism: Indications from the fascist period in France and Germany of judicial methodology's impact on substantive law', *Cornell International Law Journal*, 35, 101.

DeCoste, F. C. (1999), 'Law/Holocaust/Academy', *Modern Law Review*, 62, 792.

Demuth, F. (1936), *List of Displaced German Scholars* (London, Speedee Press Services).

Elon, A. (2002), *The Pity of It All: A Portrait of the German-Jewish Epoch 1743–1933* (New York, Picador).

Foljanty, L. (2013), *Recht oder Gesetz: Juristische Identität und Autorität in den Naturrechtsdebatten der Nachkriegszeit* (Tübingen, Mohr Siebeck).

Forsthoff, E. (1933), *Der totale Staat* (Hamburg, Hanseatische Verl.-Anst.).

Fountaine, C. L. (2020), 'Complicity in the perversion of justice: The role of lawyers in eroding the rule of law in the Third Reich', *St Mary's Journal of Legal Malpractice & Ethics*, 10, 198.

Fraenkel, E. (2017), *The Dual State: A Contribution to the Theory of Dictatorship*, trans. E. A. Shils, E. Lowenstein, and K. Knorr (Oxford, Oxford University Press).

Frei, N. (2002), *Adenauer's Germany and the Nazi Past: The Politics of Amnesty and Integration,* trans. J. Golb (New York, Columbia University Press).

Fried, G. (2014), 'What Heidegger was hiding', *Foreign Affairs*, 93, 159.

Friedländer, S. (2009), *Nazi Germany and the Jews, 1933–1945*, abridged (New York, Harper Perennial).

Gellately, R. (2020), *Hitler's True Believers: How Ordinary People Became Nazis* (New York, Oxford University Press).

Giles, G. J. (1983), 'National Socialism and the educated elite in the Weimar Republic', in P. D. Stachura (ed.), *The Nazi Machtergreifung* (London, George Allen & Unwin).

Gross, O. (2022), 'Hitler's willing law professors', in B. Levinson and R. Eriksen (eds), *The Betrayal of the Humanities* (Bloomington, Indiana University Press).

Gross, R. (2013), 'Guilt, shame, anger, indignation: Nazi law and Nazi morals', in A. E. Steinweis and R. D. Rachlin (eds), *The Law in Nazi Germany: Ideology, Opportunism, and the Perversion of Justice* (New York, Berghahn Books), 89.

Grüttner, M. (2005), 'German universities under the swastika', in J. Connelly and M. Grüttner (eds), *Universities under Dictatorship* (University Park, Pennsylvania State University Press), 75.

Hammen, O. J. (1941), 'German historians and the advent of the National Socialist state', *Journal of Modern History*, 13, 161.

Hartshorne, E. Y. (1937), *The German Universities and National Socialism* (London, George Allen & Unwin).

Herf, J. (1984), *Reactionary Modernism: Technology, Culture, and Politics in Weimar and the Third Reich* (Cambridge, Cambridge University Press).

Hilberg, R. (1993), *Perpetrators, Victims, Bystanders: The Jewish Catastrophe 1933–1945* (London, Lime Tree).

Hilgendorf, E. J. C. (2017), 'Rechtsphilosophie zwischen 1860 und 1960', in E. J. C. Hilgendorf and J. Joerden (eds), *Handbuch Rechtsphilosophie* (Stuttgart, J. B. Mezler), 160.

Jacobsen, A. (2014), *Operation Paperclip: The Secret Intelligence Program to Bring Nazi Scientists to America* (New York, Little, Brown).

Jarausch, K. H. (1983), *Students, Society and Politics in Imperial Germany: The Rise of Academic Illiberalism* (Princeton, Princeton University Press).

Jarausch, K. H. (1990), *The Unfree Professions: German Lawyers, Teachers, and Engineers, 1900–1950* (Oxford, Oxford University Press).

Jarausch, K. H. (2013), 'The conundrum of complicity: German professionals and the final solution', in A. E. Steinweis and R. D. Rachlin (eds), *The Law in Nazi Germany: Ideology, Opportunism, and the Perversion of Justice* (New York, Berghahn Books), 23.

Judt, T. (2005), *Postwar: A History of Europe since 1945* (London, Penguin).

Kater, M. H. (1989), *Doctors under Hitler* (Chapel Hill, University of North Carolina Press).

Kaufmann, A. (1988), 'National Socialism and German jurisprudence from 1933 to 1945', *Cardozo Law Review*, 9, 1629.

Klemperer, V. (1999), *I Will Bear Witness: A Diary of the Nazi Years, 1933–1941*, trans. M. Chalmers (New York, The Modern Library).

Koellreutter, O. (1938), *Deutsches Verfassungsrecht: Ein Grundriß*, 3rd edn (Berlin, Juncker & Dünnhaupt).

Koonz, C. (2003), *The Nazi Conscience* (Cambridge, Belknap).

Ladwig-Winters, S. (2018), *Lawyers without Rights: The Fate of Jewish Lawyers in Berlin after 1933* (Chicago, American Bar Association).

Larenz, K. (1934), *Deutsche Rechtserneuerung und Rechtsphilosophie* (Tübingen, Mohr).

Ledford, K. F. (2013), 'Judging German judges in the Third Reich: Excusing and confronting the past', in A. E. Steinweis and R. D. Rachlin (eds), *The Law in Nazi Germany: Ideology, Opportunism, and the Perversion of Justice* (New York, Berghahn Books), 161.

Legal Tribune Online (2016), 'Maas: "Es gibt kein Ende der Geschichte"', *Legal Tribune Online*, 10 October, https://www.lto.de/recht/nachrichten/n/rosenburg-akte-projekt-bmjv-nationalsozialismus-vergangenheit-ministerium-mitarbeiter-nsdap-drittes-reich/ (accessed 5 June 2021).

Maier, C. (2019), 'Law, morality and the Rechtsstaat in post-war West Germany', *Historical Journal*, 62, 1069.

Maunz, T. (1934), *Neue Grundlagen des Verwaltungsrechts* (Hamburg, Hanseatische Verlagsanstalt).

Mauz, G. (1993), 'Ich bin nicht nur wütend', *Der Spiegel*, 18 October, http://www.spiegel.de/spiegel/print/d-13680349.html (accessed 5 June 2021).

Morris, D. G. (2013), 'Discrimination, degradation, defiance: Jewish lawyers under Nazism', in A. E. Steinweis and R. D. Rachlin (eds), *The Law in Nazi Germany: Ideology, Opportunism, and the Perversion of Justice* (New York, Berghahn Books), 105.

Mosse, G. L. (1998), *The Crisis of German Ideology: Intellectual Origins of the Third Reich* (New York, H. Fertig).

Müller, I. (1991), *Hitler's Justice: The Courts of the Third Reich*, trans. D. Lucas Schneider (Cambridge, MA, Harvard University Press).

Naimark, N. M. (1995), *The Russians in Germany: A History of the Soviet Zone of Occupation, 1945–1949* (Cambridge, MA, Belknap Press).

NLDS [Nationalsozialistischer Lehrebund Deutschland-Sachsen] (1933), *Bekenntnis der Professoren an den Universitäten und Hochschulen zu Adolf Hitler und dem nationalsozialistischen Staat: Überreicht vom Nationalsozialistischen Lehrerbund Deutschland-Sachsen* (Dresden).

Neumann, F. (1942), *Behemoth: The Structure and Practice of National Socialism, 1933–1944* (Oxford, Oxford University Press).

Pauer-Studer, H. (2012), 'Law and morality under evil conditions: The SS judge Konrad Morgen', *Jurisprudence*, 3, 367.

Pauer-Studer, H. (2014), 'Kelsen's legal positivism and the challenge of Nazi law', *Vienna Circle Institute Yearbook*, 17, 223.

Petrović, V. (2018), 'Germany versus Germany: Resistance against Hitler, postwar judiciary and the 1952 Remer case', in B. Bevernage and N. Wouters (eds), *The Palgrave Handbook of State-Sponsored History after 1945* (London, Palgrave), 551.

Radbruch, G. (2006 [1945]), 'Five minutes of legal philosophy (1945)', *Oxford Journal of Legal Studies*, 26, 13.

Redeker, K. (1964), 'Bewältigung der Vergangenheit als Aufgabe der Justiz', *Neue juristische Wochenschrift*, 11 June, 1097, https://www.redeker.de/downloads/lehre/2017/161/Redeker%20NJW%201964.pdf (accessed 5 June 2021).

Reimann, M. (1988), 'National Socialist jurisprudence and academic continuity: A comment on Professor Kaufmann's article', *Cardozo Law Review*, 9, 1651.

Rein, A. (1933), *Die Idee der politischen Universität* (Hamburg, Hanseatische Verl.-Anst.).

Remy, S. P. (2002), *The Heidelberg Myth: The Nazification and Denazification of a German University* (Cambridge, MA, Harvard University Press).

Ringer, F. K. (1969), *The Decline of the German Mandarins: The German Academic Community, 1890–1933* (Cambridge, MA, Harvard University Press).

Ritter, G. (1945), 'Der deutsche Professor im Dritten Reich', *Die Gegenwart*, 24 December, 23.

Rottleuthner, H. (2011), 'Legal positivism and National Socialism: A contribution to a theory of legal development', *German Law Journal*, 12, 100.

Schmitt, C. (1976), *The Concept of the Political*, trans. G. Schwab (New Brunswick, Rutgers University Press).

Schmitt, C. (1986), *Political Romanticism*, trans. G. Oakes (Cambridge, MA, MIT Press).

Schmitt, C. (1993 [1928]), *Verfassungslehre* (Berlin, Duncker und Humblot).

Schmitt, C. (2011), 'The Großraum order of international law with a ban on intervention for spatially foreign powers: A contribution to the concept of Reich in international law', in *Writings on War*, trans. T. Nunan (Cambridge, Polity), 75.

Schorn, H. (1959), *Der Richter im Dritten Reich: Geschichte und Dokumente* (Frankfurt am Main, Vittorio Klostermann).

Sharpe, M. (2018), 'The being of the Volk: State, Führer and 'the political' in Heidegger's seminars during the Kairos', in T. Zartaloudis (ed.), *Law and Philosophical Theory: Critical Intersections* (London, Rowman & Littlefield International), 199.

Sherratt, Y. (2014), *Hitler's Philosophers* (New Haven, Yale University Press).

Sims, A. R. (1978), 'Intellectuals in crisis: Historians under Hitler', *Virginia Quarterly Review*, 54, 246.

Stolleis, M. (1998), *The Law under the Swastika: Studies on Legal History in Nazi Germany*, trans. T. Dunlap (Chicago, University of Chicago Press).

Stolleis, M. (2004), *A History of Public Law in Germany, 1914–1945*, trans. T. Dunlap (Oxford, Oxford University Press).

Stolleis, M. (2007), 'Law and lawyers preparing the Holocaust', *Annual Review of Law and Social Science*, 3, 213.

Taylor, F. (2011), *Exorcising Hitler: The Occupation and Denazification of Germany* (New York, Bloomsbury).

Tuori, K. (2020), *Empire of Law: Nazi Germany, Exile Scholars and the Battle for the Future of Europe* (Cambridge, Cambridge University Press).

Weber, R. G. S. (1986), *The German Student Corps in the Third Reich* (Basingstoke, Palgrave Macmillan).

Weinreich, M. (1999), *Hitler's Professors: The Part of Scholarship in Germany's Crimes against the Jewish People* (New Haven, Yale University Press).

Weitz, E. D. (2007), *Weimar Germany: Promise and Tragedy* (Princeton, Princeton University Press).

Wittmann, P. (2008), 'Tainted law: The West German judiciary and the prosecution of Nazi war crimes', in J. Matthäus and P. Heberer (eds), *Atrocities on Trial: Historical Perspectives on the Politics of Prosecuting War Crimes* (Lincoln, University of Nebraska Press), 211.

Part III

Holding Collaborators Accountable?

10

Grudge Informers and Beyond:
On Accountability for Collaborators
with Repressive Regimes

COLLEEN MURPHY*

WIDESPREAD WRONGDOING IS never solely the work of a few; it is only possible through the acts and omissions of many who are not direct perpetrators. Collaborators aid officials of repressive regimes in subjugating and controlling political dissidents specifically and the citizenry more generally. This chapter focuses on whether, why, and how to hold informers, one specific type of collaborator, accountable for blameworthy behaviour after the fall of a repressive regime. Specifically, my interest is in the moral point of accountability, that is, the moral reasons that explain why accountability for individuals who enable, facilitate, and contribute to wrongdoing matters and that shape what counts as a morally defensible response to informers. Accountability for individuals who are implicated in, but are not direct perpetrators of, wrongdoing remains a key issue in transitional justice, the process of dealing with widespread wrongdoing characteristically committed during periods of conflict and repression.

There is no single answer to the question 'Should informers be held to account?' (Espindola and Payne (Chapter 13); Drumbl and Hola (Chapter 5)). My goal in this chapter is to propose conceptual tools (1) to make moral distinctions across various cases of informing and, (2) to identify the moral reasons in favour of accountability in any specific case. The cases I consider below are illustrative and by no means exhaustive. Through my illustrative examples, I aim to show some of the ways in

* Drafts of this paper were presented at a workshop on 'The Problem of Collaboration' at the Casa de la Universidad de California, San Angel; the Political Theory Seminar jointly run by the Department of Politics and International Studies and the Faculty of Philosophy at the University of Cambridge; and Duke Law School. I am grateful for the helpful feedback received during these discussions and on earlier drafts, in particular from Matt Adler, Duncan Bell, Mark Drumbl, Juan Espindola, Matthew Kramer, and Leigh Payne.

which informers vary. These variations are, as I discuss, morally significant, influencing whether accountability is appropriate, and what form accountability should take. I am to explain in a preliminary manner this influence.

My chapter begins with the Hart–Fuller debate in jurisprudence. This debate most explicitly focused on the disagreement between legal scholars H. L. A. Hart (1958) and Lon Fuller (1958) as to whether there is a necessary connection between law and morality. Within the context of this general debate, Hart and Fuller consider the question of whether it is justified to punish Nazi-era grudge informers, those enablers of wrongdoing who take advantage of a repressive system to rid themselves of personal enemies. Their debate concentrates on identifying the moral purpose served by accountability for such individuals and the role of law in facilitating that purpose.

The Hart–Fuller debate provides a useful starting point to think through accountability for those implicated in wrongdoing, such as collaborators, because the structure of the debate allows us to distinguish three different questions. How should we characterise individuals implicated in wrongdoing? Why does accountability matter? What form should accountability take? The Hart–Fuller debate is also useful because it underscores that the picture of actors with which theorising begins shapes and informs intuitions about whether, and how, to hold actors to account for their role in wrongdoing.

I argue in this chapter that a framework for accountability for informers must move beyond the terms of the Hart–Fuller debate in three respects: we must expand and complicate (1) the pictures of informers, (2) the range of reasons for accountability, and (3) the menu of options for accountability. After presenting the broad outlines of the Hart–Fuller debate in my first section, the second section complicates the picture of informers. My discussions highlight the diversity of reasons behind a decision to inform and the diversity of consequences that informing has for the informer, as well as for the individual informed on. Grudge informers are more complicated and varied than the single case Hart–Fuller takes up, and informers are not always grudge informers. The third section turns to the question of why to hold informers to account. I argue that the reasons justifying accountability for informers are not the set of familiar deterrence and retributive considerations that Hart addresses. Fuller links accountability with the pursuit of legal reform in transitions after repression, but legal reform is only one part of a broader project to transform the structure of interaction among citizens and between citizens and officials that is the core normative aim of transitional justice. In seeking to alter this structure of interaction, I argue, it is also critical that such processes be able to acknowledge the different degrees of blameworthiness that attach to informing across cases. The concluding section underscores why we must move beyond the simple binary Hart and Fuller present. The choice societies face is not simply to punish or not to punish informers. Instead, there is a much wider range of mechanisms of accountability that may be used to hold informers to account.

Grudge Informers

One of the most important debates in Anglo-American jurisprudence occurred between legal scholars H. L. A. Hart (1958) and Lon Fuller (1958) in the aftermath of the Second World War. The debate at its most general level concerned the relationship between law and morality; specifically, the core subject of disagreement was whether or not it was correct to hold that there is a necessary connection between law and morality.

Though this was the core subject of Hart and Fuller's disagreement, the debate itself took as its point of departure Nazi Germany. Understanding the relationship between law and morality was viewed by both scholars as not simply of theoretical interest. Hart and Fuller shared a mutual sense of consternation at the role lawyers and judges had played in the Nazi era. Rather than impeding and resisting atrocity and repression, members of the legal profession instead were deeply complicit in Nazi horrors. Hart and Fuller were concerned to identify the view of the law that lawyers and judges in the Nazi era in fact adopted, believing that this would provide some understanding of why they had failed to do better.[1] They also hoped to identify what view would ensure that lawyers and judges would do morally better in the face of injustice in the future, being critical rather than submissive when faced with morally evil laws they were called upon to uphold and interpret.

As Hart and Fuller recognised, the question of the relationship between law and morality is relevant not only for promoting better action in the future, but also for understanding how to deal with moral failure from the past. Thus, Hart and Fuller extensively discuss how to handle cases of Nazi-era grudge informer. Consideration of accountability for grudge informers is important because most informing in civil wars and authoritarian regimes is of this kind (Kalyvas 2006). German authorities prosecuted some such informers in West Germany following the end of the Second World War. The question Hart and Fuller consider is whether such punishment is justified.

Their discussion centres around one particular informer, a German woman married to a German soldier. As presented by Hart and Fuller, during one of the husband's visits home in 1944, he made critical remarks about Hitler and the Nazi Party to his wife. The wife subsequently reported the remarks to the authorities, noting that 'a man who would say a thing like that does not deserve to live' (Fuller 1958: 653). Two statutes passed by the Nazis in 1934 and 1938 prohibited public comments against government officials, the Nazi Party, or government policies when such comments could be inimical to the military defence of the German people or to the government. Hart and Fuller indicate that the wife was having an affair at the time of the husband's visit, which provided a motive for reporting her

---

[1] Debates over the most accurate way to characterise the jurisprudence of Nazi lawyers continue. For recent takes see Pauer-Studer (2020) and Oren Gross (Chapter 9).

husband and the reason why she fell into the category of grudge informers. Upon being reported, the husband was subsequently arrested, put on trial, and convicted by a military tribunal, which sentenced him to death. After the trial the husband was imprisoned and eventually sent to the front line.

The next section looks in detail at variation across cases of informing. Even within the category of grudge informers, we find that not all informers share the features of the above case. The information that grudge informers passed on to authorities could be less lethal than that provided in the case that Hart and Fuller discuss. The reasons to become a grudge informer are not always as morally suspect; sometimes women became grudge informers to protect themselves from abusive husbands (Joshi 2002). While such differences would not necessarily change the arguments or conclusions that Hart and Fuller advance, they are important for the more nuanced picture of accountability developed in the sections that follow.

After the war, in 1949, the wife was charged with illegally depriving her husband of his liberty by a West German court. Illegal deprivation of liberty was a criminal offence under the German Code of 1871 and had remained so during the Nazi period. The wife argued that she could not be punished since her actions were legal at the time they occurred. The court of appeals found the wife 'guilty of procuring the deprivation of her husband's liberty by denouncing him to the German courts, even though he had been sentenced by a court for having violated a statute, since, to quote the words of the court, the statute "was contrary to the sound conscience and sense of justice of all decent human beings"' (Hart 1958: 619). The court ruled that the 1934 and 1938 laws that she had used to claim her actions were legally valid were in fact 'invalid as contravening the fundamental principles of morality' (Hart 1958: 618).

In analysing the case of the German grudge informer, Hart agrees with the court's conclusion, but disagrees with the court's claim that the laws upon which she relied in turning in her husband were invalid because immoral. In making this claim, Hart argues that the court obscured the dilemma that punishment posed. Recognising that after injustice there exists a strong desire to punish those who committed morally egregious acts, Hart sees the core challenge to be explaining how punishment was justified, given that the morally egregious actions were legal at the time of occurrence. In Hart's view, the justification is that punishment is the lesser of two evils. To refrain from punishing the grudge informer would be to respect a central tenet of the rule of law according to which *ex post facto* punishment is impermissible. However, respecting that tenet and not punishing informers would come at the cost of implicitly signalling the permissibility of grossly immoral acts. This evil is greater, in Hart's view, than the evil of violating the prohibition on retroactive punishment (Hart 1958: 619). Hart argues that retrospective legislation should have been passed that opened the door to the punishment of informers. Such legislation would have made explicit the difficult choice confronting German society and the moral dilemma punishment after repression poses. Moreover, Hart argues, such legislation would have powerfully communicated to citizens and to members of the legal profession the following: laws may be legally valid but too evil to be obeyed.

This lesson, that at certain points laws may be too evil to command our obedience, is simple yet critical for ensuring that members of the legal profession and citizens generally retain one of the most powerful tools against legally entrenched evil: a critical perspective on what law demands. Such a stance will help deter future atrocities, Hart believed.

While Fuller agrees that grudge informers should be punished, and agrees with Hart that retroactive legislation should have been adopted to open the door to such punishment, he rejects Hart's reasoning in defence of the legislation. Fuller's basic complaint is that Hart cannot explain why morally evil laws pose a dilemma (Fuller 1958: 656). For Hart, law is like a rule-structured game. Such rules may align with morality, but they may also require grossly immoral conduct. For Hart there is no necessary connection between law and morality; to be legally valid a rule need not be moral. On the positivist's own terms, Fuller claims, a judge called upon to uphold discriminatory laws should not feel a conflict between a duty to be faithful to the law, on the one hand, and the duty to do what morality requires, on the other. The only compelling duty is what morality requires. Faced with an intrinsically morally neutral datum (law) requiring X, and a clear moral obligation not to do X, only one demand has any claim on an individual.[2] Absent any explanation of the value that law has, Fuller argues, there is no reason for legal officials to be faithful to it. Instead of capturing a dilemma posed by evil laws, positivists such as Hart dissolve it (Fuller 1958: 656).

For Fuller, we can only begin to appreciate the dilemma that the punishment of grudge informers poses, and the difficult questions confronting members of the legal profession called to uphold evil laws, if we first recognise what is distinctive and valuable about law. For Fuller (1958: 642), to be effective a legal order must be accepted subjectively as good. Only if it is seen as valuable will officials and citizens be willing mutually to restrain themselves in the ways that the law requires. Legal orders constitute a particular way of exercising authority over others, by governing conduct on the basis of rules. Law, for Fuller (1958: 644–6), has its own implicit morality, a morality that needs to be respected if one is going to create law, even bad law. Constitutive of this morality are conditions that legal systems must satisfy to a threshold level for rule-governed behaviour to be possible. Such requirements include constancy in the rules governing conduct and their promulgation, as well as congruence between declared rules and the actions of government officials. In arguing for these requirements, Fuller uses a series of hypothetical and historical examples, primarily drawn from Nazi Germany, where the conditions that are implicitly presumed to exist in legal orders are absent.[3] Each violation raises

---

[2] 'Positivist' is the term used to describe the school of thought that Hart defended. One core claim of this school of thought is that there is no necessary connection between law and morality.

[3] Retroactive legislation was also used to authorise the execution of thousands in concentration camps. Secret enactment was another method used to make wholesale killing in concentration camps lawful. Such practices were in violation of the implicit morality requirements of prospectivity and publicity.

doubts about whether a legal order, as opposed to another method of governing conduct, applies. As Fuller (1958: 660) writes:

> To me there is nothing shocking in saying that a dictatorship which clothes itself with a tinsel of legal form can so far depart from the morality of order, from the inner morality of law itself, that it ceases to be a legal system. When a system calling itself law is predicated upon a general disregard by judges of the terms of the laws they purport to enforce, when this system habitually cures its legal irregularities, even the grossest, by retroactive statues, when it has only to resort to forays of terror in the streets, which no one dares challenge, in order to escape even those scant restraints imposed by the pretense of legality – when all of these things have become true of a dictatorship, it is not hard for me, at least, to deny it the name of law.

In Fuller's (1958: 656–7) view the central question confronting the postwar German courts was how to balance a concern for maintaining some semblance of legal order during a transitional period with a concern for fundamentally reforming that legal order. He recognised that there would have been morally problematic dislocations if all aspects of the Nazi order were declared unlawful, and yet, at the same time, it was untenable simply to carry on maintaining Nazi law. Germany confronted the challenge of rebuilding law (so that the legal order respects core principles of prospectivity, congruence, clarity, etc.) and rebuilding respect for justice (by declaring what happened in the past untenable).

Against this background, Fuller (1958: 661) claims, we should view the punishment of the grudge informer in largely symbolic terms. A retroactive statute invalidating the statutes to which the grudge informer appealed would serve symbolic purposes. It would function as a way of isolating the areas in which reform and rebuilding should focus from the areas in which the law would continue to function with some continuity from the previous order. It would target the areas of law where the deterioration of the internal morality of law was greatest and where legal reform most profoundly needed. And it would contribute to the cultivation of an appropriate sense of justice by identifying behaviour that would not be tolerated in the future.

In the remainder of this chapter I do not seek to resolve the core source of disagreement between Hart and Fuller as to whether there is a necessary connection between law and morality. Rather, I critically analyse the way Hart and Fuller conceptualise the question of accountability for informers. The next section complicates the picture of informers and discusses why they are not all equally blameworthy. The third takes up the question of why accountability for informers is needed, and discusses why the reasons Hart cites are not salient and why those Fuller articulates represent only a subset of the reasons that make accountability

---

Judges, Fuller claims, routinely disregarded the terms of the laws they were called upon to enforce. In the case of the grudge informer specifically, judges convicted a man for utterances made in the privacy of his home, while the statute under which he was convicted made criminal only public utterances. To say the husband's remarks were public, as the court did, would render meaningless any notion of a private statement. Moreover, the statutes were aimed at targeting deserters or those trying to escape military duty; but women were barred from military service (Fuller 1958: 648–55).

in transitional contexts important. The final section urges us to move beyond the binary choice either to hold the grudge informer accountable via trial and punishment or not to hold the grudge informer accountable at all.

Informers

This section expands our picture of informers, citizens who aid and assist in state-sponsored repression through the provision of information to authorities. Collaborators are implicated in the wrongdoing of another by causally contributing to that wrongdoing.[4] Informers are one specific category of collaborator. They causally contribute to wrongdoing by providing information that enables wrongdoing to happen. Other collaborators may causally contribute by providing tools or supplies, such as weapons.

Collaborators generally, and informers specifically, can vary in a number of ways. There can be a *range of motives* for informing on an individual to authorities. The grudge informer whom Hart and Fuller consider acts for the sake of a personal vendetta. Other informers who are not grudge informers act under coercion or the threat of coercion. Informers can be opportunists hoping to gain personally from informing without actively wishing ill on the individual upon whom they inform. They can also be true believers, sharing the ideology animating a particular repressive regime and acting out of a deep sense of civic duty.

Not only do informers vary in the reasons for their actions, acts of informing can lead to very different *consequences for the individual informed upon.* In some cases the information provided to authorities may lead to the loss of goods, such as an apartment or income.[5] In other cases a career may be stunted. An individual may find him- or herself in a position of moral hazard, confronted with the choice of collaborating in order to avoid certain negative consequences. Arrest, torture, and in some cases death may be the consequences for some individuals about whom information is given to authorities.

Informers themselves may also face different consequences as a result of their collaboration. Acts of informing may lead to rewards. The acquisition of goods in the form of income or resources such as housing, career advancement, and employment itself are possible results of collaboration. Alternatively, informing may serve as a way to end torture or avoid arrest. Informing may entail an assumption of risk on the part of the informer. Exposure of informing activity may make an informer vulnerable to retribution at the hands of former colleagues, family, or friends.

Here are two specific examples of informers who are *not* grudge informers. Both the reasons for and consequences of informing differ from the case of the

---

[4] For a masterful treatment of the idea of being implicated in wrongdoing see Rothberg (2019). For the distinction between directly committing versus causally contributing to wrongdoing see Lepora and Goodin (2015).

[5] For illustrations of this see Hisham and Crabapple (2018).

grudge informer examined by Hart and Fuller. These illustrative examples help us expand the picture of informers beyond the confines of the category of the 'grudge informer' that Hart and Fuller offer. Both examples are taken from Leigh Payne's (2001: 12–14) discussion of collaborators in Chile during the Pinochet dictatorship. The first case is Luz Arce. A member of the Socialist Party and a militant, she was arrested by the Chilean security apparatus in 1974. Subjected to severe torture, Arce eventually informed on comrades by offering names to authorities and convincing fellow detainees to create diagrams for authorities of the Socialist Party leadership. Outside detention, she would enter comrades' homes convincing them to leave with her, whereupon they were in fact delivered to torture centres. Eventually Arce was hired by the secret police as an agent, working for them from 1975 to 1979. Writing in her autobiography years later and testifying before the Rettig Commission, Luz Arce argued that her actions were the only alternative she had in the face of death. Moreover, she claimed, though she had informed, she had attempted to do so in a way that would limit harm to the Socialist Party through, for example, strategic choice of which names to give up.

The second example is Miguel Estay Reyno, a Communist Party militant captured and detained the same year as Arce (Payne 2001: 18–21). He became a security agent for DICOMAR, an intelligence unit within the militarised police, and was involved in the capture and killing of three Communist Party leaders in 1985. Estay asserted, but then subsequently denied, that he had been tortured. He later explained and defended his actions as a product of a change of ideology, whereby he came to be committed to defending the Pinochet regime. Payne (2001: 18) ends her description of Estay with these words: 'Estay may represent Sartre's archetypal collaborator: a marginal individual in a major political party, who sees collaboration with the enemy as a means to enhance his own personal power even if it involves adopting the enemy's ideology and assuming a subordinate position under the enemy's command.'

Intuitively, the relative blameworthiness of the grudge informer, Arce, and Estay is not the same. On a spectrum of blameworthiness, the grudge informer seems most blameworthy, Arce seems least blameworthy, and Estay falls somewhere in-between. Criteria for assessing the relative blameworthiness of collaborators developed by Chiara Lepora and Robert Goodin (2015) are useful in fleshing out the basis for such intuitive reactions. I will take up this issue in the next section. But to recognise blameworthiness is not sufficient to explain why informers should be held accountable. I turn first in the next section to understanding the reasons in support of accountability for informers.

Accountability for Informers: For What Purpose?

To assess the relative blameworthiness of any agent is not to settle the question of whether and how a blameworthy agent should be held to account for blameworthy action. Just as the relative blameworthiness of collaborators is more varied than the

Hart–Fuller debate indicates, so too the question of why and how to hold informers to account is more complicated than the picture Hart and Fuller present. I focus on some of these complications in this section, specifically concerning the reasons accountability is pursued at all. I then link these reasons to the constraints on fair treatment of informers, which will ensure the nuance of blameworthiness discussed in the previous section is recognised to some degree.

Implicit in Hart's discussion are two standard reasons appealed to in justifications of criminal punishment: desert and forward-looking consequentialist considerations. From the perspective of desert, the grudge informer merits punishment because of the intrinsically awful nature of the actions in which she engaged. Consequentialist considerations weighing in favour of punishment that Hart references include curbing vigilante violence and preventing future instances of similar wrongdoing by communicating the wrongfulness of the grudge informer's conduct. Fuller recognises additional reasons that do not typically figure in moral justifications of criminal punishment, but I set these additional considerations aside for now to discuss first why it is a mistake, in my view, simply to adopt standard reasoning in defence of criminal punishment to deal with the question of accountability for grudge informers in transitional contexts.

Moral defences of criminal punishment are necessary because of the very nature of what punishment entails: the intentional infliction of suffering. In justifying criminal punishment, accounts seek to explain (1) why the intentional infliction of suffering is ever morally permissible, let alone a requirement of justice, and (2) why this is a permissible action for states specifically to take. Moral defences of criminal punishment that appeal to the intrinsic value of punishment explain why it is needed to assert the moral equality of victims, and why this equality is what states must vindicate (Hampton 1992). Consequentialist moral defences point to the important societal goals that punishment furthers through deterrence and prevention (Primoratz 1989).

In making these arguments, discussions of the justifiability of criminal punishment characteristically make the following assumptions about the nature of the wrongdoing being addressed.[6] One assumption is that wrongdoing is exceptional. This implies that the number of instances of wrongdoing lies within the capacity of state agencies to address in principle. It also implies that criminal legal rules are effective in regulating conduct. Punishment thus serves a limited and targeted purpose of deterring both the individual wrongdoer himself and the few others who may be contemplating criminal action. Another assumption is that the state has legitimacy and is impartial with respect to wrongdoing. Against this background, the standing of the state to deal with wrongdoing is straightforward to establish. It is the representative of a community's values and ensures the equality of citizens. The expressive function of criminal punishment to condemn wrongdoing becomes unproblematic to stipulate, and the deterrent impact of punishment straightforward to stipulate and assess in particular cases.

---

[6] For an extended defence of the attribution of these assumptions see Murphy (2017: Chapter 2).

For the contexts in which the question of dealing with collaborators comes up, however, these assumptions do not hold. To see this it is helpful to begin by more precisely characterising contexts in which moral issues of accountability for blameworthy collaborators arise (Murphy 2017). First, as I argue in previous work, the wrongdoing to which collaborators contribute is *normalised and political*. It is normalised in an empirical sense; wrongdoing becomes a basic fact of life around which targeted citizens must orient their conduct. That wrongdoing is normalised need not entail that it is predictable; indeed, one way to terrorise a population into submission is by creating an unpredictable environment in which the basis on which particular individuals are targeted is not fully understood by victims or others. When wrongdoing, especially in the form of repression, becomes normalised it requires many individuals to carry it out and yet more to serve as secondary agents. Thus principal and secondary agents of wrongdoing are not exceptional but become the rule. The characteristically political nature of such wrongdoing is a product of the fact both that state agents are implicated in many cases of wrongdoing and that the ultimate purposes served by wrongdoing are frequently political. Maintaining a regime, terrorising a population into submission, and contesting or defending land are some of the objectives to be facilitated by normalised wrongdoing.

Resistance to a repressive regime is often sparked by a background of what I call *pervasive structural inequality* (Murphy 2017). Institutional rules and norms differentially shape the substantive opportunities that different groups within a society (on the basis of geography, ethnicity, gender, religion, or some other fault line) enjoy to do and become things of value, such as being employed, being recognised as a member of one's community, or avoiding poverty. Moreover, repressive regimes restrict who has an opportunity to define and shape institutional rules and norms themselves by restricting access to positions of political power. It is such inequality that is often partly responsible for generating moral dilemmas surrounding collaboration for members of disenfranchised and marginalised groups wishing to better their individual situation or wanting to avoid being a target of repression.

Third, societies confronting the question of how to deal with informers face specific challenges when explaining why the state should establish processes for dealing with past wrongs. There exists what I call *fundamental uncertainty about authority* (Murphy 2017). Because the state is implicated in the wrongs that are now the subject of processes such as criminal trials, it is not a neutral party to wrongdoing in the way justifications of criminal punishment characteristically assume. Nor is the state a representative of values that are defensible and were threatened by perpetrators of wrongdoing. Repressive regimes represent values in need of repudiation, and the informers, who may now be the subject of processes of transitional justice, often simply reinforced indefensible values of the state. Thus, the standing of the state to deal with past wrongs needs to be established and cannot simply be assumed.

Finally, when a repressive regime collapses or conditions for a transition to a new form of government arises, there is often what I call *serious existential uncertainty* in the political trajectory of a community (Murphy 2017). Openings for democratic reform can be a product of the toppling of a dictator, but whether those reforms aspired to will be achieved remains far from certain. Many attempted transitions away from conflict and repression fail; conflict resumes or repression recurs. In the midst of serious existential uncertainty, it becomes very difficult for citizens and officials in a transitional society to know what narrative to tell about unfolding events and how to structure their action accordingly.

Societal transformation as the aim of transitional justice

It is in the context of pervasive structural inequality, the normalisation of wrong-doing, serious existential uncertainty, and fundamental uncertainty about authority, that calls for accountability for informers of the kind Hart and Fuller considered in postwar Germany occur. But in this context the moral objectives pursued through mechanisms of accountability go well beyond standard aims of deterrence and desert. Such mechanisms of transitional justice have as their core objective, I have argued elsewhere, the *just pursuit of societal transformation* (Murphy 2017). The subject of transformation is the basic terms of interaction among citizens, and between citizens and officials. Such transformation is necessary, given the fact that existing relations were structurally unequal and enabled the normalisation of wrongdoing. Transformation characteristically requires establishing conditions such that a thin degree of political trust is reasonable and that opportunities for all members of a community to be recognised as citizens, be respected, and participate in political institutions obtain. It also characteristically entails substantial reform to legal institutions in the face of the erosion of the rule of law (Murphy 2010, 2017).

While transformation in the broad patterns of interaction among citizens and officials is the animating objective of processes of transitional justice, this goal is pursued by confronting past wrongdoing. The presence of serious existential uncer-tainty helps explain why the process of dealing with past wrongdoing becomes linked to the forward-looking pursuit of relational transformation (Murphy 2017). In a context where it is unclear whether repression or dictatorship will effectively end or whether renewed repression and conflict will ensue, how a community deals with past wrongdoing often provides evidence of the seriousness (or lack thereof) of the commitment to change. Processes of accountability can signal the serious-ness with which the need to transform terms for interaction will be taken by a new government, in this way reducing some uncertainty about whether a community is in fact heading to a place different than the repression that came before.

There are other reasons why accountability for past wrongs has implications for the possibility of societal transformation. For efforts of transformation to occur and be effective it is necessary that there be a prior recognition that transformation is needed. This is why Fuller's claim, that punishment of grudge informers for the sake of drawing a line between conduct tolerated in the past but now rendered impermissible in the present and future, was astute. Such a line reinforces the need to change interaction moving forward. By focusing the line on informers, and not simply perpetrators, processes of accountability may counter a certain type of denial commonly found in transitional contexts. This denial takes the form of rationalising what made wrongdoing possible by attributing it to the actions of a few bad apples (Espindola 2015: 178). This form of denial implies that ordinary citizens during periods of repression and conflict were not complicit in the actions that the evil few committed. Such denial can be countered by highlighting the fact that mass atrocity only becomes possible with the help of many ordinary individuals; it depends on more than bad apples. Showing the ways that ordinary folks are implicated in serious wrongdoing can counter the narrative that the commission of wrongdoing can be reduced to the actions of an evil few. Finally, beyond drawing a line, and in this way attempting to counter existing patterns of impunity, accountability for past wrongdoing can contribute to the bootstrapping into existence of the authority of a new government, which shows, by dealing with wrongs in which the prior government was implicated, that it is committed to a different standard of conduct than that which shaped conduct in the past. With respect to informing specifically, some post-Communist governments were willing to confront their encouragement of collaborationism while others were not. In reunified Germany, for example, an agency was created specifically to organise and disseminate the Stasi archives. Part of the point of creating this agency was to lend legitimacy and moral authority to the reunified government in the eyes of East Germans.[7]

Fitting and Appropriate Treatment of Informers as a Constraint on the Pursuit of Transformation

For transformation of the terms structuring interaction to be *justly pursued*, the participants of such processes must be treated in a fitting and appropriate manner. Put differently, victims, perpetrators, and/or collaborators who are the subject of processes of transitional justice must not be treated as mere means for the sake of achieving some broader societal goal such as transformation. Fair and appropriate treatment of informers requires sensitivity to the different degrees to which informers engaged in blameworthy behaviour. To treat all informers alike is to ignore the morally significant differences of the situations in which collaboration occurred.[8] This suggests the importance of a process ideally being structured in a way that can recognise and take into account the different degrees of blameworthiness of informing

---

[7] I thank Juan Espindola for drawing my attention to this point and offering this example. More generally on this point see Espindola (2015).

[8] Blameworthiness is a central factor that shapes judgements of whether informers are treated in an appropriate manner. Additional factors that influence appropriateness but are not discussed in this section include the relationship between the agent holding an informer accountable and the informer him-/herself. The state has standing to adopt processes of accountability, such as punishment, which private citizens do not. Victims harmed by informers are entitled to feel resentment toward them, whereas those who read the stories of victims are entitled to indignation but not resentment. On what makes treatment appropriate or not see Chapter 4 of Murphy (2017).

across cases. Lepora and Goodin articulate four criteria that can be used to differ-entiate cases of collaboration specifically. After summarising their criteria, I then apply these criteria to the grudge informer, Arce, and Estay. The application of the criteria highlights why the case of the grudge informer is a relatively easy one to evaluate. Both Arce and Estay are more complicated.

Collaboration, on the view of Lepora and Goodin, may or may not be blame-worthy. Assessing the blameworthiness of collaboration in any particular case requires tending to four factors. These factors are reflected in the following for-mula: the '*pro tanto* blameworthiness for an act of complicity = function of (badness of principal wrongdoing, responsibility for the contributory act, extent of contribu-tion, extent of shared purpose with wrongdoer)' (Lepora and Goodin 2015: 98). For Lepora and Goodin, any and-all-things-considered judgement of blameworthi-ness must consider the alternative courses of action available to an agent in any particular case and the relative blameworthiness of these alternative courses. In applying their criteria below I briefly articulate alternative courses of action, but my primary interest is in assessing the relative gravity of the actual actions undertaken by agents in the three cases of interest.

The first factor that informs judgements of blameworthiness is *the badness of principal wrongdoing*, or the nature of the wrong done by the principals to which a collaborator causally contributes (Lepora and Goodin 2015: 98). One is not blame-worthy if the act to which one contributed is not itself morally bad. Informing on the mafia to the police in a democratic society is in most cases not a morally bad thing to do. Informing on neighbours to the security apparatus of an authoritarian regime engaging in systematic repression typically is. In transitional contexts, the focus is typically on informing that contributes to political wrongdoing, rather than to ordinary criminality. The morally worse the principal wrongdoing, the greater the blameworthiness of the agent who contributes to that wrong. The relative moral badness of an action can be specified in a variety of ways depending on the moral framework one adopts. For example, consequentialists consider the relative harm caused as a consequence of wrongdoing. Deontologists look at the relative serious-ness of the moral rule violated in wrongdoing, or the intrinsic badness of the act itself.

Responsibility for the contributory act takes into account whether the action of the collaborator was voluntarily and knowingly committed. Lepora and Goodin (2015) view *voluntariness* as a function of the kind of control an agent had in performing the act. Some threshold level of voluntariness is needed for an agent to be responsible at all for a contributory act. Lack of voluntariness can be an excusing condition. Actions as a product of involuntary movements or accidentally carried out would not be voluntary. Acting under duress reduces and at some limit can even remove the voluntariness of an action. Above that threshold or limit, coercion comes in degrees, and therefore can be greater or lesser degrees of the voluntari-ness of an action. The *knowledge* condition for Lepora and Goodin concerns what the agent did know, or should or could have known, when committing the action. Knowledge tracks what the agent knew about the nature of the action they were engaging in, and in particular its causal connection to principal wrongdoing and the wrongness of the principal wrongdoing itself. To avoid wilful blindness consti-tuting an excusing condition, Lepora and Goodin argue that we must consider too what an agent should have known, even if they intentionally prevented themselves from knowing certain information. 'Should' tracks the kind of effort and expense one could reasonably be expected to undertake to determine the causal contribution of one's act to some principal wrongdoing. Where it was impossible to have known the contributory nature of an act or the moral wrongness of the principal wrong-doing, responsibility for the contributory act 'would be zero' (Lepora and Goodin 2015: 105). Above that limit there is responsibility to greater or lesser degrees.

The third factor in evaluating blameworthiness is what Lepora and Goodin call the *extent of contribution*. This factor takes into account the causal role of the act of collaboration in wrongdoing. In the words of Lepora and Goodin (2015: 106), 'We can think of it, roughly, as the percentage of badness of that principal wrong that might be causally attributable to the contributory agent, by virtue of her contribu-tory act.' Casual attribution is in turn a function *of its centrality*, or how essential the act was causally for the principal wrongdoing to happen. An act could be def-initely or potentially causally essential. An act is definitely essential if it is caus-ally necessary in every possible way in which the wrong may occur (Lepora and Goodin 2015: 60). An act is potentially essential if it is causally necessary in some but not all of the paths in which the wrong occurs. Assume a case of a firing squad with four marksmen, each of whom successfully hits the heart of the victim. In one scenario the shot of one marksman could be a difference-maker if the guns of the other three marksmen for some reason failed. Causal attribution takes into account *proximity to the principal wrongdoing*, either as being closest in the causal chain or as having the last chance to reverse a course of action or a tipping point. The extent to which an agent merely *carried out a plan versus contributed to the making of a plan* matters, with greater blameworthiness attaching to the latter. The *attitude of the secondary agent toward his or her contribution* is also relevant. Such attitudes are reflected in whether the agent (1) did avoid or would have avoided following a plan if they could do so easily and without cost, or (2) is committed strictly to following instructions in implementing the plan, or (3) adjusts his or her actions in light of the actions of others to ensure the plan is successful.

The extent of shared purposes with the wrongdoing is the fourth and final factor Lepora and Goodin discuss. Sharing the purposes of the wrongdoer makes an act of collaboration morally worse. In Lepora and Goodin's words, 'boarding a bus to encourage a lynching is definitely worse than boarding a bus to protest against a lynching, even if you can foresee clearly that exactly the same number of people will end up being lynched in consequence of your action in both cases' (Lepora and Goodin 2015: 109). Sharing is a scalar idea where one can share more or less in the purposes of the principal agent and share those purposes with greater or lesser enthusiasm.

Going beyond the criteria Lepora and Goodin suggest, we might evaluate the *nature of the causal contribution*. The debate between Hart and Fuller suggests another factor to take into account when evaluating the attitude of the secondary agent, namely, the legal status of the contributory action at the time of occurrence and the extent to which an action was viewed as legally obligatory to engage in. The legal status of an action does not settle the question of whether it is defensible to engage in, but can influence the attitude of an agent to her actions and the broader societal consequences of informing. Informing that is legally required may be less blameworthy than informing that is merely legally permissible. Similarly, it may be relevant when considering blameworthiness to take into account whether informing is part of a widespread and normalised pattern of behaviour versus an isolated act.

These four factors provide the basis for distinguishing the relative blameworthiness of the grudge informer, Arce, and Estay. Consider first the grudge informer as described by Hart and Fuller. The badness of the principal wrongdoing is significant: the informer's husband was sentenced to death simply for his private critical remarks of Hitler. The grudge informer was responsible for her acts of informing. She provided information intentionally and in the absence of any duress. By the information provided, we have no reason to believe she was at risk of being targeted by government officials herself for failure to report her husband's remarks. The grudge informer was also knowledgeable about the likely consequences of reporting her husband's remarks to the authorities. Indeed, punishment was precisely part of the orienting aim of her action, as stipulated, to rid herself of her husband. The grudge informer's action was central in the sense that absent her report there was no one who could have reported the husband's remarks made in the privacy of his home and, we may assume, in confidence. We have no reason to believe the husband was publicly vocal about his critical beliefs of Hitler in ways that would have risked his being apprehended by officials. Finally, the grudge informer used the wrongdoer's plans of punishing and silencing political dissent to her advantage (i.e. ridding herself of her husband). All things considered, judgements of blameworthiness require, according to Lepora and Goodin, consideration of the alternative courses of action open to the grudge informer. In this case, there exist alternative courses of action that are morally preferable. Dealing with marital issues in a manner that did not involve harming her husband is one option; divorce instead of reporting would have been morally preferable.

At the opposite end of the spectrum lies Arce. The badness of the principal wrongdoing in her case is, like that of the grudge informer, significant. Comrades she informed on were in turn tortured, and no doubt in some instances killed. However, the voluntariness of her informing activities is significantly reduced because of the fact that she informed under coercion – not only the coercion constitutive of detention but also the coercion constitutive of torture. Different than the grudge informer's case, it is unlikely that Arce was the unique pathway to information about colleagues she informed upon. Had she not given up information, other detainees probably would or could have. Arce also tried to reduce strategically the value of her information and so therefore the danger she put her colleagues in. Finally, Arce shows no evidence of sharing purposes with the Pinochet regime.

Torture led to collaboration motivated by a desire for survival, but did not precipitate a fundamental change of heart. Assuming Arce's belief that she would have been killed had she not given information is accurate, the only reasonable course of action open to her was the one she took.

Estay's case lies on a spectrum of blameworthiness somewhere between the grudge informer and Arce. The voluntariness of at least some of his acts as an informer was reduced by the fact that those acts occurred while he was in detention. However, in that context his actions were more voluntary than Arce's, because he was not subject to the additional form of coercion that torture introduces. Estay's actions do not seem to be as causally essential as the grudge informer's, in the sense that it is likely others could have aided in the plot to kill Communist leaders or provided information necessary to the plot being carried out. However, his actions are more causally essential than Arce's, in the sense that, given his commitment to the Pinochet cause, he was interested in seeing his actions be causally effective and not merely in carrying out orders unconcerned by the ultimate success of the plan into which those orders fit. This reflected shared purposes that developed between Estay and the agents in the Pinochet scheme responsible for the principal wrongdoing. Alternative courses of action were open to Estay, such as refusing employment by the security forces after his detention.

Settling upon the appropriate characterisation of any specific informer is always fraught. Ksenija Bilbija (Chapter 3) underscores the gendered nature of the way stories of informers are framed.

Complications in Stipulating Any Aim of a Process of Transitional Justice

I have argued in this section that the overarching purpose of transitional justice is to transform the structure of interaction among citizens and between citizens and officials. I also suggested that processes focusing specifically on informers may be well positioned to counter a common form of denial among citizens and officials post-atrocity that seeks to downplay or deny the role of ordinary individuals in atrocity. While these contributions to societal transformation are plausible in theory, establishing that any single process of transitional justice will achieve or further any of these aims is far from simple. In contexts where criminal justice systems are effective and legitimate, the expressive function of punishment may be straightforward to stipulate, but the expressive meaning of any process of accountability is much more fraught in transitional contexts. This is because of the background risk of moral failure that accompanies any attempt to deal with past wrongdoing in transitional circumstances.

Processes for redressing past wrongdoing are not always mechanisms of justice nor seen as mechanisms of justice. Charges of victor's justice are levied against criminal proceedings, with justification in a number of cases. Punishment may be subjectively seen not as an expression of condemnation of wrongful conduct, but rather as a vendetta against a targeted group. Against a background context in which, *de facto*, many, many principals and secondary agents will never be held to account for wrongdoing no matter what process(es) of transitional justice is established, the potential arbitrariness and morally dubious grounds for selecting those who are in fact held to account becomes more acute. Complaints that reparations aim to buy victims' silence are often made, and in many contexts that is precisely what is going on. Truth commissions are frequently cynically viewed as offering mere words and empty rhetoric, which will do nothing to facilitate substantive change or ensure robust accountability for perpetrators named. One source of the risk of moral failure stems from the background context in which such processes are established. In a context where impunity for wrongdoing was the norm and victims of wrongdoing were treated with dismissal, contempt, and suspicion by authorities, a presumption of justice being done by any process for dealing with wrongdoing is lacking. Thus, unlike in contexts where criminal justice systems are well functioning, there is an urgent task to understand better the conditions that enable the presumption of injustice to be rebutted and the justice of such proceedings be established and seen to be established.

One factor that seems intuitively relevant in shaping both perceptions and the objective defensibility of processes as processes of justice is the procedural protections of mechanisms established.[9] These can matter for the sake of contributing to the perception of justice and also ensuring that victims and perpetrators are treated fairly. There are a wide range of considerations that may shape procedural justice for any particular process, but the discussion in my second section suggests one consideration that will be salient in treating informers: ways of distinguishing different degrees of blameworthiness among informers.

Criminal trials have well-known procedural protections to ascertain guilt accurately in ways that can tease out and distinguish among various intentions and degrees of wrongdoing to which an informer contributed. But other processes of transitional justice have procedural mechanisms as well. For example, in the context of notoriously unreliable security force files where informers cannot be reliably identified, programmes of lustration or a truth commission can rely upon and incentivise voluntary disclosure of one's status as an informer. Such disclosure, to be complete, may mandate precisely the kind of detailed information that would allow for a nuanced assessment of blameworthiness.

Distinguishing treatment for informers who acted under coercion from informers who were opportunists matters both for its own sake and for the sake of contributing to a subjective perception that whatever process is established is indeed a process of justice. Thus, showing the fairness of punishment or any other mechanism of accountability necessarily will be a function of considering not only what those held to account did, but also how their actions compare to what others did that was wrongful.

---

[9] Danner and Martinez (2005) make a similar point when discussing international criminal trials.

Accountability for Collaboration

Hart and Fuller present a binary choice. Either the grudge informer is held accountable via punishment, OR the grudge informer is not held accountable because she is not punished. However, modes of accountability exist beyond punishment. Indeed, the field of transitional justice examines in detail some of the many other ways in which individuals can be held to account for blameworthy actions. Truth commissions in their proceeding and final reports, processes of lustration, amnesty provisions conditioned upon acknowledgement of responsibility for wrongdoing by the amnesty applicant, public naming for the sake of shaming, reparations duties ascribed to perpetrators of wrongdoing, and art are some of the many forms accountability can take. Thus, the failure to punish need not entail impunity. Settling on *which* mode(s) of accountability is morally appropriate to use in particular contexts will to some extent be context-dependent. But the discussion in the second and third sections of this chapter suggests considerations that will be relevant in selecting processes of accountability in any specific context. One consideration is which process can sufficiently distinguish degrees of blameworthiness among informers. Another is which process is best positioned to counter denial about the necessary and often critical role ordinary citizens play during conflict and repression in causally contributing to the wrongdoing of others.

References

Danner, A. D. and Martinez, J. S. (2005), 'Guilty associations: Joint criminal enterprise, command responsibility, and the defense of international criminal law', *California Law Review*, 93, 75–170.

Espindola, J. (2015), *Transitional Justice after German Reunification: Exposing Unofficial Collaborators* (New York, Cambridge University Press).

Fuller, L. (1958), 'Positivism and fidelity to law: A reply to Professor Hart', *Harvard Law Review*, 71, 630–72.

Hampton, J. (1992), 'Correcting harms versus righting wrongs: The goal of retribution', *UCLA Law Review*, 39, 1659–1702.

Hart, H. L. A. (1958), 'Positivism and the separation of law and morals', *Harvard Law Review*, 71, 593–629.

Hisham M. and Crabapple, M. (2018), *Brothers of the Gun: A Memoir of the Syrian War* (New York, One World).

Joshi, V. (2002), 'The "private" became "public": Wives as denouncers in the Third Reich', *Journal of Contemporary History*, 37, 419–35.

Kalyvas, S. (2006), *The Logic of Violence in Civil War* (New York, Cambridge University Press).

Lepora, C. and Goodin, R. (2015), *On Complicity and Compromise* (Oxford, Oxford University Press).

Murphy, C. (2010), *A Moral Theory of Political Reconciliation* (New York, Cambridge University Press).

Murphy, C. (2017), *The Conceptual Foundations of Transitional Justice* (New York, Cambridge University Press).

Payne, L. (2001), 'Collaborators and the politics of memory in Chile', *Human Rights Review*, 2:3, 8–26.

Pauer-Studer, H. (2020), *Justifying Injustice: Legal Theory in Nazi Germany* (Cambridge, Cambridge University Press).

Primoratz, I. (1989), *Justifying Legal Punishment* (London, Humanities Press).

Rothberg, M. (2019), *The Implicated Subject: Beyond Victims and Perpetrators* (Palo Alto, Stanford University Press).

11

Business Collaborators on Trial: Legal Obstacles to Corporate Accountability in Argentina

GABRIEL PEREIRA

THE NORTHERN ARGENTINE province of Tucumán was a notorious site for repression during the 1970s. Even before the 1976 coup that overthrew the democratic national government and implanted a highly repressive authoritarian regime, Tucumán had experienced the repressive tactics that became associated with the dictatorship. Indeed, the 1975 *Operativo Independencia* (Operation Independence) is seen as a trial run for the dictatorship's tactics. More than 700 victims were caught up in the system of illegal detentions, torture, killings, and forced disappearance (Jemio 2016). That pre-coup repression continued throughout the period of the dictatorship (1976–83). Responsibility for the level and type of violence, the victims it targeted, and its persistence for nearly a decade, cannot be attributed to state actors – political leaders and armed forces under their command – alone. Private economic actors played a key role as collaborators in human rights violations.

This chapter focuses on that business collaboration in Tucumán and the subsequent post-transition efforts to hold economic actors accountable for their complicity in human rights violations. It examines the concept of economic actors as collaborators in authoritarian state contexts, specifically who counts as a collaborator and what makes them a collaborator. It then considers whether and how transitional justice mechanisms should address economic actors' collaboration. Before presenting those two sections, the chapter first provides some brief but relevant background for understanding the context of Argentine transitional justice.

A Brief Background on Transitional Justice in Argentina

Argentina's transitional justice process emerged in response to systematic human rights violations perpetrated by the country's recent and repressive dictatorship

(1976–83). While scholars outside the country tend to refer to this period as a 'dirty war' for its emblematic 30,000 disappeared, within the country the language of 'war' – dirty or otherwise – is seen as a justification by the armed forces for its brutal repression. Human rights advocates and activists use, instead, the notion of 'state terrorism', which caught civilians in a repressive network of clandestine torture and detention centres from which the iconic 30,000 disappeared.

The language of war was used by the armed forces to justify its repressive action aimed at pre-existing left-wing revolutionary movements, perceived as threatening to impose Communist rule in the country. Yet, the small and limited armed resistance from these groups was quickly overpowered. Those involved in the armed struggle number far lower than the victims of the repression. The rest cannot be considered 'collateral damage' resulting from war; instead, the regime engaged in a concerted and vast human rights violations campaign. Regime opponents of any ilk – professionals, students, workers, and social activists, and not only those affiliated with armed insurgency – were targeted in this 'politicide'. Kidnapping from individuals' homes or on the street, forced disappearance in the network of 610 clandestine centres, torture, and execution, were the central features of the repressive apparatus in place before and following the coup. The regime cooperated with other Southern Cone dictatorships in Operation Condor, a repressive cross-border alliance that carried out abductions, rendition, torture, and disappearances of suspected subversives. This meant that some so-called subversives in Argentina were kidnapped, tortured, and disappeared or killed abroad under agreement with the Argentine Security Apparatus. That same apparatus cooperated in the Condor alliance to capture those who had sought refuge in Argentina from repressive dictatorships in their own countries.

Some survived to tell the story. In some cases they were released from clandestine centres under surveillance. In others, they remained long-term political prisoners until the end of the dictatorship. In a few rare cases, some owed their survival to collaboration-under-torture with their abductors in the armed forces, as Bilbija highlights in Chapter 3. Survivors recounted their experiences to the famous CONADEP truth commission and their testimonies are published in the final *Nunca más* report (CONADEP 1984). They also testified in the well-known Junta Trials of 1985 and the subsequent human rights trials in Argentina and abroad, including the Operation Condor trials (Lessa 2019).

What emerges from these testimonies and the transitional justice processes in which they evolved is that the workers' movement was a central target of state terrorism even before the 1976 coup. Thousands of labour activists and leaders were murdered, imprisoned, disappeared, or forced into exile (Basualdo 2021). Repressing workers also involved the regime's prohibition on union activity. The regime exerted robust control within major companies to suppress labour mobilisation, aimed, among other policies, at dismantling the union movement. Workers, particularly union members and leaders, were considered to be regime opponents for mobilising and protesting against the draconian wage repression policies, unsafe working conditions, and the absence of basic working benefits. In short, the move away from the ideals of social democracy to neoliberal authoritarianism and the activism it spawned made labour a key victim for the regime's repression.

Argentina's transition to democracy began with the regime's abrupt collapse. Each pillar of the regime's support eroded. Its neoliberal economic plan ended with a severe economic crisis. Its military prowess was undermined in its disastrous defeat in its war with the United Kingdom over control of the Malvinas [Falkland] Islands in 1982. Argentina also became an international human rights 'pariah' when the regime itself invited expert observers to the country, prompting outcry heard around the globe in defence of victims. With almost no legitimacy left, the regime attempted to negotiate a favourable exit by allowing democratic elections. In 1983, the first of the democratically elected presidents took office, a process that has continued uninterrupted until the present. Those democratic presidents initiated and advanced transitional justice processes that have received much attention: the first truth commission in the world, the first trial of regime leaders since Nuremberg, the most extensive reparations, the dismantling of the authoritarian military structure with institutional reforms, and the most extensive set of human rights trials (Balardini 2016; Engstrom and Pereira 2012).

It is the last of these innovations – criminal trials for human rights violations – that has become the focus of transitional justice mechanisms in the country. Progress toward it has not proved linear, however. More of an 'ebb and flow' process evolved: the initial judicial accountability processes for human rights crimes in the 1980s were gradually restricted and eventually foreclosed with amnesties in the '90s; by the 2000s, however, an unrestricted prosecutorial policy reopened almost 20 years after the beginning of the transition to democracy and has remained in place even when certain presidents have attempted to roll it back (Engstrom and Pereira 2012).

As a result of this long and non-linear transitional justice process, Argentina became known as the global protagonist of transitional justice innovations (Sikkink 2008; Payne *et al.* 2015). Human rights groups have developed unprecedented mobilisation since the '80s, including the use of a wide range of legal mobilisation strategies seeking to overcome accountability obstacles. Legal innovators from within courts channelled the force of civil society mobilisation. Prosecutors and judges developed novel techniques to gather and evaluate evidence supporting victims' claims. These actors, in alliances with civil society, were able to act as a powerful counterweight to impunity forces.

The number of successful criminal prosecutions for human rights violations far surpasses any other country in the world (Lessa *et al.* 2015). Yet that is not the only innovation in Argentina's transitional justice toolkit. In the last 20 years, Argentina has innovated on the set of tools to include those considered to have collaborated in state terror and its human rights violations. This has included priests, medical doctors, and judges operating as accomplices to crimes committed in torture centres (PCCH 2018). Notably, it has also included business collaborators. With more than 20 judicial cases against economic actors initiated over the past 15 years, Argentina has become a global leader in corporate accountability.

Before examining those cases, it is important to define what economic actors' collaboration in state terror means.

Business Collaboration in State Terror

The types of collaboration and collaborators broadly vary within each specific collaborative context, as discussed by Espindola and Payne (Chapter 1) and Drumbl and Hola (Chapter 5). Latin American dictatorships, and the Argentine period of state terror in particular, created a collaboration context in which economic actors became involved. The extent and type of collaboration varies, however. This section of the chapter explores both issues.

Collaboration Context

Human rights regimes and transitional justice approaches tend to focus on state actors, particularly a handful of senior and junior officers of the armed and security forces, as the primary perpetrators of the atrocities of armed conflict and authoritarian rule. Others involved in these violations and held accountable for them tend to be those in state-associated or state-like groups, including armed rebels and paramilitary forces. In the Argentine context of the 1970s, focusing solely on state actors as accountable for the atrocities committed simplistically identifies state terrorism as a mass extermination plan designed and implemented by a small number of state actors for political objectives (Verbitsky and Bohoslavsky 2015). In contrast, a more complex understanding of state terror links the economic, social, and labour-related dimensions of the atrocities (Basualdo *et al.* 2021). State terrorism, in this more complex understanding, is more than a criminal enterprise to eliminate political opponents, but instead is a project aimed at social, economic, and political transformation.

   In this transformative project, more than a small group of actors collaborated. Not all had full awareness of the extent of terror used to advance it. They may only have seen the authoritarian regime as representing and advancing their interests. Others held a central role in the design and implementation of state terror. These actors, however, came from a variety of sectors. The level and extent of collaboration, the motivations behind it, and the forms it took warrant greater exploration. In Argentina, the collaboration of religious, judicial, and business actors in the commission of crimes against humanity is perceived as so extensive that the label 'military regime' has been replaced with the term 'civil-military regime' (Verbitsky and Bohoslavsky 2015). On the 'civil' side, Latin American dictatorships in general, and Argentina's state terrorism in particular, created a business-friendly environment. As Basualdo *et al.* (2021) point out, key national and transnational actors were the natural allies of the right-wing military regimes: military rulers, concerned with 'foreign infiltration' from international Communism through labour activism, found common grounds with business actors and opposed union mobilisations, which they perceived as a threat to their business profits. This approach is consistent with Guillermo O'Donnell's (1999) notion of the 'bureaucratic authoritarian state' alliances with economic actors toward a development strategy of 'capitalist deepening'. In Argentina, the goal of eliminating the political opposition to the regime was linked to the transformation objective, specifically adopting an economic model in which the industrial sector played a leading financial role, leading to growth of external debt, and profound industrial restructuring (Basualdo 2021: 35). State terrorism, thus, rested on a political and economic plan with clear winners and losers (Verbitsky and Bohoslavsky 2015: 7). The restriction of labour rights and the regressive redistribution of income severely affected the working class to the benefit of certain businesses. The reshaping, downsizing, and concentration of the industrial sector benefited large competitive, and particularly internationally oriented, businesses at the expense of small domestic business (Verbitsky and Bohoslavsky 2015). The repressive apparatus – particularly the victimisation of workers and unions – facilitated the transformative process without resistance. The transformative project itself gained support from those who shared the development ideology and who benefited from specific economic advantages such as subsidies and tax exemptions and the market conditions generated by the repression of specific sectors of society (Verbitsky and Bohoslavsky 2015). This is the collaborative context in which state terrorism evolved.

Business Collaborators

Solely benefiting materially from the authoritarian regime does not on its own constitute collaboration. Similarly, those who share the regime's conservative, anti-Communist religious values are not necessarily collaborators. Even an anticipated opportunity to occupy prestigious positions in society by close proximity with regime forces does not by itself mean collaboration. This full set of motivations, and more, may be behind collaboration. And yet motivation is less central to collaboration than the acts committed.

For this study, business actors' collaboration requires a direct or indirect role in implementing the massive human rights violations that occurred during the period of state terror, regardless of the reason. Collaboration requires more than supporting the dictatorship and its systematic violence and human rights violations, as objectionable as such a stance may be. Collaboration involves the higher threshold of facilitating and/or participating in the state's criminal plan. In this sense, business collaborators who did not hold political office constitute collaborators by following the definition set out by Espindola and Payne (Chapter 1) of 'working together' with an illegal regime and engaging in the commission of crimes against humanity.

Even with that threshold, two levels of business collaboration – hardline and softline – can be identified. Softline collaboration plays such a small role in the perpetration of human rights violations that it falls outside transitional justice's remit. The kind of legitimacy provided by softline business collaborators – such as the Nazi law professors discussed in Oren Gross's Chapter 9 – were crucial to sustaining the regime. In Argentina, such softline business collaborations included economic think tanks; business associations; and the intelligentsia who provided technical, political, and economic support and policy proposals to the regime (Basualdo 2015). Representatives of the main economic groups also filled critical official positions within the dictatorship (Basualdo 2021), and foreign financial institutions provided financial support to the authoritarian government that sustained it (Bohoslavsky 2015). The role of these economic entities might warrant moral criticism for failing to halt egregious regime practices when they had the power to do so. While they contributed to the operation, survival, stability, legitimacy, and success of the authoritarian government, if they did not participate in its criminal and violent repressive policies there is little legal ground to hold them accountable through retributive transitional justice mechanisms.

On the other hand, hardline business collaborators made crucial contributions to state terror in Argentina. Cases included in the Corporate Accountability and Transitional Justice (CATJ) database suggest that they facilitated the government's violent crimes, even when they were not always the intellectual authors of, or masterminds behind, those crimes.[1] Collaboration in this sense is contribution to the perpetration of specific crimes against groups of people or specific individuals, or to the broad criminal policy. There are four specific criteria that could be used to identify hardline business collaboration warranting a transitional justice response: direct complicity in criminal violence (e.g. joint criminal enterprise and conspiracy to violence); specific gross human rights violations with regard to labour (e.g. slave or forced labour); financing repression, crimes against humanity, or war crimes (e.g. bank loans to sanctioned regimes, or odious debt); and enterprises or individuals engaged in illegal activity that knowingly procure or profit from, and thereby perpetuate, violence. This chapter contends that hardline business collaborators, those who enable and/or participate in the perpetration of crimes against humanity, could and should face accountability processes for their behaviour during the period of state terror in Argentina, and elsewhere.

Hardline business collaborators, in sum, contributed to the commission of crimes against humanity. Such contribution can be seen not as secondary, but rather as essential, to the regime's repressive system. By 'working together' with state officials in illegal kidnapping, detention, torture, disappearance, and killing, hardline business collaborators formed part of the criminal enterprise. When past state violence, or the extent of violence, would not have been possible without business collaboration; when businesses enabled that violence; and when businesses knowingly contributed to that violence, economic actors moved beyond immoral behaviours into breaches of international human rights law as well as domestic laws.

---

[1] A case of material commission of the crime can be found in Chile. In 2016, Juan Francisco Luzoro Montenegro, a private landholder, transportation company owner, and director of the Business Association of Truckdrivers, was tried, found guilty, and sentenced to 20 years in prison by a Chilean High Court Judge (San Miguel Appeals Court). Luzoro was convicted not only for providing the military with vehicles to conduct illegal detentions but also for shooting victims in a massacre that occurred in the Paine region (Payne *et al.* 2020).

As such their accountability for wrongdoing advances transitional justice goals of, and victims' rights to, truth, justice, reparations, and guarantees of non-recurrence.[2]

Business Collaboration and Transitional Justice: Argentina as Protagonist

Using the four criteria presented in the last section, the CATJ database tracked transitional justice mechanism efforts to hold business collaborators responsible.[3] The findings from the analysis place Argentina as the global leader in judicial processes of corporate accountability. The country includes more than 20 judicial cases against economic actors initiated over the past 15 years at time of writing. Argentina's global standing is due to the fact that it is the country with the highest number of cases initiated and still pending. Thus, as mentioned earlier, Argentina is not only the global protagonist for transitional justice innovations in general, it has added a new – corporate accountability – mechanism to its innovative approach to fighting impunity for past state terror crimes.

These judicial advances did not begin the corporate accountability process in Argentina. In the early stages of transitional justice in the 1980s, the *Nunca más* (Never Again) truth commission report, the first report of this kind in the world, named 11 companies allegedly complicit in the authoritarian regime's kidnapping, arbitrary detention, disappearances, and torture. Moreover, the Argentine National Stock Exchange (CNV) elaborated a report in 2013 accounting for its own complicity during the dictatorship. It revealed that some business community members denounced their competitors as 'subversives' leading to their illegal detention by the repressive apparatus. Additionally, the National Ministry of Justice, in partnership with the Latin American Faculty of Social Sciences (FLACSO) and the civil society organisation Centre for Legal and Social Studies (CELS), elaborated a detailed 1,000-page report accounting for the participation of 25 companies in the commission of crimes against humanity.[4] Furthermore, popular forms of accountability have also been implemented when formal transitional justice mechanisms failed to address

[2] Intergovernmental human rights bodies such as the Inter-american Commission of Human Rights (REDESCA 2019) and the United Nations Working Group on the Issue of Human Rights and Transnational Corporations and other Business Enterprises (UNOHC 2020) have stressed the need to design transitional justice mechanisms addressing corporate responsibility in transitional justice to remedy their past behaviour and contribute to truth, reparation, and guarantees of non-recurrence.
[3] Together with Leigh A. Payne and Laura Bernal-Bermúdez, I was part of the team that built the CATJ database. It tracks the full scope of accountability efforts for economic actors allegedly involved in this set of crimes against humanity during armed conflicts and authoritarian regimes. Judicial actions include international criminal trials, foreign civil and criminal trials, and domestic civil and criminal trials – a total of 104 efforts in every type of court and every region of the world. Argentina has the highest number of domestic cases (24) and a third of all judicial actions in the CATJ.
[4] An example of a failed truth mechanism is the creation of a new truth commission on corporate complicity in the human rights violations during the Argentine dictatorship in 2015. This commission marked an innovation, but it has not yet been effectively implemented.

specific hardline business collaborators. Human rights organisations publicly 'out' business perpetrators for their past abuses, raising public awareness of corporate complicity through the so-called *escraches*, and massive rallies and demonstrations.[5]

Judicial accountability, because it has become the preferred transitional justice mechanism in Argentina, as mentioned previously, has been adapted to business collaboration. Twenty-four cases of hardline business collaborators engaged in crimes against humanity have been initiated in domestic courts, and two in foreign courts.[6] Of those 24, two are civil labour court disputes, two are in administrative courts, and 20 are criminal cases. The cases include the cover-up crimes; providing information enabling military forces to identify, locate, illegally detain, and/or kill workers; allowing the military use of company premises for clandestine detention centres; providing vehicles to kidnap and transport illegally detained individuals; granting military forces access to patrol and to enter the company to detain workers illegally; and deliberately failing to fulfil employers' duties to protect workers' safety on company premises.

As Figure 11.1 shows, however, very few of the cases have reached a final outcome. From a global perspective, this is not remarkable; the CATJ shows very few final outcomes anywhere in the world. Colombia barely surpasses Argentina in achieving outcomes, and all other countries fall far behind. Data from the CATJ confirm that in Argentina and elsewhere, hardline business collaborators have faced accountability efforts rarely, and largely enjoy impunity.

If guilty verdicts and sentences in criminal cases or adverse judgments in civil cases were the only measures of accountability for business collaboration, there would be little to analyse. To focus on outcomes only also ignores the processes by which local actors have attempted to overcome barriers to holding hardline collaborators accountable. It would further prevent analysis of those barriers. My analysis of the Argentine cases, in contrast, recognises both the struggles for justice by victims of hardline business collaboration, but also the 'stop-motion' barriers to achieving those ends because of the particular power of those collaborators. Specifically, when a case presents controversial evidence that demands similarly controversial legal assessment and judicial practice, the judicial action fails to move forward. The case becomes stuck, and sometimes shelved indefinitely, to avoid pressure or criticism from both pro-accountability and pro-impunity forces. As in stop-motion animation, things change very slowly; very little is altered from one frame or one sequence to the next. Judicial processes remain pending, hence a kind of *de facto* impunity prevails when no judgment is reached.

In the next section, I provide a brief overview of the Argentine cases and how they have moved from zero accountability to full accountability and sometimes back again. I then analyse the stop-motion processes in more depth, using the case of La Fronterita sugar mill in Tucumán province as an example.

---

[5] For a discussion of these initiatives, see Payne *et al.* (2020)

[6] Only two trials of Argentine cases – Chrysler and Ford – occurred in US courts.

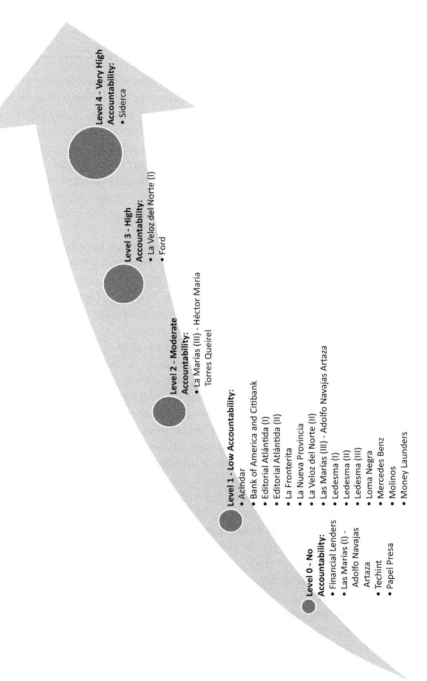

Level 0 - No Accountability:
- Financial Lenders
- Las Marías (I) - Adolfo Navajas Artaza
- Techint
- Papel Presa

Level 1 - Low Accountability:
- Acindar
- Bank of America and Citibank
- Editorial Atlántida (I)
- Editorial Atlántida (II)
- La Fronterita
- La Nueva Provincia
- La Veloz del Norte (II)
- Las Marías (III) - Adolfo Navajas Artaza
- Ledesma (I)
- Ledesma (II)
- Ledesma (III)
- Loma Negra
- Mercedes Benz
- Molinos
- Money Launders

Level 2 - Moderate Accountability:
- La Marías (III) - Héctor María Torres Queirel

Level 3 - High Accountability:
- La Veloz del Norte (I)
- Ford

Level 4 - Very High Accountability:
- Siderca

Figure 11.1 Levels of accountability of Argentine domestic cases.

Accountability Scale in Argentine Business Collaborator Cases

In our analysis of the CATJ, we found that cases fell into five stages of accountability, set out in Figure 11.1. An optimistic look at the continuum shows that the Argentine cases achieved all five levels of accountability outcome. Business collaborators escaped justice in only four cases and the highest level of accountability was reached in one. Two other cases are pending convictions. The litigation process of most cases is still open and, thus, the chances to achieve higher levels of accountability cannot be discounted.

On the other hand, our database shows that 20 cases were affected by severe delays at different stages of the litigation process: what has been referred to as the stop-motion process.[7] Legal strategies to defend hardline collaborators have proved effective in freezing or shelving cases but not to the point of foreclosing the judicial path. Argentina's cases of hardline business collaborators, therefore, allow for some understanding of how judicial processes evolve; are blocked or stuck; are reversed; and, on rare occasions, achieve a final outcome.

At the lowest (zero) stage no accountability is achieved. Acquittal or dismissal falls into this category. Even those cases that reach high accountability, but are later dismissed or reversed on appeal, are included. The final negative judgment annuls all prior accountability effects. There are four zero-accountability cases from Argentina.[8] An example of the power of hardline collaborators to achieve no accountability is the *Las Marías I – Navajas Artaza* case. The case was brought in 2006 against Navajas Artaza, owner of the company *Las Marías*, for the disappearance of a rural worker and union leader and the illegal killing of a police officer (*Patagónico* 2014). It shows how close social, political, and economic connections influence judicial processes.

Las Marías is one of the world's largest yerba mate (the main crop of Corrientes province) agroindustries (Boerr 2019). The prestigious Konex Foundation identified the company's owner, Navajas Artaza, as a model businessman in 1998 and 2008 (Fundación Konex [n.d.]). Navajas Artaza also had a noted political career during the country's authoritarian and democratic regimes. He was appointed governor of Corrientes during an earlier dictatorship in 1966–73 (*Retaguardia* 2014) and National Minister of Welfare in the 1976–83 dictatorship. He was democratically elected as mayor of Virasoro in 1985–7.

Navajas Artaza's political and social connections with judicial authorities became an obstacle to the investigations. Twenty judges disqualified themselves from prosecuting him owing to a conflict of interest related to family, friendship, or other social connections (*Retaguardia* 2018). The national public prosecutor's

---

[7] Alejandro Jasinski (2020) proposes the stop-motion idea to describe the slow pace of corporate accountability cases in Argentina.

[8] We exclude from this analysis one of the Argentine cases included in the CATJ because the outcomes do not fit the scale. In 'Minera La Aguilar', the accusation against economic actors was dropped, as one of the accused died before indictment and the second was unfit to stand trial because of mental illness.

office emphasised in a report the unjustified delays in this case (PGN 2007). Yet neither the prosecutor nor the judge used an innovative approach to advance the case. In 2008, an ad hoc judge took the unusual step of dismissing the charges without requesting further evidence collection or taking the accused's testimony. The public prosecutor failed to appeal that decision (*Sur Correntino* [n.d.]). This decision also provoked little civil society outrage. Indeed, little mobilisation within civil society was behind the case at all. Political context may partly explain the lack of mobilisation.

The first level of accountability involves legal claim-making. Preliminary investigations begin in criminal cases, or initial court papers are filed in civil cases. A low level of accountability – judicial truth-telling – is reached (Felstiner *et al.* 1980). Argentina has 65 per cent (15) of its cases at this stage. The patterns of delays and the concentration of cases in Level 1 should be analysed in the contexts of the Argentine transitional justice process. Delaying the course of judicial investigations is deployed by accused individuals of advanced age. Were they to become seriously ill or die, judicial action would be suspended, perpetuating impunity. The Attorney General's Office reports that 692 persons accused of crimes against humanity died before a ruling was passed in Argentina (PCCH 2018). The magnitude of this figure can be appreciated if we consider that 1,013 individuals received a final conviction.

Among the cases illustrating how hardline collaborators effectively manage to delay cases is La Fronterita sugar mill in Tucumán, discussed in the next section of the chapter. The case of the multimedia firm La Nueva Provincia is another paradigmatic one, which also reveals how hardline collaborators deploy strategies from outside the courtroom to influence judicial outcomes. The case investigated the newspaper owner Vicente Massot and his alleged role in the disappearance and illegal killings of two Graphic Arts Union (Sindicato de Artes Gráficas) leaders, Enrique Heinrich and Miguel Ángel Loyola. Prior to their disappearances, the two leaders had organised and participated in a workers' strike against La Nueva Provincia. In 2014, the public prosecutors of the case requested Massot's indictment for deliberately misrepresenting the incident in the newspaper *La Nueva Provincia* to cover up the disappearances (Loreti 2015).

The case failed to advance beyond claim-making, however. First- and second-instance tribunals denied the indictment request for trial, arguing that there was not enough evidence to move forward with the judicial process. Eventually, the Supreme Court confirmed these decisions in 2020, four years after it reached its docket and six years since the start of the prosecutorial investigation. The decision ordered the public prosecutor to collect further evidence. The case is still open, but no substantive progress has been made since it was initiated.

In addition to their legal defence in court, hardline business collaborators developed public campaigns to exert pressure on the judges. The media business group that represents leading Argentine newspapers, the Association of Argentine News Bodies (Asociación de Entidades Periodísticas Argentinas; ADEPA), issued public statements delegitimising the case against Massot. The campaign run by

ADEPA in the mainstream media portrayed the case as part of a series of political attacks on Argentina's news industry (*Clarín* 2014; *Litoral* 2014; *Nación* 2014). The Comisión Empresaria de Medios de Comunicación Independientes (CEMCI) made a similar claim in defence of Massot. These views resonated in some academic circles, such as the Academia Nacional de Ciencias Morales y Políticas, that decried the ideological motives and dogmatic political ideas behind the investigation. When ADEPA celebrated the indictment's rejection, it issued another public statement reaffirming the claim against the investigation as an attack on the national media and depicted Massot as an illegitimate victim of political and judicial forces (*Página|12* 2015).

The second level of accountability is achieved when a formal accusation is filed in criminal court or when the fact-finding phase of civil trials begins. The defendants are notified of the accusations against them at this stage, and evidence is presented in a court of law. In criminal cases, this stage is reached with an indictment; in civil actions, the accused receives judicial notice of the claim filed against them. The degree of accountability is moderate. In Argentina, progression from Level 1 to Level 2 is particularly challenging for business accountability forces. We found that 93 per cent (14) of the cases have remained in Level 1 four years before moving to the next. Thirteen of them are criminal cases against individuals, and the remaining one is a civil case against several banks. Only one case in Argentina stayed at this level.

The *Las Marías II – Torres Queirel* case sits in Level 2; it produced a negative outcome given the delayed criminal procedure and the – still pending – acquittal.[9] The case represents another example of the benefits business collaborators can get from delaying judicial processes. In this case, the stop-motion process to accountability affected key elements of the prosecutor's legal strategy.

This case is closely connected to the other two *Las Marías* cases. The accusations against Torres Queirel and Navajas Artaza were jointly brought to court in 2006. Although the accusation against Navajas Artaza was quickly dropped, the case against Torres Queirel and three other state officers proceeded. They were eventually accused of crimes against humanity committed against 20 workers. Twelve years later, a tribunal acquitted Queirel in 2018. The decision was based on the lack of evidence proving his participation in the disappearance of the only remaining victim in the trial. That decision is still pending review.

Torres Queirel, like Navajas Artaza, has a prominent profile within the business and political elite of Corrientes province dating back to the dictatorship. He served as mayor of Virasoro during the dictatorship while managing the farm where the crimes were allegedly committed. His business activity expanded after the dictatorship leading to his prominent national business profile.

The defence effectively engaged legal manoeuvres to delay the initiation of the trial for more than four years. The case eventually reached Level 2 accountability

---

[9] Case Reference 'Reston, Llamil; Sacco, Juan Carlos Y Torres Queirel, HectorMaria S/ Asociación Ilícita, Tortura, Privación Ilegal Libertad Pers. (Art. 142 Bis Inc. 1). Expte. Nº Fct 36001586/1991/To1'.

in 2012 when the first-instance judge made a formal request for trial. The delays weakened the case for the prosecution, however. Two of the accused died, and two others became unfit to stand trial owing to grave illness. This also resulted in the dropping from the case of 19 of the victims. In consequence, the trial included one accused, Torres Queirel, and only one victim. This implied that a substantial amount of evidence revealing how Torres Queriel had 'worked together' with army forces could not be brought to court.

The third level of accountability is a conviction or a civil judgment pending appeal, that is, the court renders judgment against the defendant, but an appeals process is under way. Because we do not yet know the outcome of the appeal process, the conviction or civil judgment is tentative. This court decision provides a high level of accountability by establishing the legal responsibility of the accused. On the other hand, these convictions or civil judgments can be – and are – reversed. Two Argentine cases fall into this category. Both cases moved slowly toward accountability and are still pending final decisions.

The case of La Veloz del Norte, initiated in 2011, has been litigated for nine years. It reached the 2016 conviction of Marcos Levin, the owner of this prominent bus company. He was convicted for providing crucial information used by military forces to identify and illegally detain a company worker. An appeals court, however, overturned the conviction in 2017. It acknowledged that torture and illegal detention had been committed against the victim and that Levin had made a substantial contribution to this, but affirmed that these human rights violations were not part of the violations committed by the state. The crimes were considered to have been committed for personal interest rather than as part of systematic human rights violations. The case has been pending final review by the Supreme Court for three years.

Similarly, the 2018 convictions of two top executives of the local branch of the transnational Ford Motor Company occurred after more than 15 years of litigation. The conviction remains pending second-instance review since that time. Because the defendants are in their 90s, it is likely that this case will never be successfully appealed. Indeed, the case against a third defendant was dropped when he died at an advanced age.

The highest level of accountability is a final conviction or adverse judgment. At this stage, final judgments cannot be appealed. The parties either lost their opportunity to do so by failing to appeal within the required period of time, or the last sentence was upheld at the highest appeals court. The figure of 12 final judgments in our database may seem relatively low in absolute terms, but it represents nearly a quarter of the total cases. Only one case reached this level in Argentina.

That case involves the Siderca company (Techint economic group). It is the only case that defies the stop-motion effect, as the case reached a final decision in six years. Oscar Orlando Bordisso disappeared after he left his job at Siderca in 1977. He was never seen again. His wife, Ana María Cebrymsky, claimed compensation from her husband's employer owing to its violation of Argentina's worker safety law obliging employers to protect workers on entry and exit from the workplace. The company claimed that the statute of limitations had run out in this case initiated in 2007. The first-instance tribunal accepted the claim against the company registering it as a crime against humanity for which statutes of limitations do not apply. On appeal, the company lost in the Provincial Supreme Court on the same grounds. The court ordered compensation to Bordisso's widow.

The presence of intense civil society mobilisation and innovative judges may explain why this case overcame the company's defence strategy, which was limited to the legal defence in court. At the end of the dictatorship, former workers of the companies owned by the Techint group and relatives of those detained/disappeared participated in a local human rights group called Comisión de Familiares de Desaparecidos de Zárate-Campana (Committee of Families of the Zarate-Campana Disappeared) to demand justice. They actively engaged in rallies condemning the disappearances of Siderca and Techint workers resulting from the civil (business)–military repressive alliance. The group provided evidence in the Siderca case on behalf of the victim's family. The group failed to achieve national resonance. This proved less significant to the accountability outcome in the context of weak veto power and a favourable political context. Similarly, the courts developed a very innovative legal reasoning, blending domestic labour law and international human rights law to recognise the company's duty to respect and protect human rights and remedy abuses. The argument on the suspension of statutes of limitations for crimes against humanity subsequently became established legal precedent in the Labour Tribunal and the Supreme Court of the Province of Buenos Aires.

In sum, judicial accountability in Argentina has faced significant obstacles. Accusations against hardline business collaborators are not rejected outright. However, several cases are regularly delayed during the pre-trial phase, illustrating the stop-motion process. At Level 1, judges do not foreclose an investigation but they manage to freeze it, preventing greater levels of accountability. The case of La Fronterita provides an in-depth examination of the criminal prosecutorial strategy initiated by public and private prosecutors against hardline business collaborators in Argentina, and how it has been stymied in the stop-motion process.

La Fronterita: A Case of Stop-Motion Justice

Stop-motion judicial processes result from the nature of the accused business collaborator.[10] The social, economic, and political power that this set of collaborators possess; their widely positive image and status in society; and a perception that they are not the primary party responsible but only benefited from an illegal regime are

[10] This section relies on several sources. I use data collected for the CATJ, including rulings issued by Argentine courts. I have also used judicial files of the case of La Fronterita to which I have access as one of the legal representatives of Jacobo Fidel Ortíz's relatives. In that regard, the chapter benefits from first-hand knowledge of the litigation process of this case. Finally, I have also used interviews with key actors in the human rights movement, judicial officials involved in causes against humanity, and relevant actors of the judicial and political field of the province of Tucumán.

the reasons that these cases have not moved forward at the same pace or rhythm as the cases against state actors. In this sense, business collaborators, not unlike the Nazi law professors discussed in Oren Gross's Chapter 9, have avoided confronting their moral and legal responsibility for crimes against humanity. In the case of Argentina, however, and in contrast with the Nazi law professors' case, transitional justice efforts have begun to raise the cost of past collaboration. The case of La Fronterita illustrates the efforts made to advance these cases and the judicial stop-motion hurdles encountered in fully achieving victims' rights of redress in those cases.

The case against La Fronterita alleges that the sugar mill, and the parent company – Minetti Group – had collaborated behind Operation Independence. By way of background, Nassif (2016) argues that the sugar agroindustry had become the main economic activity in that area of the province by the mid-1970s. At the same time, the leaders of an active labour movement had spearheaded labour rights reforms that were perceived as threatening to the sugar mills.[11] The military occupied certain urban and rural public areas, including the iconic social sites of struggle, such as sugar mills and schools, intervening and regulating all social activities. As prosecutor Camuña maintains, these areas became large open-air concentration camps, in which all citizens were captives (Camuña 2016).

Studies suggest that a specific sector of the local business community performed as hardline collaborators in the province of Tucumán. The witnesses' testimonies provided in 11 trials, albeit mainly against state actors, suggest that at least 22 business collaborators contributed to the commission of human rights violations between 1975 and 1983. Notably, 14 of these firms are linked to the sugar industry (Doz Costa *et al.* 2016). The number of victims related to alleged corporate complicity amounts to 312 people. About 55 per cent of them were workers at the same companies that participated in crimes against humanity. In addition, around 70 per cent (218) of them were involved in some union activity. Likewise, the commission of crimes against humanity against 125 victims (40 per cent of the cases surveyed) took place before the March 1976 coup, the majority (117) of which occurred during Operation Independence (Doz Costa *et al.* 2016).

In particular, the evidence collected by the public prosecutor suggests the La Fronterita made substantial contributions to the perpetration of crimes against humanity (Camuña 2016). First, the company is alleged voluntarily to have yielded sectors of its property and buildings to the armed forces to be used as a military base and clandestine detention centre.[12] The company and the armed forces also collaborated in the maintenance, logistics, and construction of new buildings for

[11] Nassif (2015, 2016, 2018) highlights that the tension among mill owners, sugarcane producers, and industrial and rural workers was a permanent feature of provincial politics. The labour movement was empowered when the Tucumán Workers' Federation of the Sugar Industry (known in Spanish as FOTIA) was created in 1944. It has since become a prominent actor in Tucumán politics and national unionism.
[12] In addition to the sugar factory and refinery, the José Minetti y Cia firm owned large tracts of land cultivated with sugar cane. In its territory there were also the *colonias*, groups of houses where workers and their families lived (MJDHN *et al.* 2016).

military use.[13] The military base allowed for regular patrolling, security activities, and control of the population of the surrounding communities and *colonias* in which abuses, such as kidnapping, illegal detention in the clandestine centre, torture, and sexual abuse, occurred (Camuña 2016).[14]

The military was not limited to its official base of operations on company grounds. The company's second contribution to human rights violations occurred when it allegedly authorised the military to access any other company properties and exercise strict public control. The armed forces patrolled internal roads and all company buildings, including the mill's plant and the workers' houses, allowing them to identify and detain workers. Examples of these abuses include the illegal detention of 12 people at a checkpoint set up in front of the military base, and the kidnapping of more than 20 employees from their houses located in the *colonias* and two more from the factory premises.

Third, the company provided the military with vehicles to carry out clandestine repressive acts. Some of these vehicles had previously been used by the company's labour union and were subsequently used by the military to kidnap, detain, and disappear the same union leaders.

The fourth contribution was the company's role in providing information on workers and their relatives to the military. Notably, the company documented those workers involved in union activities. For example, it carried out a census of the population living in the *colonias* or working at the plant, making it available to military personnel. The census included personal and labour information, as well as data on political and union activity *inter alia*, facilitating worker identification and detention.

The company's silence in the face of crimes against humanity is understood as the fifth substantial contribution. There is no record of any formal complaint denouncing the crimes at either the national or provincial truth commissions or at several trials against state actors. In fact, the public prosecutor, as later discussed, highlighted that the accused hid information he requested as evidence against state actors in an earlier trial.

The prosecutors contend that these five contributions reveal how the company engaged in crimes against humanity. The case documents human rights violations of a minimum of 68 people, of whom 44 were workers at the mill itself, 34 lived in the *colonias*, almost all were part of the company's union, eight were union board members, and 51 were detained in the company's clandestine centre (Camuña 2016).

One of the individuals affected by this collaboration between the company and the military was Jacobo Fidel Ortíz. A company worker and a recognised union leader, Ortíz defended victims of state terrorism. He made formal presentations to the authorities in defence of the kidnapped workers who, during their captivity,

---

[13] For example, upon the arrival of the armed forces, the company relocated workers housed in buildings that would be occupied by military personnel, fitted out others, and even built other buildings to ensure military installations.

[14] As we saw in n. 12, sugar mill companies such as La Fronterita owned large land extensions. Plantations, factories and workers' houses were located in these territories.

were fired by the company. Ortíz sought to avoid wrongful dismissals as well as to secure the release of his colleagues from detention.

In April 1976, Ortíz was kidnapped for the first time from his home in the *colonias*. He was transported in a company vehicle to the clandestine detention centre that operated in the mill. He was released, but kidnapped again in June of that year. During his first kidnapping, the company notified the corresponding state agency that Ortíz had supposedly resigned voluntarily, despite being detained at this time.

La Fronterita's collusions reaped significant benefits, the accusers claimed. In general terms, state terrorism substantially decreased labour protests and union mobilisation through violence. That enabled the company to implement a series of internal reforms largely resisted by the union movement, such as the mechanisation of agricultural work. Finally, the company benefited financially – an increase in production of 30.72 per cent and the purchase from the state of another sugar mill, sold below the market price (Camuña 2016).

In 2015, prosecutor Camuña began an investigation against five defendants, including directors, high-ranking officials, and mill owners. The human rights organisation Abogados y Abogadas del Noroeste Argentino en Human Rights y Estudios Sociales (ANDHES) filed a criminal petition, known in Argentina as a *querella*, on behalf of Ortíz's family.[15] Both parties pressed charges and requested that the judge indict the accused in 2018. Before deciding, the intervening judge called the accused to give testimonies between May and July 2018.

The case switched to stop-motion mode from the very moment the prosecutors requested the indictment. Although the procedural codes gave him only 10 days, it was not until May 2019 – nearly a year after – that the judge decided. He ruled that there was insufficient evidence to prosecute the accused and ordered the investigation to be redirected toward crimes committed by the state rather than by economic actors.

The decision was controversial, as the appeals briefs submitted by the public prosecutor and ANDHES indicate. First, it presents a biased perspective on the period of state terror in which state actors allegedly acted alone in perpetrating crimes against humanity – ignoring economic actors. Consistent with this view, the judge declared that the businessmen 'were victims of state terrorism' alongside sugar mill workers and community residents. Second, this view of the defendants as victims lacked evidence. The defendants had not filed a complaint attesting to their victimisation. They had not provided information to the national and local truth commission entities or courts in order to have this status conferred upon them.[16]

Furthermore, with extensive experience in crimes against humanity cases, the judge departed from consolidated national and comparative jurisprudence on the

[15] Under Argentine criminal procedure law, victims, relatives, and civil society organisations have the right to participate in criminal prosecutions and trials. As *querellantes*, they have the right actively to participate in such processes. For example, they can bring new evidence; request the judge to collect new evidence; and make their own accusations, which may be distinct from that of the public prosecutors.
[16] This position is in sharp contrast with the attitude of other businesses that were victims of state terrorism. They denounced human rights violations before state institutions, as revealed by the National Securities Commission report. That report shows 141 cases of businessmen and financiers being kidnapped and disenfranchised by the dictatorship (Perosino *et al.* 2013).

evidentiary value of testimonies in crimes-against-humanity cases. He argued that the hundreds of testimonies used by the public prosecutor to accuse the economic actors were insufficient to build an accusation. In that sense, he devalued the testimonies of victims and relatives offered by the prosecution.

The judge also concluded that the defendants had not obtained economic benefits under state terrorism. This conclusion was based on the his interpretation of an accounting report offered by the defendants. The prosecutors had provided financial evidence demonstrating that the Minetti Group had profited from the dismantling of the company's union.

This decision triggered the appeal spiral. The accusers appealed to an upper tribunal, which, in June 2020 – two years after the request for an indictment – denied the appeals. This tribunal confirmed the 'lack of merit' decision on all grounds, including a recommendation to redirect the investigation from economic actors toward state actors.

The public prosecutors and ANDHES persisted in their appeals, this time before a Cassation Chamber. This tribunal overturned the 'lack of merit' decision in December 2020. It requested the lower tribunal, not the first judge, to issue a new ruling. That tribunal required new judges, as signing a 'lack of merit' decisions disqualifies judges from making a new decision under the procedural code. As of April 2021, the appointment of new judges has not been initiated.

Notably, the Cassation Chamber (2020) asserted that the first judge and the Appeal Tribunal's decisions constituted a deviation from standard evidentiary interpretation and regular judicial practices in general and with relation to crimes-against-humanity cases in particular.[17] It highlighted that they did not address all the issues raised by the accusers and, thus, left several unscrutinised aspects to their accusation. Moreover, the Chamber highlighted that those decisions were based on wrongful criteria for assessing the evidence submitted by the prosecutors. All evidence should be assessed as an integral part of a whole accusation, rather than as fragmented pieces. In this regard, the Chamber stressed that the evidence should be evaluated according to the context in which the facts of the case took place. Additionally, the ruling stressed that such decisions undermine the values of testimonies, a crucial type of evidence in crimes-against-humanity cases. It also questioned those decisions, as they denied the value of indirect evidence in such cases.

Furthermore, the Chamber noted the possible paralysis of the type of decisions issued by the lower judge and the Appeal Tribunal. It remarked that those decisions should have included specific guidelines and investigative hypotheses to investigate the accused's potential responsibility rather than diverting the investigation toward other potential perpetrators. The Chamber concluded that a 'lack of merit' decision based on a wrongful assessment of the evidence and lack of specific guidelines might constitute an implicit 'dismissal' of the charge requests, leaving the case in limbo (Cassation Federal Chamber 2020).[18]

---

[17] Cassation Federal Chamber, 'Recurso Queja No 6 – *Imputado: Figueroa Minetti, Jorge and others v. Averiguacion de delito querrellante: Ortiz, Hortencia* (2020).

[18] *Ibid.*

As a result of the complex litigation process, the case of La Fronterita is going through a stop-motion transit to accountability. Three years have passed since the public prosecutor and the *querella* requested the accused's indictment. The case has remained at Level 1 for five years, and a final decision on the indictment remains unsettled. New appeals are anticipated, whatever the tribunal decides.

The case of La Fronterita illustrates the affect of the stop-motion process on prosecutions of hardline business collaborators. Specifically, when a case presents controversial evidence that demands similarly controversial legal assessment and judicial practice, the judicial action fails to move forward. The case becomes stuck, and sometimes shelved indefinitely, to avoid pressure or criticism from both pro-accountability and pro-impunity forces. Hardline collaborators resort to their social, economic, and political powers both to secure effective legal tactics and to exert public and covert influence over key judicial actors. As a result, judicial processes remain pending, and hence a kind of *de facto* impunity prevails when no judgment is reached.

Conclusion

This chapter addressed four central themes regarding the phenomenon of collaborations. First, the Argentine period of state terror illustrates the profound role that business collaborators played in the violence. It presents a scenario in which the transitional justice focus on the state violence ignores the key social, economic, and cultural dimensions of state terrorism, and particularly the responsibility of business collaborators in designing and sustaining crimes against humanity.

Second, the chapter suggests that while many businesses benefited from the dictatorship, not all are equally responsible. Softline collaborators did not directly support criminal activities, while hardline collaborators did, directly facilitating or participating in criminality. Making this distinction among collaborators clear is significant. Holding hardline collaborators accountable advances transitional justice goals of, and victims' rights to, truth, justice, reparations, and guarantees of non-recurrence.

Third, the chapter explores how transitional justice prosecutions have addressed hardline business collaboration in state terror in Argentina. It shows that those prosecutions have faced substantial obstacles in producing positive accountability outcomes. The chapter underscores a judicial strategy to shelve cases indefinitely to avoid pressure or criticism. Such a strategy is grounded on the controversial legal assessment of evidence and judicial practices. While judicial processes remain open, economic actors secure impunity, as several cases move in a stop-motion mode toward accountability.

Fourth, stop-motion patterns are linked to the nature of the defendants in these cases. Hardline business collaborators possess significant social, political, and economic leverage. Prosecuting them, therefore, entails significant reputational risks. Sometimes, when legal strategies are not enough to influence judicial outcomes, they are able to launch public campaigns against judges and prosecutors who are pursuing accountability.

Where these cases have advanced in Argentine and elsewhere depends on several factors to overcome what we have referred to as the veto power of businesses (Payne *et al.* 2020). This depends on civil society mobilisation to initiate cases and attract social support by demonstrating victimisation by hardline business collaborators, thereby exerting public pressure on judges and prosecutors.

Civil society mobilisation requires legal innovators willing and able to translate demands into judicial action. They are critical to the overcoming of judicial inertia in bringing powerful business figures to trial. Such legal innovation is also critical to ensuring corporate collaborators' accountability, as there is a current lack of consensus around binding and enforceable international human rights obligations on business. Without legal innovators, it is unlikely that civil society demands will advance along the accountability continuum.

International pressure from human rights bodies is also crucial to reducing the level of impunity enjoyed by businesses guilty of hardline collaboration in crimes against humanity. These agencies can play an essential role in exerting pressure on governments to implement transitional justice mechanisms and clarify states' specific obligations to protect the rights to justice, truth, and reparation. The lack of a specific treaty on business and human rights is not an obstacle for those bodies to monitor transitional justice development and establish clear legal obligations on states. The Inter-American Commission of Human Rights and the United Nations Working Group on the Issue of Human Rights and Transnational Corporations and Other Businesses Enterprises have made their very first steps. Although, that is just the beginning.

References

Balardini, L. (2016), 'Argentina: Regional protagonist of transitional justice', in E. Skaar, J. Garcia-Godos, and C. Collins (eds), *Transitional Justice in Latin America* (London, Routledge), 76–102.

Basualdo, E. M. (2015), 'The legacy of the dictatorship: The new pattern of capital accumulation, deindustrialization, and the decline of the working class', in H. Verbitsky and J. P. Bohoslavsky (eds), *The Economic Accomplices to the Argentine Dictatorship: Outstanding Debts* (Cambridge, Cambridge University Press), 75–89.

Basualdo, V. (ed.) (2021), 'Business and the military in the Argentine dictatorship (1976–1983): Institutional, economic, and repressive relations', in V. Basualdo, H. Berghoff, and M. Bucheli (eds), *Big Business and Dictatorships in Latin America: A Transnational History of Profits and Repression* (New York, Springer), 35–62.

Basualdo, V., Berghoff, H., and Bucheli, M. (eds) (2021), *Big Business and Dictatorships in Latin America: A Transnational History of Profits and Repression* (New York, Springer).

Boerr, M. (2019), 'La pelea por el mercado de la yerba mate: Las Marías lidera, pero Liebig no para de crecer y Rosamonte relegó a Molinos', *Economics*, 19 March 2019, https://economis.com.ar/la-pelea-por-el-mercado-de-la-yerba-mate-las-marias-lidera-pero-liebig-no-para-de-crecer-y-rosamonte-relego-a-molinos/ (accessed 11 February 2022).

Bohoslavsky, J. P. (2015), 'Complicity of the lenders', in H. Verbitsky and J. P. Bohoslavsky (eds.), *Outstanding Debts to Settle: The Economic Accomplices of the Dictatorship in Argentina* (Cambridge, Cambridge University Press), 105–16.

Camuña, P. (2016), 'Requerimiento de instrucción presentado por el Ministerio Público Fiscal', submission in *Ingenio La Fronterita s/averiguación de delito*, 7282/2016

Clarín (2014), 'Preocupación periodística por el allanamiento a La Nueva Provincia.' *Clarín*, 24 April, https://www.clarin.com/politica/Preocupacion-periodistica-allanamie nto-Nueva-Provincia_0_H1T4KT65vml.html (accessed 11 February 2022).

CONADEP [Comisión Nacional sobre la Desaparición de Personas] (1984), *Nunca más: Informe de la Comisión Nacional sobre la Desparición de Personas* (Buenos Aires, EUDEBA).

Doz Costa, J., Pereira, G., and Ovejero, C. (2016), 'Terrorismo de estado y complicidad empresarial: Aportes a la justicia transicional, entre el escenario internacional y el noroeste Argentino', paper presented at the IX Seminario Internacional Políticas de la Memoria, Centro Cultural de la Memoria Haroldo Conti, 20–1 August.

Engstrom, P. and Pereira, G. (2012), 'From amnesty to accountability: The ebbs and flows in the search for justice in Argentina', in F. Lessa and L. A. Payne (eds), *Amnesty in the Age of Human Rights Accountability: Comparative and International Perspectives* (Cambridge, Cambridge University Press), 97–122.

Felstiner, W. L. F., Abel, R. L., and Sarat, A. (1980), 'The emergence and transformation of disputes: Naming, blaming, claiming', *Law and Society Review*, 15:3/4, 631–54.

Fundación Konex ([n.d.]), 'Adolfo F. Navajas Artaza', website of Fundación Konex, https://www.fundacionkonex.org/b173-adolfo-f-navajas-artaza (accessed 18 June 2020).

Jasinski, A. (2020), 'STOP-MOTION: Resistencia del poder judicial a juzgar a empresarios por delitos de lesa humanidad', *El cohete a la luna*, 11 October 2020, https://www.elco hetealaluna.com/stop-motion/ (accessed 11 February 2022).

Jemio, A. S. (2016), 'Postales de la escena judicial: La megacausa Operativo Independencia', *Bordes*, August–October, 203–9.

Lessa, F. (2019), 'Operation Condor on trial: Justice for transnational human rights crimes in South America', *Journal of Latin American Studies*, 51, 409–39.

Litoral (2014), 'Adepa rechaza allanamiento al diario La Nueva Provincia', *El Litoral*, 11 April 2014, https://www.ellitoral.com/index.php/diarios/2014/04/11/politica/POLI-02.html (accessed 11 February 2022).

Loreti, D. (2015), 'The media: Uniform discourse and business deals under cover of state terrorism', in H. Verbitsky and J. P. Bohoslavsky (eds), *The Economic Accomplices to the Argentine Dictatorship Outstanding Debts* (Cambridge, Cambridge University Press), 307–22.

MJDHN [Ministerio de Justicia y Derechos Humanos de la Nación], FLACSO-Argentina, Centro de Estudios Legales y Sociales, and Sistema Argentino de Información Jurídica (2016), *Responsabilidad empresarial en delitos de lesa humanidad: Represión a trabajadores durante el terrorismo de estado*, 2 vols (Buenos Aires, MJDHN).

Nación (2014), 'Preocupación de ADEPA por el allanamiento a La Nueva Provincia', *La Nación*, 11 April 2014, https://www.lanacion.com.ar/politica/preocupacion-de-adepa-por-el-allanamiento-a-la-nueva-provincia-nid1679810 (accessed 11 February 2022).

Nassif, S. (2015), 'Protagonistas olvidados: Las luchas obreras en Tucumán en los años' 60 y principios de 'os '70', *Estudios*, 34, 159–76.

Nassif, S. (2016), *Tucumán en llamas: El cierre de los ingenios y la lucha obrera contra la dictadura (1966–1973)* (Tucumán, Universidad Nacional de Tucumán).

Nassif, S. (2018), 'Terrorismo de estado en la Argentina: Tucumán y la ofensiva contra los obreros de la agro-industria azucarera', *Revista interdisciplinaria de estudios agrarios*, 48, 57–91.

O'Donnell, G. (1999), 'Polyarchies and the (un)rule of law in Latin America: A partial conclusion', in J. E. Mendez, G. O'Donnell, and P. S. Pinheiro (eds), *The (Un)Rule of Law
and the Underprivileged in Latin America* (Notre Dame, University of Notre Dame
Press), 303–37.
Página|12 (2015), 'Busca La Impunidad de Massot', *Página|12*, 10 March 2015,
https://www.pagina12.com.ar/diario/ultimas/20-267802-2015-03-10.html (accessed
11 February 2022).
Patagónico (2014), 'Buscan llevar a juicio por delitos de esa humanidad a Navajas Artaza',
El Patagónico, 10 September 2014, https://www.elpatagonico.com/buscan-llevar-jui
cio-delitos-esa-humanidad-navajas-artaza-n667671 (accessed 11 February 2022).
Payne, L. A., Lessa, F., and Pereira, G. (2015), 'Overcoming barriers to justice in the age of
human rights accountability', *Human Rights Quarterly*, 27, 728–54.
Payne, L. A., Pereira, G., and Bernal-Bermúdez, L. (2020), *Transitional Justice and
Corporate Accountability from Below: Deploying Archimedes' Lever* (Cambridge,
Cambridge University Press).
PCCH [Procuraduría de Crímenes contra la Humanidad] (2018), 'Informe estadístico sobre
el estado de las causas por delitos de lesa humanidad en Argentina diagnóstico 2018',
https://www.fiscales.gob.ar/wp-content/uploads/2018/12/LESA_informe-estadistico-
annual-2018.pdf (access 11 February 2022).
Perosino, M. C., Napoli, B., and Bossisio, W. (2013), *Economía, política y sistema
financiero: La última dictadura cívico-militar en la CNV* (Buenos Aires, Comisión
Nacional de Valores).
PGN [Procuración General de la Nación] (2007), 'Algunos problemas vinculados al trámite
de las causas por violaciones a los DDHH cometidas durante el terrorismo de estado'.
REDESCA [Relatoría Especial sobre Derechos Económicos Sociales, Culturales y
Ambientales] (2019), 'Empresas y derechos humanos: Estándares interamericanos
arte de la portada', http://www.oas.org/es/cidh/informes/pdfs/EmpresasDDHH.pdf
(accessed 11 February 2022).
Retaguardia (2014), 'Suspendieron el juicio por los crímenes de lesa humanidad en
la yerbatera Las Marías', *La Retaguardia*, 5 November 2014, http://www.lareta
guardia.com.ar/2014/11/suspendieron-el-juicio-por-los-crimenes.html (accessed 11
February 2022).
Retaguardia (2018), 'Más de 40 años y 20 jueces después hay juicio por lesa en el
establecimiento Las Marías', *La Retaguardia*, 5 July 2018, http://www.laretaguardia.
com.ar/2018/07/las-marias.html (accessed 11 February 2022).
Sikkink, K. (2008), 'From pariah state to global protagonist: Argentina and the struggle for
international human rights', *Latin American Politics and Society*, 50, 1–29.
Sur Correntino ([n.d.]), 'Reactivarían causa por desaparición de trabajadores contra Navajas
Artaza', *Sur Correntino*, http://www.surcorrentino.com.ar/vernota.asp?id_noticia=
14799 (accessed 18 June 2020).
UNOHC [United Nations Office High Commissioner] (2020), 'Business, human rights and
conflict-affected regions: Towards heightened action', https://www.ohchr.org/EN/Iss
ues/Business/Pages/ConflictPostConflict.aspx (accessed 11 February 2022).
Verbitsky, H. and Bohoslavsky, J. P. (2015), 'Introduction. State terrorism and the
economy: From Nuremberg to Buenos Aires', in H. Verbitsky and J. P. Bohoslavsky
(eds), *The Economic Accomplices to the Argentine Dictatorship: Outstanding Debts*
(Cambridge, Cambridge University Press), 1–16.

12

International Law and Collaboration: A Tentative Embrace

SHANE DARCY

THE PHENOMENON OF collaboration, including in situations of armed conflict, is rarely studied through the prism of international law, in large part because international law itself seems to have overlooked the practice.[1] This is despite its enduring prevalence during wartime and the widespread reliance on informers by police forces and by national security and intelligence agencies. There is no explicit reference to informers or other collaborators in the Hague and Geneva treaties of international humanitarian law, notwithstanding their obsessive categorisation of the participants in armed conflict. A similar silence is found in the various international human rights conventions, which have an even broader application. Nevertheless, as this chapter discusses, international law consciously tolerates collaboration and permits the recruitment and use of informers and other collaborators by public authorities, and in some instances encourages or even obliges it. At the same time, international humanitarian law and human rights law are attuned to the risks associated with collaboration and seek to place restrictions, often indirectly, on the conduct of recruiters, collaborators, and those that may seek to punish such betrayal.

The tentative embrace of collaboration by international law is characterised by its long-standing general permissiveness toward the practice, coupled with a steadily increasing application of key standards of international humanitarian law and human rights to some of collaboration's most harmful aspects. The first section of this chapter reviews international law applicable to collaboration in situations of armed conflict, but also beyond such contexts. The emerging expectation of

---

[1] Recent exceptions include (Galvis Martínez 2020; Darcy 2019; Cheah 2018).

Proceedings of the British Academy, **248**, 244–267, © The British Academy 2022.

regulation that emanates from international human rights law holds the potential for a more forceful engagement by international law with collaboration. The second section then turns to explore the embedding of international law standards, such as they are, in national legislation and military doctrine. It considers the application of international human rights law and domestic United Kingdom legislation to a par- ticularly prominent class of collaborator – the informer – in the context of armed conflict. This part analyses the operation of the Regulation of Investigatory Powers Act (RIPA) 2000 and the extent of its application to British armed forces during wartime. This analysis is conducted against the backdrop of an increasingly strident domestic opposition to the application of human rights law during armed conflict, particularly overseas, based on the alleged 'judicial encroachment' of domestic courts, human rights bodies, and international criminal tribunals (Tugendhat and Croft 2013: 28).

Turning a Blind Eye? International Law and Collaboration

In the 1950s, Hersh Lauterpacht wrote that '[a]lthough a belligerent acts lawfully in employing spies and traitors, the other belligerent, who punishes them, like- wise acts lawfully' (Oppenheim 1952: 422). His summary of international law's stance toward collaborators during times of war would have been equally accurate if made prior to the adoption of the 1949 Geneva Conventions. It also continues to capture, in a general sense, the present position of international law regarding the phenomenon. While parties to an armed conflict not only regularly recruit and use collaborators of various types – whether as informers, defecting fighters, or local functionaries – they also understand that the practice is largely permissible under international humanitarian law. In the context of intelligence gathering, for instance, the United Kingdom's *Joint Service Manual* states that '[i]nformation can lawfully be gleaned in many different ways, for example, by the employment of informers or agents in enemy-held territory' (UKMOD 2004: 63). Requiring fighters to take part in hostilities against their own side during a non-international armed conflict is also viewed as lawful: the United States *Law of War Manual* puts it that 'captured insurgents who are nationals of that State could be required to serve in that State's armed forces or to take part in operations directed against their former comrades'. [2] The laws of occupation can be read as requiring local administrators, officials, and judges to remain in their positions and serve under an

---

[2] United States Department of Defense (2015: 1039–40). See, however, the concept of 'abusive forced labour' as addressed in *Prosecutor v. Blaškić*, case no. IT-95-14-A, Appeals Chamber, Judgment, 29 July 2004, para. 597.

occupying power, while also attempting to act in the interests of the local population (Redse Johansen 2013: 206–7).

Although the various treaties of international humanitarian law neither outlaw
collaboration nor identify collaborators as a group of participants in armed conflict
to which specific rules apply, there is an implicit recognition of the existence of
the practice, of the likely treasonous nature of certain acts of collaboration under
domestic law, and of the harsh reality faced by those that serve the enemy in any
of the various ways that might be considered collaboration.[3] International humanitarian law seeks to prohibit parties to an armed conflict from forcing individuals to
provide assistance to an opposing side against their will, but accepts the punishment
of alleged collaborators, albeit not in the cruel or inhumane ways that frequently
accompany the practice – what the Special Court for Sierra Leone has described as
'the gruesome repercussions for collaborating'.[4] As with its approach to armed conflict itself, international humanitarian law seeks to mitigate the harm associated with
collaboration by outlawing particular acts, rather than prohibiting the practice itself.[5]

International human rights law, which applies both during and outside situations of armed conflict, takes a largely similar approach. Human rights treaties
do not refer directly to the practice of using informers or other collaborators, but
their general protections, especially those addressed to the right to life, freedom
from torture, and the right to privacy are of relevance where state authorities are
engaged in the deployment of collaborators, most commonly in the context of
the use of informers. The application of human rights law to covert policing or
intelligence gathering has been acknowledged by human rights courts and treaty
bodies. The European Court of Human Rights, for example, observed that police
'are increasingly required to make use of undercover agents, informers and covert
practices, particularly in tackling organised crime and corruption'.[6] The United
Nations Convention against Transnational Organized Crime not only recognises
the resort to the practice of using informers, but encourages states' parties to use
those 'who participate or who have participated in organized criminal groups' as
a source of information.[7] The application of human rights law to the practice of
using informers or other collaborators remains nascent. However, it is evident, as
will be discussed further later in the chapter, that this body of law goes further than
international humanitarian law in one respect: by creating an obligation on states'
parties to relevant treaties to ensure the proper regulation of the use of informers,
given the obvious risks to human rights that arise.

---

[3] On the meaning and practice of collaboration see the introductory chapter by Espindola and Payne;
Kalyvas 2008; Deák 2015; Dethlefsen 1990; Brook 2005; Cohen 2008; Rings 1982.
[4] *Prosecutor v. Sesay, Kallon and Gbao*, case no. SCSL-04-15-T, Trial Chamber I, Judgment, 2 March
2009, para. 1125.
[5] See Moyn (2018); Jochnick and Normand (1994).
[6] *Ramanauskas v. Lithuania*, app. no. 74420/01 (ECtHR, 5 February 2008), para. 49.
[7] Article 26(1), United Nations Convention against Transnational Organized Crime (2000), 2225
UNTS 209.

International Humanitarian Law

The self-interest of states in seeking to use an opponent's personnel or people against it has led to the arguably hypocritical approach of international law in shielding the pursuit of betrayal of an opposing belligerent by its soldiers or citizens, while at the same time accepting that states will subject such treasonous behaviour to stern sanctions under domestic law.[8] States actively seek cooperation from an enemy's nationals or from those loyal to an opposing side in internal conflicts, but condemn collaboration with an opposing side in the strongest of terms when it is to their detriment. International humanitarian law remains indifferent to the choice by individuals or the domestic lawfulness of providing assistance to an opposing party to an armed conflict, and instead demands humane treatment of all those who are not taking an active part in hostilities, irrespective of which side they fought for or supported. In this respect, and in one of the clearest acknowledgements of both the practice of recruiting informers in times of armed conflict and the temptation of recruiters to resort to forceful techniques, the Fourth Geneva Convention states plainly that '[n]o physical or moral coercion shall be exercised against protected persons, in particular to obtain information from them or from third parties'.[9] The Third Geneva Convention forbids parties from forcibly extracting information from prisoners of war or compelling them to fight in the enemy's armed forces.[10]

The prohibition of coercion in the context of international armed conflicts, and the similar though not identical rules applicable in non-international armed conflicts, constitute a core contribution of humanitarian law to the legal framework applicable to collaboration during wartime.[11] Parties to an armed conflict are not denied the opportunity to deploy informers or other collaborators, but are restricted by and large to making use of only voluntary collaborators. While it remains difficult to draw clear lines between compelled and consensual collaboration during armed conflict, humanitarian law has at the very least moved away from the previous toleration of coerced collaboration.[12] The Fourth Geneva Convention's prohibition on coercion against civilians applies to both physical and moral forms, 'whether the pressure is direct or indirect, obvious or hidden' (Pictet 1958: 219–20), whereas the predecessor rule in the 1907 Hague Regulations was narrower, decreeing to belligerents that it is 'forbidden to force the inhabitants of territory occupied by it to furnish information about the army of the other belligerent, or about its means of defense'.[13] A number of states lodged formal reservations to this article, evidence of the strongly held view that coercion of enemy civilians for

---

[8] As has been the case with espionage generally; see Chesterman (2011: 27).
[9] Article 31, Fourth Geneva Convention.
[10] Articles 17, 50, 130, Third Geneva Convention.
[11] See for example Common Article 3, 1949 Geneva Conventions; Article 4, Additional Protocol II.
[12] See Chapter 5 by Drumbl and Holá for a discussion of this issue outside the context of armed conflict.
[13] Article 44, 1907 Hague Regulations.

purposes of intelligence gathering should be permissible (Darcy 2019: 52–70). The
Lieber Code had considered it permissible to force citizens to act as guides – that
an army could 'impress them if they cannot obtain them otherwise'.[14] While severe
punishments were contemplated for so-called 'war traitors' under the Lieber Code,
it sought to exclude sanctions for those that may have collaborated under duress.[15]

The drafters of these early laws of war had to reconcile the evident tension
between military demands for local intelligence and other forms of assistance, and
humanitarian considerations towards the civilian population. Permitting belligerents
to demand information from civilians would create a 'fatal position' for the inhab-
itant of an occupied territory: 'on the one hand, if he betrays his country he will be
guillotined, hung or imprisoned for life; on the other hand, if he refuses he will be
shot'.[16] After lengthy and at times fractious debate, the states participating in the
Second Hague Peace Conference voted against embedding such an 'incubus' in
international law.[17] The new rules in the 1907 Hague Regulations, it was stressed,
did not outlaw willing cooperation; they did not apply 'to services offered voluntarily and without compulsion'.[18] There was, in the words of one delegate, 'no
doubt on this point. To accept and to demand are two entirely different things.'[19]

Voluntary collaboration from the civilian population might be obtained in
various ways according to the delegates at the Peace Conference. The Dutch representative, den Beer Poortugael, had advocated for a humanitarian approach,
pressing the delegates to do 'what is moral and right', without having to relinquish
their power to recruit voluntary collaborators.[20] During an intervention infused
with antisemitism, he told fellow delegates that international law should not submit
entirely to the demands of warring parties, given that collaboration could be secured
by the promise of financial reward:

> If in the occupying army, the information and spy service is well regulated, it will
> find many cosmopolitans, individuals without heart and without country, Judases who
> would betray even the Messiah for a sequin. If this service is not well regulated,
> whose is the fault? Should the inhabitants who must remain apart from the struggle
> be forced to supply the lack of instruction and foresight of the invader? If a State has
> not sufficient means to make war let it keep the peace or make peace. It is not for us to
> make war easy. The best means the belligerent has to obtain his end in the minimum
> of time is to prevent the inhabitants of an occupied territory from going to join the

[14] Article 93, Instructions for the Government of Armies of the United States in the Field, prepared by
Francis Lieber, promulgated as General Orders no. 100 by President Lincoln, 24 April 1863.
[15] *Ibid.*, Articles 94–6.
[16] Third meeting of the Second Commission: First Subcommission, 24 July 1907 (Brown Scott
1921: 120).
[17] *Ibid.*
[18] Fourth meeting of the Second Commission: First Subcommission, 31 July 1907 (Brown Scott
1921: 133).
[19] *Ibid.*
[20] Third meeting of the Second Commission: First Subcommission, 24 July 1907 (Brown Scott
1921: 120).

armed forces of the adversary. To that end there is no more efficacious means than to pay in cash for everything that one takes and never to force the inhabitants to commit villainies.[21]

Through the introduction of rules against compelling the inhabitants in occupied territories to divulge information, take part in military operations, or pledge allegiance to the hostile power, and by requiring the humane treatment of prisoners of war, including their exclusion from work connected with military operations, the Hague Regulations introduced significant restrictions of relevance to collaboration but did not completely exclude the potential for belligerents to recruit and deploy collaborators.[22]

The 1949 Geneva Conventions, as supplemented by the 1977 Additional Protocols, did not significantly alter humanitarian law's overarching approach to collaboration during armed conflict, although these treaties clarified and expanded the scope of the prohibition of coercion against prisoners of war and civilians, further enshrined the obligation of humane treatment, and introduced universal jurisdiction for the crime of forcing protected persons to serve in hostile forces.[23] Regarding voluntary cooperation, some additional rules were introduced. For instance, the Fourth Geneva Convention prohibits 'pressure or propaganda which is aimed at securing voluntary enlistment' of civilians.[24] It is argued that the rules in the Third Geneva Convention regarding denunciation of rights effectively outlaw voluntary defection by prisoners of war to the armed forces of the opposing side (D'Argent 2015: 148–9; Sassòli 1985: 10, 24–5; ICRC 2016: para. 995).

Notwithstanding these legal developments, the treaties also conceive of situations where individuals may have to engage in certain activities that might be viewed as tantamount to collaboration. In situations of occupation, where an occupying power is obliged to 'take all the measures in his power to restore, and ensure, as far as possible, public order and safety',[25] public bodies may have to continue to function under the authority of an occupying power. The Fourth Geneva Convention, for example, specifies that the occupier 'shall, with the cooperation of the national and local authorities, facilitate the proper working of all institutions devoted to the care and education of children'.[26] Public officials and judges are offered some protection where they decline to serve under the occupying power: 'The Occupying Power may not alter the status of public officials or judges in the occupied territories or in any way apply sanctions to or take any measures of coercion or discrimination against them, should they abstain from fulfilling their functions for reasons of conscience.'[27] However, given that protected persons can be compelled to carry

---

[21] Second meeting of the Second Commission, 14 August 1907 (Brown Scott 1921): 10.
[22] See Articles 6, 23(h), 44–45, 52, Hague Regulations 1907.
[23] Article 130, Third Geneva Convention; Article 147, Fourth Geneva Convention. See also Articles 8(2)(a)(v) and 8(2)(b)(xv), Rome Statute of the International Criminal Court.
[24] Article 51, Fourth Geneva Convention.
[25] Article 43, 1907 Hague Regulations.
[26] Article 50, Fourth Geneva Convention.
[27] Article 54(1), Fourth Geneva Convention.

out work that is 'necessary either for the needs of the occupying army, or for the public utility services or for the feeding, clothing, sheltering, transportation or health of the population of the occupied territory', an occupying power could seem-ingly refuse to allow public officials or judges to abstain from fulfilling their roles.[28] As stated at the 1949 Diplomatic Conference, 'it might be necessary for certain of these officials or judges to be compulsorily employed'.[29] Judges may be 'the natural guardians and protectors' of the population under occupation (Pictet 1958: 306), but no doubt face risks in trying to navigate a successful course between perceived collaboration and benign cooperation. Regarding regular policing, the *Commentary* to the Fourth Geneva Convention also states that 'the occupation authorities, being responsible for maintaining law and order, are within their rights in claiming the co-operation of the police'.[30] The rule outlawing coercion is therefore neither abso-lute nor clear-cut.

International humanitarian law as developed by states demonstrates some awareness of the prevalence of collaboration during armed conflict, and has sought to exclude, albeit not entirely, resort to compulsion in the recruitment of informers and other collaborators. The principle of humane treatment has underpinned this approach, and is particularly relevant to the punishment of those considered to have collaborated with an opposing side, while there are limited circumstances where activities performed by informers and other collaborators may amount to direct participation in hostilities, such as intelligence gathering or identifying individuals during military operations, thus rendering such individuals as legitimate targets under the law of armed conflict (ICRC 2009: 48), the consequences for collabor-ation are most often felt outside the context of hostilities, and often after the end of a conflict.

States have nevertheless sought to limit the protections afforded to those that have assisted an opposing side in an international armed conflict, as is evident in the general exclusion of a state's own nationals from the categories of prisoners of war and protected persons under the Third and Fourth Geneva Conventions. That being said, the elevation of the fundamental guarantees of Common Article 3 to customary international law and the expansion of the protective rules of the Additional Protocols mean that:

> Persons detained for reasons related to an armed conflict without being entitled to a status specifically protected under the Geneva Conventions, such as the detaining power's own nationals who may have collaborated with the enemy, likewise benefit from the fundamental guarantees of IHL [international humanitarian law] with regard to humane treatment and fair trial until their final release, repatriation or return. (Melzer 2016: 207)

---

[28] Article 51(2), Fourth Geneva Convention.
[29] Report of Committee III to the Plenary Assembly, *Final Record of the Diplomatic Conference of Geneva of 1949*, Vol. II, Section A, 829.
[30] *Ibid.*, 307. See Chapter 4 by Luis de la Calle in this volume, discussing the portrayal of the Basque police as collaborators with Spain.

States retain the right to punish collaboration under national law, but must do so in accordance with fundamental guarantees. For non-state armed groups, the questions regarding punishment of collaboration and complying with applicable fair trial standards are acutely challenging (Darcy 2019: 162–70; Somer 2007; Sivakumaran 2009; Klamberg 2018; Murray 2016: 224–6).

The punishment of wartime collaborators has frequently failed to accord with the rules and principles of international humanitarian law, as parties purposefully and often publicly resort to cruel displays of retributive violence that is also aimed at deterring others from cooperating with the opposing side. As regards the potential criminality of these acts under international law, the concept of war crimes has traditionally been concerned with offences perpetrated against enemy personnel or civilians, thus having excluded the killing or ill treatment of alleged collaborators from its purview. However, with the significant development of the law of war crimes in non-international armed conflicts, and recent jurisprudence from the International Criminal Court seeking to expand the scope of the law of war crimes to include offences perpetrated against members of an armed group by members on the same side, it would seem that crimes against those alleged to have assisted the other side now fall more squarely within the purview of international humanitarian law.[31]

International humanitarian law is not oblivious to the practice of collaboration during armed conflict, and its often severe consequences, although it has addressed the phenomenon partially, and most often indirectly. It aims to exclude reliance on coerced collaboration, although not completely, and to enjoin that alleged collaborators are treated humanely, even though their punishment is permissible, at least by states. Its approach is limited by the reliance on general prohibitions of abusive conduct, compounded by relatively limited means of enforcement, such as criminal prosecution for transgressors. This seems inadequate given the widespread prevalence of collaboration, which is at times covert in nature, but is often accompanied by violations of international humanitarian law. The attendant harms, whether associated with recruitment, the actions of collaborators, or their punishment, are often inherent in the practice and may form part of a deliberate strategy, rather than being mere isolated examples. Permitting the practice in principle may contribute to the associated abuse in practice. Notwithstanding the applicable restrictions, international humanitarian law does not challenge the legitimacy or indeed the wisdom of resort to the practice. Its engagement with the phenomenon is less than wholehearted. The next section turns to consider the contribution of international human rights law to collaboration, including in the context of armed conflict.

---

[31] See *Prosecutor v. Ntaganda*, Appeals Chamber, Judgment on the appeal of Mr Ntaganda against the Second Decision on the Defence's challenge to the jurisdiction of the Court in respect of Counts 6 and 9, case no. ICC-01/04-02/06 OA5, 15 June 2017; *Prosecutor v. Ntaganda*, Trial Chamber VI, Judgment, case no. ICC-01/04-02/06, 8 July 2019, para. 965.

International Human Rights Law

International human rights law is increasingly recognised by national armed forces as being applicable in situations of armed conflict, alongside international humanitarian law.[32] The International Court of Justice has been of this view at least since the 1996 *Nuclear Weapons* Advisory Opinion, and has confirmed and somewhat refined its understanding on the relationship between human rights law and humanitarian law in a number of decisions.[33] Regional human rights courts and United Nations human rights bodies have also applied human rights law to situations of armed conflict, including outside the territory of states' parties to relevant treaties.[34] As to the interaction between international human rights law and international humanitarian law, the two bodies of law are 'complementary, not mutually exclusive', in the words of the United Nations Human Rights Committee.[35] While the co-application of human rights and international humanitarian law is not without challenges, the increased acceptance of human rights law in times of armed conflict offers an avenue for addressing particular harms that may have evaded the attention of international humanitarian law to date or been neglected by its limited means of enforcement.[36]

Despite clear differences in origins, functioning, and outlook, international human rights law and international humanitarian law share a broadly similar approach to collaboration during armed conflict. None of their treaties explicitly addresses the practice of using informers or other collaborators either during, or indeed outside, situations of armed conflict, yet a number of their general rules and standards can be brought to bear on the practice and its consequences. In contrast to international humanitarian law, however, international human rights law has generated a nascent body of judicial and quasi-judicial decisions that have examined human rights concerns related to various aspects of the use of informers in domestic contexts. Moreover, while human rights law generally accepts the permissibility of the use of informers, and arguably other collaborators, it is evident that relevant human rights standards give rise to an obligation upon states to ensure

---

[32] See for example Norwegian Ministry of Defence (2018), 25–7; New Zealand Defence Force (2019), 2–4; UKMOD (2004), 282.

[33] International Court of Justice (ICJ), 'Legality of the threat or use of nuclear weapons', Advisory Opinion, 8 July 1996, general list no. 95, para. 25. See also ICJ, 'Legality of the construction of a wall in the occupied Palestinian territories', Advisory Opinion, 9 July 2004, General List no. 131; *Case Concerning Armed Activities on the Territory of the Congo (Democratic Republic of the Congo v Uganda)*, Judgment, 19 December 2005, general list no. 116, paras 178–80.

[34] See for example European Court of Human Rights (ECtHR), *Al-Skeini and others v. United Kingdom*, application no. 55721/07, Grand Chamber Judgment, 7 July 2011; Inter-American Court of Human Rights, *Case of the Massacres of El Mozote and Nearby Places v El Salvador*, Judgment, 25 October 2012.

[35] General Comment no. 36, para. 64.

[36] See for example ECtHR, *Georgia v. Russia (II)*, application no. 38263/08, Grand Chamber Judgment, 21 January 2021.

adequate legal regulation of such practices. The operation of 'unregulated systems' of informers not only gives rise to clear dangers (Cohen and Dudai 2005: 229), but may also run afoul of emerging understanding of international human rights law.

International human rights law has had more to say about the use of informers than other forms of collaboration, on account of its being a common tactic of national authorities in the context of policing, criminal justice, and national security, and one that 'often leads to human rights violations of and by informers' (Cohen and Dudai 2005: 229). The key rights at issue in this context include freedom from torture and cruel or inhuman punishment or treatment, fair trial rights, the right to life, and the right to privacy. Each will be discussed briefly in turn.

The Convention against Torture and Other Cruel, Inhuman or Degrading Treatment or Punishment prohibits torture absolutely and recognises that such ill-treatment is used for purposes of obtaining information.[37] As regards less severe forms of coercion, which would clearly be relevant in the context of recruiting informers, these are not explicitly addressed in the key human rights treaties, compared with the reference to 'physical and moral coercion' in the Fourth Geneva Conventions, although at least one convention obliges states to have respect for 'physical, mental, and moral integrity'.[38] There is, however, some recognition that detained persons in particular are in an especially vulnerable situation; United Nations principles concerning prisoners and detainees prohibit the taking of 'undue advantage of the situation of a detained or imprisoned person for the purpose of compelling him to confess, to incriminate himself otherwise or to testify against any other person'.[39] While detained persons may volunteer to cooperate as informers, threats or so-called 'legal blackmail' often play a role in recruitment, and in circumstances involving limited, if any, oversight (Sanders *et al.* 2010: 329; Jones-Brown and Shane 2011: 9; Dunningham and Morris 1996: 7; Shamas 2018).

The use of information provided by both willing and reluctant informers in the context of criminal investigations or prosecutions can give rise to fair trial concerns (Bloom 2002; Natapoff 2009; Gilliam 2011). The European Court of Human Rights, for example, considered that the use of anonymous informants as trial witnesses in one case 'involved limitations on the rights of the defence which were irreconcilable with the guarantees contained in Article 6'.[40] Individuals who give evidence in

---

[37] Article 1(1), Convention against Torture and Other Cruel, Inhuman or Degrading Treatment or Punishment (1984) 1465 UNTS 85.

[38] Article 5(1), American Convention on Human Rights (1969), entered into force on 18 July 1978; 1144 UNTS 123.

[39] Principle 21, 'Body of principles for the protection of all persons under any form of detention or imprisonment', General Assembly Resolution 43/173, 9 December 1988.

[40] *Kostovski v. the Netherlands*, app. no. 11454/85 (ECtHR, 20 November 1989), para. 44. See further *Texeira de Castro v. Portugal*, app. no. 44/1997/828/1034 (ECtHR, 9 June 1998); *Jasper v. United Kingdom*, app. no. 27052/95 (ECtHR, 16 February 2000); *Rowe and Davis v. United Kingdom*, app. no. 28901/95 (ECtHR, 16 February 2000); *Fitt v. United Kingdom*, app. no. 29777/96 (ECtHR, 16 February 2000); *Donohue v. Ireland*, app no. 19165/08 (ECtHR, 12 December 2013).

criminal trials, or act as informers for police or national security authorities, may face serious risks to their lives or persons, or to those of their families, as a result.

Human rights law has been more prominent in addressing state obligations concerning the right to life and freedom from torture in the context of informing, possibly on account of the occasionally overt consequences of being an informer, compared with the usually covert nature of recruitment and informing. The European Court of Human Rights has examined such issues through the lens of Articles 2 and 3 of the European Convention, clarifying in one case that:

> national authorities have an obligation to take all steps reasonably expected to prevent real and immediate risks to prisoners' physical integrity, of which the authorities had or ought to have had knowledge ... This obligation is all the more true in cases when prisoners run a particularly heightened risk of ill-treatment by their fellow inmates, such as is the case with sexual offenders and police collaborators.[41]

The obligation extends beyond places of detention or imprisonment, such as in the context of the 'life-threatening vengeance' that a collaborator and his family were facing from organised criminal groups.[42] Similar concerns have come before relevant human rights bodies in the context of petitions relating to the deportation of failed asylum seekers and *non-refoulement*.[43]

International human rights law makes its most significant contribution to the legal framework governing the use of informers not through the obligations arising from the non-derogable right to life or freedom from torture, or to fundamental fair trial guarantees, but perhaps, somewhat surprisingly, by way of the right to privacy. This right is enshrined in several of the core human rights treaties, each of which seeks to prevent arbitrary, unlawful, or abusive interference by public authorities in the lives of individuals.[44] The recruitment or deployment of an individual as an informer by state authorities may entail an interference not only in their private life but also in that of the individuals about whom an informer might share information. To comply with international human rights law, interferences of this nature must be neither unlawful nor arbitrary.

The European Convention elaborates that an interference in the right to private and family life is only permissible where it is 'in accordance with the law and is necessary in a democratic society in the interests of national security, public safety or the economic well-being of the country, for the prevention of disorder or crime, for the protection of health or morals, or for the protection of the rights and

---

[41] *DF v. Latvia*, app. no. 11160/07 (ECtHR, 29 October 2013), paras 83–4.

[42] *RR and Others v. Hungary*, app. no. 19400/11 (ECtHR, 4 December 2012), para. 32.

[43] See *X and X v. Denmark*, communication no. 2186/2012, views adopted by the Committee at its 112th session (22 October 2014), CCPR/C/112/D/2186/2012, 17 November 2014; *H and B v. UK*, app. nos 70073/10 and 44539/11 (ECtHR, 9 April 2013); *S. G. v. Netherlands*, Decision, communication no. 135/1999, CAT/C/32/D/135/1999 (Committee against Torture, 14 May 2004).

[44] See Article 17, International Covenant on Civil and Political Rights; Article 11(2), American Convention on Human Rights; Article 8, European Convention on Human Rights.

freedoms of others'.[45] The European Court confirms that measures entailing interference with rights under Article 8 must have 'a specific legal basis' in domestic
law.[46] For the Human Rights Committee, such laws 'must specify in detail the precise circumstances in which such interferences may be permitted', while a decision
to make an authorised interference 'must be made only by the authority designated
under the law, and on a case-by-case basis'.[47] Relevant domestic laws must
adequately provide an indication to citizens as to when and how public authorities
may be permitted to undertake such interferences.[48]

International human rights law thus accepts the permissibility of the use of
informers by state authorities, but insists on effective regulation of the practice. This
stance confers a certain legitimacy on the recruitment and deployment of informers,
while states also enjoy a degree of latitude in their application of the requirements
of necessity and proportionality in relation to measures taken. Nevertheless, the
elaboration of domestic legislation concerning the use of informers should see the
processes involved in the practice of recruiting and deploying informers subjected
to oversight, and at the very least outline how state authorities purport to comply
with applicable human rights standards. Recent scholarship has elaborated a human
rights based approach to the practice of using informers (Sambei 2015: 221; Walsh
2009: 176–7).

Despite the requirements of international human rights law, particularly in
relation to the right to privacy, states have been very reluctant to legislate in this
area. Only a handful of states have adopted legislative frameworks governing the
use of so-called covert human intelligence sources (CHIS), with authorities often
engaging in self-regulation through reliance on internal codes of conduct or executive guidance (Neyroud and Beckley 2001: 173; Fishwick 2009: 126). The United
Kingdom's Regulation of Investigatory Powers Act 2000 stands out amongst the
limited examples of national legislation, given that it is expressly aimed at ensuring
compliance with the state's international human rights law obligations, and
provides for a system of internal authorisation and external oversight. Notably, it is
considered to apply to the activities of the armed forces during situations of armed
conflict, including those that may take place outside the territory of the United
Kingdom. The next section thus turns to explore the application of this legislation during armed conflict and other more recent relevant legislative developments,
including those which push back against the application of human rights standards
to armed forces during wartime.

[45] Article 8(2), European Convention on Human Rights.
[46] *Big Brother Watch and Others v. United Kingdom*, app. nos 58170/13, 62322/14, 24960/15 (ECtHR, 13 September 2018), para. 305.
[47] Human Rights Committee, General Comment no. 16: Article 17 (Right to Privacy), 28 September 1988, para. 8.
[48] *Kopp v. Switzerland*, app. no. 23224/94 (ECtHR, 25 March 1998), para. 64.

Regulating Hidden Aspects of War?

The United Kingdom's Regulation of Investigatory Powers Act 2000

When introducing the Regulation of Investigatory Powers Bill in the House of Commons in March 2000, the Home Secretary, Jack Straw, sought both to emphasise the significance of the proposed legislation and to explain its purpose:

> This is an important Bill, and represents a significant step forward for the protection of human rights in this country. Human rights considerations have dominated its drafting. None of the law enforcement activities specified in the Bill is new. What is new is that, for the first time, the use of these techniques will be properly regulated by law and externally supervised. That will serve to ensure that law enforcement and other operations are consistent with the duties imposed on public authorities by the European convention on human rights and by the Human Rights Act 1998.[49]

Although there was no specific reference made in Parliament at that time, there is little doubt that the consequences of the widespread unregulated use of informers in Northern Ireland over the course of the preceding three decades of conflict played a role in the promulgation of this legislation.

As discussed by Dudai and Hearty in Chapter 8, informers were recruited and deployed by MI5, the British counter-intelligence and security agency, the British Army, and the Royal Ulster Constabulary throughout the so-called 'Troubles' (Moran 2013: 23–66; Moran and Walker 2016; Leahy, 2020; Edwards 2021). Informers were implicated in serious criminal activity, including murder, and were at times themselves the victims of torture or extrajudicial killings, although some victims may have been mistakenly identified or deliberately misidentified as 'touts' (Toolis 1995: 194; Coogan 1994: 176).[50] Despite the prevalence of the practice of deploying informers in Northern Ireland, the independent de Silva review found that there had been 'a wilful and abject failure by successive governments to provide the clear policy and legal framework necessary for agent-handling operations to take place effectively and within the law'.[51] In the words of the Chief Constable of the Police Service of Northern Ireland, the successor of the Royal Ulster Constabulary, there were 'no rules ... [t]here was no regulatory framework for handling of informants' (McCann 2016).

The lack of a formalised legal framework applying to the use of informers in Northern Ireland during the Troubles may have been intentional. According to McGovern (2016: 302), this void created 'a space of legal obscurity and plausible

---

[49] *Parliamentary Debates*, Vol. 381, 6 March 2000.
[50] See also Police Ombudsman for Northern Ireland, Statutory Report: Public Statement by the Police Ombudsman in Accordance with Section 62 of the Police (Northern Ireland) Act 1998. Relating to a complaint by the victims and survivors of the Murders at the Heights Bar, Loughinisland, 18 June 1994, Belfast, 2016, 3, 37, 62, 82–3, 134, 137, 142–6.
[51] Rt Hon. Sir Desmond de Silva, *The Report of the Patrick Finucane Review*, 12 December 2012, H.C. 802–I, 7.

deniability that facilitated counterinsurgency practice rather than hampering it'. The de Silva review did not take issue with the use of informers per se, finding that the running of agents was 'one of the most effective methods by which the security forces could frustrate terrorist activity and save lives'.[52] While this may be so in certain circumstances, Dudai and Hearty elaborate in Chapter 8 on how it may also be the case that the use of informers can be counterproductive and lead to further violence. Notwithstanding the high value of informers who may be involved in criminal activity, and the difficulties in drawing up the necessary 'detailed legal and policy framework', de Silva did not exonerate the failure to regulate.[53] Internal guidelines had been relied upon by certain authorities, as legislation was considered 'politically unobtainable' on account of the potential involvement of informers in criminal activities.[54] One result was that informers were often effectively protected from prosecution despite their involvement in unlawful activity. A Police Ombudsman Commission report described as 'indefensible' the shielding of informers from police questioning despite their apparent involvement in a particular series of murders.[55]

The adoption of RIPA 2000 came shortly after the 1998 signing of the peace agreement to end the Northern Ireland conflict and the adoption of the Human Rights Act implementing the European Convention on Human Rights at the national level. It sets out a scheme for the authorisation and oversight of both the conduct and use of CHIS, drawing on the principles of necessity and proportionality in line with Article 8 of the European Convention.[56] The Act requires authorisation by a designated individual within the relevant public authority, which includes the police, intelligence services, and armed forces, rather than externally, such as by a judge.[57] Oversight, record-keeping, and to a limited extent the security and welfare of informers are also addressed in the legislation. In relation to protecting covert sources, for example, it states that 'there will at all times be a person holding an office, rank or position with the relevant investigating authority who will have day-to-day responsibility for dealing with the source on behalf of that authority, and for the source's security and welfare'.[58] Regarding external supervision, as mentioned by Jack Straw, the legislation provided for the creation of various Commissioners to exercise an oversight role, as well as an Investigatory Powers Tribunal to hear complaints regarding alleged breaches.[59]

The Regulation of Investigatory Powers Act 2000 went some way toward meeting the United Kingdom's obligations under the European Convention by

[52] *Ibid.*, 68.

[53] *Ibid.*, 68–9. See also Moran (2013: 57).

[54] Moran (2013: 83).

[55] Police Ombudsman for Northern Ireland (2016), Statutory Report, 144.

[56] RIPA 2000, Section 29(2)–(3).

[57] *Ibid.*, Sections 29–30, Schedule I.

[58] *Ibid.*, Section 29(5)(a).

[59] *Ibid.*, Sections 61–3, but see, however, Section 32A. For an example of the reporting provided by the relevant Commissioners see Mark Waller, *Report of the Intelligence Services Commissioner for 2016*, HC/298, 23–6.

placing the requirements of authorisation and oversight on a statutory footing. There were remaining concerns, however, such as the permitted use of juveniles or 'vulnerable individuals' as CHIS (Gayle and Cobain 2018a, b), as well as the failure of the original legislation adequately to address the issue of informer involvement in criminal activities. The Home Office has issued a Code of Practice that offers guidance on the application of RIPA 2000 in the context of the deployment of human intelligence sources, which it recognises as a 'high-risk covert technique',[60] and the Code states, without much elaboration, that neither the legislation nor the Code 'is intended to affect the existing practices and procedures surrounding criminal participation of CHIS'.[61] The de Silva review pointedly raised doubts as to whether RIPA 2000 and the accompanying Code of Practice provided 'a real resolution to these difficult issues given that it provides little guidance as to the limits of the activities of covert human intelligence sources'.[62]

To this end, the British government introduced the Covert Human Intelligence Sources (Criminal Conduct) Act 2021, aimed at creating a system of authorisation of criminal conduct by informers. The Act entails an amendment to RIPA 2000 that would allow relevant authorities to grant a 'criminal conduct authorisation' if considered necessary – in the interests of national security, for the purpose of preventing or detecting crime or preventing disorder, or in the interests of the United Kingdom's economic well-being – and proportionate, that is to say that the aim could not be reasonably achieved by other conduct that is not criminal.[63] While the Intelligence and Security Committee of Parliament broadly welcomed the legislation, civil society organisations raised serious concerns about the absence of any explicit limits on potential criminal conduct.[64] The Act introduces specific safeguards for juveniles and vulnerable adults, but does not go so far as to prohibit their use as informers, or their engaging in criminal activity.[65] The legislation refers without elaboration to 'the need to take into account other matters so far as they are relevant (for example, requirements of the Human Rights Act 1998)'.[66] The authorisation by state agents of criminal conduct by informers sits uneasily with the duty to prevent, investigate, and prosecute serious human rights violations. The proposed legislation as it stands does not grant immunity from prosecution to those informers who participate in criminal conduct, although, as MI5 has previously set out, an authorisation for criminal conduct and accompanying records 'may form the basis of representations by the Service to the prosecuting authorities that prosecution is

---

[60] Home Office, Covert Human Intelligence Source Code of Practice (2014), 10.

[61] *Ibid.*, 7.

[62] De Silva, *The Report of the Patrick Finucane Review*, 91.

[63] Covert Human Intelligence Sources (Criminal Conduct) Act 2021, Section 1(5).

[64] Intelligence and Security Committee of Parliament, *Statement on the Covert Human Intelligence Sources (Criminal Conduct) Bill*, 24 September 2020; Sabbagh (2020).

[65] Covert Human Intelligence Sources (Criminal Conduct) Act 2021, Sections 2–3.

[66] *Ibid.*, Section 1(5).

not in the public interest'.[67] The Court of Appeal has considered the absence of any explicit granting of immunity in this context as supporting the lawfulness of the 'indispensable' deployment of informers by the British Security Service.[68]

Turning to the context of armed conflict, RIPA 2000 explicitly applies to British armed forces with no evident distinction being drawn between situations of armed conflict and otherwise.[69] The legislation left open the question as to whether it might apply overseas and in the context of military activities. The Home Office, however, considers that this legislation, as with the Human Rights Act itself, can apply extraterritorially, given the objective of giving effect to the European Convention:

> The Human Rights Act 1998 applies to all activity taking place within the UK. This should be taken to include overseas territories and facilities which are within the jurisdiction of the UK. Authorisations under the 2000 Act may therefore be appropriate for overseas covert operations occurring in UK Embassies, military bases, detention facilities, etc., in order to comply with rights to privacy under Article 8 of the ECHR [European Convention of Human Rights].[70]

This is a *prima facie* narrower interpretation of the jurisdictional scope of human rights law, particularly given that the European Court of Human Rights has accepted the application of the Convention in situations beyond military bases and detention facilities.[71] On the equivalent provision concerning privacy of the International Covenant on Civil and Political Rights, the International Court of Justice has held that this applies to Israel as a party to the Covenant in its own territory and throughout the Palestinian territories it occupies.[72]

The United Kingdom Ministry of Defence accepts the application of RIPA 2000 during situations of armed conflict, including overseas, although as a matter of policy rather than of formal legal application. Its 2018 doctrine publication *Legal Support to Joint Operations*, for instance, explains that in relation to intelligence operations, '[s]ome UK legislation applies overseas as a matter of law. Where it does not, policy may apply it' (UKMOD 2018: 68). The Regulation of Investigatory Powers Act 2000 is identified as falling within the latter category:

> Covert human intelligence and surveillance operations conducted by UK Armed Forces are planned, authorised, executed and recorded in a manner consistent with UK legislation, principally the Regulation of Investigatory Powers Act 2000. Although that Act does not apply to overseas operations as a matter of law, it is applied as a matter of policy.

[67] 'Guidelines on the use of Agents who participate in Criminality (Official Guidance)', March 2011, para. 9, available at https://reprieve.org.uk/press/tribunal-to-consider-whether-mi5-covert-agents-can-commit-serious-criminal-offences/ (accessed 22 February 2022).
[68] *Privacy International et al. v. Secretary of State et al.* [2021] EWCA Civ 330, paras 8, 59, 76, 85–6, 99.
[69] RIPA 2000, Schedule 1, Part 1, 5–6.
[70] Home Office, Covert Human Intelligence Source Code of Practice (2014), 32.
[71] See, for example, *Al-Skeini and others v. UK*, app. no. 55721/07 (ECtHR, 7 July 2011), paras 138–42. See further Lubell (2012).
[72] ICJ, 'Legality of the construction of a wall', para. 128.

The Regulation of Investigatory Powers Act requires, in particular, those authorising the use of covert techniques to give proper consideration to whether their use is necessary and proportionate. It strictly limits the people who can lawfully use covert techniques, the purposes for, and conditions in which they can be used, and how the material obtained must be handled. (UKMOD 2018: 69)

A 2009 British Army field manual on countering insurgency, which also notes that the legislation applies 'by reason of MOD policy',[73] acknowledges that gathering intelligence from within the civilian population 'may challenge human rights and liberties, or open those who provide intelligence to threats of reprisal', and states that RIPA 2000 'provides a well-established regulatory framework for such operations and reduces the chances of improper conduct and abuse', even if it may, 'at first sight, appear to be cumbersome on operations'.[74]

Notwithstanding such endorsements, the decision to treat RIPA 2000 as applying as a matter of policy rather than law is telling. This arguably provides for some flexibility in its application, and perhaps allows the maintenance of a more lightly regulated space for intelligence gathering, including through the deployment of informers. It may also reflect enduring opposition towards the application of human rights standards during armed conflict. While the Ministry of Defence has acknowledged that international human rights law, as well as RIPA 2000, may have a role in 'identifying the freedoms and constraints' applicable to intelligence exploitation activities (UKMOD 2018: 68), the fourth edition of the Ministry's *Captured Persons* (2020) makes no reference at all to RIPA 2000, and sets out its less than unqualified embrace of the application of international human rights law:

Compliance with all international and domestic law is fundamental to our Armed Forces. In some circumstances, regional human rights instruments, including the European Convention on Human Rights, may apply to [captured persons] during operations. The applicability of the European Convention on Human Rights to CPERS [captured persons] has, and continues to be, subject to scrutiny and ongoing interpretation in the UK courts and the European Court of Human Rights .... The MOD's position is that the International Covenant on Civil and Political Rights and the United Nations (UN) Convention against Torture and Inhuman or Degrading Treatment do not always apply extraterritorially and, therefore, they will apply only by exception to [captured persons] during operations overseas. (UKMOD 2020: 129–30)

This is an evident pushback against an overly broad application of human rights law to the conduct of armed forces, an argument that has been made much more forcefully elsewhere.[75]

---

[73] British Army Field Manual, *Countering Insurgency* (2009), Army Code 71876, Vol. I, Part 10, 3-36, 12-20.
[74] *Ibid.*
[75] See for example Tugendhat and Croft 2013: 21, arguing that human rights law contributes to a new legal environment that 'may constrain Britain's armed forces in ways that undermine their speed, flexibility and effectiveness'; and Ekins, Morgan and Tugendhat 2016: 11, claiming that the application of human rights law gives rise to 'judicial imperialism'. See, however, Waters (2008).

A key component of RIPA 2000 is that it provides for some external oversight of the use of CHIS. In the context of governance and oversight of human intelligence operations relating to captured persons, the Ministry of Defence references certain oversight mechanisms that have their genesis in this legislation. Referring to an 'additional and separate mechanism' relating to intellegence collected from human sources, or HUMINT, detailed within an unpublished Ministry of Defence policy document,[76] *Captured Persons* explains that 'a monthly case management board will report to the Investigatory Powers Commissioner during regular inspections' (UKMOD 2020: 154). The Investigatory Powers Commissioner's Office was set up under the Investigatory Powers Act 2016, with the role of keeping under review 'by way of audit, inspection and investigation' the exercise of functions covered by relevant parts of RIPA 2000, including the use of CHIS.[77]

Notwithstanding these references to RIPA 2000 and related mechanisms in a number of official documents regarding military doctrine and policy, it is difficult to determine the full extent to which the measures required under the legislation relating to the use of CHIS have been embraced in British military practice. The annual reports of the Investigatory Powers Commissioner's Office provide some indication. Its 2017 report noted the relatively low reported numbers of CHIS authorisations outside law enforcement and stated that the Ministry of Defence had, 'generally speaking, properly authorised CHIS activity during the period covered by this report', although some concerns were raised, such as the need to maintain 'an up-to-date record of intrusion into the lives of the family members of a CHIS'.[78] The Office offered a brief summary of its inspection of the use of informers by the Ministry of Defence in its 2018 report:

> We inspected the internal review mechanisms for agent running activity in place at the MOD and were pleased to note a regular, centralised process was in place. This is used by the MOD to oversee the ongoing necessity of their use of covert powers in relation to a range of missions. Our inspection noted good consideration of the proportionality of conducting each action authorised and of the likely collateral intrusion.[79]

The Office did not consider the use of CHIS overseas by the Ministry of Defence for its 2019 report, but indicated that it would do in the next reporting period.[80]

The Investigatory Powers Tribunal has not been confronted with the issue of the deployment of informers in situations of armed conflict, although it did issue a judgment in December 2019 concerning the use by MI5 of covert human intelligence sources and their involvement in criminal activities, which seems to have prompted the adoption of the Covert Human Intelligence Sources (Criminal Conduct) Act 2021.[81]

---

[76] DI ICSP/4-2-02-06-07, MOD Policy on Defence HUMINT Data Management, 10 February 2011.
[77] See Regulation of Investigatory Powers Act 2016, Sections 229(3)(e), 233(3).
[78] IPCO Annual Report, 2017, 14–15, 19–20.
[79] IPCO Annual Report, 2018, 57.
[80] IPCO Annual Report, 2019, 73.
[81] *Privacy International et al. v. Secretary of State et al.* [2019] UKIPTrib IPT_17_186_CH, 20 December 2019.

The Court of Appeal has found that the Security Services have, and have always had, the power 'to run agents who participate in criminality'.[82]

The Regulation of Investigatory Powers Act 2000 meets key requirements of Article 8 of the European Convention of Human Rights by establishing the legal foundation for the state interference that is inherent in the use of informers, and by requiring adherence to the principles of necessity and proportionality. Nevertheless, the legislation adopts a model of 'self-authorisation' that relies heavily on the honesty of public authorities and a willingness to comply (Sanders *et al*. 2010: 331–3; Hirsch 2001; Williams 2006: 152–3). This is deeply problematic given the express power to authorise criminal activity. One view of the legislation's impact on the use of police informers is that it has given rise to a 'more secret, and thus less controllable, system of informers over which RIPA merely draws a presentational veil' (Sanders *et al*. 2010: 321–34). Bethan Loftus's ethnographic study of covert policing in the United Kingdom (2019: 2083) reveals that RIPA 2000 has been embedded in police practice, policy, and training, although she finds that, 'in contrast with custodial investigation, employing covert methods was considered by officers to impose fewer constraints'. No such study exists for the application for RIPA 2000 in the context of military operations. Moreover, other legislative moves are currently under way to restrict the application of human rights law in military operations.

In September 2020, the *Sunday Telegraph* reported that the British Prime Minister Boris Johnson was preparing to 'opt out of human rights laws', particularly in those areas where judges had 'overreached' (Malnick 2020). In addition to the issue of deportation of migrants and asylum seekers, prosecutions and human rights claims relating to British military activities were also specifically highlighted. The Overseas Operations (Service Personnel and Veterans) Act 2021 introduces a 'presumption against prosecution' of members of the armed forces operating overseas.[83] International crimes and torture are formally excluded from this presumption, although no such exclusion was included in the original proposed Bill.[84] The Bill had also put forward a 'duty to consider derogation' from the European Convention on Human Rights, thus signalling a regressive approach to the application of human rights during situations of armed conflict.[85] Article 8 of the European Convention is a right that may be derogated from during a state of emergency, thus its suspension during a state of emergency would clearly jeopardise the application of RIPA 2000. Its precarious application to the armed forces during time of conflict is underscored by its application as a matter of policy rather than law, which suggests a possibility for its being set aside irrespective of any formal derogation by the United Kingdom. These ongoing legal battles regarding the application of human rights during wartime and the activities of recruited informers serve to

---

[82] *Privacy International et al. v. Secretary of State et al.* [2021] EWCA Civ 330, para. 86.

[83] Overseas Operations (Service Personnel and Veterans) Act, 2021, Section 2.

[84] *Ibid.*, Section 6.

[85] Overseas Operations (Service Personnel and Veterans) Bill, 2020, Section 12. On derogations see Milanović 2016.

demonstrate how the expected regulation under international human rights law of the use of informers – what could amount to a potentially more purposive embrace by international law of at least one form of collaboration – remains to be realised in the context of armed conflict.

Conclusion

Given the frequency with which parties to an armed conflict, as well as national policing, security, and intelligence authorities, resort to the use of informers and other collaborators, it would be naive to consider that international law could have contemplated an absolute prohibition of the seeking or obtaining of assistance of this nature. States have agreed, albeit reluctantly at first, to rules that forbid forced collaboration. Several restrictions laid out in the 1949 Geneva Conventions and related treaties apply to the phenomenon of collaboration, even if in an indirect manner, but make clear that in most circumstances individuals should not be compelled to serve an opposing belligerent. This legal framework allows some exceptions, such as the case of officials in an occupied territory. Yet, by and large, international humanitarian law has maintained a permissive stance toward the practice, subject to restrictions often based on the principle of humane treatment. Voluntary collaboration is largely unaddressed by this body of law, although national courts have on at least one occasion treated this as being at odds with the laws of armed conflict in certain narrow circumstances.[86]

While the practice of deploying informers and other collaborators may provide valuable intelligence on opposition forces, ensure greater accuracy in targeting during the conduct of hostilities, or facilitate the maintenance of order during a situation of belligerent occupation, there is little doubt that there are negative impacts on human rights that frequently occur in this context (Gordon 2014; Gross 2015: 109; Hewitt 2010: 3–5; Dudai 2012: 33; Sarma 2005 178; Cohen and Dudai 2005: 239–40). This chapter examined how international human rights law mirrors the approach of humanitarian law to an extent, by insisting on the protection of relevant rights, including the right to life, freedom from torture, and fair trials guarantees, but through the right to privacy insists on regulation of the practice of using informers in particular. Human rights standards, which apply during times of armed conflict, including those occurring extraterritorially, require a clear legislative basis for any interference by public authorities in the private lives of individuals, subject to the principles of necessity and proportionality. Nevertheless, the application of international human rights law to the practice of using informers and other collaborators remains underdeveloped, particularly in the context of armed conflict.

---

[86] See, for example, HCJ 3799/02, *Adalah et. al. v. GOC Central Command, IDF et al.*, Supreme Court sitting as the High Court of Justice, 23 June 2005.

With national law often the vehicle that serves to embed international rules and principles in domestic systems, the chapter considered the role of the United Kingdom's Regulation of Investigatory Powers Act 2000 in embedding human rights standards in the legal framework applicable to the use of informers. This legislation applies to a range of public authorities, including the armed forces, and it is applied as a matter of policy to British armed forces during situations of conflict occurring extraterritorially. While there is little doubt that the legislation creates an advanced system involving authorisation and oversight, it belatedly addressed the question of informer participation in criminal activities, albeit without unambiguous limits, and the extent and effectiveness of its application during situations of armed conflict is not fully apparent. Although covert activity by state authorities is rarely adjudicated upon (Perina 2015: 549), the Investigatory Powers Tribunal has begun to address certain aspects of covert human intelligence activities in the United Kingdom. The genesis of this legislation lies in the human rights obligations of the United Kingdom, particularly under the European Convention on Human Rights, a foundation that is now openly disdained in certain quarters. The legislation offers an elaborated model that could influence the future evolution of international law in how it addresses aspects of collaboration, albeit entailing an approach that leaves much of the regulation and oversight in the shadows and refrains from upending the law's ultimate permissiveness in this context.

References

Bloom, R. M. (2002), *Ratting: The Use and Abuse of Informants in the American Justice System* (Westport, CT, Praeger).

Brook, T. (2005), *Collaboration; Japanese Agents and Local Elites in Wartime China* (Cambridge, MA, Harvard University Press).

Brown Scott, J. (1921), *The Proceedings of the Hague Peace Conferences: The Conference of 1907*, Vol. III, *Meetings of the Second, Third, and Fourth Commissions* (New York, Oxford University Press).

Cheah, W. L. (2018), 'Dealing with desertion and gaps in international humanitarian law: Changes of allegiance in the Singapore war crimes trials', *Asian Journal of International Law*, 8, 350–70.

Chesterman, S. (2011), *One Nation under Surveillance* (Oxford, Oxford University Press).

Cohen H. and Dudai, R. (2005), 'Human rights dilemmas in using informers to combat terrorism: The Israeli–Palestinian case', *Terrorism and Political Violence*, 17, 229–43.

Cohen, H. (2008), *Army of Shadows: Palestinian Collaboration with Zionism, 1917–1948*, trans. H. Watzman (Berkeley, CA, University of California Press).

Coogan, T. P. (1994), *The IRA: A History* (Boulder, CO, Roberts Rinehart).

D'Argent, P. (2015), 'Non-renunciation of the rights provided by the conventions', in A. Clapham, P. Gaeta, and M. Sassòli (eds), *The 1949 Geneva Conventions: A Commentary* (Oxford: Oxford University Press), 145–54.

Darcy, S. (2019), *To Serve the Enemy: Informers, Collaborators, and the Laws of Armed Conflict* (Oxford, Oxford University Press).

Deák, I. (2015), *Europe on Trial: The Story of Collaboration, Resistance, and Retribution During World War II* (Boulder, CO, Westview Press)

Dethlefsen, H. (1990), 'Denmark and the German occupation: Cooperation, negotiation or collaboration?', *Scandinavian Journal of History*, 15, 193–206.

Dudai, R. (2012), 'Informers and the transition in Northern Ireland', *British Journal of Criminology*, 52, 32–54.

Dunningham, C. and Morris, C. (1996), 'A risky business: The recruitment and running of informers by English police officers', *Police Studies*, 19, 1–25.

Edwards, A. (2021), *Agents of Influence: Britain's Secret Intelligence War against the IRA* (Dublin, Irish Academic Press).

Ekins, R., Morgan, J., and Tugendhat, T. (2016), *Clearing the Fog of Law: Saving Our Armed Forces from Defeat by Judicial Diktat* (London, Policy Exchange).

Fishwick, M. (2009), 'The European perspective', in R. Billingsley (ed.), *Covert Human Intelligence Sources: The Unlovely Face of Police Work* (Sherfield on Loddon, Waterside Press), 123–36.

Galvis Martínez, M. (2020), 'Betrayal in war: Rules and trends on seeking collaboration under IHL', *Journal of Conflict and Security Law*, 25: 81–99.

Gayle, D. and Cobain, I. (2018a), 'UK intelligence and police using child spies in covert operations', *Guardian*, 19 July.

Gayle, D. and Cobain, I. (2018b), 'Home Office pressed for details over use of child spies', *Guardian*, 17 August.

Gilliam, M. W. (2011), 'Whispering sweet nothings: How jailhouse snitches subvert American justice', in S. Guerra Thompson, J. L. Hopgood, and H. K. Valderrama (eds), *American Justice in the Age of Innocence: Understanding the Causes of Wrongful Convictions and How to Prevent Them* (Bloomington, IN, iUniverse Books), 195–234.

Gordon, N. (2014), 'Talking about collaborators', *Los Angeles Review of Books*, 25 February.

Gross, M. L. (2015), *The Ethics of Insurgency* (Cambridge, Cambridge University Press).

Hewitt, S. (2010), *Snitch! A History of the Modern Intelligence Informer* (London/New York, Continuum).

Hirsch, C. (2001), 'Policing undercover agents in the United Kingdom: Whether the regulation of investigatory powers acts complies with regional human rights obligations', *Fordham International Law Journal*, 25, 1282–34.

ICRC [International Committee of the Red Cross] (2009), *Interpretive Guidance on the Notion of Direct Participation* (Geneva, ICRC).

ICRC [International Committee of the Red Cross] (2016), *Commentary on the First Geneva Convention: Convention (I) for the Amelioration of the Condition of the Wounded and Sick in Armed Forces in the Field*, 2nd edn (Cambridge, Cambridge University Press).

Jochnick, C. af and Normand, R. (1994), 'The legitimation of violence: A critical history of the laws of war', *Harvard International Law Journal*, 3, 49–96.

Jones-Brown, D. and Shane, J. M. (2011), *An Exploratory Study on the Use of Confidential Informants in New Jersey* (Newark, American Civil Liberties Union of New Jersey).

Kalyvas, S. N. (2008), 'Collaboration in comparative perspective', *European Review of History – Revue européenne d'histoire*, 15, 109–11.

Klamberg, M. (2018), 'The legality of rebel courts during non-international armed conflicts', *Journal of International Criminal Justice*, 16, 235–63.

Leahy, T. (2020), *The Intelligence War against the IRA* (Cambridge, Cambridge University Press).

Loftus, B. (2019), 'Normalizing covert surveillance: The subterranean world of policing', *British Journal of Sociology*, 70, 2070–91.

Lubell, N. (2012), 'Human rights obligations in military occupation', *International Review of the Red Cross*, 94, 317–37.

Malnick, E. (2020), 'Boris Johnson set to opt out of human rights laws', *Sunday Telegraph*, 12 September.

McCann, E. (2016), 'State role in killings by IRA changes everything', *Irish Times*, 28 January.

McGovern, M. (2016), 'Informers, agents and the liberal ideology of collusion in Northern Ireland', *Critical Studies on Terrorism*, 9, 292–311.

Melzer, N. (2016), *International Humanitarian Law* (Geneva, ICRC).

Milanović, M. (2016), 'Extraterritorial derogations from human rights in armed conflict', in N. Bhuta (ed.), *The Frontiers of Human Rights: Extraterritoriality and Its Challenges* (Oxford, Oxford University Press), 55–88.

Moran, J. (2013), *From Northern Ireland to Afghansistan: British Military Intelligence Operations, Ethics and Human Rights* (Farnham, Ashgate).

Moran, J. and Walker, C. (2016), 'Intelligence powers and accountability in the UK', in Z. K. Goldman and S. J. Rascoff (eds), *Global Intelligence Oversight: Governing Security in the Twenty-First Century* (Oxford, Oxford University Press), 289–314.

Moyn, S. (2018), 'A war without civilian deaths? What arguments for a more humane war conceal', *New Republic*, 23 October.

Murray, D. (2016), *The Human Rights Obligations of Non-State Armed Groups* (Oxford, Hart).

Natapoff, A. (2009), *Snitching: Criminal Informants and the Erosion of American Justice* (New York, New York University Press).

New Zealand Defence Force (2019), *Manual of Armed Forces Law*, Vol. IV, *Law of Armed Conflict* (Wellington, New Zealand Defence Force).

Neyroud, P. and Beckley, A. (2001), 'Regulating informers: The Regulation of Investigatory Powers Act, covert policing and human rights', in R. Billingsley, T. Nemitz, and P. Bean (eds), *Informers: Policing, Policy, Practice* (London, Routledge), 164–75.

Norwegian Ministry of Defence (2018), *Manual of the Law of Armed Conflict* (Oslo, Chief of Defence).

Oppenheim, L. (1952), *International Law: A Treatise*, ed. H. Lauterpacht, Vol. II, 7th edn (London, Longmans).

Perina, A. H. (2015), 'Black holes and open secrets: The impact of covert action on international law', *Columbia Journal of Transnational Law*, 53, 507–83.

Pictet, J. (1958), *Commentary IV Geneva Convention* (Geneva, ICRC).

Redse Johansen, S. (2013), 'The occupied and the occupier: The case of Norway', in K. Mujezinović Larsen, C. Guldahl Cooper, and G. Nystuen (eds), *Searching for a 'Principle of Humanity' in International Humanitarian Law* (Cambridge, Cambridge University Press), 206–32.

Rings, W. (1982), *Life with the Enemy: Collaboration and Resistance in Hitler's Europe 1939–1945*, trans. J. Maxwell Brownjohn (New York, Doubleday).

Sabbagh, D. (2020), 'UK set to introduce bill allowing MI5 agents to break the law', *Guardian*, 24 September.

Sambei, A. (2015), 'Intelligence cooperation versus evidence collection and dissemination', in L. van den Herik and N. Schrijver (eds), *Counter-Terrorism Strategies in a Fragmented International Legal Order: Meeting the Challenges* (Cambridge, Cambridge University Press), 212–39.

Sanders, A., Young, R, and Burton, M. (2010), *Criminal Justice* (Oxford, Oxford University Press).

Sarma, K. (2005), 'Informers and the battle against republican terrorism: A review of 30 years of conflict', *Police Practice and Research*, 6, 165–80.

Sassòli, M. (1985), 'The status, treatment and repatriation of deserters under international humanitarian law', *Yearbook/International Institute of Humanitarian Law*, 9–36.

Shamas, D. (2018), 'A nation of informants: Reining in post-9/11 coercion of intelligence informants' *Brooklyn Law Review*, 83, 1175–1226.

Sivakumaran, S. (2009), 'Courts of armed opposition groups: Fair trials or summary justice?', *Journal of International Criminal Justice*, 7, 489–513.

Somer, J. (2007), 'Jungle justice: Passing sentence on the equality of belligerents in non-international armed conflict', *International Review of the Red Cross*, 89, 655–90.

Toolis, K. (1995), *Rebel Hearts: Journeys within the IRA's Soul* (London, Picador).

Tugendhat, T. and Croft, L. (2013), *The Fog of Law: An Introduction to the Legal Erosion of British Fighting Power* (London, Policy Exchange).

UKMOD [United Kingdom Ministry of Defence] (2004), *The Joint Service Manual of the Law of Armed Conflict* (Oxford, Oxford University Press).

UKMOD [United Kingdom Ministry of Defence] (2018), *Legal Support to Joint Operations*, 3rd edn (Swindon, UKMOD, Joint Doctrine and Concepts Centre).

UKMOD [United Kingdom Ministry of Defence] (2020), *Captured Persons*, 4th edn (Swindon, UKMOD).

United States Department of Defense (2015), *Law of War Manual* (Washington, DC, Office of General Counsel, Department of Defense).

Walsh, D. P. J. (2009), *Human Rights and Policing in Ireland: Law, Policy and Practice* (Dublin, Clarus Press).

Waters, C. P. M. (2008), 'Is the military legally encircled?', *Defence Studies*, 8, 26–48.

Williams, V. (2006), *Surveillance and Intelligence Law Handbook* (Oxford, Oxford University Press).

13

Conclusion: Reckoning with Collaboration

JUAN ESPINDOLA AND LEIGH A. PAYNE

THIS VOLUME BEGINS with the story of Judas and the harsh penalty he faced for his collaboration in Jesus's death: chewed by Lucifer in the pit of hell. Even in alternative versions of Judas's story of betrayal, there comes a day of reckoning. Judas recognises the results of his actions and takes his own life; he could not live with what he had done. Moving past Judas, the chapters in this book have grappled with what collaboration is, what factors motivate it, and how much harm it engenders or even diminishes, to arrive at a discussion of the mechanisms that societies emerging from autocracy or civil strife put in place to confront the actions of collaborators. In this conclusion, we bring together some of the main insights developed from the distinct disciplinary perspectives of the authors, and from the various collaboration contexts they have examined.

Who Is a Collaborator?

The efforts of the authors in this volume to identify who is a collaborator seek to raise complexity rather than reducing it. A set of chapters take on the collaborator-as-informer who feeds information to state enemies that perpetuates violence against rebel forces and resisters in Northern Ireland (Dudai and Hearty; Darcy), Argentina (Bilbija), Chile (Murphy), and Czechoslovakia (Drumbl and Holá). Yet each chapter suggests that collaborators do not always intend to betray their side, if there is even a clear 'side' to which they supposedly belong. The different motivations behind collaborators' actions do not minimise their role but rather complicate it, questioning the assumptions that lead to branding and social stigma. In other cases examined in the volume, a population is 'betrayed' by some of their members working for the enemy force: Basques in the Spanish police (De la Calle); Colombian security force members in paramilitary groups (Arias and Prieto); Black South Africans in the colonial and apartheid security apparatus (Dlamini); and enslaved Blacks who work on behalf of the slave owners (Dennis). In these cases, the authors probe why we expect individuals, because of their nationality, race, or official allegiance, to be loyal to that identity and service. The authors reveal collaborators' multiple identities and loyalties that defy a simple story of treachery. Indeed, the betrayal dimension is further questioned by those authors who examine a kind of inside collaboration: that is, those who not only failed to resist evil, but sustained it by contributing financially, ideologically, and morally, such as businesses in Argentina's dictatorship (Pereira) and law professors in Nazi Germany (Gross). Some have blood on their hands; others have blood in their hearts. And, yet, in many cases it is the observers' expectation that these groups and individuals should have known better, and were in a position of power to do something, that constitutes their betrayal.

What Form Does Collaboration Take?

Collaboration involves actions of very different sorts, many of which are portrayed in detail in the chapters of the volume. Some collaborators act in the open and maintain a close, if secondary, relationship with the main actors, as in the case of economic actors' complicity in the Argentine dictatorship's violent repression of workers and the labour movement (Pereira). The Basque police force also cooperated overtly with the national Spanish government; not interpreting its own law-enforcement actions as collaborative in a negative sense, it saw little need to conceal them (De la Calle). But many forms of collaboration take place outside the public eye. Informers are perhaps the most ubiquitous kinds of collaborators. Some are professionals who infiltrate insurgent organisations or the state with the clear intent of harming it and with a clear idea of the intelligence they need to seek and share (Dudai and Hearty). Others are victims who inform on other victims, as exemplified by slaves in antebellum United States (Dennis) and victims of the Argentine military dictatorship (Bilbija). Yet others acquire information by happenstance, and share it, often without any awareness of the use authorities will make of that information, as in the case of denunciators for the secret police in the Czech Republic during the Communist era (Drumbl and Holá). Finally, collaboration may occur in the context of weak institutions, and the collaborator may be a public official who covertly advises or provides critical information to groups he would be expected to confront, thus becoming a sort of intermediary. Arias and Prieto offer one such example in their examination of José Miguel Narváez, one of the highest-ranking public officials of the Colombian state security agency and an adviser to the army, and his collaboration with paramilitary groups in the prolonged civil war in Colombia.

Why Collaborate?

Collaborators have many motivations. The chapters in this collection examine cases where material rewards were offered. Sometimes these were salaries or single payments in a pay-per-give model. Salaries were paid to the Basque officers working for the Ertzaintza (De la Calle), the Black members of South African colonial and apartheid police forces (Dlamini), agents working for the Pinochet repressive apparatus (Murphy), and law professors in Nazi Germany (Gross). Material rewards such as an apartment, education for children, and jobs were offered in exchange for collaboration in the Czechoslovak case (Drumbl and Holá). In the case of tortured victims-turned-collaborators, the material reward could be one's life (Murphy; Bilbija). Enslaved Blacks were offered small sums, lenient sentences, or legal exculpation, and even emancipation, working papers, and the freedom to migrate in exchange for information (Dennis). Economic actors' collaborations led to protection from workers' and union demands, workplace disruptions, and wage repression, as well as offering beneficial terms of trade, borrowing and lending advantages, and legal impunity (Pereira). Even coerced forms of collaboration provide some sort of material reward or incentive – a way to survive or postpone imminent death, for example (Bilbija; Murphy; Dennis).

Yet these material rewards may prove to be side benefits rather than the underlying motivation for collaboration. Advancing a shared ideology is a less tangible, non-material reward. Oren Gross discusses the role that law professors in the most prestigious German universities played in bolstering the Nazi regime. These professors did not have to be recruited; they flocked. Not only did they remain silent as Jewish professors and students were purged from the universities. In their actions and their silence, they conferred 'a veneer of legality on the actions of the regime' (181). This kind of collaboration did not necessarily directly cause anyone's death, but it gave legitimacy to a killing machine. Gross explains that National Socialism embraced an anti-positivist understanding of law according to which Hitler was the interpreter of the will of the people, conceived in racial terms. By erasing the frontiers between law and morality, allowing Nazi ideology to achieve moral value, and defending a 'distorted and depraved variant of irrational and communal natural law, founded in biology', law professors lent support to the idea that the Führer's will must be law. Pereira also presents the idea of a joint enterprise between the military and business in Argentina, which together promoted the repressive apparatus, not only to enhance profits, but to create a political and economic system consistent with the Cold War ideology of national security and neo-liberalism.

De la Calle, Dennis, Dudai and Hearty, and Dlamini expound on the multiple dimensions of collaboration that cannot be reduced to material motive alone. A shared respect for law and order, or moral standards of behaviour, or religious principles may lead to collaboration with a presumed enemy, and ignores the set of underlying beliefs that trump an identity derived from racial or ethno-nationalist origins. Dlamini argues in his chapter, for instance, that while the actions of some informers in South Africa could be seen as a way to compensate for their thwarted ambitions (they were highly educated Blacks who, despite their education, faced multiple unfair barriers), other collaborators may have informed for colonial authorities as a way of directly alerting them to the grievances of the local population.

When to Collaborate?

The discussion so far hints at the ubiquity of collaboration. The evidence presented in this volume suggests that there is nothing historically or contextually unique about collaboration, the forms it takes, the reasons behind it, its ease, or its consequences. Even where movements prided themselves on eschewing the temptation to collaborate, examples have been found (Gross, this volume). Arendt (1994) and others (Jegstrup 1986) have identified Denmark as one of the bright lights in terms of avoiding Nazi collaboration, while others cast doubt on the assumed intrinsic goodness of 'rescuers' (Dudai 2012).

The study of collaboration has focused on reviled figures at key historical moments of unconscionable betrayal of one's country to an enemy power, such as Vidkun Quisling or Benedict Arnold. Yet collaboration in this volume does not hinge on a particular historical context. It is widely extended; used by both sides in civil conflicts (Dudai and Hearty; Arias and Prieto), by both sides in nationalist liberation struggles (De la Calle; Dlamini), by repressive regimes against internal enemies (Bilbija; Drumbl and Holá; Murphy; Gross; Pereira), and in repressive social and economic systems (Dennis); and is recognised as an intractable and permanent feature of interstate and even intrastate conflict by international law (Darcy), which tolerates its occurrence, outlawing only some of the excesses associated with the practice, such as coerced collaboration or harsh and inhumane punishment against collaborators.

Understanding the contexts of collaboration – particularly when they emerge under duress – may also allow for greater comprehension of how anyone, under a specific set of conditions, might become a collaborator. Ksenija Bilbija explores the case of Mercedes Carazo, a high-ranking member of the Montoneros, an urban guerrilla group that rebelled against the dictatorship in Argentina and was eventually crushed by it. Carazo turned into a collaborator for the military dictatorship, which used the information she provided, and later her services, to conduct counterinsurgency activities leading to the arrest and disappearance of former Montoneros. Carazo was framed as a collaborator by her erstwhile comrades and others. They displayed no sympathy or empathy for her brutal torture, nor for how informing might have seemed to her the only option to escape a violent death. Her critics never asked nor attempted to answer the question 'What might I have done in such a situation?' It is easier to condemn collaboration as morally wrong than to consider the complex set of factors behind the act. That Carazo took a top official in the enemy authoritarian regime as her lover further confirms, for her critics, her reprehensible nature. Only one author, and a few fellow political prisoners, discussed by Bilbija offered an alternative perspective. That Carazo does not attempt to tell her own story may suggest that she cannot fathom redemption, comprehension, or compassion in the aftermath of her betrayal.

And yet collaboration stories could also be told as forms of resistance. Bilbija recounts a view that Carazo may have informed only after her comrades were safe, or gave up names only of those she already assumed to be known by the repressive apparatus. In other cases, as chapters by Drumbl and Holá and Dudai and Hearty reveal, feigning collaboration can produce misinformation that distracts the enemy and wastes their time and resources chasing concocted stories. Or, by providing countless irrelevant details, would-be collaborators may bog down the apparatus, making it less efficient.

The transformative process that the collaborator undergoes – from reprehensible figure to a comprehensible and even responsible one – occurs over time and with some change in context. The dynamics behind collaboration, thus, defy static and fixed notions. This complicates the question of how to deal with collaborators in transitional justice contexts. These dynamics also reveal the political uses of collaboration. Denigrating collaboration justifies harsh treatment and sends a warning to would-be informants of the severe cost associated with betrayal. Condemning collaboration reinforces loyalty but also certain standards of behaviour. Paradoxically, collaboration itself is ubiquitous because it enhances power. It breaks down the unity of – weakens – the other side.

How to Respond to Collaboration: Social Stigma

These chapters show how collaborators have faced social stigma as the truth about their roles in past atrocities was revealed. Consider, for example, the killing or attempted killing of alleged and admitted collaborators such as Jean McConville, Martin McGartland, and others in Northern Ireland (Dudai and Hearty), or the call for violence against slave collaborators (Dennis).

Female collaborators are sometimes denied the opportunity to atone for or provide an account of their actions, as with the French women whose heads were shaved as punishment for their sexual 'treason'. If they are given the opportunity to do so, their testimonies may be given deflated credibility. And if a female collaborator fails to offer a public account of her actions, for instance because she was also a victim and chose silence and retreat as the best way to cope with the past, her voice may be usurped by commentators. Bilbija illustrates the latter possibility through the case of Carazo. Because of her collaboration and intimate relationship with one of her captors, several writers fictionalised her story, demonising her. They failed to recognise her collaboration as involuntary in the context of imprisonment in the infamous ESMA clandestine torture centre. Carazo's collaboration was taken up and engaged with by several writers in a set of semi-fictional works. Bilbija notes that not only was Carazo denied the right to tell her own story, she was also denied the empathy that she deserved under the circumstances of torture/sexual aggression.

As Bilbija shows, not all collaborators choose to tell their stories for comprehension or atonement. In the confusion of violence, some manage to evade moral and legal culpability. They remain unrepentant and receive light reproach. Because their contribution is intangible, ideological collaborators commonly fall within this category. Gross shows how law professors in Germany continued their academic careers unperturbed, or subject to minor disturbances only, some of them finding accommodation in post-Nazi Germany, and one, Theodor Maunz, even participating in the drafting of the West German Constitution. The chapters on wrongdoing and collaboration in Czechoslovakia by Drumbl and Holá and in South Africa by Dlamini further illustrate that at times there is very little punitive response at all. Societies sometimes choose to close the book and move on.

Social stigma when it is aimed at collaborators tends toward silencing the individual, ostracism, and a brand of popular justice. These processes impede learning the truth about systems of coercion within the regime and insiders' knowledge of those regimes. The Chilean victim-turned-victimiser in Murphy's chapter provides that information. Having first betrayed her comrades in the Socialist Party, she then betrayed the regime repressors who saved her life by collaborating with the Chilean Truth Commission. Even then, the valuable information she provided did not redeem her in Chilean society. She left the country. Mercedes Carazo, Bilbija recounts, gave testimony at the trials against the repressive force that she had collaborated with, but she did so from a distance, in Peru, and never told her own story.

Social stigma prevents collaborators from finding an opportunity to repair the damage they have done. Gross mentions the reparations policies in postwar Germany, but these did not provide redress to Jewish law professors who had lost their jobs, their salaries, their status in German society – all of which had been taken by their Nazi colleagues' collaboration. Even if such reparations were paid by the postwar German state, they will not have come from the collaborators themselves. Would an apology from collaborators have mattered? What could be done to offer redress for these wrongs?

Because collaborators tend to be seen as reprehensible figures and beyond redemption, harsh actions are often proposed and taken to address their betrayal. Understanding collaboration, however, also means questioning the assumption that in every case collaborators are reprehensible and incomprehensible figures who have carried out unforgiveable acts of betrayal. This complicates a simple way of dealing with collaborators. Executing those assumed to be collaborators, as the desperate members of the resistance did in the Warsaw Ghetto, is a revenge response to gross injustices without a consideration of contexts of collaboration. Given the stigma associated with, and the almost irredeemable quality of, collaborationism, their use by political actors may be intractable for processes of coming to terms with the past as commonly promoted.

How to Respond to Collaboration: Transitional Justice?

Beyond social stigma and informal or spontaneous responses to collaboration, the question of how political institutions must deal with collaborators is one that many chapters in the volume confront head-on. While most contributors make the case that some form of accountability is desirable, they also express their concern that transitional justice efforts tend to be ill prepared to grapple with collaboration. This is either because national and international institutions have yet to develop effective tools to confront collaborators, or because the main focus of these efforts are violations of human rights as characterised in international law, as well as the political motivations of the conflict (as when amnesties are only granted for political crimes).

Legal standards, international law, and legal action are what Darcy argues for in Chapter 12, as a way to reduce the ubiquity of collaboration in armed conflicts – international and domestic – but also as an alternative to the forms of violent vengeance that have been used by communities in meting out their own forms of justice against collaborators' impunity. As he shows, however, collaborators, and particularly informers, continue to be among the most vulnerable parties within conflicts, as states are reluctant to bind themselves to these legal constraints in their relations to them. International law is therefore too underdeveloped internationally to be useful for domestic processes and to avoid committing atrocities against the collaborators themselves, perpetuating cycles of distrust.

Despite the limitations of the international legal framework, domestic processes have held collaborators accountable, such as the stiff prison sentences for the two ageing Ford Motor Company executives in Argentina (Pereira) and the public official–paramilitary collaborator José Miguel Narváez in Colombia (Arias and Prieto). Pereira's chapter, in particular, considers ways in which judicial processes have moved forward to address collaboration. Specifically, as part of its judicial orientation in transitional justice, Argentina has begun to put business collaborators on trial for their involvement in crimes against humanity during the last dictatorship.

Drawing on philosophical discussions about the justification of punishment, Murphy explains some of the main reasons why punishing informers in transitional justice contexts is ethically appropriate. Punishment is commonly justified retrospectively: they deserve to be punished if they are complicit in the perpetration of wrongdoing. Forward-looking grounds may also be used: society must openly censure the behaviour of collaborators, to discourage others from such acts. Murphy argues that with respect to communities emerging from extraordinary violence, punishment and deterrence, as traditionally understood to apply to consolidated democracies, fail to capture why collaborators must be punished. In societies transitioning out of extraordinary violence, the state lacks moral legitimacy, and the kind of wrongdoing committed in its midst tends to be inflicted on groups, as with genocide, and to be politically motivated. These features, among others, make it unlikely that punishment will accomplish the goals normally attributed to it. Murphy then contends that the punishment of perpetrators, including that of collaborators, must be part of a process of just societal transformation, that is, of fundamentally altering the institutional framework that structures interactions between citizens and officials in transitional communities. Such a framework lies at the root of past wrongdoing. Punishing perpetrators in general, and collaborators in particular, is a way for public officials to express the depth of their commitment to overhauling this framework and to drawing a line between conduct tolerated in the past but now deemed impermissible. The punishment of collaborators in particular contributes to the debunking of some of the kinds of rationalisations of wrongdoing that are typical in transitional justice (e.g. that wrongdoing was the action of a few bad apples).

Punishment of collaborators, or any other accountability mechanism that societies deem fit for addressing collaboration, must be extremely sensitive to the different degrees to which, and conditions under which, they engaged in blameworthy behaviour. Some chapters in this book probe the impossibility of even considering legal action against widespread 'collaborationist societies'. The Czech Republic opened up files to expose the ubiquitous petty informing carried out for instrumental and ideological reasons (Drumbl and Holá). How could these extensive numbers of cases be tried? The transitional justice system opted instead for lustration, a flawed process by nearly all accounts.

But the wrongs of collaboration are not always amenable to this paradigm. They may involve breaches of community trust, or intimate or non-ideological violence, as was discussed previously (see Drumbl and Holá). The case of Northern Ireland shows that collaborators have been excluded from practices of reconciliation, with important consequences not only for them but also for their families, who often remain ostracised from the community, or end up leaving it.

The range of explanations for collaboration and its harmful or relatively benign results suggests that solutions are also likely to vary. The ubiquity of collaboration behind past violence in armed conflict and authoritarian rule does not mean that one approach will fit the variation within and across these situations. The following questions warrant further investigation. What kind of light does collaboration shed on transitional justice's concern for victims and for accountability for the collaborating perpetrators of human rights violations? Are the most popular institutional mechanisms to address wrongdoing in transitional contexts (criminal trials, truth commissions, lustration) appropriate for holding collaborators accountable? What hitherto unnoticed challenges does the existence of a network of collaborators and informers pose for societies transitioning away from conflict?

These are questions that this volume only begins to examine. Future studies should take this further to explore how transitional justice has dealt with collaboration, and whether and how it might deal with collaboration in a way that avoids the problems just discussed.

References

Arendt, H. (1994), *Eichmann in Jerusalem: A Report on the Banality of Evil* (New York, Penguin).

Dudai, R. (2012), '"Rescues for humanity": Rescuers, mass atrocities, and transitional justice', *Human Rights Quarterly*, 34, 1–38.

Jegstrup, E. (1986), 'Spontaneous action: the rescue of the Danish Jews from Hannah Arendt's perspective', *Humboldt Journal of Social Relations*, 13, 260–84.

Index

absolute truth 57
Abu Ghraib 91n8
academic elites and the Third Reich 179–99, 270, 273
accuracy of information 33, 35–9; *see also* quality of information
Aceh conflict 70
Actis, M. 51, 59n14
acts of collaboration, defining 13
Adams, G. 160, 162, 168, 169
ADEPA (Asociación de Entidades Periodísticas Argentinas) 232–3
ad-hoc recruitment 172
Adorno, T. W. 3, 55
African National Congress *see* ANC
agency 101, 107, 113, 215
agent provocateurs 167n7
Al Qaeda 73, 158
Alexievich, S. 87–8
alien rule 68
Améry, J. 54
amnesties 109n48
ANC (African National Congress) 29, 32, 34, 35, 38, 41, 44–5, 106
anonymous informants 253–4
anti-Communist motives 92, 140, 141, 145, 146, 153, 226
anti-informing motives 119–21
apartheid 12, 29–49
Apor, P. 101
appeals against punishment 234, 239
appearance of treachery/betrayal 8
appearances of collaboration 128
Aptheker, H. 114, 117, 118, 119, 121, 122, 126, 127
Arce, L. 210, 215, 217
archival sources 35, 97n22, 163, 169, 214, 219
Arendt, H. 3, 271
Arens, M. 14
Argentina 50–67, 171, 222–43, 269, 270, 271
Arjona, A. 148

armed groups: Argentina 223, 225; civil wars 69, 205, 271; internal armed conflicts 132–56; local militia groups 70–2; Northern Ireland 157–78
Asociación de Entidades Periodísticas Argentinas *see* ADEPA
Assaf, D. 14
assassination: avoiding, as motivation 124; as consequence of informing 209, 272; as punishment for collaboration 14, 170; *see also* survival maximisation
atonement 15
AUC (Autodefensas Unidas de Colombia) 136, 137, 139, 140, 142, 143, 144
Auden, W. H. 179, 182
authoritarianism 108, 109, 134, 205, 224, 226
authority, fundamental uncertainty about 212
autobiography/memoirs 162–3, 165, 166, 210
Autodefensas Unidas de Colombia *see* AUC

'bad apple' explanations for collaborators 149, 214
Baer, R. 158
'banality of evil' 3
Barrera, V. 148
Basque country 68–84, 161, 269
Basualdo, E. M. 225, 226, 227
Beinart, W. 35
Benda, J. 179, 180, 184
Bennett, L., Jr. 126, 127
Ben-Yehuda, N. 6, 9, 12, 16n9
Berman, B. 31
Bernal-Bermúdez, L. 228n3
betrayal 5–7, 8, 30, 106n42, 126, 134, 157, 171, 268
Bhola, M. 40–1
Bibb, H. 122, 123
Bílek, L. 94, 95
Black identity: collaboration during American slavery 5, 112–31, 270; South Africa 30–1, 37–8, 39–44, 47–8, 270, 271
Black Lives Matter 83, 113